Africans of the Diaspora

Africans of the Diaspora

The Evolution of African Consciousness and Leadership in the Americas

(From Slavery to the 1920s)

Vincent Bakpetu Thompson

Africa World Press, Inc.

P.O. Box 1892
Trenton, NJ 08607

P.O. Box 48
Asmara, ERITREA

Africa World Press, Inc.

P.O. Box 1892
Trenton, NJ 08607

P.O. Box 48
Asmara, ERITREA

First Printing 2000

Cover and Book Design: Jonathan Gullery

This book is set in Berling Roman and Tiepelo

Library of Congress Cataloging-in-Publication Data

Thompson, Vincent Bakpetu.
Africans of the disapora : the evolution of African American consciousness & leadership in the Americas / by Vincent B. Thompson.
p. cm.
Includes bibliographical references (p.) and index.
ISBN 0-86543-668-1. -- ISBN 0-86543-669-X (pbk.)
1. Afro-American leadership. 2. Afro-Americans--Politics and government. 3. Afro-Americans--Ethnic identity. 4. African diaspora. I. Title.
E185.615T56 1999
305.896'073--dc21 98-52240
CIP

This book is dedicated to Basil Davidson
and the late Dr. Walter Rodney.

Contents

Prologue

The present text, *Africans of the Diaspora*, is a sequel to the author's earlier work, T*he Making of the African Diaspora in the America's 1441-1900* (Longman Group England/Longman Inc., New York, 1987 and seven subsequent reprints). The current book examines the evolution of leadership in the same Diaspora in the Americas. The focus here, of course, is on leadership in North America, where that kind of leadership that could be identified among Africans of the Diaspora has been persistent. It does explore the other regions into which Africans were taken, the Caribbean and South America, but the latter two areas have not displayed this African consciousness with the same consistency as in North America. "African" leadership in the Caribbean and South America has been overshadowed by the policies pursued in those theaters of operation by the ruling slavocracy and their successors, which have dampened, curtailed, minimized, and almost destroyed an African consciousness, despite an African presence. It was policy in these societies to destroy all memory of Africa, to eliminate it entirely, so that it did not interfere with the workings of the plantation systems which were the mainstay of those societies in the early times. In some sense, it could be insisted that they all still are plantation societies.

Afrocentric leadership in these regions was perfunctory or nonexistent until recently, with few exceptions. There was, for instance, Brazil, where enslaved Africans provided leadership by the creation of the phenomenon of marronage known variously as *Quilombos*, *Mocambos*, and *ladeiras*, and a notable one which constituted itself into an African State in Brazil in the province of Alagoas in Pernambuco. (Kent 1965). They were to be celebrated by some writers as "The Famous Negroes of Palmares" (or the palm forests) (Pierson 1946; Diggs 1953) while to others they were the "*Quilombos Dos Palmares*" (Bastide 1971). There was also the phenomenon of African Muslim revolts which were led at various times and especially in the first part of the nineteeth century by the Hausas, Yoruba, and Malians (including Senegambia and Male Muslims, in Bahia). These latter leaders used counter-violence against the system of violence inaugurated by the plantation system, conceiving of their struggles in *jihadist* (Holy War of Islam) terms which gave it a moralistic tone, thus creating a leadership that was an amalgam of physical force, moral suasion, and activism all at once. For, as has been observed elsewhere in the text, sometimes one type of leadership (e.g., physical force) combined these attributes with those of moral suasion or activism or all of them. The leaders of the Maroon communities as well as leaders of slave revolts, including the Muslim rebels in Brazil, provided that form of leadership quite early [with the establishment of the plantation system throughout most of the Americas] and persisted until the final abrogation of slavery in all the territories, Brazil and Cuba (1880s) being the last two theaters to abandon slavery.

In the other parts of the Americas, currently less well-studied in terms of the evolution of an African-oriented leadership [or a leadership conscious of its African origins and emphasizing this] much of their efforts were directed early in the nineteenth century to the struggles for independence from Spain and Spanish control. Thus, many of them were in the army of Simon Bolivar in his bid for the liberation of South America and he received assistance from the Haitian leader, Alexander Petion, in his independence struggles. But the end of the independence struggles tended to eliminate the African orientation in political and societal matters, as the various successor states had recourse to varying expedients for minimizing, controlling and undermining the African presence (Rout Jr. 1976). But despite these, there continued to be African-descended populations in various parts of South America having had their voices muted or their consciousness of their Africaness eroded. But assimilation devices, as Brazil has tried to promote, have not prevented the growth of an African consciousness in more recent times - even in Brazil. A more recent development is the emergence of this consciousness in the celebration of the exploits of the men and women of Palmares - an African hegemony which survived for about a century and was destroyed about three hundred years ago by the Portuguese whose authority it had challenged. It was a movement that had the potential for creating an African rather than a Portuguese Brazil - at least in the northeast part of the country.

Palmares has now been installed by the government of Brazil as a public holiday to be celebrated in the month of November. Whether or not the government understands its significance is immaterial. It is a concession to the African presence in Brazil and an acknowledgment long overdue. It is clear, however, that the African-descended people have taken it to heart and in the future more manifestations of the gravity of that famous republic will emerge in diverse media such as studies, art, language, history, poetry, folk-tale, and legend. Some awareness of Palmares has surfaced in orature, and songs are emerging about Palmares, an image that has lain in obscurity for a long time but will not soon be laid to rest.

In Cuba also between the beginning of the nineteenth century through to the beginning of the twentieth (1812 and 1912) the African presence expressed itself in the physical force as well as moral suasionist and activist leadership that were manifested especially in the so-called *Aponte Revolt* of 1812, *La Escalera* of 1843-44, and the African contributions in the wars of independence in Cuba, the so-called Ten Years War (1868-78) and that of 1895 with the contributions of the Maceo brothers, José and Antonio and others but which, when independence had been won, resulted in the denial to the Africans of their rightful share of the fruits of independence (Helg 1995), all of these rebellions leading up to the revolt of 1912 and its merciless suppression by Euro-Cubans. The episodes contributed to the dampening of that leadership's public expression of its Africanness. The spirit of Africanness has not been destroyed in Afro-Cuba but have been denied their rightful share of influence and have been forced into exile in the metropolitan and urban centers of North America in the second half of the twentieth century.

The emergence of leadership after 1920 falls outside the scope of the present work but is a topic ripe for future study.

Other areas of the Americas have yet to be seriously studied to see whether the lull which descended on them from the early nineteenth century has been transformed into a consciousness of Africa in the twentieth century or not.

While time does not stand still, the study of leadership patterns that emerged and continued to emerge in North America and the inspiration which that emergence provided for a later generation of activists and leaders in South America (such as Abdias do Nascimento in Brazil) and the emergence of cultural nationalism in that region are worthy of study. It is an awareness of this gap which has induced this study of leadership in an area where it has been persistent and varied in kind and where it has also confronted with remarkable success the machinations of its detractors such as the American Colonization Society. The fact that, despite such opposition, leadership continued to emerge is a testimony to the tenacity and success of the African Diaspora in the Americas.

While the bulk of this study reflects specific North American peculiarities, it does touch on those other theaters in which Africans played a vital part, i.e., the Caribbean and South America. Further studies of the latter areas and the twentieth century studies of leadership perceptions, advocacies, and activities after 1920 should enlighten us further on the development of this African-conscious diasporan leadership.

The current study has been undertaken to fill a specific need to document the evolution of leadership in a theater of constant and continuous struggle for the enhancement of their stature as human beings of African stock.

The work divides into two parts, the first five chapters dealing with the early leadership and the last three with the later leadership. The penultimate chapter (Epilogue) compares the African Diaspora and the Jewish Diaspora from the perspective of the leadership of prelates, persistent in the North American experience, a fact which has given the concept prominence in the contemporary world.

Since I embarked on the writing of this book a few studies of individual personalities have appeared. These studies have provided me with deeper insights into the personalities of these leaders, their struggles, aspirations, and achievements. As most of them appeared after my work was completed, it became imperative to examine them prior to sending out this MS. Among those works are the following:

Carleton Mabee (with Susan Mabee Newhouse), *Sojourner Truth: Slave, Prophet, Legend* (New York and London: New York University Press, 1993); Orville Vernon Burton, *Born to Rebel: Benjamin E. Mays An Autobiography* (Athens GA and London: University of Georgia Press, 1987). David E. Swift, *Black Prophets of Justice: Activist*

Clergy Before the Civil War (Baton Rouge: Louisiana State University Press, 1989). Leon Litwack and August Meier (eds.), *Black Leaders of the Nineteenth Century* (Urbana and Chicago: University of Illinois Press, 1988); and John Hope Franklin and August Meier (eds.), *Black Leaders of the Twentieth Century* (Urbana and Chicago: University of Illinois Press, 1982).

My indebtedness to these writers is evident not only in the bibliography of this work but also in the body of the work. Their contributions have been immense and further studies of other leaders in the eighteenth, nineteenth, and twentieth centuries African Diaspora are necessary to provide a composite picture of the nature and character of this leadership and their ideas, activities, and achievements within the African Diaspora in the Americas.

There are probably other studies that have so far eluded this writer. As more studies of individual personalities or groups are conducted, a clearer perspective is bound to emerge to enhance our knowledge of the preoccupations of these worthy descendants of Africa in the New World diaspora of the Americas. It should also reveal their respective levels of affinity with Africa. Until then, this remains a pioneering endeavor.

Acknowledgments

This work has been long in gestation and the assistance, the author has received from many people and institutions deserve expressions of his deep appreciation. Among these are the encouragement and steadfastness of Professor Edward Reynolds and Godfrey Uzoigwe. Both read several chapters of the manuscript and gave useful advice. For the many who hosted this writer during his many travels and excursions, he asks them to accept a comprehensive thank you. The hospitality of Dr. Eileen Babb, her daughter Alethea, and her mother Mrs. Irene King cannot be fully repaid for their warmth, kindness; their faith in this writer nurtured his endeavors and their home during several return visits provided a safe and quiet retreat and sanctuary for contemplation and writing.

The inspiration and friendship of Basil Davidson is acknowledged in the dedication.

The following libraries assisted this researcher and he is deeply grateful to them: The British Library (formerly British Museum); the Public Record Office, London; the Libraries of the University of the West Indies in Trinidad, Barbados, and Mona Jamaica; The University of Miami at Coral Gables in Florida; The University of Michigan at Ann Arbor; The Schomburg Center for Research in Black Culture; London University and the London School of Economics and King's College Library London; The Howard University Moorland-Spingarn Collections; and last but not least, the libraries of Connecticut College, the University of Brasilia, and the University of Salvador Bahia have been most helpful.

Thanks are also due to Connecticut College for the Sabbatical leave which helped the rethinking and overhauling of the entire manuscript, and shortening it. The University of Miami at Coral Gables (Florida) and especially Don Spivey (Chair) and the entire History Department,who invited this writer to spend his Sabbatical as a Research Professor and to jumpstart their African History program, deserve this writer's gratitude. They not only provided a congenial and intellectual atmosphere but also the facilities for research and writing as well as excellent resources. The cordiality and assistance of the library staff made quick references possible.

The devoted service and patience of Mrs. Diane T. Monte in typing the entire manuscript as well as the patience endured by members of her family are acknowledged with humility. Additional thanks go to Mrs. Harriet Gaynor for introducing the author to Mrs. Monte.

Sincere thanks to Frank Blissard for the superb editing of this work. The same appreciation is expressed to Wanjiku Ngugi, editorial coordinator, for the interest she has taken in this work and also to the publisher K. Checole for his willingness to publish this work. This writer hopes it is the beginning of a fruitful association.

Every research effort in which documents and published texts are involved must suffer from the tyranny of sources. Under the circumstances, they must also carry some responsibility for errors of fact.

Thanks are also due to Sage Publications the publishers of *Journal of Black Studies* for their permission to use some material which had appeared in a previous article on "Early leadership."

Part 1

Early Leadership

CHAPTER 1

A PERSPECTIVE ON LEADERSHIP

This work encompasses the period of the African dispersion into the Americas from the inception of the slave trade to the end of the second decade of the twentieth century. While the work distinguishes neatly between leadership before the 1860s and the period following the American Civil War (1860-1865), this work focuses on the evolution and development of that leadership from the eighteenth century through the first two decades of the twentieth century. While there are certain common strands running through the leadership of both phases, the leadership was varied in kind, quality, and advocacy, but, essentially, was preoccupied with the fortunes and destiny of African descendants in the Americas and especially in the United States. These preoccupations surfaced in society in many ways: on the pulpit, on the political platform, in moralistic arguments and debates, in the press, in meetings and conventions, among the small but increasing population of African-American intellectuals, and even in the homes of private individuals.

The qualities which this writer regards as leadership qualities are those which sustain individuals, groups, and peoples during times of tribulation or acute crisis, enabling them not only to endure their existing hardships, but to challenge them sufficiently to achieve a transcendence of those problems. For Africans enslaved in the

Americas, many of whom had previously enjoyed the status of free people and the benefits of liberty in their native land, not only was their enslavement perceived as a calamity, but the experience must have posed many dilemmas for them. Not all of them would have been capable of working out stratagems to upset the system which held them in check, but there were those capable of being actuated to follow the suggestions and guidance of a more daring as well as perceptive person or persons with the wherewithal and the persistence to undermine, cheat, and defeat the system.

The modern system of slavery in the Americas challenged some of its victims to inveigh against it with acts of daring. These budding attempts at the crystallization of leadership among the early African-Americans have hardly been given sufficient attention, except by a few writers. It is these endeavors that concern this writer, and the work here undertaken is seen as one among the introductory excursions into the subject of leadership in the African diaspora in the Americas. There is much that we do not know and much more that needs to be known, but the effort must be made to ascertain the facts.Hitherto, fragments of lives, often autobiographical, have been depicted or reconstructed revealing the activities of this vocal and sometimes heroic leadership.[1] The voices of the silent leaders are stilled as they were never recorded or only fragmentarily recorded. It does mean that the discussion in this work focusses on an aspect of leadership that belonged to an enlightened wing within the entire body of Africans in the diaspora in the Americas, whose views on their conditions generally could be appropriated because they are documented as conveying the goals of the silent masses of their peoples. Essentially, the goal was the same for both the mass and the enlightened group in the period under consideration, namely, freedom and the right to enjoy the benefits of freedom unmolested. Most other things flowed from their confrontations with the opposing position of the majority of Euro-Americans to deny them those rights and the dignity that went with the attainment of those rights. The situations as they developed were conflictual and full of heartaches and frustrations.

Importance of the Question

The importance of the question of leadership in the context of this work arises, in the main, for two reasons: first, because the enslaved children of Africa in the Americas, for a protracted period, were given no guide for their elevation by those who had enslaved them. This is understandable because elevation was not a preoccupation of their enslavers. However, the realities of slave societies and the degradation of the African people were bound to produce conflictual situations in which some form of leadership would manifest itself no matter how draconian the measures employed to suppress opposition. Accordingly, they had to evolve their own leadership out of sheer necessity and these emerged out of the crises of finding their bearings through the maze of confusion created by the techniques employed by the slavocracy to keep them in a state of confusion. A second reason is that the leadership posed possible and alternative paths for the future in terms of destiny. Among the alternatives was one which sought to identify Africans in the dispersion with the continent of their origin—Africa—and this helped to delineate the contributions of the African-derived people in the Americas to the African struggles for their regeneration and efforts at unity.[2] In short, out of this leadership crisis arose the notion of Pan-African unity and the creation of a Pan-African tradition.[3]

Although we have argued in another context[4] that slavery on the plantations of the West Indies and the rest of the Americas was a remote cause of Pan-African activity, it was in North America that the activities of the enslaved Africans, their descendants, and the free Africans (misnamed free people of color) aided the crystallization of a leadership that impelled the formation of Pan-African ideas and goals. This is not to suggest that the entire body of people of African origin felt the need to return to Africa. Such a mass movement was to come later, but there was always a group constituting a kind of leadership that always thought about Africa and felt some kinship.[5] There was no universal notion of a return to Africa either physically or spiritually. Yet the thought of Africa did not emerge out of nothing. It matured out of the strivings of the children of Africa in North America to uplift themselves from the degradation of slavery in the Americas generally. Their strivings were part and parcel of the history of the children of Africa in the New World dispersion and it was in the process of evolving that history that the Pan-African sentiments found their natural spokesmen and led to the establishment of a Pan-African tradition. But we must first consider the various stages passed in order to crystalize this leadership.

In the early period of dispersion of the African peoples into the Americas, visible leadership hardly existed. Individuals could decide on a course of action, such as revolt on board a slave ship, and others might join them, but this was not sustained as the revolts, except in a few cases, were put down with merciless severity. Leadership as such is a feature that emerged only with increasingly greater and better organization, although the voices of leaders were heard before they actually formed organizations. Their voices sometimes called forth the organizations and the emergence of such organizations either strengthened or weakened them. The social milieu also determined whether leadership could emerge and the type of that leadership. Within the context of slave societies, the emergence of even a single vocal personality was deemed a danger to the system and was promptly discouraged as the slavocracy also had its own sanctions against would-be "troublemakers". Thus, the kind of leadership that could emerge would be among those not in bondage or those in bondage who had the capacity to conceal their organization and ambition for a time. The former kind of leadership was represented by the many religious prelates and founders of free African Churches to be joined later by professional men including artisans and intellectuals, often those who had never been enslaved or had secured their freedom through one of many expedients available. Whereas the latter belonged to those represented by Gabriel Prosser, Nat Turner, and Madison Washington (in the USA), Henri Christophe and Jean J. Dessalines (St. Dominque, Haiti), Tackey [Teshi] and Samuel Sharpe (Jamaica), Cuffey and Agidi (Berbice, British Guiana), Zumbi (Palmares, Brazil), Joseph Cinque (Cuba), and many others who led or plotted slave revolts, both types lived under severe constraints and threats and often were not approved of. Their sheer persistence has immortalized their names and their struggles.

In this evolution of leadership (for evolution it was), there were many individualistic expressions of leadership that were emulated by some but not the majority. Such persons merely demonstrated the revulsion, but also their sense of worth, to a system which sought to stifle and restrain not only life and limb but the very process of thought itself. They rejected all these impositions and demonstrated that rejection in numerous ways. Some of them became the folk heroes of later times. Examples of this leadership may be found among people who raised slave revolts on board ship either at home before transportation, or during the middle passage, or on the plantations. Many among such leaders ran away from the plantations soon after landing, like the various maroon communities of many lands. The most celebrated of these were the seventeenth-century founders of the Republic of Palmares in northeastern Brazil, the Surinamese Maroons, those of Jamaica, and those of Florida (the Seminoles). Their actions declared that others could follow their example. Individuals who ran away and expected others to follow their examples do not feature in this work, although they constituted leadership after another fashion, but they were not in any way concerned with the plight of their brethren in bondage. By contrast, the Maroon communities fought to the death to defend and sustain the survival of their communities. They were, therefore, celebrated for being illustrious and inspirational, as we do today the famous Republic of Palmares under its last leader Zumbi especially, because for about a century they sustained themselves against the buffettings and repeated assaults of their European enemies, the Dutch and the Portuguese. Nothing was simple for that period, for paths to elevation were strewn with hazards and frustrations. But leaders who sought to carry some of or all their brethren with them (the concern of this work) knew the trials and tribulations of trying to lead a disparate, disarranged, often mesmerized, and down-trodden people. But in their endeavors and in their capacity to inspire they constituted the real leadership of the people. Much of this kind of identifiable leadership belonged to the second half of the eighteenth century, at a time when the enslavement of Africans and their transference to the Americas was more than two centuries old. It became stronger and more articulate in the nineteenth century. It was diverse in kind but its ends were identical - upliftment from degradation and elevation from the status of property and thing to that of human beings who could realize their potential. For the sake of clarity and precision, the leadership before 1860 is herein termed "early leadership" and begins with the arrival of the Africans in the Americas, but focuses principally on the late eighteenth century. The leadership emerging after 1860 is designated "later leadership". Yet the period prior to 1860 overlaps with the succeeding period and so it is to be seen that some of those who had been identified in the earlier period recur in the later period, although, because of style and emphasis, the later leadership merits separate treatment. The earlier period was essentially the period of slavery with its sprinkling of a few free blacks with a quasi-free status, while the beginning of the second period saw the antislavery drama working itself to a logical conclusion with the demise of slavery in sight and the shift in emphasis to the rehabilitation of the victims of slavery in the post-slavery era. It was, of course, concerned, as with its predecessors, with its destiny in a milieu previously overtly hostile and forbidding but where manifestations of that hostility still abounded.[6] It also manifested signs of assimilation to aspects of the wider Euro-American society and its cultural patterns, while struggling to retain some of its own, not by any means a mean feat.

Divisive Techniques in Operation

There were numerous techniques by which the operators of the slave system in the Americas tended to divide peoples of African descent. They also divided the progeny of the intermingling and intermixtures of peoples of many origins (but principally African, European, and Native American [alias Amerindians] as well as "creole"[7] mixtures). These were validated by some legal stipulations. Despite these "divide and rule" techniques of color differentiations (with privileges for some whose colors were lighter,) they were all classified as Negroes notwithstanding that one or other of their parentage was of European or Euro-American origin. Thus, by the broad definitions of North American society, the mulatto, known to the societies of the Caribbean and South America, was unknown in law and custom in the United States of America. The mulatto was still classified as "negro" unless he had first escaped the color net or hatch by the phenomenon of "passing" for white. Thus "negro" slaves and free mulattoes [alias "colored" - slave and free,] found themselves collectively thrown into the same mold and the general struggles for their common elevation. Where, of course, the color-shade complex had wreaked its havoc through a prolonged period of inculcation, custom, and even legal stipulations, as in the Caribbean and in South America, these congeries of people found cooperation difficult and operated as separate classes, separated not only by color-shade gradations, but defined also by economic levl and social status, apart from the attitudes that had earlier been induced and fostered until they became the received tradition. The tragedy of this manifested itself in the St. Domingue struggle for liberation, as both struggles (that of the mulattos and that of the Negroes) were conceived as separate until the stark realities dawned on both groups that they stood to lose the struggle by the petty indulgences of color differentiations which they themselves had not instituted but had inherited from an uncaring slavocracry. They soon realized that to persist along a weather-beaten track of color-superiority and inferiority would condemn them to the misery of perpetual enslavement instead of the freedom for which they had unfurled their separate banners. But despite this cooperation in St. Domingue, modern Haiti is still plagued by this infamous color or mulatto legacy introduced by the French in St. Domingue and in the other Caribbean theaters of enslavement of the Africans.

CATEGORIZATION OF LEADERSHIP

In perceiving this leadership, three broad types emerge. The first, the "physical-force" types, emerge out of the milieu of their enslavement itself. Slavery sustained itself by, in the first instance, brute force: violence was predominant and ubiquitous, and punishments were dished out for minor and major transgressions alike or even assumed transgressions. As violence was the order of the day, it tended in turn to beget violence. Both the enslaved and the nominally free were its victims and so provided leadership of this kind.

The second category consisted of moralists, who existed both among the slaves and among the free people, and whose attitudes and outlook were sometimes conditioned by religious principles inherent in either the African or the Euro-Christian tradition. There was such a large variety of this leadership at various times in this long period of evolution of leadership. Third were the activist types, whose methods were fundamentally different from those of the moralists, although some of them were motivated and guided by moral suasion. But they argued (through available channels of communication) and agitated on anti-slavery platforms, from pulpits and other forums, and through the agency of the press, whether African-American supported or those of the Euro-Americans that allowed an airing of their opinion, such as *The Liberator*. They organized their people and, to some extent, became involved either directly or indirectly in political activity. They were among those who assailed the American Colonization Society, when it sought to remove the free colored of the United States to Africa during the larger part of the nineteenth century. This category of leadership included the first "Civil Rights" leaders from the period of the emergence of the Convention movement and even earlier. The distinction between the second and the third categories of leadership was sometimes blurred and sometimes also that between the second and first categories.

SUMMATION

This study begins with an examination of the "physical-force" type of leadership, which was ever-present from the beginning to the end of the slavery era. But a caveat is necessary in dealing with the three broad categories of leadership mentioned above: periodisation is difficult since these three types were operating simultaneously. All said and done, these categories are arbitrary. Thus, we find that moral leaders sometimes showed awareness of and acquiesced approvingly in the doings of the "physical-force" leaders; or again physical force leaders had moral arguments for choosing the path of violence or vice versa. The men and women who made good their escape from the citadel of slavery by one means or another, or who secured manumission through one of the many available avenues (e.g., service in the army or militia, or purchase through hard work), or who escaped and returned to rescue others, were certainly the first identifiable leaders and pointed the way for others to do the same and even better. But these were individuals taking independent action on their own initiative and not with a view to elevating the entire group or even a sizeable group of the slave population. Their achievements, though inspirational, were minimal in terms of elevating the whole, even if they caused consternation in the hearts of slaveholders. But the leadership which kept the plantation societies alive with agitation and fear, which tended to demoralize the slaveholders and their sympathizers, and which eventually sought to give substance to the lives of the freed people after complete emancipation was secured within an ambivalent and hostile society, has immortalized itself and is the main concern of this study. Since it was in the United States of America that these categories of leadership were evolving long before the abolition of slavery in Brazil and Cuba, it is there that this study shall focus. Hopefully, future researchers will bring to the surface the reasons for the non-evolution of Africa-oriented leadership in these other theaters prior to the middle of the twentieth century. Leadership which grew among descendants of Africa in the Americas seemed more persistent in the United States of America than elsewhere in the Americas. Against this background of the rest of the Americas this profusion of leadership on the American mainland, especially in the northern states, merits our attention. There are reasons for this: first, because it was here more than anywhere else that a variant leadership emerged with a clear vision of their destiny. Second, because the quality of that leadership was such that its advocacies could not be ignored as it posed problems and dilemmas for their constitutional advancement in American society. In this work, a shortened formula is used to categorize the various modes of leadership. We have already mentioned the three principal categories in the earlier phase. Each leader that emerged could be visualized in this work within one or more of those overlapping categories. The categories, though arbitrary, are harnessed in order to generalize the nature of leadership. Although these categories of leadership were sometimes personified by women, it was predominantly a leadership of men in an era and society where women were given very little opportunity to demonstrate the capacity for leadership. While it is a sad commentary on the state of the society in which these categories of leadership emerged, it was not itself a deliberate act on the part of African-American leaders to exclude women, except in some of the exclusive organizations that were formed in those times.

In the earlier period, which ended in 1860 at the time of the American Civil War, women were found in the revolt against slavery, though their acts of poisoning slaveowners or participating in killing them or by participating in slave revolts if not leading them (as in the case of Nanni of the maroons of Jamaica or the prophetesses or so-called "Sage-matrons" of the Surinamese society as John Stedman called them), or those who became the catalysts for revolt. But with the proliferation of these leaders, there were leaders who typified the categories. In order to make this study more manageable, those representative of the leadership have been singled out as typifying the rest. Hence among activist leaders two women and three men are briefly discussed in order to present a picture of their own respective manners of leadership and its achievement. It is by no means exhaustive since the aim is not to achieve a biographical study of each person but rather to distill what is gleaned from each life in an era when the Africans of the diaspora were groping for direction.But these women activists observed in the earlier phase at times mirrored their moral guiding principles based on their religious convictions. Yet they were active in a manner that would qualify them as activist leaders. Despite the fact that the categories were not watertight, they did mirror those who were essentially in one camp or the other. Thus, Richard Allen, who epitomized the moral leadership in an earlier period, was a moralist through and through, and by conviction and inclination, and could not have been recruited into the rank of the physical- force leadership, for instance. But some moralists were activists and, in effect, fell into one or other category as the opportunities presented themselves and determined the category into which they would fall. While prominently of one kind they still fitted easily into another category. The activists like Frederick Douglass, the Rev. Samuel Ringgold Ward, Charles Lenox Remond, the Rev. Henry Highland Garnet and many more, were also guided by certain moral principles and even in their agitation for rights or emancipation they were always employing their moral arguments to advance their cause and sought to be persuasive to those yet unconvinced of the cause they espoused. Yet, periodically, in their speeches, they expressed approval of the actions of the physical-force leaders. Thus we saw the activist, the Rev. Henry Highland Garnet, recall the exploits of Nathaniel (alias Nat) Turner[8] in Virginia in 1831 in a speech he delivered to the National Convention of Colored People in 1843; while Frederick Douglass spoke approvingly of the murder by runaway slaves of a slaveholder, Mr. Gorschurch, who in 1851 attempted to recapture his escaped slaves against the spirited defense of other slaves and whose resistance had such fatal consequences in what came to be known as the "Christina Affair." Douglass was gleeful because, as he saw it, "man-stealers" were receiving their just deserts.[9]

There were also leaders in the earlier period whose leadership continued in the second phase. These included Garnet and Douglass. The latter's leadership towered above all others, despite periodic episodes of rivalry with Charles Lenox Remond, Samuel Ringgold Ward, John Mercer Langston and some others. But Douglass remained the acknowledged leader until his death in 1895. Yet there were others who were already exerting their influence in the same period, such as Dr. Martin Robinson Delany, Bishop Henry McNeal Turner, the Rev. Alexander Crummell, and Dr. Edward Wilmot Blyden. Although the latter's leadership had more impact in West Africa, his advocacies filtered back into the United States through his periodic visits to that country, through his correspondence with influential personalities in both black and white communities, and through his publications. Blyden always took advantage of his visits to the United States to persuade African-Americans to be committed to Africa through emigration there or support for would-be emigrants with a view to enhancing the African personality and its stature in the world. A notable feature of the leadership that was emerging from the eighteenth century onwards was that of prelates and men of the cloth, a feature which has persisted into our own age. They would be among the advocates of the many issues which agitated the minds and hearts of African Americans in every waking moment. Thus, they were either integrationists, emigrationists, or "separate identitists" and those branded as "nationalists." But not all of the leadership in one or other of these persuasions were religious prelates; some were lay people, but they all had one thing in common—they were all free within the meaning of that term as it pertained to descendants of Africa in the United States.

The preoccupation with emigration, whose chief spokesman in the 1850s was Dr. M. R. Delany, lost its fervor after the Civil War, when prospects for integration and full citizenship seemed within their grasp. But the aftermath of Reconstruction and the long-term implications of its aftermath revived the idea, and when in the 1880s and 90s disfranchisement became enshrined in pro-intimisation legislation of the various states (thanks to the failure of nerve by some Euro-American liberals in the north and the emergence of what was termed the "New South", the political pendulum for African-Americans swung between integration and emigration, in time even incorporating the notion of "separate identity." It polarized the African-American professional men and their intellectual leadership from the masses sandwiched between them and ground down by peonage, poverty, rancid racism, racial discrimination, and share-cropping. The debates and arguments from both sides were passionately posed with much conviction and logic. Even the South from which much of the emigrationist ethos was issuing forth continued as in the days of slavery to display its ambivalence to the presence of African-Americans in its midst. The South in its new mood would be content to deny citizenship to the African-Americans while at the same time expecting them to occupy submissively the lowest rungs of the political, economic, and social ladders and remain docile to the dictates of white southerners.

While the integrationists focused their attention and efforts on securing these ends, to achieving enfranchisement and playing some part in that society, others—keenly aware of the failure of Reconstruction—despaired of these possibilities and became preoccupied with a destiny outside the United States, in Africa, beyond the ebb and flow of racism. Among the leaders disappointed with the aftermath of Reconstruction were Dr. M. R. Delany, Bishop McNeal Turner of the A.M.E. Church, and even leaders like the Rev. Alexander Crummell and Dr. Edward Wilmot Blyden (who was denied, on racial grounds, the opportunity for higher education in the U.S.A. after coming there from the Danish Island of St. Thomas). Yet, this resourceful man came to play many parts—a classical scholar (in Greek, Latin, and Arabic), conversant also with Hebrew and French, in addition to being a lay preacher, he also became President of Liberia College, twice served as Ambassador to the Court of St. James (Britain) and France, and became an authority on Islam, occupying, for a time, the post of Director of Muslim Studies in Lagos, Nigeria. He was also the author of many books which were to influence budding West African nationalists in the late nineteenth and early twentieth centuries. But despite the fact that there emerged so many resourceful men and women in the second phase of the later leadership, the personality and ideas of one person tended to tower above all others. Accordingly, in the post-Civil War period, it was Frederick Douglass who dominated the scene, and his principal preoccupation was with integration and elevation through education, industry, and group effort as well as cooperation with sympathetic Euro-Americans. These became his obsessions until his death in 1895. He was also an advocate of women's rights and often spoke on their platform. So the period until his passing departure was known as the "age of Frederick Douglass." He was also the chief assailant of emigrationists like Delany and

McNeal Turner and others like H. H. Garnet and Alexander Crummell. It was always his contention that individuals could emigrate, but never nations.

But the 1880s also saw the rise of Booker T. Washington to prominence and his accomodationist tendencies in thought, word, and action made him the successor to Douglass, even though they differed fundamentally in their orientation. For while Douglass placed implicit faith in the importance of the vote, Mr. Washington discounted and minimized it. It was obviously not priority for him as it had been for the integrationist leadership. He acquiesced in segregation. It is often thought that Booker T. Washington was the first to lay emphasis on industrial education, without taking into account that Douglass had also advocated it long before Washington.[10] But Douglass did not slavishly endorse industrial education at the expense of higher education. He himself had been a caulker before he became a journalist, public servant and public figure, yet he insisted that all fields of education should be embraced by African-Americans with the capability just as he urged them to press into the professions and into all fields of endeavor.[11] Booker T. Washington, by contrast, insisted on industrial education as the only form that had any meaning and thus sought to circumscribe African-Americans within its narrow limits, consequently limiting their opportunies. This posture was to bring him into conflict soon with other African-American radicals, the most prominent of them being Dr. W. E. B. DuBois, the Harvard Ph.D. of 1895, just at the time Mr. Washington was stepping into the shoes of Frederick Douglass as the "Negro Leader" by virute of the speech he delivered at the Atlanta Cotton Exposition that year, a speech thereafter dubbed "The Compromise".[12] No sooner had Mr. Washington assumed the mantle of leadership than he found himself challenged by the radicals, of whom the most prominent were William Monroe Trotter (founder of the *Boston Guardian*), Ida B. Wells Barnett (also a newspaper editor and an assailant of lynchings), and DuBois. But there were middle-roaders and critics such as Mary Church Terrell, wife of Judge Terrell, who obtained his position as a patronage through the influence of Mr. Washington. The first three were Washington's arch critics till the end of his life in 1915-a period during which controversy raged between integrationists (exemplified by DuBois and the founders of the Niagara Movement whose ideals and energies went into the formation and sustaining of the inter-racial National Negro Committee in 1901 and which, the following year adopted the name of the National Association for the Advancement of Colored People, the longest-surviving civil rights movement in the United States of America. Against these, until Mr. Washington's death in

1915, were the accomodationist stances, which rejected integration for segregation, stressed "harmony" rather than what he termed "strife and confrontation," industrial rather than higher education, and, on the issue of the vote, disfranchisement and gradualism instead of enfranchisement of African-Americans.

All these activities were conducted within the United States. But parallel to this was the emigrationist ethos which continued to rear its head during the period to the end of the second decade of the twentieth century, when the African-American status was at its lowest point, despite progress that had been made in education (both lower and higher) as well as in the professions. Although Mr. Washington himself was an opponent of any kind of emigration from the south, even those which carried African-Americans to northern and western cities, he continued to urge them to remain in the south and, as he so frequently put it, "cast your bucket where you are!" Despite his admonishments, however, the 1880s saw not only advocacies for emigration out of the south to the north and west but some also to Africa.

The year 1879 is remembered for the great "Exodus" from the South-from Mississippi and Tennessee to Kansas, and from Louisiana, Georgia, and Alabama to Texas, led respectively by Benjamin (alias "Pap") Singleton (described as the "Moses of the Colored Exodus") and Henry Adams. These mammoth movements of a disillusioned population seeking redemption elsewhere were symptomatic of the malaise of the South and reflected the frustrations, dashed hopes, and disabilities which had taken over after the Compromise of 1877, when Federal troops were withdrawn from the South and the region was left to its own devices in dealing with African-Americans. It is still remarkable that neither Singleton nor Adams was literate in the conventional sense. Singleton in particular displayed a capacity to persuade effectively and manifested the ability to instill confidence among a disillusioned people who felt cheated out of the legacy they had expected to receive at the conclusion of the Civil War. The south had become hellish to these disillusioned people for numerous reasons which have been noted by other authors.[13] The organizational abilities of Singleton and Adams were amply demonstrated at this point in time.

That emigration as an ideal persisted was demonstrated by the occurrence of the National Convention on Emigration in North Carolina in 1889.[14] Emigration seemed to be idea that would not just go away. Even a National Convention in Nashville (Tennessee) in 1879 was reported to be enthusiastic about the Singleton exodus of that year, observing the many ills which blacks continue to suffer. In

1890 the Afro-American League was formed to press for migration to the northwest in order to counteract southern "persecution".[15] Many northern leaders were said to have approved of the exodus. The persistence of these tendencies resulted in the setting up of a Senate Committee to investigate the Kansas Exodus, before which Singleton appeared and explained that he was the "whole cause of the Exodus."[16]

Singleton might have exaggerated his own role without taking account of many factors which impelled the response to his advocacy. However, many factors, such as oppression, persecution, lynchings, intimidation, economic factors such as depression, unproductivity of land, as well as ambition for betterment all contributed to the periodic resurfacing of the emigration obsession which by then had become a tradition. The situation must have been desperate for one of the veterans of the emigration movement, Dr. Delany, to restate his earlier thesis counselling emigration through the question: "Where is a more fit place to seek new homes than in the land of their fathers and mothers, especially provided for them by nature?"[17] Delany threw his energies into emigration again and his advocacy was reinforced by the persuasive voice of Bishop Turner. He and some African-Americans in Charleston, South Carolina, floated the Liberian Exodus Joint Stock Company in 1877 to enhance African emigration. The Company's ship made the first and only voyage in 1878 captained by a white man. Loss attended the venture and resulted in a court case. This failure was followed by another effort in 1890, with Delany being associated again even in his old age. It arose due to the deteriorating political, economic, social and psychological conditions of blacks in the south and these propelled them into other emigration ventures for Africa. It was a situation which challenged leadership to be well focused and, as one author has observed:

> To focus such unrest in a practical movement, however, required leadership and organization and the narrative of African emigration from 1890 to 1910 is a story of the search for effective leadership and organization for the many unhappy blacks who despaired of making a home in the United States.[18]

This leadership was to issue forth from divergent quarters. By this time the nationalist element, within America or outside it. was coming increasingly to the fore of discussions and deliberations. Until his death in 1915, Bishop Turner was one of the most prominent advocates of this version of black nationalism, which still saw emigration as necessary, if not essential. He had become a vice-president of the American Colonization Society, a society which was intensely disliked by many blacks for reasons discussed below in Chapter five. Some people had gone out to Africa under its auspices and while some stayed there others returned to America. In a period of desperation and destitution, some of these African-Americans resorted to the ACS in the 1890s when the organization itself lacked resources and, in fact, was in debt. It was unable to fulfill the dreams of so many for transplantation to Africa.

THE MESSAGE FROM LIBERIA

From Liberia in West Africa, Edward Blyden, another of these nationalists and a respected intellectual voice in much of West Africa, ardently advocated that African-American emigrants proceed to Africa to realize their potential and aid their kith and kin in their regeneration, a task for which he felt the European colonizers of Africa were no match, despite earlier support of European colonization during the scramble for Africa, especially for the British. When the opportunity arose during his recurrent visits to the United States, he expressed that desire for black emigration, which he qualified to mean those genuinely black, rejecting the mulatto, whom he felt could not maintain the determination required for the task in hand. He too was one of the vice-presidents of the ACS and had come to Africa under its auspices. Until his death in 1912, he continued to hold the belief that emigration to Africa was the best solution to the race problem and the plight of the African diaspora in the Americas in the United States. His arguments were numerous and in his writings and lectures he ranged over many subjects and addressed Africans, Europeans, Euro-Americans, and African-Americans alike. He was the foremost intellectual of the West-African scene in his lifetime, inspiring many others who were not only to pay him homage but were also to play significant roles in the formation of Pan-African organizations such as the National Congress of British West Africa, formed by Joseph Ephraim Casely-Hayford[19] of the Gold Coast in 1920.Blyden received the welcome of some Southern whites intent on seeing the removal of blacks. But the South, ever ambivalent about its black labor force, felt the need to reduce the black population of the south yet had to contend with the objections of large landowners who understood the implications of the massive loss of their sources of labor and wealth. These landowners saw the blacks as the "economic backbone" of the south and knew they could ill afford their departure, a sentiment also expressed by President Harrison.[20]

When two United States Southern Senators, Butler of South Carolina and Morgan of Alabama, through expediency in 1890, attempted to promote what has become known to posterity as "The Butler Bill" for the settlement of African-Americans in Belgian King Leopold II's so-called "Congo Free State" in the heart of Africa, they were acting out their prejudices, shared by some vocal southerners who wished to see the expatriation of African-Americans. The bill however, was aborted![21] The Congo Free State at the beginning of the twentieth century revealed such excesses and brutalities against defenseless Africans that shocked even the sensibilities of imperialist Europe and the U.S.A. The suggestion of the Belgian Congo as a place for settlement taxed the ingenuity of the African-American leadership, which therefore sought integration of their brethren within American society. The implication was that the threats of their deportation from the country were not far from their reflections and continued to hang over their heads like the sword of Damocles. However, it is appropriate that we now examine the nature and character of this leadership evolution and the paths it had trodden to the end of the second decade of the twentieth century, after this brief perspective on leadership among Africans of the diaspora. The work divides into four broad parts. Part 1 deals with early leadership as it evolved. Part 2 which falls between the early and later leadership phases, forms a watershed in that it coincided with the time when the leadership of the African diaspora was being forged and yet found itself confronted with a forged false humanitarianism which sought to discourage them from remaining in British and American societies. Thus, the formation of the British Sierra Leone Company and the American Colonization Society, in the eighteenth and nineteenth centuries respectively, injected a distractive element into the thoughts of these African descedents. Part 3 deals with the issues and controversies that arose as these descedants of Africa sought to map out their destiny in a hostile environment and, also, due to previous and contemporary experiences forged a tradition of ambivalence towards the continent of their forbears. This was the phase of leadership up to 1920. Part 4 seeks to confront the validity of an African diaspora. Here it examines the symbolism and experience which African prelates in the Americas harnessed from the Jewish experience to equate with theirs and deriving inspiration therefrom to emphasize the doctrine of "Providential Design" which led some African descedents in the Americas to conceive of their four centuries in the Americas as consistent with an African Diaspora. The intensity of this thought process was more manifest in the second phase of the evolution of leadership from the mid-nineteenth century into our own day. It is an arbitrary conception, but it makes for another examination of the issues which preoccupied leadership in each phase. The chapters are as follows.

The first chapter (this introduction) reflects a perspective on that leadership. The second chapter deals briefly with the physical force leadership by reference to three leaders in the United States as reflecting the logic of physical force. The third chapter deals with moral suasion, especially Bishop Richard Allen as the epitome of that leadership. The fourth chapter discusses the activist aspect of leadership, taking a few as representative of the rest who expressed similar sentiments, with Frederick Douglass becoming the most dominant voice of the era. As the issues agitated related to securing freedom, they are seen within the framework of the anti-slavery endeavors and the elevation of the rest. In the fifth chapter the American Colonization Society comes under a searchlight in terms of the humanitarianism claimed for it and the British Sierra Leone venture, both activities concerned with uprooting free Africans (especially those formerly enslaved) from their original societies. They are examined in terms of their general aims and objectives and responses to them as well as the way they attempted to detract from the evolution of leadership by the introduction of a red herring instead of allowing the struggles to be focused on the termination of slavery.In the second phase of leadership evolution, commencing after 1860, chapter six examines the crises in the objectives of this leadership, while chapter seven briefly considers the tradition of ambivalence towards Africa by some of the leadership. It should come as no surprise that Africa was deflated in the thoughts of African-Americans, except for the enlightened few. This devaluation of Africa among African-Americans arose from the imagery that the slavocrats and their supporters had foisted and fostered since the arrival of Africans in the country. Africa's image included "savage," "wild," less desirable and many other epithets lurid in their import which had been invented to portray it as an uninhabitable place and its inhabitants as subhuman. These images had served the rationalizations of the slavocracy well but had also worked themselves into the psychology of the African-Americans, and were to be reinforced in the post-emancipation period by adverse propaganda both from internal and external sources. It had led to the belief that Africans were not part of the human race. With more knowledge, however, more and more African-Americans began to see Africa in a more favorable light, but that development belongs to the second half of the twentieth century and is beyond the scope of this work. Thus, ambivalence had been injected into the thoughts of African-Americans and it is this ambivalence that is briefly examined here although it is a fertile area of research. The eighth chapter examines, albeit in a cursory way, points of convergence and divergence between the African diaspora and the Jewish diaspora, a concept deserving indepth study in its own right. But this writer is cognizant of Jewish symbolisms, especially religious ones, adopted by the Africans of the diaspora in the United States based on their prelates' perception of both peoples experiences, leading to their elaboration of the doctrine of "providential design." The conclusion, while observing that the crises in the perspectives of leadership survive into the latter part of the twentieth century, simply describes the situation at the end of the second decade of the twentieth century.The degree of success of that leadership-and its sustenance- depended on evolved ideas, its own organizing ability and that of the organizations it controlled, and its capacity to broaden the basis and the perceptions of those led. In many senses, before 1920, the leadership was, in the main, elitist and failed to take account of the masses by recruiting them or inviting them into their deliberations.

Such mass leadership was not to be seen until the advent of the Universal Negro Improvement Association and the African Communities League of Marcus Mosiah Garvey from Jamaica (which became a mammoth movement, in fact, the largest mass movement ever seen in the United States prior to that date) and Dr. Carter G. Woodson's Association for the Study of Negro Life and History which he founded in 1915. But the American Negro Academy of 1897 and the Negro Society for History Research (1916) at Yonkers (New York), although vital in providing an intellectual focus, were still elitist organizations which did not seek to include the masses of African-Americans. Woodson, however held the annual meetings of his Association sometimes in churches which meant a larger participation; he also tailored his *Negro History Bulletin* to inform the mass of African-Americans and others so as to make them conscious of history, and especially, their history as a factor in their regeneration and elevation as well as inspiration.

Leadership of the Elitist Kind: Some Reflections

Another kind of leadership which emerged in this period of the evolution of leadership in the African diaspora in the Americas was that provided by the founders of the elitist "Greek Letter Societies," known as the fraternities and sororities which is amply documented elsewhere.[22] This kind of leadership and those mentioned in the few succeeding pages of this chapter have not been featured in this work in an exhaustive manner. This leadership seemed to have taken its cue from the Euro-Americans who had first established the fraternities and sororities but were unwilling to open their doors to African-American aspirants, as also occurred with the Masonic Orders prior to Prince Hall's founding of his own Masonic Order. Prince Hall having bypassed Euro-American objections to gain the necessary license from Europe was able to establish his own Masonic Order in the eighteenth century. Another in this genre of leadership not discussed in this work is that which expounded socialism or adhered to its European proponents. In the forefront of this activity was the Rev. George Washington Woodbey, whose activities were centered in Omaha (Nebraska) and San Diego (California). As this writer is currently researching Woodbey, not much is discussed here. But this writer finds it baffling, and sometimes instructive, that not once did W. E. B. DuBois refer to this socialist prelate, despite DuBois' professions to have embraced socialism first, of the "Path," and later Marxism shortly before his death. Although Woodbey was DuBois' elder by a full generation, having been active at the time of DuBois' birth, nonetheless, his leadership was certainly contemporaneous with that of DuBois. Although he was of humble origins and did not have the kind of academic training which DuBois had, nevertheless, he was a spirited speaker and a man of ideas, who drew large crowds to his rallies. He was very eloquent and his style was easy to understand. Furthermore, this Reverend gentleman expounded some interesting socialistic ideas even before the Soviet leader Vladimir Lenin, despite the fact that some of those thoughts tended to be credited to Lenin and yet were actually the brainchildren of Woodbey. Of course, owing to the prejudices of those times, Woodbey lost his post as Minister in San Diego because it was said that he was too socialistic for black religious conservatives. The other leadership with socialist affiliations falls outside the scope of this work but belongs to the succeeding period of the evolution of leadership in the African diaspora. There was also the elitist leadership of the late nineteenth century founders of the American Negro Academy (1897) who set themselves up as the intellectual leading lights among their people, devoted to intellectual pursuits and the discussion of ideas, as well as providing the leadership of the "Talented Tenth" introduced in the writings of Crummell and expounded by DuBois. The Rev. Alexander Crummell himself became its first President, with DuBois succeeding him as the second president of the Academy. The Academy published *Occasional Papers*. The impact of this leadership on the masses of African-Americans is difficult to determine, although it might have been inspirational to the intellectual members of the African-American community and some of its members must have contributed to the founding, of the Niagara Movement and, later, the National Association for the Advancement of Colored People. Their leadership impact might have been overshadowed by the one-man domination of leadership which emerged in the latter part of the nineteenth century, until Crummell's death in 1895, when the age of DuBois actually took off, even before his assault on the pronouncements and leadership of Booker T. Washington. Yet, despite the domination of these personalities and their ideas, other leaders were expressing their thoughts and providing leadership according to their own lights in the same period. Among these men were Martin Robinson Delany and Bishop Henry McNeal Turner. Yet the question of destiny of the African-Americans continued to agitate the minds of many in this period, and the contributions of leaders whether elitist or commoners all poured into the melting pot of ideas in the face of growing racial hostility from the Euro-American quarter in general and from the white South in particular.

The emergence of numerous publications which tended to place the blacks outside the pale of humanity forged the leadership that was to emerge in the early twentieth century and even well into the second half of the twentieth century. The succession of African-American leaders were men and women forged in the hard and harsh school of suffering, struggle, and discrimination; and each successive age contributed to the forging of the Africans of the diaspora in the United States and other parts of the Americas as they appear today. Their labors have been sisyphean. They might not have achieved their objectives but their contributions cannot be ignored, despised, or minimized. This leadership of the elitist kind hovered between the integrationist orientation of leadership and the separate identitists but were more often integrationists than anything else. Only on one occasion, as has been shown in this work, did the elitists express the emigrationist perspective and that was in the petition which Prince Hall and some of his followers submitted in the eighteenth century to the Legislature of Massachusetts to be aided to emigrate to Africa.

The question that remains unanswered is: Could it be that the founding fathers of the United States of America, by creating a constitution which accepted slavery, had foreordained the destiny of the descendants of Africa in the United States such that they should never attain equality in the United States, and that if they remained on American soil the concession of full equality would not be made? The further examination of the travail of the Africans of the Diaspora in the U.S.A. belongs to the next period of the evolution of leadership between 1920 and the contemporary period. It does not fall within the purview of this work, although this work informs the succeeding period in the evolution of Africans of the Diaspora, first in the United States, second in the other parts of the Americas, and third the manner in which they have worked and will work for reconnection to Africa.

NOTES

1. See for example Rev. William J. Simmons, *Men of Mark, Eminent, Progressive and Rising*, New York, 1887, reprint 1968.
2. See for instance, G. Shepperson, "Notes on Negro-American Influences on the Emergence of African Nationalism," *Journal of African History*, Vol. 1, No. 2, 1960.
3. J. E. Harris, "The Pan-African Tradition," Lecture delivered at the University of Nairobi, 1972 unpublished manuscript. Also Tony Martin, *Race First*, The Majority Press.
4. V. B. Thompson, Africa and Unity: The Evolution of Pan-Africanism, London and New York, 1969, 1977, 1984, p. xxi-xxiii, 3-7.
5. See *Africa Times and Orient Review*, London, Vol. 1, No. 3, Sept. 1912, p. 89 for a letter of protest to the editor by activists of the A.M.E. Church of British Guiana (later Guyana) concerning the flogging of two Southern Nigerian clerks for refusing to be subservient to a Third Class Resident (equivalent to a District Commissioner in Eastern Africa). They regarded the punishment meted out to the clerks as highly repulsive and inhuman.
6. See for instance, George M. Fredrickson, *The Black Image in the White Mind... 1817-1914*, Hanover, New Hampshire, 1987.
7. See Thompson, V. B., *The Making of the African Diaspora in the Americas*, London and Harlow, 1987, Chs. 5 & 6 and Appendix 2.
8. H. H. Garnet at the National Colored Convention of 1843 in C. G. Woodson, *Negro Orators and their Orations*, Washington, D. C., 1925, pp. 150-57.
9. F. Douglass, *Life and Times of Frederick Douglass*, London, 1882, New York, 1881, also William Still, *The Underground Railroad*, Philadelphia, 1899, pp. 348-57.
10. See Douglass, *Life and Times, op. cit.* pp. 248-52. His letter to Mrs. Harriet Beecher Stowe dated 8 March, 1853 also in H. Brotz, *Negro Social and Political Thought* (Documents) pp. 220-26. The early National Negro Convention movement had at various times advocated it for the unlettered black masses as a prerequisite for their elevation but did not slavishly adhere to it as the only path to their elevation.
11. Brotz, *op. cit.*, pp. 12. C. G. Woodson, *Negro Orators and their Orations*, pp. 579-93.
12. DuBois, W. E. B., *Souls of Black Folk*, Ch. 3.
13. See J. Saunders Redding, *The Lonesome Road*, New York, 1958; Edwin Redkey, *Black Exodus*, New Haven, 1969, p. 5 *et seq.*; August Meier, *Negro Thought in America 1880-1915*, CH. IV, pp. 60-62, 64-65; Benjamin Brawley, *A Social History of the American Negro*, New York, 1921;p C. G. Woodson, *A Century of Negro Migration*, Washington, D.C., 1918, p. 130.
14. Meier, August, *op. cit.* p. 60.
15. *Ibid.*
16. Redding, *op. cit.* also Arna Bontemps, *Any Place But Here*, Walter L.Flemming, "'Pap' Singleton, The Moses of the Colored Exodus," *American Journal of Sociology*, XV (July, 1909), pp. 77-80; see also, W. E. B. DuBois, *Black Reconstruction*, New York, 1935, p. 693. Of the numbers involved Singleton took two colonies to Kansas of 7,432 blacks. Henry Adams' was greater claiming about 92,800 from Louisiana, Texas,

Arkansas, Mississippi and Alabama. About 60,000 went to Kansas, two-thirds of whom were destitute on arrival.

17. Meier, August, *op. cit.* pp. 65-66.
18. E. Redkey, *op. cit.* p. 23.
19. See various references to Blyden in J. E. Casely-Hayford, *Ethiopia Unbound.*
20. Redkey, *op. cit. loc. cit.*
21. For the proceedings see Congressional Records, 51st Congress, First Session, pp. 419-430, 623-630, 802-807, 966-973, 1046-1988, and 4364.
22. See Frazier, E. F., *The Negro in the United States.* Revised edition, 1961, pp. 381-86.

Chapter 2

Physical Force Leadership

The logic of physical force was obvious from the very operation of the slave system.[1] In our consideration of the strategy of the slavocracy and of most people who wielded power in slave societies, it was observed how violence was perfected to the point of being a cult - violence being a notable feature of slave societies often unabating and unrelenting. Violence was ubiquitous and ever-present and channels through which grievances could be ventilated were often non-existent, deliberately blocked, and where they existed they could hardly be relied on to achieve a redress of those grievances. Decisions were arbitrary and the just were always the oppressors not the victims. Left with no alternative, the desperate slave, the determined slave, or the slave of indomitable spirit repaid his ill-usage in kind; thus violence begot violence and so we find that slave revolts were numerous and recurrent.[2] Such revolts did not uphold the widespread assertion that the African slaves were docile, such docility being frequently "noted" in the writings of certain travellers and visitors to the plantations, who often (though not always) shared pro-slavery sentiments. The recurrent revolts testified to the opposite of docility and revealed the yearning for freedom even when the chances of securing this seemed remote. The records reveal that, in desperation, slaves were prepared to commit suicide, or poison their progeny as well as their masters rather than succumb to the indignities inherent in the slave system. Hence the plantocracy and their agents sought ways and means of preventing such occurrences. Slave revolts (the violent ones) were often initiated by slaves themselves, sometimes in collaboration with freemen, as in the case of Denmark Vesey's revolt of 1822. Where free blacks or free colored people did not initiate revolts, they sometimes manifested sympathy for their enslaved brethren by numerous activities, as agitating the slave question on anti-slavery platforms, or facilitating the escape of slaves or defending them against slave catchers after their escape. Such free men formed the natural leaders in an era in which they could be the only spokesmen for their oppressed brethren. The peculiarities of the situation were bound to make the emergence of leadership so haphazard. The men and women who led those violent revolts against their enslavers formed the initial leadership for the Africans of the diaspora. They are not nameless, but they are too numerous to name. Nonetheless, partiality is shown in this text by singling out a few as typical of that leadership. These revolts rocked the foundations of slavery in North America. The most successful revolts were those of the Africans of St. Domingue (Haiti) led by Toussaint L'Overture, Jean Jacques Dessalines and Henri Christophe, Claiveaux, *Capoi dit la mort* (alias Capoix Death), La Plume, Tackey (Teshi) in Jamaica and Samuel Sharpe (Jamaica) and Cuffy (Kofi in Berbice, later British Guiana) and Boni in Surinam.[3] Yet the three major revolts on the North American scene showed their organizers to be men of ability. But, even more important were the motives for revolt freedom. This observation does not, however, discount the leaders of slave revolts in the West Indies or the men and women of Palmares (the "famous Negro Republic" in Brazil) or those of other *Quilombos*. Furthermore in singling out the three North American revolts, consideration is given to the fact they have become symbols of revolt among African-Americans and Afro-Caribbeans who look back on their long and painful history in the house of bondage in the Americas. In further singling out this North American peculiarity, we are made aware of the fact that it was on the North American scene that a clear line of leadership persisted and has continued to be maintained into the contemporary period. This factor alone justifies the study of that emergent leadership.

Gabriel Revolt 1800

The revolts under consideration occurred between 1800 and 1832. The first of these was led by Gabriel, slave of a certain Mr. Thomas H. Prosser in Henrico County, (around Richmond), Virginia, in 1800. Not much is known of Gabriel's background, but his elaborately laid-out plan marked him as a leader of consequence. It is even suggested that he used the Bible to actuate his brethren into revolt by assuring them that they could, like the Israelites of old,[4] cast off the yoke of slavery with God's assistance. As the attempted insurrection occurred at a time when Thomas Jefferson was leading a democratic movement, his opponents, the Federalists, blamed the attempted insurrection of Gabriel on this democratic tendency of Jefferson[5] and his adherents, who seemed to favor the ideals of liberty issuing forth from the French Revolution.

It was even rumored that the rebel slaves intended in their revolt to spare French lives. With the betrayal of the projected revolt by two of his fellow slaves, Gabriel, on being captured, refused to reveal the names of any of his adherents. This firmness of will marked him out as a leader of some consequence.This projected revolt struck fear in the hearts of the Virginians and this led the Governor into a secret correspondence with Thomas Jefferson for the purpose of securing land somewhere to banish truculent and refractory slaves. The same proposal made to Jefferson was formulated in the form of a resolution in 1805 and passed by a secret session of the Virginia legislature. Even though no action seemed to have been taken, this incident revealed the state of unease within the stronghold of the slave-holding communities.

Denmark Vesey Revolt 1822

The second major revolt occurred in 1822 but before we discuss this, it is essential to note what one modern American authority on slave revolts has said of the period. According to Professor Herbert Aptheker, "The 1820's... is one of the periods of most intense slave revolts."[6] Viewing those revolts within the context of a world setting of democratic and militant awakenings, Aptheker observed that in the United States the period was marked by a Jacksonian[7] triumph and there were the beginnings of a politically conscious labor movement. It was also a period of revolutionary ferment in Spain (even observed by David Walker in *The Appeal*), Turkey, Greece, Italy, France, Belgium, Poland, South America, Mexico, and the West Indies. Of the last, slaves were involved while the ferment in South America and Mexico aided the cause of anti-slavery. Mexico abolished slavery in 1829. Slave owners in the South were alarmed by these revolutionary trends, and since accounts of most of these revolts were often published in North American newspapers outside the South, the alarm of the slavocracy went unabated. In this same period Martinique, Puerto Rico, Cuba, Antigua, Tortola, Demerara, and Jamaica experienced revolts which did not go unnoticed in the United States.

Some fugitive slaves in the South described as "Maroons" disturbed outlying districts and accordingly southern cities like Petersburgh (Virginia), Mobile (Alabama), and Augusta (Georgia) experienced frequent incendiarism. Even the domestic slave trade was disturbed by the revolts on board such slave trading vessels, and two such revolts in 1826 were sensational.[8] It was under this pervasive atmosphere of plots and insurrections that Denmark Vesey (Veazie) in Charleston, South Carolina made his revolt in 1822. This revolt was said to have involved thousands of slaves. Vesey himself was a free man, having secured manumission in 1800 by purchase for $600 after a successful lucky dip or lottery in Charleston in which he gained $1500. When a boy, Vesey had been sold at San Domingo by his owner, the captain of a ship, but was returned when he exhibited signs of epilepsy and seemed physically weak. He was returned to his master in Charleston and faithfully served the latter for twenty years before his manumission. On being manumitted, he became accomplished as a carpenter and enhanced his reputation both among slaves and the free colored people of Charleston. He was literate and seemed well informed on events such as the success of the Haitian revolution and on the ideas guiding the French Revolution. His use of the Haitian example to inspire the slaves of Charleston mirrored again how the specter of St. Domingue haunted other slave societies in the Americas. He briefed himself succinctly with Congressional debates on the Missouri Compromise of 1820.

Vesey sought to instill confidence into his brethren of African descent and aimed at impressing on them the notion of equality with the Euro-Americans. This self-assertion manifested itself often in Vesey and surfaced in an "Official Report" relating to the trial of Vesey and his associates after his revolt had failed. The report suggested that when walking through the streets in the company of another of his color, he would reproach his companion for kowtowing to a "white" person and would launch into a dissertation "all men were born equal" and express his amazement that anyone would choose to demean himself by undue subservience. He let it be known that he would never cringe to any white person, and that no one who felt himself a man ought to. But when his companions answered: "We are slaves," Vesey replied sarcastically and indignantly in the characteristic Aristotelian assertion: "You deserve to remain slaves." When asked how subservience should be transcended his characteristic reply was: "Go and buy a spelling book and read the fables of Hercules and the Wagoner."[9] He was concerned that his brethren should understand their degradation and rise above it by organization and violence if need be.The names of Vesey's four lieutenants in the revolt were coded. As was usual in the plantations of the Americas there was always a "faithful house Negro"[10] and it was one such fellow who refused to be persuaded to join the revolt and subsequently betrayed the rest. The reprisals, as with all slave revolts, were summary. Vesey's lieutenants, except one, refused to reveal the names of their adherents and collaborators. It was rumored that some members of the Negro Methodist Church were participants, although their leaders refrained from joining the revolt. But by craft, cunning, and threats, some of the leaders of the plot were discovered. Thirty of them were hanged, thirty-seven deported from the U.S., and Vesey, defiant to the last, refused to reveal the names of his associates and died bravely. One of Vesey's lieutenants exhibited that courage and steadfastness previously noted in one incident of discovery of a slave plot in the West Indies, when he admonished his condemned associates not to betray others by admonishing them thus: "Do not open your lips...Die silent as you shall see me do."[11]

The next revolt to shake the complacency of the Southern Sates and to re-awaken the conscience of the north to the evils of American slavery occurred in Southampton County, Virginia in 1831. It was organized and led by Nathaniel (alias Nat) Turner. Of the leader so many conflicting opinions have been held, but one of the most serious attempts to re-evaluate the Turner Revolt was first undertaken by Herbert Aptheker in 1937 as a research project for a degree and published in 1965, a hundred and thirty five years after the event. The Turner Revolt in more recent times has generated much controversy of interpretation. One William Styron carried out his own researches and produced a more jaundiced view of Turner and his associates.

His book was titled *The Confessions of Nat Turner*. His methodology sparked off controversy and there have been rejoinders to his work, one example being the John Henrik Clarke anthology of responses by ten black writers.[12] Despite this controversy, it must be reasserted that what a people believe is important in their perception of events is often entrenched in their folklore. In this folklore of the majority of African-Americans, Nat Turner is a celebrated folk-hero. But we should first consider the viewpoint of one African-American activist in the movement for the abolition of slavery before proceeding to discuss the event.The Reverend Henry Highland Garnet, at the age of 29, addressing the National Convention of Colored Citizens in Buffalo, New York, in 1843, said of Turner: "The patriotic Nathaniel Turner followed Denmark Veazie. He was goaded to desperation by wrong and injustice. By despotism, his name has been recorded on the list of infamy, and future generations will remember him among the noble and brave."[13] That this was the considered opinion of a man who was to become one of the leaders of thought and action among Africans of the Diaspora not only in the United States but in the West Indies-and for a short time in Africa itself-is significant. It also showed the influence which both the Turner episode and the experience of slavery exercised on his mind.[14] But we must observe that it is his partial fulfillment of Garnet's prediction that "future generations would remember Turner among the noble and brave" that gives Professor Aptheker's excellent study[15] its significance; for, in it, with painstaking and careful study, he has been able to re-appraise the revolt within the framework of the general revolutionary ferment of those times and its continuity in the contemporary world. There is no reason to paraphrase Aptheker's work, for it deserves to be read in full and remains unsurpassed. Yet we must examine some of the points made by that author in order to see how he placed the revolt of Turner within the framework of world history; for, the Turner Revolt was not an isolated incident, although the prejudiced opinion of those times preferred to treat it as such. This attitude of treatment of events in isolation was similar to that of George Washington at the time of the Africa slave revolt in Haiti.[16] Washington, it had been observed,[17] while extolling the French Revolution, and being one of the champions of the American Revolution, could not bring himself to extend its spirit and content to the down-trodden Africans, whose degradation was worse than those of their European and Euro-American counterparts. Yet Washington was glad to see the children of Africa in America join the Euro-Americans in their revolt against England, just as in later times African-Americans would be called upon to fight on behalf of their "fatherland," America, which was still unprepared to concede them the full benefits of citizenship. It should also be recalled that Washington himself owned African slaves.

But what is of interest is that George Washington reflected an attitude of mind which pervaded the entire official thinking of the time. Revolt for the children of Africa (the so-called Negroes) was deemed heinous! Thus, while rightly observing that the 1830s was a period of revolution throughout the world (in fact, between 1830 and 1850), Aptheker saw these agitations and strivings as those of people engaged in self-immolation to secure more freedom and the right to assist in determining national policies; he also observed the ambivalence of the press of the United States, which, while approving revolts such as those of the Poles, lamented those of the "Negro" slaves. Aptheker noted that the *Richmond Enquirer* (Virginia) of August 23, 1831 had carried a poem of Thomas Campbell in celebration of the Polish people's revolutionary struggles and yet seventy-five miles away, unknown to the editor of the paper a revolt of "Negro slaves," led by Nat Turner, was raging. Yet when the editor of the paper commented on the latter incident three days later he saw nothing "noble" in the latter eruption while he had eulogized the former. He characterized it as an "insurrection" and not (as he had that of the Poles and other Europeans) "a revolution." The weight of prejudice against the children of Africa in America and the notion of inferiority dominated most of the writings of the pro-slavery protagonists. Such was the irony. Aptheker saw beneath this veil of opposite interpretations and his deductions and cynicism are obvious and clear: "This sword is raised by Negroes, by Blacks, by those whom God very obviously put on this earth to serve and work for the white man. For that they were made, and only for that."[18] For a pro-slavery Professor, Rev. Thomas Roderick Dew, of William and Mary College, the distinction was made in the following rhetorical question: "Has it come out at last to this: that the hellish plots and massacres of Dessalines,[19] Gabriel,[20] and Nat Turner are to be compared to the noble deeds and devoted patriotism of Lafayette, Kosciusko and Sckrynecki?"[21] Dew could not bring himself to give an affirmative answer to this question for based on his racial prejudice, a liberated "Negro" was the incarnation of Satan. The image-molding activities of the pro-slavery group and those hostile to descendants of Africa in the Americas were persistent and even so callous as to deny the slaves' humanity. The prejudice was reinforced in the citation which follows:Mr. William Preston speaking in the anti-slavery debates precipitated in the Virginia legislature of 1831-32 by Nat Turner's revolt said "... if those who are slaves here, were not what they are; if, Mr. speaker they were white men in oppression and bondage, I would rejoice in a revolution here".[22]

A young slaveholder on reading Dr. Channing's "Slavery" was also reported to have said "that if it could be proved that negroes are more than a link between man and brute, the rest follows of course, and he must liberate all his."[23] We see from the above that this perverted prejudice of imbuing the "Negro" with inferiority prevented many commentators on the Turner revolt from evaluating it in true perspective within the context of a society sustained on slave labor and the excesses which breed revolts, just as in another time and place prejudice and blindness prevented a dispassionate appraisal of a more contemporary African-American leader, Malcolm X.

Thus William Sidney Drewry, in his account of the Southampton episode, could not see the contradictions in his thought when in several places he asserted not only the inferiority of the "Negro"[24] but that only the deluded, cowardly, and stupid ever took part in a slave revolt[25] while, in an earlier description of Nat Turner, he had referred to him as a "man of considerable mental ability and wide information."[26] This pointing out of contradictions in the thoughts of those who justified revolution for whites and condemned it for blacks, all because of acquired habits of thought, perception, action, and ingrained prejudices, is one of the real merits of Professor Aptheker's study of Nat Turner. Referring to the works of modern anatomists, anthropologists, and psychologists who refute this nonsense about inferiority, Aptheker concludes that "one need not find one man a martyr because he is white, and calling another man a wretch because of some degree of coloration. Specifically one may then, and should consider the followers of Nat Turner not as deluded wretches and monsters (unless all revolutionists may thus be described) but rather as further examples of the woefully long, and indeed veritably endless, roll of human beings willing to resort to open struggle in order to get something precious to them peace, prosperity, liberty, or, in a word, a greater amount of happiness."[27]

The successes and failures of those revolts are not very important, as most of them failed initially. Yet, the success of the Haitian revolution was a landmark in the history of the children of Africa in the Americas and in the world. However, what is of greater importance than the success of slave revolts is the effect of these revolts on the minds of people within and without slave societies, - their impact on the enslaved, the free people of color, the slaveholders and their sympathizers, as well as the anti-slavery groups and societies. For in them we are likely to find the seeds which germinated to terminate slavery and all its works. This is a gigantic task which has been undertaken by many stalwarts including Professor Aptheker.[28]All we can do here is to state some broad outlines which had their influence on the emergence of leadership for the downtrodden descendants of Africans in the New World diaspora. There is another point of significance about the Turner revolt, for it followed so closely on the publication by David Walker, another free colored man of Boston, of his *Appeal to All the Colored Citizens of the United States*. The first copy of this revolutionary book was published in 1829.[29] This publication ran into three editions, the final being published in 1830. Walker did not live to see the impact of his Appeal, for, before the end of the year 1830, Walker had died at the young age of 44 years. The circumstances under which Walker died are shrouded in mystery but William Lloyd Garrison's paper *The Liberator* of 22 January 1831, under the heading "Death of Walker" published a letter signed by a colored man which sheds some light on the possibility of foul play at the instigation of some member of the slavocracy.[30] Two modern American historians (confirmed by a third) have testified to the fact that Walker's *Appeal* was one of the greatest contributions to the anti-slavery literature.[31] In the *Life of Benjamin Lundy*, a Quaker stalwart and a pacifist but an abolitionist, who published *The Genius of Universal Emancipation*, we learn that: "It is supposed, by some, that the pamphlet of Walker was the cause of the massacre of whites at Southampton, Virginia, which took place in the following year."[32] As Turner was literate, it was widely believed that he had seen and read the Walker pamphlet; but he had also read the Bible, perhaps observing the contradictions between the teachings of Christianity and the actions of professed Christians, especially in holding their fellow men in bondage. As Walker's pamphlet was in circulation at the time, there is the probability that Turner had seen and read it. This, however, is immaterial, for the harsh realities of slavery for those who had neither seen nor read Walker's *Appeal* had led them to revolt again and again against slavery. By the kind of argument often advanced by detractors, Walker's text was both the cause and effect of Nat Turner's revolt.[33] Prior to the Turner Revolt the slavocracry had sought by ingenuous "laws" to militarize their society and secure the slave system. They are too numerous to mention and we do well to omit them here. The tightening of regulations and security following the revolt of 1831 merely intensified what had already been in existence and was part of the established practice of slave societies. But the pre-Turner revolt laws and stipulations might have themselves been among the causes of the revolts that they sought to prevent. Aptheker's researches led him to say that "an examination of the evidence reveals a highly intelligent man (Nat Turner) who finds it impossible to accept the *status quo* and discovers his rationalization for his rebellious feelings in religion."[34] The causes and the motivations of the Turner Revolt have been at various times grossly distorted; thus, over the years, a false imagery has been built around the revolt, portraying Turner in a bad light.

These distortions have been assailed by Aptheker,[35] who argues that liberty was obviously the prime aim—a viewpoint implicit or explicit in most of the later commentaries concerning the event. Implicit in the flimsy and many accusations levelled at the abolitionists of having probably instigated the revolt is the implication that freedom was the motivation. But this accusation against abolitionists was rebutted by William Lloyd Garrison, editor of *The Liberator*, who wrote "We have circulated no papers extra in any part of our country. We have not a single white or black subscriber south of the Potomac. We have no travelling agent or agents. It is not the real or `avowed object' of *The Liberator* to stir up insurrections but the contrary."[36] While protesting the innocence of the abolitionists with no intention of inciting revolt, Garrison's reporting of the Turner incident left no doubt as to the effect his words would have had on the slaves. In *The Liberator* of September 3, 1831, he castigated the slaveholders and their sympathizers thus: "Ye patriotic hypocrites! Ye panegyrists of Frenchmen, Greeks, Poles! Ye Fustian declaimers for liberty! Ye valiant sticklers for equal rights among yourselves! Ye haters of aristocracy! Ye assailants of monarchies! Ye republican nullifiers! Ye treasonable disunionists! Be Dumb! Cast no reproach on the conduct of slaves, but let your lips and cheeks bear the blisters of condemnation."[37]

Effects

The effects of the Turner Revolt on all classes and various shades of opinion in the United States have been dealt with by Aptheker[38] and not even a summary is attempted here, only a few generalized points. Restlessness of the slaves increased and fears of impending insurrections were reiterated at regular intervals. But drastic measures were taken to prevent the recurrence of these revolts by the slaveholders and the white community. What were considered to be harsher laws were introduced and restrictions imposed on the movements and activities of free colored people as well as the slaves (these related to the denial of opportunities for assembly, for receiving religious instruction, or any kind of education). Contact with any Northern or abolitionist agencies were severely punished, and the receipt of any abolitionist newspapers, pamphlets, or propaganda tracts or other printed material was regarded as seditious. But in the slave states it seemed as if a volcano had been smothered and had the potential of erupting again. There seemed to have developed a determination by the defenders of slavery to maintain it at all costs. But so also were the abolitionists impelled to persist in the efforts to secure the eradication of this evil. Thus, while abolitionists established vigilance committees to prevent the abduction of fugitives back into slavery, the slaving states set up vigilante committees and organized mobs to ensure that no impostor or "subversive element" penetrated the watchful eye of these committees. What is relevant is that Nat Turner was one in the chain of physical force leaders who saw no alternative to asserting the humanity of African-American, other than the methods used by his oppressor to keep him in bondage. Repressive measures did not stem the tide of revolt among the bondsmen and bondswomen and those nominally out of bondage. The period succeeding the Turner Revolt down to the outbreak of the Civil War saw recurrent revolts. Even reports from Brazil, Tortola, and Jamaica between 1831 and 1832 added to the panic in the slave strongholds.[39] The peace of mind of the slavocracry if ever there was any, was gone. One frenzied act of legislation led to another and the authorities used terror tactics on "Negroes" while their Euro-American spokesmen pontificated on the "wretchedness" of the free blacks and their "religious adventures" which often led them to foment slave revolts.

Thus, at one stroke, the authorities aimed to deny both the freeman and his kinsman in slavery the right to enlightenment, freedom of worship and assembly, as well as the opportunity for mental growth, development, and opportunity for progress in society. These factors, apart from the hounding of freemen out of some cities and states, compelled some of them to escape to the North. Free black people were denied the right to possess firearms; and even ideas of colonization of the free blacks outside the U.S., especially in Liberia, persisted and even in some cases, as in Maryland, became the preoccupation of legislatures. Laws prohibiting the importation of slaves for sale in some Southern states were passed, but soon became dead letters. In North Carolina "Negroes" found preaching earned a punishment of thirty-nine lashes. Death was the penalty in Florida after February 12, 1832 for any kind of incitement to revolt or insurrection of slaves or through statements likely to achieve the same results. Thus the action of killing slaves during a revolt was *"justifiable homicide."* [40] Association between free "negroes" and the enslaved without slaveholder's permission was also prohibited. Yet the abolitionists only became more determined in their crusade. One issue of *The Liberator* in which Garrison had commented on the Turner Revolt contained this statement: "Insurrections are the natural and consequent productions of slavery—experience has proved this in all ages and in all nations where slavery has existed. Slavery *ought* to be, *must* be and shall be abolished in the United States."[41] The positions of the North and the South became polarized - the latter hardening on the question of slavery, the former winning more people to the abolitionist ranks. A consequence of the Turner Revolt was to increase Southern intransigence in its resistance to the abolition of slavery. But this inward looking and regressive trend was far from being a sign of strength. It was to be tested a generation later.

But the chief legacy of the revolts, especially the Turner Revolt, is the memory and legacy of struggle which has remained fresh in the minds of African-Americans in the diaspora to this day, seeing Turner and those before as the pioneers of the struggle to realize the dignity of the African-derived people. Among some African-Americans the Turner Revolt is seen as belonging to the tradition of progressive struggle. The late Dr. W. E. B. DuBois, the veteran scholar and one of the earliest Pan-Africanists, expressed the Euro-American attitude towards the African-American striving thus: "There are ever those about him whispering: `You are nobody; why strive to be somebody? The odds are overwhelming against you—wealth, tradition, learning and guns. Be reasonable. Accept the dole of charity and the cant of missionaries and sink contentedly to your place as humble servants and helpers of the white world. "[42] As if to imply that Turner pointed the way among the physical force leaders, Aptheker wrote: "Nat Turner was one who refused to `be reasonable,' and it is believed that as the present-day stirrings of the American Negro people grow, the significance of the Turner Revolt as a tradition of progressive struggle will increase." [43] Although the individual activities of the physical force leadership failed in some quarters (but by no means in the long-run), we leave the last word on this type of leadership during the anti-slavery struggle to Professor Aptheker, who wrote: "If and when humanism arrives and animalism is driven from the world, Nat Turner will be labelled as one who fought against the latter. His motives will be admired and sadness, and amazement perhaps, will grip the observer who will realize that, with those admirable motives, society, as then arranged, made his bloody deeds necessary." [44] If this chapter is thin it is simply because opposition of enlsaved Africans to slavery and the slave trade and the endeavors to freedom have been discussed in another text[45] and the accounts of slave exploits are ubiquitous. What seemed important was to identify the tendency to physical force and the rationale behind it and how some outstanding leaders of this tendency typified the rest and for the same reason have become folk heroes and represent adequately the traditions of struggles of the Africans of the Diaspora in the Americas. Furthermore, even in the twentieth century, there has emerged a leadership in the United States of America that has restated the need for the activation of this tradition of struggle, stating them in more explicit and more vehement terms. Among them have been the Black Panther Party. Even in the discussions and lectures of the late Malcolm X, El Hajj El Malik Shebazz, these issues had again arisen, the typical ones appearing in his "Message to the Grass Roots" and "Ballots or Bullets." Moreover, some modern African commentators insisted after the assassination of the moral suasionist leader, Martin Luther King, in 1968, that his death by an assassin's bullet once again re-emphasized that the path of moral suasion had failed and that the violence of a violent society must be met with violence.

This has sometimes given gravity to the Marxian analysis of conflict in society. In fact, the inclination results from perception and the working of the dialectic in the struggles for full citizenship in contemporary America. But all these considerations belong to a later period in the evolution of leadership of the Diaspora and fall outside the scope of this work.

THEATERS OTHER THAN NORTH AMERICA

There were numerous slave revolts and attempted revolts which were aborted in the many theaters of slavery in South America and the Caribbean, including Cuba. In Cuba, none caused so much consternation as the alleged "conspiracy" of *La Escalera* in 1844, resulting in excessive reprisals against the slaves, the *morenos* (black and brown), the free colored, and the *pardos* (colored and some whites) who were believed to be associated with that conspiracy. Not only was much done under the Captain-General for Spain, Leopoldo O'Donnell, to decimate and whittle down the influence of the free colored people, but a generation later it had recovered sufficiently and produced the momentum to be in the forefront of the "Ten Years War" inaugurated in 1868 for Cuban liberation and that of 1895. *La Escalera,* in fact, resulted in the emergence of the modified slave regulations of 1844 as a supplement to the Slave Code of 1842, which in many respects was an advance on previous Slave Codes. By this time it had begun to dawn on slavocrats and civil authorities that the restiveness of slaves implied some dissatisfaction with the existing system. Moreover, the experiences of emancipation in St. Domingue (Haiti) in 1804 and the British West Indies in the 1830s and the campaigns by Britain to terminate the slave trade and slavery in other theaters were imbuing even the slaves in Cuba with aspirations for their own liberation. But coupled with this fear of a mass uprising against Spain by the local authorities and the push for independence was the fear of the Africanization of Cuba because of its large African and colored population. The United States, with its own racist system, conscious of the existence of the Black State of Haiti, and fearful that common cause would be made by Cuba and Haiti, did not welcome that development, with its clear implications for slave states in the southern United States. There was also the ever-present fear that the British might aid the Cuban struggle against Spain (and, indirectly, against the United States) and thus extend their hegemony to areas in the Caribbean, South America, and even parts of the United States thus undermining U.S. sovereignty. To forestall the British in such designs, various high officials and dignitaries in the United States contemplated and advocated the annexation of Cuba. A first step towards achieving this was taken in 1840 when the United States intruded its commercial activities in the quest not only for large profitable returns, but also in a bid to establish U.S. ascendancy in Cuba's political affairs, as the alternative to a highly Africanized liberated Cuba.[46] A recent study[47] has shown how the Afro-Cubans who participated in significant numbers in the Ten Years War (1868-1878) and in the second and final struggle for independence from Spain (1895-1898) contributed their quota immensely in the hope not only that their liberation from Spain and from slavery would come about but that complete equality with the whites would also be achieved. But subterfuges by Cuban whites with divergent perspectives used the myth of an "African takeover of Cuba"[48] and their own aspirations for attaining (nay, continuing) white supremecy, to frustrate and destroy Afro-Cuban aspirations. With many subterfuges and discriminatory practices, they did much to close many of the avenues towards enhancement of the status and stature of the Afro-Cubans. Those racist attitudes were also informed and bolstered up by the racial supremacist attitudes and practices of Cuba's nearest neighbor, the United States. *La Escalera* (1844), which had resulted in the massacre of many Afro-Cubans, including the celebrated poet Placido, found a generation later that these Afro-Cubans had recovered sufficiently to be in the vanguard and in a strong position to express once again their aspirations for national independence.

Despite their significant contributions acknowledged in Cuban history in the second war of liberation in 1895, they were rewarded, to use the language of Christ, with a "stone instead of bread," and were downgraded by deliberate, subtle, and conspiratorial methods and policies to the bottom of society in Cuba by the determination of the white racial supremacists to confine them there and diminish them even further.

The Afro-Cubans (who, according to recent studies of the period, had fashioned the first political party in the hemisphere) found their endeavor destroyed forever in a move to realize what Brazil was later to enunciate as "racial democracy"[49] (in which everyone was in the melting-pot). Consequently, a pretext was found for massacring a sizeable number of Afro-Cubans in 1912. History seemed to repeat itself, bearing in mind the Apponte massacre of 1812. Vilification of the Afro-Cubans took the same vicious form that was being spread internally in the United States and especially in the South between the 1880s and the 1920s.

The result was that the "Afro-Cuban problem" - created by suspicions, craftiness, skullduggery, deceit, and hegemonic ambition of white Cubans - was relegated to the background of any serious considerations. It still remains one of the legacies of the enslavement of Africans in Cuba, despite the pretext of a socialist and socialized society. It indicts the Cuban *bourgeois* pretence in the period of the 1920s to have achieved democracy for only one group, the whites, while deliberately denying it through nuanced palliatives and expressions to its compatriots, who had borne the brunt of the liberation struggles of the second half of the nineteenth century against Spain, for the realization of a "free Cuba."

But their efforts resulted in a supreme irony. Their massacre in 1912 was a culmination of sinister white efforts, since the commencement of the nineteenth century, to achieve total castration and genocide (both physical and cultural) of the Afro-Cubans, with all the avenues to enhancement of their stature and status in Cuban society firmly closed to them. The history of their experiences are only now being revealed, but the white hegemony in Cuba has not emerged exonerated. The final judgement of their disreputable record still remains to be pronounced. But their excesses against their Afro-Cuban compatriots prevented a clear emergence of Afro-Cuban leadership with a Pan-African perspective. That emergence belongs to the second half of the twentieth century well into the 1980s, about twenty years after Fidel Castro's Revolution and its initial Marxist orientation. Nevertheless, before and after the emancipation of slaves in 1886 in Cuba, some Afro-Cubans left for West Africa, [50] where, in mingling with the Afro-Brazilians who had also returned to West Africa as well as some Sierra Leone repatriates (rescued from slave vessels and beached in Freetown Sierra Leone and later allowed to return to their homeland, many of whom returned to Nigeria), some of these Afro-Cubans reintegrated into African society, even while keeping a distinctive identity as repatriates, whereas others continued to be in touch with their relations in Cuba and Brazil respectively.

This aspect of the study has yet to be completed. But it is known, even in the official records of the British in West Africa, that these Afro-Cubans and Afro-Brazilians were in the forefront in generating the African nationalist sentiments in Nigeria[51] against colonial policies, even if they were themselves exploited by British colonialism in West Africa. A reflection on Palmares is pertinent here in order to complete the cycle of the physical force leadership.

Dos Palmares: An African Constellation in the Western Hemisphere (1595-1696)

The emergence of an African state within the slave colonial setting of Palmares in the Northeastern portion of Brazil in the Portuguese province of Pernambuco, was a phenomenon as much as a cause for celebration. It was founded in the late sixteenth century (the date often quoted is 1595) by Africans who immediately escaped from the plantations to establish their own community, governed by their own rules derived from Africa and used to guide their internal relations with one another and, later, with their external foes. It was a phenomenon for many reasons, even though it was not the first and only community established by Africans fleeing the plantations. It was still early in time and was the longest lasting, excepting the smaller community of maroons of Suriname, who have lasted into the late twentieth century. The reason is because it established a state, a republic with a king as head of state, who was elected, and guided by a council. Third, it was the result of bringing together into one fold Africans from various parts of the continent into one Pan-African arrangement with a "give and take" principle at work, which sustained them in unity for a long time. Fourth, it allowed others such as Native Americans and some Europeans who disliked slavery (and who were often designated poor whites) to become members of the state. (Some of these Native Americans later revealed the path which produced the chink in the formidable wall of their defenses, through which the Portuguese in the final assault were able to infiltrate and later penetrate its defenses.) Fifth, according to a modern Brazilian writer-historian (and he was right), it was the first real effort to establish a democratic system in the entire hemisphere in modern times. [52] (Readings of its system of governance would establish this assertion, as time and space do not allow this writer such an indulgence.) Sixth, its existence emphasized this adherence to freedom and those who escaped to it immediately became liberated. Those who were captured from the plantations had to redeem themselves by bringing in other enslaved Africans from the plantations. Their numbers were also reinforced by new arrivals from Africa, who soon fled the plantations to join them. Seventh, from the point of view of the slavocrats, it was an unusual, remarkable occurrence, undreamed of by them in their blinkered prejudices against the African people. Eight, because its existence in a slave theater and its formidable and sustained attacks on the plantations threatened the very existence of the slave order in the first instance, both in Brazil's northeast and elsewhere in the region. Had the *Palmaristas* succeeded in throwing out their Portuguese adversaries, Brazil might have emerged as an African Brazil and not a Portuguese Brazil.Ninth, from the point of view of the enslaved Africans and those who continued to join them and swell their ranks, it remained for nearly a century a bastion of freedom which the plantations were not. For the *Palmaristas*, it was a logical progression of Africans formerly free, once they had tasted enslavement and degradation and felt the urgency of regaining their freedom by any means necessary, even the same violence so ubiquitous in slave societies for sustaining the system.

Furthermore, the formation of the Famous Republic of Palmares was itself an act of defiance towards the slave order, and a manifestation of independence by being a separate entity outside the framework of the slave system. Moreover, the formidable nature of its periodic confrontations with the slave order (often provoked by the slavocracy) in actual combat constituted a concrete threat to that order's survival as a strong and seemingly invincible Palmares (as it was for a protracted period), and threatened to undermine the Portuguese pursuit of wealth and power in the western hemisphere. Tenth, the success of Palmares, had it ultimately driven the Portuguese out, as later the Haitians were to do with the French, would have been inspirational in other slave theaters to attempt the same. Furthermore, it would have heightened the consternation felt in various slave societies both on the American mainland and in the islands, as they continued to be haunted well into the twentieth century by the specter of the Haitian Revolution.[53] The many revolts in slave theaters from 1795 on (beginning with the Jamaican Maroons, the Caribs of St. Vincent (1796), with revolts in Grenada, Dominica about the same time) were felt in both official and unofficial circles to have been inspired by the St. Domingue (Haitian) revolt *cum* revolution.

While the slavocrats would have over-exaggerated the impact of Haiti on their local revolts (as there were disagreeable factors prevailing within those slave societies), it would be misleading to discount the inspiration that Haiti had provided. But were all the territories able to communicate freely, and obtain as well as secure weapons, especially firepower, they would have been formidable against the minority of the slavocracy.

The success of Palmares lay in its location at a considerable distance from Salvador, then the capital of Brazil, and also because it was located in difficult terrain among mountain fastnesses. To have experienced the terrain of Palmares is to be able to contemplate the formidable obstacles to penetration to the respective colonial powers, the Portuguese and the Dutch, in assailing it. For a protracted period success eluded them and they swallowed their pride and nursed frustrations (although their official records are instructive). Inaccessibility was also made more certain by the wooded nature of the surroundings, while the palm forests also gave it an aura of mystery that intimidated the superstitious Portuguese and their Euro-Brazilian progeny. It also had the protection of a huge landmass unlike the islands which were surrounded by water and easily encompassed by a determined navy. Its organization was a factor which made it formidable against the foes from the capital and elsewhere in the country. It was also a state which devolved power, but with a central voice of control. Following from this, since the kings were elected, they held their position by popular acclaim and they retained their position, if they did not compromise the integrity of the state and as long as they were guided by the rules (laws and customs) which guided the society, as was the case with rulers in African societies from whom most of them sprung.The fact of its democratic set-up needs to be stressed, for not even the colonies of North America which later formed the United States had at the time of Palmares' destruction evolved a democracy. It should be borne in mind that one factor in the North American colonies' revolt against England was because they rejected taxation without representation. That goal was not reached in the United States until the Civil Rights Act of 1954. The United States was still a slave society and many in the population did not even count for representation and the voting principle was encumbered by such limiting factors as the property qualification. The formidable nature of Palmares's defenses and its systems of intelligence (both in ascertaining what the enemy was up to and in preparing a prolonged siege) all helped to sustain the republic. But, above all, the citizens of Palmares had an implicit belief in their State and knew the consequences of failing to be vigilant and failing to defend it. It was, therefore, in keeping with this conviction and signal attitude of mind that in the Portuguese final onslaught on their State in 1696, the Palmaristas (Spanish, *Palmarenos*) put up such a determined struggle and died valiantly in a manner that brings credit to their memory. They knew the consequences of failing in their struggles against a slave power obsessed with revenge and chose the path of heroism instead of ignominy. The recent recognition by the Brazilian government of these people, declaring November 20th, a public holiday, is a testimony to their belated recognition of a foe formidable in battle, nonetheless, a foe who, had it triumphed, would have given Brazil a different history and destiny. But that recognition of a public holiday did not come before much agitation for it by Afro-Brazilians, who demanded evenhandedness. They shamed the Brazilian regime into a concession in order to continue its myth of the existence of a "racial democracy" in Brazil.The exploits of the illustrious people of *Dos Palmares* has reverberated throughout the hemisphere and now the world during the last years of the twentieth century. Its symbolic significance will grow with increasing studies of the period and works of Afro-Brazilian writers, artists, musicians, historians, and archaeologists.

There is still much more to know about *Dos Palmares*, even though only three of their kings' names have surfaced in the annals-

Ganga Zumba, Zumbi, and Kamunga. Zumbi opposed the former when he attempted to reach a dangerous compromise, with the Portuguese colonial authorities. Often those compromises embodied in so-called treaties, were only temporary expedients, palliatives for gaining time to attack these Maroon communities. The history of the relations of the colonial powers with Maroons revealed many examples of broken pledges by the slavocracy. Another significant fact which makes *Dos Palmares* a symbol of freedom is that with its destruction by the Portuguese - the destruction of a democratic experiment at a time when Portugal was governed by dictatorial regimes - the Portuguese in the colonies had not even begun to understand what was implied by having a democratic system of government. Only in recent times, and then not for more than two decades, did another anti-colonial struggle against them (this time) in Africa itself, by the people of Guinea Bissau, Angolans, Mozambicans catapult the Portuguese home onto the democratic platform and compell them to renounce their dictators. Portugal, in the last years of the twentiwth century, still remains a fledgling democracy, with some proponents and practitioners of fascism still vocal and hankering for the day of their return to power.

The main weakness of Palmares was not its organization but rather its technological deficiency, which it could not have overcome being beleaguered on all sides by slave societies determined to maintain their systems and with the Portuguese slave regime bent on Palmares's destruction, just as the ancient Romans were in their final confrontation with another African state, Carthage. The destruction of Palmares was comparable in nature and vehemence with that of Carthage. Without comparable weapons and with no sources to obtain them, as was the case with Haiti, it was only a matter of time before they would be undermined. The absence also of any free African states in the hemisphere as independent entities (as was the case with Haiti which helped Bolivar in his South American struggles) made the destruction of Palmares inevitable, but the state lasted for upwards of a century when the modern world was young. Knowledge of Palmares is bound to increase in the future and even its last leader, Zumbi, will be appreciated not as a "rebel without a cause," but as a leader guided by principles, as a national and patriotic leader imbued with a consciousness of the need to preserve the dignity and integrity of his people and their state. *Dos Palmares* was the most famous *Quilombos* (from the Ambundu word, *Ki-lombo*). It was first and foremost in its confrontation with its European adversaries, the Portuguese and the Dutch, a physical force leadership which understood the vital nature of the use of this force which its

European assailants used against it without compunction. It remains a symbol of the African tradition of struggle in the Americas and a source of pride among African people because it harnessed its resources for governance and organization, drawing from the African experiences brought with them from the parent continent to guide their conduct of affairs.

CONCLUSION

Those who had earlier embarked on physical force, and, especially, the celebrated ones like the *Palmaristas* of the Republic of Palmaris in Bahia, Brazil, Tackey (Teshi) and Samuel Sharpe (Jamaica), Gabriel Prosser, Denmark Vesey, and Nat Turner (United States), Toussaint L'Ouverture, Dessalines, Henri Christophe, Alexander Petion, LaPlume, *Capoix dix la Mort* (St. Domingue- Haiti), Cuffy and Agidi (Berbice-British Guiana) and many of the Muslim Hausa, Yoruba, and Tapa revolts in Bahia, Brazil between 1720 and 1838, all had a logic to their endeavors. This was to be poetically expressed by a later descendant, Claude McKay, Afro-Caribbean poet of the Harlem Renaissance, who articulated it thus:

> If we must die, let it not be like hogs
> Hunted and penned in an inglorious spot,
> While round us bark the mad and hungry dogs,
> Making their mock at our accursed lot.
> If we must die, Oh let us nobly die,
> So that our precious blood may not be shed
> In vain; Then even the monsters we defy
> Shall be constrained to honor us though dead!
> Oh, Kinsmen! We must meet the common foe!
> Though far outnumbered let us show us brave,
> And for their thousand blows deal one deathblow!
> What though before us lies the open grave?
> Like men we'll face the murderous, cowardly pack,
> Pressed to the wall, dying but fighting back! [54]

The logic of those sentiments had begun to engulf the apartheid regime of South Africa in the 1990s, a logic thrown back at Africans in the parent continent by the earlier struggles of the Africans of the diaspora to rid themselves forever of slavery and degradation. It was enshrined in the organization of numerous independent maroon communities in many parts of the Americas, and especially that now known to the annals as the "Famous Republic of Palmares" in Brazil. A little reflection on Palmares, because of its long endurance, despite the repeated and relentless onslaughts by two European powers of the slavery era, Portugal and Holland, has been appropriate here.

NOTES

1. See V. B. Thompson, *The Making of the African Diaspora in the Americas 1441-1900*, Longman Group, Harlow, and New York, 1987. Chapter 7, esp. pp. 193-97.
2. They were more frequent in some theaters than in others —more in Brazil, the West Indies and on a gigantic scale than in the U.S.A. or Canada but they were there all the same.
3. Some of these revolts have been partially recaptured in the works of modern novelists—see for instance: Edgar Mittleholtzer, *Kaywana Stock, Children of Kaywana*, Corgi Books, London, (1976) earlier 1954: *Kaywana Heritage*, esp. chapter headed: "Twenty-sixth of February, 1763." Corgi Books, London, 1976 (earlier 1953).
4. We see the examples and symbolism of the earlier diaspora that of the Israelites influencing the thoughts and actions of a secondary diaspora, that of the African peoples. The points of convergence and divergence are discussed in a subsequent chapter. A text by Arna Bontemps has recently been re-published on the Gabriel Revolt titled: *Black Thunder*. It was previously published by the MacMillan Company in 1936 and then in 1963. The reissue of 1992 has an introductory note by Arnold Rampersad, Beacon Press. Beacon published a hardback edition in 1968.
5. E. Franklin Frazier, *The Negro is the United States*, New York, The MacMillan Company, revised edition, 1957, 1961, p. 87 (also fifth printing).
6. Herbert Aptheker, *`One Continued Cry': David Walker's Appeal to the Colored Citizens of the World (1829-1839) Its Setting and Its Meaning, etc.*, New York, Humanities Press, 1965, p. 33.
7. Reference to Andrew Jackson, a U. S. President. See *Concise Dictionary of American Biography*, (ed. Joseph G. E. Hopkins), Charles Schribner's Sons, New York, 7th President of the U. S. A., 1964, pp. 481-82.
8. H. Aptheker, *op. cit., One Continued Cry, etc.*, pp. 33-4.
9. *An Official Report of the Trials of Sundry Negroes Charged with An Attempt to Raise An Insurrection in the State of South Carolina, Prepared and Published at the Request of the Court by Lionel Kennedy and Thomas Parker*, p. 19 quoted in E. Franklin Frazier, *The Negro in the United States*, Revised Edition, Macmillan and Company, New York, 1961, pp. 87-88.
10. Faithfulness in this sense related to the slave owner not to the cause of liberation.
11. *An Attempt to Raise an Insurrection, op. cit.*, pp. 87-99. For a comparable example see Edmund D'Auvergne, *Human Livestock*, London, 1933, pp. 107-08.
12. John Henrik Clarke (ed.) *William Styron Nat Turner: Ten Black Writers Respond*, Boston, Beacon Press, 1968. See especially Clarke's introduction, pp. vii-x. For another documentary study see Henry Irving Tragle, *The Southampton Slave Revolt of 1831: A Compilation of Source Material*, The University of Massachusetts Press, Amherst, 1971 see especially his introduction and his observation that "It takes nothing away from the memory of John Brown to recall the first real blow struck at the roots of the

`peculiar institution' in Virginia, came twenty-eight years earlier, and that it was delivered by a man who was born, lived and died a slave.' - Nat Turner," p. 3.

13. Henry Highland Garnet, "An Address to the Slaves of the United States of America: 1843." Quoted in Carter G. Woodson, *Negro Orators and Their Orations*, Washington, D.C., 1952, pp. 156-57.
14. Garnet had been born in slavery but his father and the entire family fled from slavery into freedom. See also *Great Lives Observed: Nat Turner*, Prentice-Hall, Inc., Englewood Cliffs, N. J. 1971, ch. 6, pp. 66-74 for the perception of enslaved Africans on the Turner episode.
15. Herbert Aptheker, *Nat Turner's Slave Rebellion*, together with the full text of the so-called `Confessions' of Nat Turner made in prison in 1831, New York, Humanities Press, 1965.
16. The Haitian slave revolt began in 1791 two years after the outbreak of the first French Revolution. See *The Writings of George Washington*, J. C. Fitzpatrick (ed.), Vol. 31, 1931-40, pp. 375-453.
17. See my chapter on the special case of St. Domingue (Haiti), Chapter 11 in V. B. Thompson, *The Making..., op. cit.*
18. H. Aptheker, *Nat Turner's Slave Rebellion*, p. 2.
19. A leader of the Haitian revolution.
20. The Gabriel revolt of 1800.
21. Professor T. R. Dew, *The Pro-Slavery Argument*, "Review of the debate in the Virginia Legislature of 1831 and 1832," pp. 448 and 450. Quoted in Aptheker, *Nat Turner, op. cit.*, p. 2.
22. Speeches delivered in the House of Delegates, January 16, 1832, in *Richmond Enquirer*, 9th February, 1832. Quoted from Aptheker, *Ibid.*, p. 3.
23. Harriet Martineau, *Society in America*, Saunders and Othley, New York and London, 1837, 4th Edition, 2 Volumes, Vol. 1, p. 371.
24. W. S. Drewry, *The Southampton Insurrection*, The Neale Company, Washington, 1900, pp. 154, 174, 184 and 192. Quoted in Aptheker, *Nat Turner, op. cit.*, p. 3.
25. Drewry, *Ibid.*, pp. 63 and 192. Aptheker, *Ibid.*, p. 3.
26. *Ibid.*, p. 27. Aptheker, *Ibid*, p. 3. There is an irony here for the African's (alias Negroes) humanity had been accepted by this assertion. Yet under slavery he was not man but property.
27. H. Aptheker, *Nat Turner, op. cit.*, Introduction, p. 5.
28. See H. Aptheker, *American Negro Slave Revolts*, New York, 1943
29. David Walker, *Walker's Appeal, in four Articles together With a Preamble*, Boston, published by David Walker 1856 (Reprint). Also Herbert Aptheker, *One Continual Cry: David Walker's Appeal to the Colored Citizens of the World*, (1829-1830), New York, 1965.
30. See documents section for a copy of this letter. *The Liberator*, 1830.
31. John Hope Franklin, "Slaves Virtually Free in Antebellum North Carolina," in *The Journal of Negro History*, Vo. 28, No. 3, July 1943, p. 288.
32. Benjamin Lundy, *Life, Travels and Opinions of Benjamin Lundy*, Philadelphia, 1847, pp. 237-38. The reference is to Nat Turner's revolt. Also *Slavery and Abolition*, 1831-1841, Vo. 16 of the American Nation Series, A. B. Hart (ed.), New York and London, 1906, pp. 217-18. Also Hilary A. Herbert, *The Abolition Crusade and its Consequences, etc.*, New York, 1912, p. 60.
33. This is too simplistic a viewpoint. The most obvious one and so often

glossed over is in keeping with Professor Aptheker's conclusion "that Nat Turner sought the liberation of the Negro people." (See H. Aptheker, *Nat Turner's Slave Rebellion*, p. 35). In more recent times controversy has attained a new dimension by the publications of William Styron's *Confessions of Nat Turner*. The latter's strictures on Nat Turner have since been rebutted by African-American writers. See for instance J. H. Clarke (ed.), *William Styron's Nat Turner; Ten Black Writers Respond*, Boston, 1968. The popularity of the discussion is shown by the fact that the publication which was first made in 1968 had by October of that year gone into its third printing. But the controversy goes on. For a clearer reappraisal of the Turner Revolt, see Henry Irving Tragle, *The Southampton Slave Revolt of 1831: A Compilation of Source Material*, The University of Massachusetts Press, Amherst, 1971, Introduction

34. H. Aptheker, *Nat Turner, etc.*, p. 35.
35. *Ibid.*, pp. 38, 45-46. Also the *Confessions of Nat Turner* in *Ibid.*, p. 139.
36. Quoted in *Life, Times and Opinions of Benjamin Lundy*, p. 248, from *The Liberator*, 24th September, 1831, Vol. 1, No. 39, p. 155.
37. *The Liberator*, Boston, Vol. 1, No. 36, September 3, 1831, p. 143. Also quoted in part in W. P. And F. J. Garrison, *William Lloyd Garrison 1805-1879*, New York, 1885, Vol. 1, p. 250. Also Aptheker, *Nat Turner, Op. cit.*, pp. 41-42.
38. Aptheker, *Ibid.*, pp. 57-107.
39. *Ibid.*, p. 71.
40. *Ibid.*, p. 78. Also F. Tannenbaum, *Slave and Citizen*, New York, 1947, p. 72
41. Aptheker, *op. cit.*, p. 97. Also *The Liberator*, 22 October 1831 (quotation from Westfield Phoenix)
42. W. E. B. DuBois, *John Brown*, (American Crisis Biographies), E. P. Oberholtzer, (ed.), Philadelphia, 1909, p. 390. Almost at the end of the twentieth century similar sentiments are being hauled at the oppressed Africans in South Africa—the majority population. It is in essence the same psychological warfare which Turner and others before and after him had rejected. Will it succeed after failing several times and several centuries previously?
43. Aptheker, *op. cit.*, p. 107.
44. *Ibid.*, p. 110.
45. See for instance: H. Aptheker, *American Negro Revolts* and other works of his on David Walker and Nat Turner.
46. Robert L. Pawuette, *Sugar is Made with Blood: The Conspiracy of La Escalera and the Conflict between Empires over Slavery in Cuba*, Wesleyan University Press, Middletown, CT, 1988, p. 187; see also his Ch. 7 esp. pp. 188-90. La Escalera had been preceded by the conspiracy of 1812 by a *moreno* militia man named José Antonio Aponte. That conspiracy was to have involved both slaves and free people in a series of conspiracies, in short a collaboration of free men and slaves, but it was stillborn. See pp. 123-26 of the text cited on *La-Escalera*.
47. Aline Helg, *Our Rightful Share: The Afro-Cuban Struggle for Equality*, 1886-1912, Chapel Hill and London, The University of North Carolina Press, 1995. The entire book deals with this struggle but see especially the introduction, pp. 2-21, Chapters 2, 3, & 6 as well as conclusion.
48. See Rafael Duharte Jimenez, "The 19th Century Black fear", Excerpts from

Dos temores de nuestro pasado colonial" (The Two Old Fears of Our Colonial Past) in the author's *Seis ensayos de interpretación histórica*) Six essays in historical interpretation) Editorial Oriente, Santiago de Cuba, 1983, pp. 83-100. Editor's Title and subtitles, quoted in *AfroCuba: An Anthology of Cuban Writings on Race, Politics and Culture,* (eds.) Pedro Perez Sarduy and Jean Stubbs, New York, Ocean Press, 1993, pp. 37-46. A modern Afro-Brazilian scholar has affirmed that the same fear and obsession has been ever-present in the thoughts and actions of the Brazilian ruling class in the entire course of their history. See Abdias do Nascimento, *Brazil: Mixture or Massacre,* Dover, MA, The Majority Press, 1979 and 1989, introd. pp. 8-10

49. For an arch critic of the concept as well as the pretentious practice see Abdias do Nascimento, *Brazil: Mixture or Massacre,* Dover, MA, The Majority Press, 1979 & 1989, pp. vii-xv, 57-90.
50. See for instance, Rodolfo Sarracino, "Back to Africa," Excerpts from Ch. 2, "Encuentros en Lagos y Matanzas," (Encounters in Lagos and Mantazas) in *Los que Volvieron a Africa* (Those who Returned to Africa), *Ciencias Sociales,* 1988, pp. 47-50, 51-52, 54-64 in *AfroCuba: An Anthology, etc. op. cit.,* ed. Sarduy and Stubbs, pp. 67-76.
51. George Shepperson, "The African Abroad or The African of the Diaspora," in T. O. Ranger (ed.), *Emerging Themes of African History,* Nairobi, Kenya, East African Publishing House, 1968, pp. 164-67.
52. See Abdias do Nascimento, *Mixture or Massacre: Essays in the Genocide of a Black People,* Dover, MA, The Majority Press, 1978 & 1989, pp. 10, 29.
53. Aline Helg, *Our Rightful Share: The Afro-Cuban Struggle for Equality, 1886-1912,* Chapel Hill and London, 1995, pp. 17, 47, 49-51, 54, 78-82, 86-87, 89, 121, 123, 163, 165, 174, 234, 238-40. One of those obsessions were seen in Cuba when the Afro-Cuban political party sought legitimacy in 1912 in the country for which it had made a huge sacrifice to secure its freedom that was being denied to Afro-Cubans. Several revolts or attempted revolts raised the fear even in the United States of another Haiti. See also the Diary of Lady Nugent for the specter of Haiti and the bloody massacre there.
54. Claude McKay, *A Long Way From Home,* p. 222

Chapter 3

Moral Suasionists

This category of leadership emerges in society whenever the assumption prevails that the rulers of society are open to reason and can be persuaded to change courses of action and policies in the light of certain moral arguments. The Americas were no exception to this rule. In fact, inherent in the abolitionist crusade was the belief that the moral and religious arguments could be employed to achieve the demise of slavery. Yet some of the men we feature here as moral leaders were also active on the pulpit and political platforms and to this extent associated themselves with certain organizational activities for the advancement and enhancement of the welfare of their brethren as well as humanity in general.It has been stated in the previous chapter that the three categories of leadership we termed activist, moral suasionist, and physical force tended to overlap. Thus, we might find that a moral force leadership was just as much committed to activism and that an activist leadership might or might not be a physical force type. Men like Denmark Vesey and Nat Turner certainly had some moral philosophy inspiring their revolt. For instance, they used the Christian teaching of the equality of all men before God and, therefore, felt it was morally wrong for some men to enslave and subordinate others to their whims and will. Such ideas went into the making of Christian socialism and what today is called humanism. Thus we might come upon a moral leader like Richard Allen, first Bishop of the African Methodist Episcopal Church of the city of Philadelphia, who would preach pacification based on solid religious convictions and yet would understand the restiveness of slaves and their recurrent revolts against their condition.[1] The leadership of moral suasion of the Africans of the diaspora in the West Indies and the United States seemed to be emerging simultaneously about the last quarter of the eighteenth century. But the profusion of leaders was greater on the North American mainland than elsewhere. The few who emerged from the West Indies were outstanding, but they had just begun making an impact when they quit the West Indies for Britain,[2] whereas their counterparts in the United States made their debut on American soil. The reasons for this are not far to seek.

Writing of the West Indies towards the end of the nineteenth century, Reverend Caldecott had referred to the West Indian scene during slavery as barren in the output of literature, art, and culture. According to him the social climate was unfavorable to such development and only Bryan Edwards, the historian, and E. Long made up for this West Indian deficiency.[3] Thus, while this incentive was lacking in the various groups into which the European community was split, there was hardly anything like enlightenment for the children of Africa settled there, neither in rudimentary education of reading and writing nor in the embracing of the Christian faith. The exception being the abysmal experiment (more appropriately non-experiment) on the Barbados plantation of Christopher Coderington bequeathed to the Society for the Propagation of the Gospel in the early eighteenth century.[4] Caldecott tells of a Moravian Minister to the West Indies, in 1816, who rejoiced at having found a black man who could read.[5] The plantocracy frowned on the idea of literacy for slaves and regarded such indulgences as dangerous for the survival of their system. Therefore the little enlightenment received by the slaves came through the efforts of some of the non-conformist religious sects —the Wesleyan Methodists from England, the Baptists from America, and the Moravian Brethren or *Unitas Fratrum* from Germany, and the kindness of individual Europeans as well as the exertions of the slaves themselves. The zest for learning no matter how rudimentary was part of that preparation for leadership, as is shown throughout man's history.

The slavocracy and other vested interests in the West Indies were hostile to the activities of these missionaries, fearing that they might imbue the slaves or the free Africans with the notion of social equality, thereby disturbing their paradise based on the sweat of another's brow. Yet, in 1815, the Jamaican Legislature had accepted the right of slaves to be instructed. But, as with the United States, some slaves through patronage of one kind or another, or through their own clandestine efforts and organizations, learned to read, and by dogged persistence and perseverance had embraced some tenets and ethics of Christianity. From among these there emerged that leadership among the Africans of the Americas who were able to document their sentiments on the slave trade and its corollary, slavery. Since there was such a large crop of these leaders in the United States, we have chosen a few of the most outstanding.

The leadership of prelates among the Africans of the diaspora in the United States is a situation that has persisted to the present day, despite the rise of secular leaders. It is a study that has yet to be undertaken in depth, and is long overdue. A few such studies have recently appeared, but much more work is needed.

Leadership from the West Indies

Cugoano and Equiano

From the West Indies, two stand out distinctly and we begin our discussion with these. They were Ottobah Cugoano (christened James Stuart) from the Gold Coast (modern Ghana), [6] and Olaudah Equiano (otherwise known as Gustavus Vassa), an Ibo from an area of West Africa that came to be part of modern Nigeria. They are worthy to be called the first black abolitionists although they were more than that, for they were also among the first of the emergent leadership of the Africans of the diaspora to be humanistic and internationalist in outlook. Cugoano had written a book, published in 1787, entitled *Thoughts and Sentiments on the Evils of That Wicked Traffic Slavery in Human Species* (a title later abridged to *Thoughts and Sentiments on the Evils of Slavery* and here-in-after referred to as such) The year 1787 was significant in that it was also the year of the establishment, on the inspiration of the "Clapham Sect," of the first antislavery organization in England. Cugoano in his text expounded the notion of equality of all men before God, employing a combination of Christian teaching and eighteenth-century humanitarianism to shore up his argument. The book was a synthesis of Cugoano's African background and his European experience, but couched in legalistic language. Equiano's work on the other hand, was published in two combined volumes in 1789 (the year of the first French Revolution) and went through several editions in a matter of months. Entitled *The Interesting Narrative of the Life of Olaudah Equiano or Gustavus Vassa, The African,* it was autobiographical in nature. From both of these men of African origin, impassioned protests against the slave trade and slavery issued loud and clear. Both denounced the beastly treatment of the African which robbed him of his dignity, and both pleaded for complete abolition. While Cugoano provided theoretical arguments against the slave trade and slavery, Equiano used examples of day- to-day cruelties and brutalities of both the slave trade and the slavery system. As Professor July aptly observes, the result was that Equiano "lent authenticity and immediacy to Cugoano's reasoning."[7]Both works appeared, as Professor July has also observed, at an opportune moment, when the abolitionist campaign was already beginning to make its initial impact on British society. Both works constituted an early African commentary, disquisition, and judgement on aspects of European "civilization" and its effects of Africa. Cugoano assailed theoretical arguments of prelates who justified slavery by claiming biblical authority. He also argued that the color of the skin was a mark of environment and not an emblem of slavery. His arguments were at once an amalgam of the humanitarianism of the times and his own deeply Christian convictions. Religion here gave the moralist leader his ammunition. Much of Equiano's book was narrative and descriptive while Cugoano provided the philosophical and explanatory basis of the case against slavery. Both deeply impressed the abolitionist mind. The contradictions and duplicity of Europe were laid bare in Cugoano, who saw her simultaneously as enslaver and humanitarian. Apart from consideration of the moralistic and humanitarian arguments against the slave trade and the institution of slavery, both writers showed awareness of the economic aspects as well. For them the slave trade was destroying Africa rather than aiding her development. They therefore expressed the hope that the abolition of the slave trade would provide the opportunity for mutually profitable commerce between Britain and Africa. Both of them seemed to have been supporters of the idea of colonizing manumitted slaves in Africa, but they had their reservations as to some of the shortcomings of the Sierra Leone venture. Vassa had himself been one of the Commissioners for the Sierra Leone expedition headed by Granville Sharp, but his misgivings and criticisms of its leadership and sense of timing led to his dismissal from the post. Cuogoano's Africanism also surfaced in his criticism of the undertaking. He did not ignore the genuineness of the initiators of the scheme. His doubts rather centered on a number of points: first, that no treaty had been concluded with the indigenous people on whose territory the venture was intended to encroach; second, he was also critical of the administrative failings which proved a menace to the health and welfare of the expedition; and third, he saw clearly the danger of re-enslavement of freed men. This factor alone was enough to deter others from offering to join the venture; many men and women of African origin opted for exile in England rather than risk re-enslavement in Africa. It was, in, fact a choice between real freedom in England (even if they were second or third class citizens) and a dubious liberty in Africa. But, above all, Cugoano addressed his fears to the British government as to whether a "free colony" was feasible in the vicinity of British-maintained forts and garrisons for ensnaring and transporting men into captivity. In fact, his book was one of the first eloquent attempts to question the consistency of European intentions in Africa.From the writings of these men emerge clearly their moral philosophies bolstered up by their Christian convictions. Both were untiring fighters for the equality of man and while among the first black abolitionists, they were also among the earliest (if not the very first), to express notions of an "African personality" while making no apology for their Africaness.Cugoano went to the Sierra Leone while Vassa remained in England and married an English lady named Susan Cullen, the daughter of James and Ann Cullen of Ely (Cambridgeshire), on April 7, 1792. [8] While Vassa recounts his most interesting experiences in Britain and many other countries in Europe as well as America and the West Indian islands, not much surfaced on the later career of Cugoano. Vassa died in London, England on March 31, 1797, only four years after his marriage. But he had two daughters, Anna Maria and Johanna; the first died in the year of her father's demise age 4, on 21 July 1797. Cugoano from Sierra Leone lamented the absence of Vassa. Vassa wrote with a kind of refinement and presented his work as an appeal (or petition) to the British Parliament (both Lords and Commons) so as to persuade them to bring the cruel system to an end. He revealed the excesses of plantation slavery in a refined style, which, in his modesty, he said was "devoid of any literary merit." But literary merit that work certainly has even when read today. But even more, it contained the strivings and cravings of the human spirit and revealed a magnanimous and forgiving heart.

As both writers offered what was essentially their moral philosophy bolstered up by their Christian beliefs, justice can only be done to their protests by reading their works in full. Only by doing so could one clearly perceive the nature and language of that protest. However, they were far from equivocal in condemning the slave trade and slavery. Here is a typical sentiment of disapproval by Cugoano: "Every man of any sensibility, whether he be Christian or a heathen, if he has any discernment at all, must think that for any men, or any class of men to deal with their fellow-creatures as with the beasts of the field, or account them as such, however ignorant they may be, and in whatever situation or whatever they may find them, and whatever country of complexion they may be of that those men who are the procurers and holders of slaves, are the greatest villains of the world."[9]

Here is Equiano to complement the argument in protest:

> Surely this traffic cannot be good, which spreads like pestilence and taints what it touches! Which violates that first natural right of mankind, equality and independence, and gives one man a domination over his fellows which God could never intend! For it raises the owner to a state as far above a man as it depressed the slave below it; and, with all the presumption of human pride, sets a distinction between them immeasurable in extent, and endless in duration! Yet how mistaken is the avarice even of the planters. Are slaves more useful by being thus humbled to the conditions of brutes, than they would be if suffered to enjoy the privileges of men.... When you make men slaves you deprive them of half their virtue, you set them in rapine and cruelty, and compel them to live with you in a state of war; and yet you complain that they are not honest or faithful! You stupefy them with stripes, and think it necessary to keep them in a state of ignorance; and yet you accept that they are incapable of learning, that their minds are such a barren soil or moor, that culture would be lost on them; and that they come from a climate where nature, though prodigal of her bounties in a degree unknown to yourselves, has left man alone and scant and unfinished, and incapable of enjoying the treasures she has poured out for him! Are they fit to be applied by one rational being to another? And are you not struck with shame and mortification, to see the partakers of your nature reduced so low? But above all are there no dangers attending this mode of treatment? Are you not hourly in dread of an insurrection?[10]

These were the sentiments of men who had experienced servitude before their manumission. They were, in fact, the voices of the first abolitionists of African origin in the West and they were unmistakenly forthright. From these citations we can infer that they saw themselves as nothing less than men and members of the human family, but they also saw themselves as Africans; thus they were among the first in modern times to express the concepts known as the "African Personality." Equiano's use of the term "The African" in reference to himself in the title of his book is significant. So also was Cugoano's use of it in much of his book. For instance, he wrote:

> Liberty and Freedom, where people may starve for want, can do them but little good. We want many rules of civilization in Africa; but, in many respects, we may boast of some more essential liberties than any of the civilized nations in Europe

> enjoy; for the poorest amongst us are never in distress for want, unless some general and universal calamity happen to us.[11]

In his plea for the abolition of the system, Cugoano called on all the efforts of mankind and in his advocacy he and others, who later joined the rank and file of the anti-slavery crusades, symbolized the abolitionists of the world. He said:

> Wherefore it ought to be the universal endeavor, and the ardent wish of all the lovers of God and the Savior of men, and of all that delight in his way of righteousness, and of all the lovers of their country, and the friends of mankind, and of every real patriot in the land, and of every man and woman that dwelleth therein, and of all those that have pretense to charity, generosity, sensibility and humanity, and whoever has any regard to innocence and virtue, to plead that slavery with all its great and heinous magnitude of iniquity, might be abolished throughout the British dominions; and from henceforth to hinder and prohibit the carrying on of that barbarous, brutish and inhuman traffic of the slavery and commerce of human species, wherever the power and the influence of the British Empire extends it.[12]

Leadership in London

Ignatius Sancho

Besides Equiano and Cugoano, whose leadership role was given prominence in London, there were also in London some men of African origin associated with literary circles as well as the arts and music of the eighteenth century among the leadership of moral suasion. One of the most outstanding was Ignatius Sancho. There are conflicting versions about the manner in which Sancho found his way to England. Nevertheless all versions agree that he was brought to England at about the age of two. One account indicates that he was rescued from a slave ship bound for the West Indies and then brought to England. Another version indicated that he was born in 1729 on a slave trading ship bound for the Spanish West Indies a few days after the vessel had left the shore of Guinea (West Africa). He was baptized at Carthagena in present day Columbia and given the name of Ignatius. His mother died shortly of a disease resulting from unfamiliarity with the climate while his father, in order to defeat slavery, committed suicide. Ignatius was brought by his master to England while under two years old and was given to three maiden sisters resident at Greenwich. Those women (who were racially prejudiced) felt that he looked like the "Squire of Don Quixote" and so named him Sancho. They also felt that ignorance was the only security for the obedience of the Negro and did not believe it necessary to enlarge the mind of their "slave." Nevertheless, the Duke of Montagu, a frequent visitor to the home of the three sisters, lived at nearby Blackheath and because of his admiration for this African, who demonstrated frankness of manner, a man who had not experienced servitude, and unrefined by education, the Duke frequently brought Sancho home to the Duchess and indulged him in reading by giving him gifts of books and recommended to his mistresses to "cultivate a genius of such apparent fertile mind." The Duke became a patron of Sancho but the three sisters were not keen on cultivating Sancho's mind. Nevertheless, Sancho himself, preoccupied with notions of freedom, eventually abandoned the three sisters, who had at various times threatened to return him to servitude. As the Duke of Montagu had died, Ignatius Sancho sought the protection of the Duchess who, at first, reproved him and dismissed him. Down to his last five shillings and yet with freedom pulsating within his bosom, he purchased an old pistol to safeguard his personal freedom. The Duchess secretly admired his character and eventually admitted him to the household. Sancho remained a butler at the home of the Duchess until her death. In her will she bequeathed a small fortune to him and by his own industry he was able to possess 70 pounds sterling in money and an annuity of 30 pounds. But his new situation led him to be indulgent. This annuity appeared to him an inexhaustible sum of money and in his profligacy he exhausted the money and once more became penniless. He was said to be a great favorite of women, and he was addicted to cards, but an unsuccessful contest at cribbage with a Jew, who won his clothes, determined him to abjure such indulgences.

His Artistic Pursuits

Sancho was such a great lover of the theater that he is said to have spent his last shilling to visit the Drury Lane Theater. In time of adversity he was induced to consider the stage as a source of livelihood. Because of his complexion he was seen as a possible Othello or Oroonako, but with his defective articulation he could not accede to the theater. Today, Sancho is remembered for the exquisite letters he wrote, although his name was associated with that of eighteenth-century African composers of music in London-among whom were George Augustus Bridgetower, a virtuoso violinist and a friend of Beethoven; and Julius Soubies, a dandy, reputed to be a favorite of women and who was more of a fencing expert than a musical composer, though this fencing did not detract from his genius. Sancho eventually married a young woman of West Indian origin and the family were able to establish a grocery shop, but Sancho suffered from gout and increasing corpulence from 1773, which led him to set up his own private business. He died in December 1780 as a result of "complicated disorders."

Sancho's Leadership Qualities

Sancho's qualities of leadership, especially that of moral suasion, were manifested in certain of his letters, preserved in two volumes.[13] From them one can obtain gleanings of some of his preoccupations. They reveal his concern for his race apart from his interests in the worlds of poetry, music, and painting. He was well known in English cultural circles and was consulted for advice.[14] Sancho did plead periodically for his unfortunate brethren, who were held in slavery on the Western plantations. In one of his letters he explained that the first part of his life was unlucky, as he was placed in a family who judged ignorance the best and only security to obedience. He then told how he struggled to acquire literacy—through "God's blessings"—and, in his humility, remarked that the latter part of his life he had spent in service in the home of one of the best families of the United Kingdom. In this letter, dated July 1776,[15] addressed to a certain Mr. Stern, he admonished the latter to give one hour's attention daily to slavery as practiced in the West Indies, exhorting Stern to "hear their supplications...and addresses."[16] In another letter Sancho describes himself as a "Black-a-moor."[17] In his letters we see the dogged determination of this sable son of Africa to enlighten himself and overcome many of the obstacles placed in his path to prevent his advancement. In an early letter of Sancho's to a Mr. M. he wrote: "May they all unite their endeavors... and rescue this once manly and martial people from the silken slavery of foreign luxury and debauchery."[18] As this letter is dated 1772, the year of the Mansfield judgement about James Sommersett, it might well have been an address to Chief Justice Mansfield, who liberated the slave Sommersett, having pronounced that the "state of slavery was unknown to English law."One letter which seemed to be a spirited defense of his race was written in 1778 to a Mr. J-W-E. In it he observed: "In one of your letters which I do not recollect... you speak (with honest indignation) of the treachery and chicanery of the Natives.... My good friend, you should remember from who they learnt these vices.... the first Christian visitors found them a simple, harmless people... but the cursed avidity for wealth urged these first visitors (and all succeeding ones) to such acts of deception... and even wanton cruelty... that the poor ignorant Natives soon learnt to turn the knavish... and diabolical arts which they too soon imbibed upon their teachers.... I say it with reluctance that I must observe your country's conduct has been uniformly wicked in the East-West Indies—and even on the Coast of Guinea. The grand object of English navigators - is money - money - money - for which I do not pretend to blame them. (Then he justifies commerce)...."[19] Sancho proceeded in that letter to explain that in Africa the poor wretched natives, who were blessed with the most fertile and luxuriant soil, were rendered so much more miserable for what Providence intended as a blessing and that the Christians' abominable traffic for slaves, and the horrid cruelty and treachery of the petty kings, encouraged their customers, who carried them strong liquors to inflame national madness and powder and bad firearms to furnish them with the "hellish means of killing and kidnapping...." He further explained that it was a subject that soured his blood but his mention of it was to prevent his friend (J-W-E.?) from making too hasty a condemnation of the knavery of a people who, though bad as they may be, were possibly made "worse by Christian visitors."[20] His views on colonization of freed blacks are not known, but one portion of a letter in the second volume of his letters seems to indicate that he might have favored some colonization scheme.[21]

Leadership in North America

Slave Poets

Phyllis Wheatley (1753-1784)

Phyllis Wheatley's form of leadership was inspirational rather than active in the enhancement of the descendants of Africa in bondage in the West. Through the good fortune of being kept as a domestic, she was able to cultivate her mind and attained the reputation of a poetess. She dedicated some of her poems to George Washington (a slave owner and the first President of the United States of America) and others to William Earl of Dartmouth, Colonial Secretary, the very man who had stated English policy vis-à-vis the slave trade at a time when agitation was building up against the activity. He had said that "a trade which had proved so beneficial to the nation could not be abolished."[22] Phyllis Wheatley herself had been abducted from her home as a very small child and her exact age was never ascertained, but it was guessed that she would have been about six or seven when she was brought to America. This then must explain in part her loss of memory of her original homeland. Although it was against the laws in North America in those days to teach a slave or black person to read or write, her mistress taught her. In time her distinction as a poet emerged. But the late African-American poet, Langston Hughes, tells us that she was not the first black poet to appear in the Americas; that among the early black poets, who had published in North America were Lucy Terry of Deerfield, Massachusetts, who in 1746 had written, among other verses, *Bars Fight*, an account of an Indian raid on the town in which she lived. Another was Jupiter Hammon, who lived in bondage. According to Langston Hughes, Hammon's poems began to be published as broadsides in Queens Village, Long Island, in 1760. Although he had never met Phyllis Wheatley (the Boston slave girl), he paid her tribute in a poem in 1778 entitled *A Poetic Address to Phyllis Wheatley.*[23] But Phyllis Wheatley was not a leader of consequence, for she failed to demonstrate in her poems any awareness of her origins or of the sufferings and yearnings of her enslaved brethren in the Americas. Her eulogy of George Washington during the time of the confrontation of the thirteen colonies with England earned a gracious reply in the form of a letter from Washington himself.[24] But in spite of the fact that she composed poems such as *Liberty and Peace* (relating to the U.S.A. and its success against Britain), not having experienced personally the harshness and brutality of slavery, she demonstrated little or no awareness of its consequences on her people. Accordingly, she hardly wrote of bondage at all. Only in one poem of hers (the one dedicated to William Earl of Dartmouth) was a flicker of awareness revealed. That poem was contradicted by another, *On Being Brought Back From*

Africa to America which began:

It was mercy that brought me from my pagan land
Taught my benighted soul to understand
That there's a God—that there's a Savior too;
Once I redemption neither sought nor knew.
Some view our sable race with scornful eye -
"Their color is a diabolic dye."
Remember, Christians, Negroes black as Cain
May be refined, and join the angelic train. [25]

Yet the only poem with faint echoes of Africa reads:

I, young in life, by seeming cruel fate
Was snatch'ed from Africa's fancy'd happy seat:
What pangs excruciating must molest
What sorrows labour in my parent's breast?
Steel's was the soul and by no misery mov'd

That from a father seiz'd his babe belov'd
Such, such my case. And I can then but pray
Others may never feel tyrannical sway.[26]

There is a moral note in the last two lines of the above quoted poem, but nothing more. The poem was romantic and visionary and far from being aware of the realities which beset black people in the Americas at the time they were written. Nevertheless, in terms of a practical contribution to the crusade against slavery, Phyllis Wheatley made none. J. H. Franklin, the eminent African-American historian, said of her, and with justification: "Her writings are, perhaps, a good example of the search for independence through the method of escape, which was to become a favorite device of the Negro of a later century."[27] People who referred to her in the early years of the twentieth-century or in the late nineteenth century only used her as inspiration to demonstrate what a black person was capable of achieving when given the opportunity.[28] In our *exposé* we study leaders who failed as well as those who succeeded.Thus, as a leader of thought or action, her contributions to the upliftment of her people were negligible, but she represented an inspirational pioneer, occupying the middle position between servitude and freedom. She demonstrated no substantiel awareness of the gravity of the slave condition and its dehumanizing characteristics. She seemed content to live in her own sheltered world, a cocoon sheltered by induced values which were unquestioningly accepted by her, [29] the values of those who had rescued her from the jaws of abject misery that her blindness led her to say: "T'was a mercy that brought me from my pagan land," a land which she hardly knew since she was a little girl when she was abducted into slavery. Yet her contemporaries in slavery with far less opportunities showed themselves capable of more mature reflection and employed the art of persuasion with the hope of convincing the heady slavocrats and their adherents of the necessity for change. It is in this light that we must view the leadership of George Moses Horton, another slave poet in the United States of America during the second decade of the nineteenth-century.

George Moses Horton

Another poet of note was George Moses Horton, whose name should be associated with those of black abolitionists and whose poems were published in 1829[30] under the title *The Hope for Liberty*. Unlike, Wheatley, his poems contained the preoccupations of a mind that rejected slavery. Horton lived in North Carolina, was nominally free, and so was able to read widely and write extensively.For about thirty years he continued to write for students of the University of North Carolina and for many newspapers especially the notable Raleigh Register. But he remained in bondage for about thirty-two years and was to be kept in that condition unless he accepted passage to Liberia (which was rejected).[31] By 1837 Joshua Coffin was to confirm that George Moses Horton was still in servitude.[32] By this date a second edition of his poems (by another publisher) appeared, but the original title was altered to read: "Poems of a Slave." Some of the titles of his poems are noteworthy: "On Liberty and Slavery"; "The Slave's Complaint"; "Lines: On Hearing the Intention of a Gentleman to Purchase the Poet's Freedom."[33]

Two distinguished modern historians suggest that George's interest in poetry later waned with his becoming a drunkard, a preoccupation purported to be the result of frustrations at not being manumitted.[34] Some such sentiments can be gleaned from the following lines:

> Bid slavery hide her haggard face,
> And barbarian fly:
> I scorn to see the sad disgrace
> In which enslaved I lie. [35]

Of his craving for liberty he wrote:

> Come melting Pity, from afar,
> And break this enormous bar,
> Between a wretch and thee,
> Purchase a few short days of time
> And bid a vassal soar sublime,
> On wings of Liberty. [36]

George's preoccupation with liberty was intense. The Quaker journalist, Benjamin Lundy, observed George in the *Raleigh Register* (North Carolina) by describing him as "an extraordinary young slave." George at the time was twenty-five years of age. He was portrayed as having a mild and humble disposition and deportment. [37] But his poems did not save him from bondage and he only found liberty with the coming of the American Civil War. Yet his legacy is the legacy of the moral suasionist, the epitome of which was the Rt. Rev. Richard Allen, first Bishop of the African Methodist Episcopal Church of the city of Philadelphia.

The Leadership of Bishop Richard Allen

In an assessment of the circumstances of the eighteenth and nineteenth-centuries, Allen towers high among the moral leaders in the

African Diaspora in North America. His form of leadership is typical of the moral leadership which Africans of the Diaspora provided for their people in times of acute crises. It is no surprise that in the second half of the twentieth century religious prelates and leaders like the late Congressman Rev. Adam Clayton Powell Jr. and Martin Luther King Jr., and even the Rev. Ralph Abernathy, the Rev. Jesse Jackson, and the Rev. Andre Tory should emerge among the leaders of thought and action among their downtrodden brethren. Such leadership also arose in the West Indies and among Africans of the Diaspora in Canada. In fact, the prelates of this century belong to the tradition of leadership which was first established by both Richard Allen and Absalom Jones in the latter part of the eighteenth century. North America and the West Indies have produced many leaders of thought and action who had first been reared and nurtured on the pulpit. They were also among the first political leaders of the Africans of the Diaspora. Richard Allen himself had a slave background. He was born about 1760 in Philadelphia and while still young was sold to a planter in Delaware. He became a Methodist preacher quite early and through earnings as a wagon driver during the Revolutionary War was able to raise money to purchase his freedom in 1777. He was a gifted speaker and attracted the attention of many to the pulpit. In those days the Methodist Community of St. George (Philadelphia) consisted of free and slave as well as colored and white (Euro-American) people. But the increase in number of colored adherents in the Church led to a white (i.e., Euro-American) clamor that segregation be practiced within the Church. It was this attempt to foster segregation which brought the final break of Allen and his associates, Absalom Jones and William White, with the white Methodists. [38]

It occurred one Sunday when these three among others were earnest in prayer and an usher attempted to relegate them to what had come to be described as "Negro pews." [39] Allen and his group, finding this intolerable, rose up and walked out of the church *en-block*. They then founded the Free African Society (April 12, 1787). This was a religious as well as a civic organization and ultimately laid the foundations for the Bethel Methodist Episcopal Church in Philadelphia in 1794. At the time, the organizers aimed at establishing a peaceful place of worship for black people.

Epidemic of Yellow Fever in Philadelphia, 1793

Prior to the emergence of Bethel Church in 1793 there had occurred an epidemic of Yellow fever in the city of Philadelphia. While many whites fled the city, the responsibility for tending the sick and the dead devolved on the shoulders of "free Negroes" (apart from the slaves who were bonded to labor). As many of the white doctors had died, Allen and Jones enlisted as assistants to a surgeon, Dr. Benjamin Rush, [40] who taught them the preliminaries of ministration to the victims of the disease. Many "colored" people offered their services and served with enthusiasm. The fact should also have taught the prejudiced whites some object lessons. Some black men lost their lives in the process. While the services of Allen and Jones received commendation, there ensued from the pen of one detractor, a journalist, Mathew Carey, a deflation of their contributions and those of the other colored people. It was later discovered that Carey was not even in the city at the time of the outbreak of yellow fever. As a result, the Mayor of Philadelphia drew up resolutions expressing thanks to the "colored" contributions during the epidemic. Allen's and Jones' reply to Carey was entitled A Narrative of the *Proceedings of the Black People During the Late Calamity in Philadelphia.*[41] This reply is said to have enhanced Allen's and Jones' reputation.

Preoccupation with the Church

But let us return to the new Church, for Allen and his associates were concerned with establishing a place where their brethren could worship unmolested. The aim was not to establish a segregated Church but one in which self-respect was a ruling principle. After Allen and his associates had withdrawn from St. George's Methodist Episcopal Church in 1784, they were faced with the problem of creating an effective union among themselves. On April 12, 1787 they established the Free African Society, which became the first mutual aid society among African-Americans. It aimed at achieving self-improvement for the brethren. Its meetings were held in the Allen's home until May 1788, when, with the increase in numbers, they found sanctuary in the home of one Sarah Dougherty up to the end of 1788. Sarah later became Allen's wife. After that they removed to Friends' Free African School House, where monthly meetings were held until 1791.In the preamble to the articles of association, we see that both Richard Allen and Absalom Jones were responsible for the organization. This mutual aide society laid the foundations for the establishment of the first African Methodist Episcopal Church. In the articles of association adopted on May 17, 1787, the following statement appears: "We the free Africans and their descendants of the City of Philadelphia, in the state of Pennsylvania, or elsewhere, do unanimously agree for the benefit of each other, to advance one shilling in silver Pennsylvania currency a month; and after one year's subscription from the date thereof, then to hand forth to the needy of this society, if any should require, the sum of three shillings and nine pence per week of said money; provided this necessity is not brought on them by their own imprudence."[42]

Some of the rules guiding the organization were intended to inculcate discipline. The organization thus rejected, first, drunkenness and disorderly behavior and such persons were disqualified from membership. Second, failure to pay dues could lead to termination of membership. Third, attendance at monthly meetings was to be punctilious. Fourth, fines were imposed in case of non-attendance, except in cases of illness. Fifth, benefits were available for widows of deceased members; these were to receive benefits of the society in order that they might be able to educate their children, if these could not attend free schools.And although the organizers of Bethel Church agreed to be governed by the "doctrine of the Methodists," yet because of the existence of the spirit of independence within their rank and file they declared their independence on November 3, 1794. Thereafter, the membership of the Church was only open to people of African descent, though for some time they continued to labor under the shadow of the Methodist Episcopal Church, ministers from which community preached on Bethel's pulpit. But the spirit of independence was strong and with the incorporation of Bethel as the African Methodist Episcopal Church in 1816, complete independence was declared. [43] Among some of the practical proposals and achievements of the African Church organizers were the following: apprenticing of children to trades and teaching of lessons in thrift, sobriety and industry in the black population. They rendered assistance to the needy brethren in the Society. The way was paved for an extensive cooperation in the social progress of a much larger "Negro" population and later "Negro" fraternal organizations. Some whites, as a result of their humanitarianism, or observing the Black efforts, were also induced to establish schools for Negroes. Among the early white pioneers were Whitfield of Pennsylvania, who in 1740 purchased in Pennsylvania a plot of land to organize a Negro school. His resources failed to bring the plan to fruition. Then there was the Quaker gentleman Anthony Benezet, who, from 1779, conducted an evening school for African-Americans. Another Quaker school was established soon after Benezet's. In 1789 a *Society for the Free Instruction of Orderly Blacks and People of Color* was founded. [44] The title of this society, of course, mirrors some white assumptions and prejudices.

Of the black effort we observe that from the founding of St. Thomas Episcopal Church under Absalom Jones, a school was begun there. Richard Allen, with these precedents before his eyes, embarked on school organization. This fact debunks the assertion of the Rt.

Rev. Daniel Payne (who himself became an AME bishop), in his history of the African Methodist Episcopal Church, that neither Allen nor Jones thought of school and education for black people because "they were ignorant men."[45] Allen in 1795 had founded a day school at Bethel Church in which sixty were in attendance. In October 1796, the Trustees of Bethel African Methodist Episcopal Church sought the assistance of others and organized the First Day School—Sunday School—in their building and a night school. This was the beginning of the first Sunday School in the AME Church. Education as conceived at that time was intended both for children and adults and Allen was in the forefront of these endeavors. It was even said that no man of his group was more interested than he in the education of his people. He gave encouragement and solace to prospective high school or college students and his perspicacity led him to see the value of trained leadership, though his main emphasis was still on ecclesiastical leadership. Against the background of the evolution of leadership, Allen was, in some respects, more forward-looking than the nineteenth-century African-American leader Booker T. Washington. Allen saw this leadership as the prerequisite for black independence, especially in ecclesiastical matters. Allen kept it constantly in mind that persons of African descent (alias, the Negroes) in American society would remain discriminated against unless they responded by developing their own leadership, articulated through the Negro Church, Negro School, and Negro Economic Organization—all involving group action. This awareness of the vital nature of Negro Church leadership expressed through group action put him miles ahead of Booker T. Washington two generations later. The operative word in this organizational activity was "Independence," but guided by consecrated leadership so as to prevent his people being crushed, insulted, ignored or assigned to a subordinate place in society in general. He was able to see that if Negroes were not organized they would be degraded further and their spirits broken. Thus, he was more forward-looking than his lay successor, Booker T. Washington.

SUMMARY

What we have tried to convey is that African Methodism in the United States of America arose because of the failure of the non-conformist (white) sects to eschew racism. Among these religious sects were the Methodist Episcopal Church, the Protestant Episcopal Church, and the Presbyterian Church. Independence of spirit among the African Methodists led by Richard Allen stemmed from the failure of non-conformist Churches to banish racism and their relegation of black worshippers to what were called "Negro Pews." These religious sects succumbed to the will of the slavocracry and subscribed to the dominance of black by white and failed to demonstrate courage of conviction when Christian principles involving human equality were being flouted. They, therefore, lost their African members. This independence of spirit of the African Methodists led by Allen, was to extend beyond the confines of Philadelphia to other parts of the country, contributing to a proliferation of Independent African Churches in North America, as Methodism, which began as a religion of the masses, was failing to live up to its pretensions; hence the fission which resulted in the establishment of black Methodism.

Daniel Coker

Daniel Coker provides another example of this early moral leadership. He was born of a slave father and an English indentured mother and learned to read and write through association with the young son of his master. He escaped from slavery in Blatimore, Maryland to New York and was converted and ordained Deacon in the Methodist Episcopal Church by Bishop Asbury. Coker returned to Baltimore and remained in hiding until he could arrange for the purchase of his freedom. Then he had the opportunity of employing his talents by founding a school. It was known as "The African School," the first of its kind in Baltimore in the early nineteenth century. Coker began with seventeen pupils and eventually attracted one hundred and fifty pupils before joining Richard Allen in organizing[46] the AME Church. He later emigrated (1820) to West Africa to become one of the leaders returned from the Diaspora to make his contributions to the new state of Liberia. At this point an evaluation of Allen's leadership becomes essential.

Richard Allen Evaluated

In the light of what has been said above, some evaluation of the Rt. Rev. Bishop Richard Allen, first Bishop of the African Methodist Episcopal Church of the City of Philadelphia, becomes imperative. The leadership provided by him was the first of its kind, which was to recur in the African Diaspora and especially in the United States of America. Allen pointed the way, according to his lights, to salvation for his people through their exertions in the sphere of religion, acquisition and accumulation of property, industry and education, independence of spirit, as well as organizing some form of unity. But he was not blinded by his own acquisition of property to the plight of his people. Thus, he was one of the early African-American philanthropists. He was a constant petitioner for the abolition of slavery, using his position as leader of the Free African Society to advocate this. He contributed articles to the first-ever African-American newspaper in the United States, *Freedom's Journal*, founded by John Russwurm, the first African-American to graduate (1826) from an American college (Bowdoin in Maine). This journal was founded the following year in cooperation with the Rev. Samuel B. Cornish and emerged even before the much celebrated *Liberator* (1831) of William Lloyd Garrison, the stalwart white abolitionist. Thus even before the second phase of the campaign against slavery had gathered force, Africans of the Diaspora in the United States were expressing their sentiments on the subject. This phase began after 1830. It was in one such issue of the journal that Richard Allen expressed himself in no uncertain terms against plans for the colonization of the African-Americans outside the United States.[47] It was also through him that some 3,000 opponents of colonization among the African-Americans assembled in Philadelphia in 1817 to reject the program of the recently founded American Colonization Society, which sought to transport free colored people to Africa as a way of resolving the racial problems of the United States of America. Methods of intimidation had been employed as well by their supporters to induce blacks to accept the program of transportation back to Africa. These happenings induced the blacks of New York, Pennsylvania, Delaware, and Maryland to organize themselves to defend their interests against mob violence and mob law. But laws continued to be enacted to abridge the liberties of the Free People of Color in the United States and called for the effective organization of blacks, and it was out of the efforts to cope with these contingencies and perplexities that there emerged the Convention Movement of Colored People in 1830. Richard Allen was no less an inspiration to the emergence of this movement. He was among the participants of the first National Convention in 1830, which assembled in the city of Philadelphia. Allen was elected President. The aim of the Convention was to seek ways and means of swift elevation of the "colored" people to a more exalted status than slavery and the slave codes had allowed them.[48]

This new movement, urged on by Allen, admonished the African-Americans to be diligent, purchase land, work for unity, and seize every opportunity presented by the benevolence of friends of humanity to elevate their conditions and those of their brethren. In this respect, Allen and his associates seemed more far-sighted than a later leader in the Diaspora, Booker T. Washington, for they insisted on full citizenship in the United States while rejecting transfer to Africa. A Constitution for the Convention Movement was worked out, but Richard Allen was dead when the next Convention met in 1831. Yet Allen's name is immortalized in the African Methodist Episcopal

Church, the Church from which men like Bishop Henry McNeal Turner (1834-1915) were to emerge, first as activist leaders and later as advocates of emigration to Africa and the idea of "Africa for Africans." H. M Turner visited West Africa in November 1891 and organized the first AME Conference there; in April of the same year, he visited South Africa and organized the First AME Conference there and ordained some of the ministers, who manifested the phenomenon described in another context as "Ethiopianism."[49] But Turner's advocacy of Ethiopianism was ardent.[50] Allen was always the voice of moral suasion, often reasoned and backed by logic, whose pronouncements are rooted in a deep religious conviction: his arguments were based mostly on his adhesion to the tenets of Christianity and the fundamentals of the Bible. He was, of course, a fundamentalist. He asserted that God was the first to plead the cause of the slaves by his reference to the ancient enslavement of the Israelites in Egypt. He argued that even God, who knew the extent of a slave's loathing for his oppressor, had strictly forbidden hatred of this sort, hence the quotation from *Deuteronomy*, Chapter 23, v. 7: "Thou shalt not abhor an Egyptian because thou was a stranger in his land." Allen pleaded for the commandment of love even on behalf of adversaries; thus, he sought to impress the spirit of forgiveness for their oppression on the minds of the African slaves and ex-slaves. Equally did he appeal to slaveholders to abandon the enslavement of man. He implored them in the name of their children, country, and God, lamenting the bloodshed which had resulted from the severities of slaveowner actions and the responses to them by the enslaved. In thus thinking, Allen stuck to the fundamentalist position of "thou shalt do no murder."

He further argued that the slaveholders could not justify the reproach of "inferiority" of the Africans after having reduced the Africans to an abject state and that this could not provide justification for enslaving Africans. Refuting the notion of the "contented slave," he had once said: "I have shown cause, I will also show why they appear contented as they can in your sight, but the dreadful insurrections they have made when opportunity has offered, is enough to convince a reasonable man that great uneasiness and not contentment is the inhabitant of their hearts."[51]

But Allen's mistake was the assumption that most slave owners were reasonable and open to persuasion. The irrationality of slavery itself disproved any reasonableness on the part of slave owners, and the way they worked the slave to death hardly proved more reasonable. Yet, the method of Richard Allen, though that of a suppliant in a weaker bargaining position, was not based on weakness, but on moral strength. But the fact is not altered that the pleader in a stronger position would have used his strength to achieve his aim, a feature very often manifested in human experience. Thus, for the American South, it was only the Civil War that could ultimately compel emancipation. Even after this the South continued to fight a rearguard action for a lost cause. Nevertheless, the religious coloring of Bishop Allen's thoughts also made him hold a prophetic vision in the assertion that "God himself had pleaded their cause; He hath from time to time raised up instruments for that purpose [e.g., Moses among the Israelites in Egypt], sometimes mean and contemptible in your sight, at other times He hath used such as pleased him with whom you have not thought it beneath your dignity to contend." But implicit in his plea was the appeal for what later came to be known as "equality of opportunity." [52] Allen said that it was not enough to subject enslaved Africans to an abject state and then plead their incapacity. He argued that despite the exertions of Moses for the children of Israel, their acquired slave habits persisted. Thus, he said "We believe if you would try the experiment of taking a few black children, and cultivate their minds with the same care and let them have the same prospect in view as to living in the world, as you would wish for your own children, you would find upon the trial, they were not inferior in mental endowments.... Men must be willfully blind and extremely partial, that cannot see the contrary effects of liberty and slavery upon the mind of man: I truly confess that vile habits often acquired in a state of servitude, are not easily thrown off; the example of the Israelites shows, who with all that Moses could do to reclaim them from it, still continued in their habits more or less; and why would you look for better from us? It is in our posterity enjoying the same privileges with your own, that you ought to look for betters things."[53] The leadership question had surfaced from very early times in the struggles of the Africans abroad to defeat and transcend slavery. Those who strove on their own initiative constituted the natural leaders. But the necessity for this leadership was not less felt by one of the foremost leaders of the eighteenth and early nineteenth centuries, the Rt. Rev. Bishop Richard Allen.

The themes of Allen's addresses were down to earth and were constantly concerned with championing the cause of the downtrodden. Thus we had his "Address to the People of Color" and "A Short Address to the Friends of Him Who Hath No Helper." In the former address directed to his brethren, Bishop Allen spoke to them with affectionate sympathy of their condition, recounting how he had been a slave and how at times all hopes of liberty had eluded him. But his primary concern was with their welfare and he claimed to have understood their yearning for the bonds of slavery to be broken. In mentioning his experiences of this longing for liberty, he wanted them to place their implicit trust in God and recommended that they should be affectionate towards their masters and mistresses. But by suggesting this, Allen was ignoring the economic realities of slavery, which made the slaveowners less permeable to reason; for a display of affection sometimes led some slave owners to suggest that the African slaves were contented with their lot. Allen's Christianity made him commend the slaves to prepare their lives for the hereafter; for, he believed, that the powers of the most cruel masters ended with the death of the slave. Such advocacies would hardly have commended themselves to the physical force leaders discussed in the previous chapter, as it must have struck them as nihilist. For those who had secured manumission, Allen admonished them not to show ingratitude or rancor or ill-will because of their past maltreatment, for he saw such an attitude as a transgression of God's law. He entreated the "free Negroes" to recognize their obligation and by their example he believed the cause of freedom would be served. Accordingly, he remarked: "We who know how bitter the cup is of which the slave hath to drink, O, how ought we to feel for those who yet remain in bondage! Will ever our friends excuse - will God pardon us - for the part we act in making strong the hands of the enemies of our color?" [54] Modern revolutionaries would hardly attend to this guidance, but Allen was a man of his time and represented one category - but by no means all - of the leadership that competed for the loyalty of the Africans of the diaspora.

Conclusion

This category of leadership spread over many fields of endeavor. Some were religious prelates, others speakers and protesters on anti-slavery and political platforms, some musical composers and music makers. Others were authors and literary geniuses such as writers of prose and poetry while some were active in the arts and some were fencing experts. Their interest varied but the outstanding ones showed themselves concerned with the immediate and future plight of their people, making their preoccupations known, whether in forthright or oblique ways. But in the main, their approach was through the language of reason and moral appeal. One type of leadership in this category that was first and recurrent was that of the religious prelates, and the emphasis given in this section of the work to the leadership of Richard Allen typifies the stature of this kind of leadership from the Church, as the Negro Church was itself one of the first significant social organizations among the Africans of the Diaspora in the Americas.

We now consider the third category of leadership evolved so early in time in the Americas despite the limiting factor of slavery.

NOTES

1. See for instance Richard Allen, "An Address to Those Who Keep Slaves and Approve the Practice" in *The Life Experience of the Rt. Rev. Richard Allen* with an introduction by G. A. Singleton, Nashville, 1960, p. 71.
2. In fact, they had no impact on the West Indian scene. The West Indies, at the time, were run as "White men's countries" in spite of a preponderance of an African and mixed population.
3. A. Caldecott, *op. cit.*, London, 1898, p. 38.
4. See F. J. Klingberg (ed.), *Coderington Chronicle*, pp. 85-103. Bennett, who wrote the article, exaggerated the position especially because of the earlier profession of faith by enthusiastic Bishops. His claims have since been discounted by later research. (Klingberg also exaggerated in his introduction to the text, pp. 3-12). Bennett changed his views in his book: *Bondsmen and Bishops*, etc., Berkeley, 1958.
5. Klingberg, op. cit. above, p. 86; see also J. H. Buchner, *The Moravians in Jamaica: History of the Mission of the United Brethren Church to the Negroes on the Island of Jamaica from the year 1754 to 1854,* London, Longman and Co., 1854.
6. See C. Fyfe, *A History of the Sierra Leone*, for the way they were initially associated with the scheme for the settlement of freed slaves in the Sierra Leone. Also R. July, *The Origin of Modern African Thought*, London, Faber and Faber, 1968, Ch. 1.
7. R. July, *op. cit.* , p. 36 et seq.
8. see Peter Fryer, *Staying Power*, London, Pluto Press, 1984, p. 110.
9. C. Cugoano, *Thoughts and Sentiments on the Evils of Slavery*, London, 1787, pp. 24, 111-113.
10. O. Equiano (Gustavus Vassa), *The Interesting Narrative of the Life of Olaudah Equiano or Gustavus Vassa, The African*, London, 1789, Vo. 1, pp. 223-27.
11. O. Cugoano, *op. cit.* , p. 138.
12. *Ibid.* , pp. 123-26.
13. *Letters of the Late Ignatius Sancho: An African in two Volumes* to which he prefixed *Memories of his Life,* London, J. Nichols, 1782.
14. *Ibid.*, Vo. 1, pp. xii-xiv.
15. *Ibid.* , Vo. 1, Letter xxv to Mr. Stern dated July 1776.
16. *Ibid.* , Vo. 1, pp. 95-98.
17. *Ibid.* , Vo. 1, Letter dated 9 May 1778 to Miss C., p. 189.
18. *Ibid.* , Vol. 1, Letter xiv, pp. 156, *et. seq.* , dated 8 November 1772 to Mr. M.
19. *Ibid.* , Vol. 2, Letter dated 1778, pp. 3-6. He then proceeded to justify commerce. Compare this observation with that of Dr. Thomas Winterbottom, a physician to the coast of the Sierra Leone in the 18th century, who observed that contact with the European slave traders had "tutored Africans in the arts of deceit." See Thomas Winterbottom, *An Account of the Native Africans in the Neighbourhood of Sierra Leone, etc.* , London, 1803, 2 Vols., Vol. 1, p. 206. Printed by C. Wittingham: sold by John Hatchasol.
20. Sancho, *op. cit.* The sentiments here would have coincided with those of Cugoano observed earlier in his criticism of Europeans in their dealings

with Africans.

21. *Ibid.* , Vol. 2, pp. 163-165 signed Africans. Letter ixv for the *General Advertiser,* dated 29 April 1890 to the Friend Editor.
22. Quoted in E. D. Morel, *The Black Man's Burden,* London & Manchester, 1919, p. 21. Also Chapman Cohen, *Christianity, Slavery and Labor,* 1931, p. 54. See Benjamin Brawley, *Early Negro American Writers,* Chapel Hill, N.C., 1934, pp. 39-40; also pp. 52-53.
23. Langston Hughes, *Famous American Negroes,* New York, 1954, pp. 5-6.
24. Oscar Wegelin, *Jupiter Hammon: American Negro Poets: Selections From His Writings and A Bibliography,* (Hartman's Historical Set No. 13, New York, Charles Fred Hartman, 1915); also Vernon Loggins, *The Negro Author: His Development in America,* New York, Columbia University Press, 1931, pp. 9-16; also Benjamin Brawley, *Early Negro American Writers: Selections and Biographical and Critical Introductions,* Chapel Hill, University of North Carolina Press, 1935, pp. 52-53); also Sydney Kaplan, *The Black Presence in the Era of the American Revolution 1770-1800,* Greenwich, Connecticut, New York Graphic Society, 1973, pp. 171-78.
25. Phyllis Wheatley, *Poems on Various Subjects, Religious and Moral,* A. Bell, London, 1773, p. 18; also *Poems of Phyllis Wheatley,* Julian D. Mason, Jr. (ed.), Chapel Hill, University of North Carolina Press, 1966, p. 7. See also Benjamin Brawley, *Early Negro American Writers,* Chapel Hill, N.C., 1935, p. 40 and previous page.
26. Langston Hughes, *Famous American Negroes,* p. 9.
27. J. H. Franklin, *op. cit.* , p. 156.
28. See Mukhtar Ali Isani, "The British Reception of Wheatley's Poems on Various Subjects," *Journal of Negro History,* LXVI (1981), pp. 144-149 (How youth, sex, race, condition of servitude all conditioned the reception by others of her poems.)
29. Lunsford Lane, another ex-slave wrote in his autobiography: "Indeed I, with others, was often told by the minister how good God was in bringing us over to the country from dark and benighted African, and permitting us to listen to the sound of the gospel." Lunsford Lane, *Narrative, etc.* in W. L. Katz (ed.), *Five Slave Narratives,* New York, 1969, p. 20. Emphasis not in original. The quotation and response of Phyllis Wheatley showed how the prejudice was distilled and inculcated into the descendants of Africa in slave societies and after. It even appears in a poem of Hannah Moore in the 18th century entitled: *The Sorrows of Yamba.* These infusions in doses were among the first breeders of ambivalence among Africans of the diaspora. Other prejudices were to be ingrafted on their consciousness once slavery had been officially abolished.
30. The year 1829 is of some significance for it saw the publication of David Walker's *Appeal to the Colored Citizens of the United States* (a strong anti-slavery pamphlet by an Afro-American) and the *Ethiopian Manifesto* of Robert A. Young (See H. Aptheker, One Continual Cry, etc. Also J. H. Franklin *From Slavery to Freedom,* Vintage Books Edition, 1969, p. 250.
31. See *Poems of a Slave,* published by Isaac Knapp, Boston, Massachusetts, 1837, "Explanation dated Raleigh July 2, 1829, pp. 119-123, editor of the *Raleigh Register* where some of George's poems appeared because it sought to raise sufficient funds to secure his emancipation. Mr. Weston R. Gales of Raleigh (in 1829 George was 32 years old) labored in the fields on his

master's farm, a field hand owned by Mr. James Carlton of Chatham County, at Chapel Hill, North Carolina. George then could read and was learning to write and employed it on poetry. "He was described as a 'faithful, honest and industrious slave.'" How his spirits were stirred within him are mirrored in this poem:

Come melting Pity, from afar
And break this vast enormous bar,
Between a wretch and thee,
Purchase a few short days of time,
And bid a vassal soar subline,
On wings of Liberty.

Raleigh Register, *Op. cit.*, p. 11. Also J. H. Frankin, *op. cit.*, p. 232.

35. "On Liberty and Slavery" by George M. Horton in Hope for Liberty, 1829. Poems of a Slave, Second edition, 1837, p. 131, Stanza 8. Compare with lines below in "Liberty and Slavery," p. 131

Come liberty, thou cheerful sound
Roll through my ravished ears!
Come, let my grief in joys be drowned,
And drive away my fears
George Moses Horton

36. *Ibid.*, p. 121.
37. Benjamin Lundy, Life, Travels and Opinions of Benjamin Lundy, Philadelphia, 1847, pp. 222-223.
38. Charles H. Wesley, Richard Allen: Apostle of Freedom, Washington, DC, 1935, p. 50. Professor C. H. Wesley, now deceased, had written the most comprehensive and admirable account of the life of Richard Allen. This part of the chapter has been in the main drawn from the work of Charles Wesley and supplemented by information from other sources. This author is particularly indebted to Professor Wesley and expresses the hope that the work would induce someone to do a similar study of Allen's associate Absalom Jones, and Rector of St. Thomas from 1794. It is also to be regretted that this scholarly book published in 1935, the year of the invasion of "Abyssinia" has become rare today.
39. *Ibid., loc. cit.* Also, see text, Carol V. R. George, Segregated Sabbaths.
40. Two modern historians of the United States of America had some interesting observations on the career of Dr. Benjamin Rush of Philadelphia but in terms of his medical performance during the yellow fever epidemic of 1793 they wrote; "sometimes he [Rush] is remembered for his bold attempt to reform the military hospitals of the continental Army and sometimes for his energetic and selfless work during the great fever epidemic of 1793, but more often his medical career stands damned by history because his drastic cure of yellow fever - copious bleeding followed by a violent purge - helped to hasten the death of George Washington." R. B. Ney and J. E. Morpurgo, A History of the United States, Penguin Books, 1955, p. 22 et. seq.
41. The Life Experience of the Rt. Rev. Richard Allen with an introduction by George A. Singleton, New York, Nashville, 1960. Also C. H. Wesley, Richard Allen: Apostle of Freedom, The Associated Press, Washington

DC, 1935, pp. 100-106 et. seq. See also Benjamin Brawley, Early American Writers, op. cit. , pp. 89-95.

42. C. H. Wesley, op. cit. , pp. 59-62.
43. C. H. Wesley, Richard Allen: Apostle of Freedom, The Associated Publishers, Washington DC, 1935, pp. 84-85. Also Chapter 7, especially pp. 79-82, pp. 152-53, 155, 158.
44. C. H. Wesley, op. cit., pp. 92-93.
45. Daniel Payne, *A History of the African Methodist Episcopal Church.*
46. C. H. Wesley, op. cit. , pp. 130-31, 154.
47. See C. H. Wesley, op. cit., p. 34; see also p. 161 for earlier objection.
48. See a subsequent chapter of this work for details of the Convention Movement.
49. See George Shepperson, "Ethiopianism and African Nationalism" in Phylon, Vol. XIV (Spring 1953), pp. 9-18. See Edward Roux, *Time Longer than Rope*, Madison, Wisconsin, 1972, 2nd Edition, pp. 77-86 for a discussion of the Ethiopian movement. For mention of H. M. Turner, see D. Thwaite, *The Seething of African Pot*, Constable & Co., London, 1936, pp. 35-39, 82, 248-49.
50. Redkey, Black Exodus, New Haven, 1971, Ch. 2. Also A. Wilkerson Jordan, The African Methodist Episcopal Church in Africa, n.d. (1973), also Shepperson, op. cit. , in n. 48 above, p. 9.
51. Richard Allen: "An Address to those Who Keep Slaves and Approve the Practice," in *The Life Experience of the Rt. Rev. Richard Allen*, with introduction by George A. Singleton, New York, Nashville, 1960, p. 71.
52. Ibid. , p. 71.
53. Ibid., pp. 69-70.
54. Richard Allen, *The Life Experience of the Rt. Rev. Richard Allen*, G. Singleton, (ed.), pp. 73-74

Chapter 4

Activist Leadership

Like the other two categories of leadership discussed above, the activist leaders were many, but again we will here single out a few who typified that kind of emergent leadership: two women and three men. The women were Isabella, known to posterity as Soujourner Truth, and Araminta (alias Minty), known to posterity as Harriet Tubman.The three men are The Reverend Henry Highland Garnet, Charles Lennox Remond, and Frederick Douglass. All of them were active in the anti-slavery movement and made their contributions among those un-named blacks whose role earned for them the appellation "black abolitionists."

Sojourner Truth and Harriet Tubman

Both Sojourner Truth and Harriet Tubman were born in slavery and began their activities against slavery after they had obtained their freedom. Both of them were women of indomitable spirit whose examples inspired other abolitionists in spite of the handicap of being unlettered. While Sojourner Truth was know to many anti-slavery platforms as a speaker agitating the question of abolition and emancipation, as well as women's rights, Harriet Tubman's name is associated with the effective working of the Underground Railroad. A full length biography of Sojourner Truth is now readily available. [1] Born a slave on a Dutch Slave Estate in New York about 1797, she should have secured her manumission as a result of the New York State emancipation proclamation of 1827, but her owner decided to retain her in slavery a year longer. She, however, escaped with an infant daughter and later successfully fought to rescue her son, Peter, who had been illegally sold to an Alabama slaver. She herself had experienced the pangs of slavery for about forty years. Although an activist, elements of moral leadership were prominent in her. She was deeply religious and on one occasion, while Frederick Douglass was discussing the anti-slavery agitation and had despaired that bloodshed might be necessary in order to terminate slavery, Sojourner Truth in awe and with characteristic adherence to good moral standards asked Douglass: "Is God Dead?"[2] But Douglass' reply that God was not dead did not blind him to the fact that the slave question was heading for a bloody confrontation. By her forthrightness and determination she was able to ingratiate herself into the favor of the author of Uncle Tom's Cabin, Mrs. Harriet Beecher Stowe. Mrs. Stowe called her the "Libyan Sybil." Her slave experiences were in the North, although after 1843 she began campaigning in New England and the West. She personally hawked her own narrative in order to raise funds for the anti-slavery crusade, but she worked incessantly for the anti-slavery cause and at the time of the Civil War, she was not only a "freedom rider," who strove to desegregate public transport, but also received her commission from President Abraham Lincoln and worked in hospitals and among the freedmen for four years. In addition to her anti-slavery activities, she was an untiring fighter for equal rights for women and was a strong advocate of temperance. An outstanding feature of her career is that she made her presence felt at two separate Women's Conventions in Ohio and gained the recognition of the American women in general. Initially, others were inclined to exclude her from participating. With her capacity for cutting repartee she had chided the white women there assembled (Akron), most of them probably middle class, who would not have had a quarter of her experience in work and suffering.

She was not hesitant in reminding them that they complained too much about the highhandedness of men. Complaint was not what was required, she thundered. She herself did not depend on men to do things for her or help her into or off carriages (implying that some of them did and cherished this). She wanted to see them take the initiative for themselves and take the struggle headlong into the men's arena not just sit back and whine. She bared her hands to show them how they had not shirked arduous toil, explaining that she needed no men to confer rights on her. With good humor also she added: "The slaves in the south were talking about rights, now the women were talking about rights. The white man will soon be in trouble."[3] When one male challenger dared her to bare her breasts in order to prove she was not a man masquerading as a women, she did so promptly, not only embarrassing him but others there assembled who felt the request was impertinent. But Sojourner Truth dared the man to come and suck the breast if he so wished. [4] She demonstrated by that incident that she was an indomitable fighter capable of giving as many blows as she took. She died in 1883 having become a legend in her own lifetime.

Harriet, by contrast, was a slave in the South of the United States, born in Maryland about the year 1823 (but this date is uncertain). She escaped from slavery at about the age of twenty-five. The interesting narrative of that escape is told by her biographer, Sarah Bradford.[5] It was known that on the eve of her escape she had been singing a song about a train which she hoped to board to freedom, and by dawn of the next day she had escaped, never again to be enslaved. The song went like this:

> When that old chariot comes.
>   [When dat ole chariot comes]
> I'm gwine to leave you.
>   [Ah'm gwine t'lebe you;]
> I'm bound for the Promised Land.
>   [Ah'm bown for de promised lan'.]
> I'm gwine to leave you.
>   [Ah'm gwine t'lebe you.] [6]

From the moment of her escape she employed all her talent and resourcefulness to defeat slavery as best as she knew how. Having cultivated her intelligence within the citadel of slavery, she then used that intelligence to advantage in spiriting away slaves from the south into "free territory."While the price on her head continued to rise, she is said to have visited the South about nineteen times and rescued as many as three hundred slaves, not losing any of her escapees. She is also said to have rescued all the members of her family, except one who died in slavery. Her chief role in the anti-slavery crusade was played in the development of the Underground Railroad and she was one of its most active and successful conductors, comparing favorably with men conductors.

Through this activity she achieved fame in the North and notoriety in the South. She was well known in Philadelphia where she had unloaded her first cargo of slaves. But after the passing of the Fugitive Slave Law of 1850, she preferred to escort her slaves all the way to Canada because of her distrust of "Uncle Sam." the implication was that she could not rely on whites conveying the slaves to their final destination and felt compelled to see the task through herself.Harriet was well known to many of the activists of the abolitionist movement - Frederick Douglass, the Rev. H. H. Garnet, and many more. It is said that she had a vision or premonition of the emancipation while staying at the home of the Rev. H. H. Garnet, three years before the actual proclamation.[7] Although she was a combination of moral, activist, and physical force leadership, she was an activist through and through. Her moral principles, like those of many others in her position, were derived from her assimilation of Christian doctrine; it is said, for instance, that she was the kind of person who would pray for a dead slave master to be restored to life although she would also pray for God to make the slave master recoil from the practice of slavery. But while she placed implicit faith in God, she at the same time believed that action was needed against slavery. The physical force aspect of her belief is seen in that she was a confidant of the celebrated John Brown (the white abolitionist) of Harper's Ferry fame. Furthermore, her use of the gun to persuade faint-hearted blacks who sometimes lost hope on the flight from slavery and wished to return to slavery was another example of the use of physical force to achieve an end. She frowned on cowardice and on those who expressed a desire to be returned to slavery, often using the words, "Dead Negroes tell no tales!"[8] Furthermore, the role she played on behalf of the Union Government during the American Civil War in serving as a scout (spy) certainly marked her out as a courageous woman and one who understood the necessity for using all methods at one's disposal to eliminate the evils of slavery. Even the celebrated John Brown of Harper's Ferry fame, who, in speaking of her, while introducing her to the abolitionist, Wendell Phillips, said that she was one of the "best and the bravest on the continent" and referred to her as "General Tubman."[9] But essentially she was not a physical force type. As an activist, her activism was conditioned by her moral conception of man in relation to God and to his fellow man. Her contributions to the Civil War effort on the Union side in South Carolina as a scout (spy)[10] earned her the commendation from William H. Seward, Secretary of the State of the Union.

Her qualities of self-immolation for worthy causes in the face of difficulty and overwhelming odds marked her out as a leader of consequence. When Frederick Douglass was asked to write a testimonial on behalf of Harriet Tubman, he replied that he needed such words from her more than she needed them from him and insisted that her labors and devotion were far superior in the cause in which they had both been involved. [11] But Harriet, having determined that she would never return to slavery, retained her freedom and was a source of encouragement to others to seek freedom.

She settled her parents in Auburn, New York, in 1857 where she also took up residence the following year. Her services to the Union Army in the Civil War as a scout and as part of the effort to undermine the slave system eventually earned her a small state pension, after sympathizers had championed her cause. Her activities in combination with those of others helped to cast doubts on the survival of the slave system.

At the time of her demise, the *Afro-American Ledger* of Baltimore for March 15, 1913 eulogized her as "Queen of the Underground" and "one of the foremost Women of her times." Even the white American Suffragett, Susan B. Anthony, who had had a long and cordial relationship with Harriet Tubman, wrote of her as "the most wonderful woman-Harriet Tubman." As a tribute to her, one American vessel of the Second World War was named the Harriet Tubman.[12] She lived to a ripe old age, until March 13, 1913, and also became a legend in her own lifetime. In the rank and file of people engaged in a righteous struggle, she continues to be an inspiration, but even more so for the liberation of women, whether black or white.

Similarities and Divergences

Despite the similarities of these two women, there were also differences in terms of their activities and personalities. The following are some points of convergence: They both had been enslaved and both had escaped from slavery, so they both knew slavery first hand the pains it inflicted. Both were illiterate and slavery had not given them the opportunity to be formally educated. Both were deeply religious and believed so implicitly in "Divine Providence" and retribution that it sustained them in their assault on the citadel of slavery. Despite their status, they developed courage and wisdom which sustained them in times of crisis. Although both of them appeared on anti-slavery platforms, much of Harriet's activities were conducted away from the glare of publicity, unlike Sojourner Truth who by virtue of her activities was more in the limelight (into which she sometimes intruded herself because of the nature of the anti-slavery crusade). Both of them had cultivated their intelligence in such a way as to enable them to overcome obstacles.

In terms of divergences, while Harriet Tubman was self-effacing Sojourner Truth had no qualms in approaching the crowd and coping masterfully with their heckling. In the effort to undermine slavery by spiriting away slaves, Harriet knew it made sense to begin her journey under cover of darkness. traveling at night and avoiding open places by daylight, hiding and using disguises to avoid identification and capture, and this proved singularly successful. She also used the

North Star to guide her in a trail that initially was unfamiliar and where she could not be guided by a map, as she was illiterate. Sojourner Truth, however, despite her lack of education and lack of fluency in English (as she had first been enslaved in a Dutch settlement and Dutch remained her primary language), she still was astute enough to escape and then use the emancipation law of New York to rescue her son from slavery.

There were many differences between both women, especially in their outlook on life and their reactions to situations. Sojourner, for instance, would normally resist violence and would not herself initiate it for any purpose, but would be guided by logic, as in her participation in the American Civil War in a nursing capacity. Her question to Douglass when he had lost hope that slavery would ever be resolved by peaceful means was a case in point. But Harriet's carrying of a gun for protection and to facilitate the process of spiriting away slaves as well as her use of threats to use it on the faint-hearted were clear indications that, faced with the necessity to use violence, she would do so, even if she was not by nature a violent type. But it was also clear that, having experienced slavery's excesses, she knew instinctively that in order to be successful in confronting it and the slavocracy it would still be necessary, at times, to employ the enemy's methods - intimidation and violence. It would, therefore, be in character for her to play the role of scout against her enemies, the southern slavocracy, breaching their frontiers and lines in order to supply the Union side with intelligence.

While Sojourner Truth courted the limelight, Harriet Tubman shied away from it. While Sojourner was quite effusive with her sentiments, Harriet was taciturn, and their respective postures suited their respective temperaments. But they both knew that struggles for a worthy cause always eventually yielded results and this partly explains their dogged persistence. They were both sincere and honest and, despite divergences in methods and outlook, they had more in common than not and their goal in each case was the goal of liberty in a society that had denied it to their brethren. Thus, they engaged in their struggles in a selfless way and it carried them into a long life in which both of them became legends both in their own lifetimes and after death. In fact, it is no surprise that so late in the twentieth century they continue to inspire others as symbols of struggle and models of persistence and resilience of the human spirit. At this point a consideration of the male activists is appropriate.

Charles Lennox Remond

Remond lived in Salem, Massachusetts, where he had been born. He was well educated and was much sought after as a speaker. He was respected by the anti-slavery forces and feared by the pro-slavery advocates, who dreaded the capacity of his sharp and eloquent tongue and his spirited onslaught on the "peculiar institution." He was a courageous person, despite the hazards of assailing slavery. Like other African descendants in the United States who assailed slavery, he was equally an internationalist; for, he had made contact with anti-slavery people abroad. One of his finest speeches was one delivered to the British and Foreign Anti-Slavery Society in 1841 when he rose to second a resolution. [13]

One of the most outstanding and pioneering of African-American historians, Dr. Carter G. Woodson, observed that Charles Lennox Remond, as precursor of Frederick Douglass, was easily "the most famous Negro in the United States prior to the rise of the latter." We also learn that Remond was one of the seventeen members of the first anti-slavery society formed in North America. [14] Woodson, who made a commendable effort to collect valuable documents of those early African-American leaders, informs us that Remond did not leave much of his writing behind. Nevertheless, he was able to rescue some of Remond's orations and letters from anti-slavery publications such as *The Liberator.* From them we get a glimpse of the man and his beliefs. He was passionately anti-slavery, and defiant towards those who tried to diminish the dignity of his people. His dedication to the cause was unquestionable. For example, he once said while addressing the New England Anti-Slavery Convention of 1854:

> ...I would rather be ten thousand times blacker than I am than be the proudest pale face that walks State Street today, doing the bidding of the slave holder. [15]

In another context he explained why he championed the great cause of anti-slavery. He insisted that it was not because the slave was poor, ignorant, or lowly that he professed himself the slave's friend but rather because the slave was despised, outraged, trampled on, and brutalized - in short, a man who, though a man among men, was herded among things that crawled and the beasts that grovelled. [16]

His orations were always interspersed with logic and conveyed the passion and conviction of a man already determined against slavery and all its works. On one occasion he asked: "Where is the man, who, if asked to become a slave would not hurl back the offer indignantly in the teeth of the oppressor? Nay where is the woman - where is the child?" [17] But in keeping with his oratory of defiance he had indicated that he did not plead for sympathy but was simply asking the majority for the opportunity[18] to develop the faculties with which the Creator had endowed them. He continued, "I tell you friends if we were equal in numbers tomorrow, we should not ask your aid: into our hands we would take the vindication of our rights." [19] As he grew impatient with the slow pace of emancipation in the United States of America, he delivered on July 4, 1856 a more vitriolic speech to the Massachusetts Anti-slavery Society in which he said that: "If the Union shall be dissolved, if for no other purpose than for the emancipation of the slave, it will be glory enough for me to engage in it." [20] This statement earned the applause of the audience. Like other activists of the anti-slavery era, most of his activities were carried out on anti-slavery platforms throughout the country and abroad in Europe. Even with this leader, however, we have an amalgam of moral, physical and activist leadership.

Charles L. Remond was President of the Essex Anti-Slavery Society for about five years (1840-1845). He was a fighter against the disfranchisement of blacks. [21] In keeping with this, in 1837 he appeared before the Massachusetts House of Representatives Committee and protested against "Jim Crow" practices on the railways and steam boats. He advocated the elective franchise for "Negroes" in Massachusetts and in other states of the American Union.[22] He was a determined fighter against the Fugitive Slave Law of 1850 expressing strong denunciations of the measure at Anti-Slavery meetings.[23] He opposed colonization as advocated by the American Colonization Society, an opposition which he extended to the organizers of the African Civilization Society under the leadership of the Rev. Henry Highland Garnet, another stalwart of the abolition era.[24] Earlier still, in the 1840s he, as a Garrisonian abolitionist (the term Garrisonian here relates to the pacifist wing of abolitionists led by William Lloyd Garrison, which eschewed political action) expressed unpacific sentiments relating to anti-slavery. While in the British Isles attending the World Anti-Slavery Convention of 1840, Remond informed the Glasglow Anti-Slavery Society that he would welcome a war between the United States and England over the Canadian border if the development would bring ultimate freedom for the slaves. He earned the reproof of the *Anti-Slavery Standard* for being over zealous. But Remond, undaunted, declared to the Hibernian Anti-Slavery Society that the dissolution of the American Union would lead outraged slaves to embrace their hitherto friendless and weakened torturers.[25]

He was a relentless fighter for the creation of a Negro Military forces to take its place beside the white military contingent of the nation. In keeping with this he and Robert Morris (a black Professor), another African-American stalwart, in May 1852 appeared before the Military Committee of the State of Massachusetts to press the case. In advocating this, they cited contributions of blacks to the cause of American freedom at the time of the Revolution and in the War of 1812. [26] At the time of the Dred Scott decision, delivered by Chief Justice Tanney of the Supreme Court of the United States against Negro-America citizenship, Remond expressed his defiance of the decision. At the Convention of Colored Citizens of Massachusetts held at New Bedford in August 1858, Remond proposed that a committee be appointed to prepare an address to the slaves inviting them to revolt. This proposal produced a divergence of viewpoint between him and Josiah Henson (for long assumed to be the Uncle Tom of Harriet Beecher Stowe's novel). But Remond's proposal was rejected by a small majority.[27] Nevertheless, Remond, among others, continued to denounce the Tanney Judgement in the Dred Scott case of 1857. His memory is dimmed by time, but he certainly merits the full-length biography which has since appeared.

The Rev. Henry Highland Garnet (1815-1882)

Equally distinguished in the activist rank-and-file was the Rev. Henry Highland Garnet. He stood on a par with another activist of that period, Rev. Samuel Ringgold Ward. Reveered as a scholar, lecturer, minister of religion, and newspaper editor and proprietor, Garnet was born a slave in Kent County, Maryland, on December 23, 1815, to Colonel William Spencer. From the writings of Alexander Crummell[28] and others we gather that he was the "grandson of a Mandingo Chieftain and warrior" who had been taken prisoner in a fight and sold into American slavery. According to Crummell the fires of liberty were never quenched in his family. On the death of Colonel Spencer in 1824, his slaves were distributed among various relatives. Garnet's father (George Garnet), using the pretext of attending another slave's funeral, escaped with his family (comprising himself, his wife, his son Henry, and his only daughter) in a covered wagon to Wilmington, Delaware. They were sheltered by Thomas Garret, a Quaker and a white abolitionist, and were aided by him to repair to Bucks County, Pennsylvania. The family moved on to New York in 1825. Between the years of 1825 and 1840 young Henry Garnet devoted his time to acquiring education. The family lived next door to the home of the Crummells and there his association with Alexander Crummell began.

Garnet had a varied career and at one time had to spend two years as a cabin boy owing to the needy state of the family. His attempts with Alexander Crummell to obtain admission to an academy in Cannan, New Hampshire were frustrated by a mob but he eventually entered Oneida Institute Whitesboro, a Manual Labor Seminary, and graduated in 1840. Thereafter, he settled in Troy, New York, continued for a while as a teacher, and then studied theology, entered the ministry, and served congregations in New York and the District of Colombia. He was licensed to preach in 1842. He also became President of Avery College in Pittsburgh for about three years and was a successful educator.

Among his early publications was the *Clarion*,[29] a newspaper which he edited. From Crummell's account we get a glimpse of Garnet's capabilities. He always excelled at school and had an originality of mind despite a physical disability that eventuated in the amputation of one of his legs.

At the age of 19, Garnet was invited by Nathaniel Peabody Rogers (one of the earliest of distinguished American philanthropists and abolitionists in the state of New Hampshire and friend of William Lloyd Garrison) to an anti-slavery convention in Plymouth, New Hampshire and had the opportunity of making his first anti-slavery speech on the 4th of July, 1835.[30] But his most celebrated anti-slavery speech was made at the age of twenty-nine (in 1843) at the Buffalo, New York National Convention of Colored People where he made his "Address to the Slaves of the United States of America."[31] Another celebrated speech was made in Detroit, Michigan in 1865. The first speech was so radical that it was not adopted by the Convention, though John Brown of Harper's Ferry fame published it six years later. The speech was not only a tirade against slavery but an appeal for the slaves to strike for their freedom. Not only did Garnet recall the pioneers of black liberty, such as Joseph Cinque (1839) and Madison Washington (1846), but he admonished the slaves to die as freemen rather than live as slaves. He continued: "Remember that you are Four Million! Let your motto be resistance! Resistance! No oppressed people have ever secured their liberty without resistance!"[32] The speech was again the subject of correspondence between H. H. Garnet and a Mrs. Maria Chapman, who had condemned the National Convention of Colored People in Buffalo of August that year. He mildly reproved her for being an abolitionist and yet being against his speech for the liberty of the slaves. He criticized her for upbraiding him without having read his speech but only acting on hearsay. How then could she feel competent to criticize it with fairness? The letter closed with the words: "Be assured that there is one black American who dares to speak boldly on the subject of universal liberty."[33]

The anti-slavery agitation at the time also made its demand for the genius and talent of the ablest of the colored people, and Garnet, Douglass, C. L. Remond, and Samuel Ringgold Ward also supplied these. According to Alexander Crummell, to hear Garnet was a "privilege and high delight." [34] His oratorical gifts did not disappoint his audience. He was passionate, eloquent, and persuasive. As long as slavery persisted in the United States of America, he was determined never to celebrate the 4th of July, American Independence Day, a resolution which he had made while yet an adolescent. The United States were too narrow for his energetic frame. He visited Britain in 1850, the year of the Fugitive Slave Law in the United States, and spoke in most of the cities of the United Kingdom agitating the question for the emancipation of slaves. In so doing, he, like Douglass and other abolitionist stalwarts from the United States both black and white, constituted themselves into abolitionists of the world. Their broad international outlook marked them out as men of merit. He was also a delegate to the peace conference at Frankfurt-on-Main and traveled through France and Prussia. His international activities led him for a brief spell to become a Minister in Jamaica and only illness caused his return to the United States.

At first he was an opponent of any form of emigration for the colored people from the United States. In 1848 his strong feelings on the subject had been couched in the following manner: "We are planted here, and we cannot as a whole people, be re-colonized back to our fatherland. It is too late to make a successful attempt to separate the black and white people in the New World . . . . America is my home, my country, and I have no other. I love what ever good there may be in her institutions. I hate her sins, loathe her slavery, and I pray heaven that ere long she may wash away her guilt in tears of repentance."[35] Yet ten years later, (after disillusionment with the Fugitive Slave Law of 1850), in 1858, he was to be one of the chief promoters of the *African Civilization Society* and his meeting three years later with the chief advocate of emigration in the 1850s, Dr. Martin Robinson Delany, reinforced his beliefs about emigration but the aim was not for a general emigration, rather it was to be select. The aim of that society was stated to be "the civilization of Africa."[36]

His Labors Summarized

Garnet, as his life indicates, was a Presbyterian minister and pastor to several congregations, an anti-slavery orator and advocate, foremost friend and active agent of the fugitive slaves. He acted as agent to Gerrit Smith for the disposal of land grants to colored men in New York and was a temperance lecturer and promoter and a delegate to

Europe on behalf of temperance as well as freedom. He was an untiring fighter for the rights of African-Americans to vote. His association with the Liberty Party was in keeping with these aspirations. He was a leading member of the Liberty Party and at the time of his departure for Africa was distinguished in the Republican Party. Not only was he a confidant of John Brown but he sympathized with John Brown's preoccupations for liberty and believed that the man died in a righteous cause.

In 1881 he was appointed Minister to Liberia, arriving in Monrovia (Liberia) on December 28, 1881 and died two months later {in 1882). There is no more fitting tribute to the work of this stalwart of the abolitionist era and relentless fighter for the dignity of man than the tribute which his associate and colleague, the Rev. Alexander Crummell, paid him at the time of his death. Crummell observed: "They buried him like a prince, this princely man, with the blood of a long line of chieftains in his veins, in the soil of his fathers."[37]

The Leadership of Frederick Douglass (1817-1895)

Next in this activist line was Frederick Douglass, whose emergence challenged the existing leadership of other activists, notably C. L. Remond. The period from 1840 until just before Douglass's death in 1895 (and before the rise of Booker T. Washington in the 1880s) has been aptly called the "age of Frederick Douglass." Among the leaders of the era, both African-American and European-American, Douglass towered high and made his mark by his oratorical powers, by his powers of persuasion through the publication of his newspapers, and by fearlessly championing worthy causes (concerned first with slave emancipation and elevation and, later, with Civil Rights and opportunities for self- and social improvement).

This writer first came upon the name of Frederick Douglass as a young high school student at the age of eighteen when the play *Abraham Lincoln* by John Drinkwater was one of the set books for English literature. Without knowing the background of the playwright it is still not unfair to say that the play is a disservice to the memories and accomplishments of Frederick Douglass. The portrayal of Douglass in that play was that of an "ignorant" and "uneducated" black man. The strictures are unworthy of a modern playwright and what is more deplorable is that the play is still read in schools today. The image of Douglass therein presented, either as man or as the representative symbol of his aspiring people, is hardly creditable; although Douglass had no formal education yet, in an America in which the legend of the self-made man is often commendable, one could hardly reproach Douglass for the manner in which he strove to become a leader of consequence within the United States. Gleanings from his journalistic excursions, from his autobiographies, as well as the many speeches delivered, and from the tributes paid him while he was alive, and at his death, the man who emerges is, in fact, a remarkable leader of men. His techniques adopted in order to acquire literacy both in the home in which he was a slave and from his white urchin playmates, his unfaulted journalism, his acquisition of enough reading ability to be conversant with *The Colombian Orator* at the age of thirteen (a book which he had purchased with the fifty cents he had earned shining shoes), all testify to his single-mindedness. His efforts to master its contents and further efforts he made at achieving enlightenment and to impart the little he knew to his own brethren in the secrecy of slave societies, riddled by draconian laws, hardly justify the slurs on the worthy career of Douglass, which Drinkwater's play attempts to cast. For in his oratory, Douglass remains in the realm of celebrated world orators. Yet, his sense of logic and his numerous dissertations and expositions were not easily assailed and as a symbol of progress of his degraded brethren Douglass acquitted himself admirably. Not only was his journalistic output prolific, but it was exquisite in style of execution, and in content was pregnant with meaning. This was the man, unfairly maligned and dismissed as a nonentity, an ignorant negro, and a revanchist in what essentially is a "trash" of a play. Not only does Drinkwater's play Abraham Lincoln misrepresent Douglass' nature, character, and deportment but it ignores his capabilities, his rise through adversity, his perceptiveness, perspicuity, influence and magnamity. But no doubt the play panders to popular prejudice in a racist social setting, and the image of Douglass as therein contained is wide of the mark. Here are samples of Drinkwater's introduction of Douglass:

> Susan: And who *in the name of night* might you be?
> The Negro: Mista Frederick Douglass. Mista Lincoln tell me to come here. Nobody stop me, so I come to look for him.
>
> * * *
>
> Douglass: Mista Lincoln live here. You his servant? A very fine thing for young girl to be servant to Mista Lincoln.
> Susan: Well, we get on very well together.
> Douglass: A very bad thing to be slave in South.
> Susan: Look here, you Mr. Douglass, don't you go mixing me up with slaves.
> Douglass: No, *you not slave*. You, servant, but you free body. That very mighty thing. A poor servant, born free.[38]

Let us now proceed to explore the real rather than the fictional Douglass. Frederick Douglass, born in slavery in Maryland in 1817, escaped in 1838. His narratives reveal his rebelliousness against wrong and efforts to quench his thirst for knowledge.[39] He was certainly an exceptional slave and as a freeman he had a heart larger than life - in fact, larger than the society which had bred him. We need not go into details of how he himself by subtleties and dogged determination and persistence succeeded in teaching himself to read and write. The reproof which one of his masters gave his own wife that she desist from teaching a slave (Douglass) how to read led him to say that from that moment he knew the path to his freedom.[40] In his autobiographies he tells of the various stratagems which he employed to acquire literacy: through interacting with white urchin playmates, occasionally "stealing" the copybook of his master's son or borrowing the spelling books of his white playmates in order to master the alphabet and words of his master's literature. Eventually, he even organized (secretly, in the woods), a Sabbath school for some young blacks in order to teach them how to read and write, a school that was later transferred to the home of a free colored man. Once literate, he was able to read the Bible and newspapers, copying passages from the Bible in the loft where he slept at night. He thereby perfected his reading and writing. One cannot but be impressed by his generosity in trying to share his newly acquired knowledge with his unfortunate brethren.

After his escape to the north he was recruited into the anti-slavery movement and from 1841 he began his labor in earnest as a platform speaker until he became a Garrison in 1847. He had heard of Garrison and the Garrisonians while still in bondage, but now, knowing who they were, he was able to say that no matter who they were they could not be enemies to slaves. In 1845 he was spirited away to England (to prevent his falling into the hands of slave-catchers), where he remained for about two years until his freedom was purchased by his friends. He later returned to the United States of America, but his Garrisonian ardor had waned and, with a schism in the anti-slavery movement, he became part of the new faction under the leadership of the Tappans—the American Foreign Anti-Slavery Society - which believed in political action. The English experience contributed to his maturity and gave fresh impetus to his anti-slavery exertions. He again returned to England in 1859, at the time of the crisis which had arisen over John Brown's abortive attempt to bring slavery to an end in the United States by his attack on Harper's Ferry in Virginia. Douglass had to seek safety because of alleged complicity in the raid, but the outbreak of the Civil War soon saw him back in the United States, where he directed his energies towards that war, urging Lincoln to identify the Union cause with the emancipation of slaves, vehemently proclaiming that without the elimination of the slave situation the Union cause could never triumph. [41]

His oratorical and persuasive powers did not go unnoticed and his associates, black and white, in the cause of human freedom commented favorably on them. He seemed triumphant in most of the causes he espoused. His journalistic excursions, eloquent masterpieces laced with persuasive logic, were no less crusading. So were his addresses to numerous conferences, conventions and meetings. He became a phenomenon in American society and his fame spread beyond the confines of the United States of America. With the establishment in 1847 of his newspaper *The North Star* (later the *Frederick Douglass Paper,* 1857), his news items, commentaries, and analysis broadened beyond the subject of slavery and the plight of "the Negro" to include presidential addresses and congressional matters; it became, in fact, a "political organ" rather than a mere news outlet, but it did not shirk the task of demanding universal emancipation.

Outside the United States, but chiefly in Britain and Ireland, his activities and pronouncements revealed him to be an internationalist on anti-slavery and a range of other issues. In London in August 1847 he addressed the Temperance Convention at Covent Garden (famed for its market and Opera House). It was such a stirring address that it led the white American delegates to protest at what they considered Douglass' unfairness (as well as the spirit animating his delivery). But Douglass received the acclaim of the English delegates, especially for the poignancy of his address and its content arguing that he was not a delegate to the Convention; at least, not in an official capacity, because those who could have elected him were wallowing in abject slavery. In spite of the protest of the white American delegates Douglass was able to make his point and impress upon the Convention his sincerity and ardent desire to see slavery eliminated in an England that had already turned its back against slavery. [42]

Through his journalistic pursuits he not only enhanced his reputation but did credit to his own people, for by enhancing his dignity he enhanced theirs. Increasingly, he came to doubt that slavery could be abolished by any other means than bloodshed; even when reproved by Sojourner Truth on one occasion, he was still not sure that pacific means could bring down slavery. [43] In making this observation, he demonstrated that he was capable of being persuaded by the facts. He earned many invitations to speak on numerous platforms and on divergent subjects, earning the acclaim of others and advancing the cause for which he fought.

At the Free Soil Convention of Buffalo, New York in 1848, he further assailed slavery in North America. He became associated with the Convention Movement of the Colored People, becoming its President in 1848. At one of these Conventions, held in Rochester, New York in 1853 under Douglass' leadership, it was decided that an Industrial College be established for blacks; that Harriet Beecher Stowe, the author of Uncle Tom's Cabin, be approached to solicit funds from Britain for the purpose; and that a register of colored mechanics be compiled together with names of persons willing to employ them or teach colored boys trades. It was also urged that statistical and other information be published on the actual conditions of African-Americans, so as to combat effectively false propaganda mounted against them. One of these agencies disseminating that propaganda was the American Colonization Society, about which more shall be said presently.

DOUGLASS AND PRINCIPLES

Douglass gave free reign to his thoughts and these revealed the principles which guided his actions. He argued that, in reforming movements, "measures change but never principles." [44] Faced, after the passing of the Fugitive Slave Act of 1850, with the dilemma of whether to quit the United States for Canada, as his colleague Samuel Ringgold Ward had done, he was persuaded to remain after consultation with Dr. Daniel Payne, Bishop of the African Methodist Episcopal Church. Yet, the new law had infused insecurity into the lives of colored people, who could be abducted into slavery on the slightest pretext. Hence Douglass rejoiced when slave-catchers failed to recapture their slaves and he expressed his approval in the fatality that resulted from an incident known to the annals as the Christina Affair,[45] when a slave owner, Edward Gorsuch, was killed in a violent attempt to recover some black men whom he alleged were his former slaves. Since Douglass saw these slave-owners as "man-stealers," he showed himself in sympathy with the slaves who attempted to defend themselves and prevent their being returned to slavery. In this respect Douglass found himself at one with the physical force leaders. Douglass found the emancipation proclamation of January 1863 so defective as to be critical of it and suggested that it was not a proclamation of liberty throughout the land but was a measure hedged about by discrimination and reservations. He could not understand men like Lincoln who could say they were willing to fight for the preservation of the Union but not for the liberation of the blacks. Believing that the way to break down an unreasonable custom was to contradict it in practice, his arguments thereafter led him to dispute with both blacks and whites about rights and the best means of achieving them.

Civil Rights

Even after slavery had been abolished, Douglass saw that the freed men and women were still gagged by restrictive legislation and practices, and so he launched into the movement for civil rights. Unlike his successor, Booker T. Washington, Douglass saw the necessity for the free colored people to be enfranchised and to have access to the jury box as well as the "cartridge box" - without which, he argued, no class of people could live and flourish in the United States of America. He therefore directed his energies into the quest for this power for the recently emancipated millions. It was one of the saddest experiences of his old age that this power, which had seemed within the grasp of those African-Americans, was curtailed and a large section of the African-Americans were disenfranchised in some parts of the American Union. [46]

There are authors who have attempted to liken his leadership to that of Booker T. Washington, but this is misleading. Douglass argued for the ballot whereas Booker T. Washington sanctified the disenfranchisement of the people whom he claimed to lead. Washington's Atlanta Exposition speech in 1895 (pejoratively called the "Atlanta Compromise.") generated much controversy, some favoring it and others denouncing it, although it received the acclamation of many southern whites and some northerners as well. But within the ranks of the African-Americans it received rebuttals from such eminent names as those of William Monroe Trotter, Charles Chestnutt, and W. E. B DuBois, the latter challenging Washington relentlessly until Washington's death in 1915. But the controversy belongs to a later period in the evolution of leadership among Africans of the diaspora and is discussed at length elsewhere. [47]

The argument for enfranchisement Douglass developed at such length that it would do him justice to here include one of his typical arguments. He adduced some reasons for demanding the ballot, arguing that opponents had misgivings because they felt that the Freedmen would be brought in conflict with the old master class in particular and with the white South in general. These fears had been advanced as reasons for denial of the franchise in order to avoid conflict. Furthermore, it had been argued that the new freedmen were unfit to exercise the ballot because of their ignorance, servility, and degradation, especially as such an exercise of the ballot affected the destiny of the nation. Douglass argued that such reasons employed for denying the new freedmen the ballot were, in fact, good reasons for conceding it. On the conflict that was likely to arise between the freedmen and the old master class of the south he contended that this presupposed that both classes were antagonistic to each other and that the maintenance of one would prove inimical to the other. This being the case, he argued, then the question resolved itself thus:

> If the negro had the means of protecting his civil rights, those who formerly denied him these rights would be offended and would make war upon him. Experience had shown, in a measure, the correctness of this position. The old master was offended to find the negro whom he lately possessed the right to enslave and flog to till casting a ballot equal to his own; and he resorted to all sorts of meanness, violence, and crime to dispossess him of the enjoyment of this point of equality. In this respect the exercise of the right of suffrage by the negro has been attended with the evil, which the opponents of the measure predicted, and they could say; `I told you so,' but immeasurably and intolerably the greater would have been the evil consequence resulting from the denial to one class, of this natural means of protection and granting it to the other, and the hostile class. It would have been to have committed the lamb to the care of the wolf - the arming of one class and disarming the other - protecting one interest, and destroying the other making the rich strong and the poor weak - the white man a tyrant, and the black man a slave. The very fact, therefore, that the old master classes of the south felt that their interests were opposed to those of the freedmen, instead of being a reason against their enfranchisement, was the most popular one in its favor. Until it shall be safe to leave the lamb in the hold of the lion, the laborer in the power of capitalist, the poor in the hands of the rich, it will not be safe to leave a newly emancipated people completely in the hands of their former masters, especially when such masters have not ceased to be such from enlightened moral convictions, but by irresistible force. [48]

Thus Douglass saw the arming of the weak as the counterweight to the domination of the strong, and although the class struggle would be exacerbated, this would also be resolved and the weak protected against the strong. The thesis of white domination and the anti-thesis of black ballot power and solidarity becomes resolved in conflict. This came near to being dialectical. It was also characteristic of Douglass to argue that if the Negro knew enough to pay taxes for the support of the government, he knew enough to vote and if he knew as much when sober "as an Irishman knew when drunk, he knew enough to vote."

In advocating the ballot Douglass was not unaware of the abuses[49] which might arise; but he believed that trial and error would in time eliminate this. He therefore agitated tirelessly for civil rights. Thus, when the United States Senate Committee proposed granting the rebel states the complete option of enfranchisement of their colored citizens or not, Douglass criticized the measure for its half-heartedness. The suffrage, he insisted, was the only means of preventing the colored Americans from being plunged back into slavery, a sentiment echoed by a later successor and civil rights fighter, Dr. W. E. B. DuBois.[50]

On education, Douglass was the first African-American to suggest the suitability of industrial education for the "Negroes"-an idea later appropriated by so-called "philanthropic friends of the Negro," who sought to bestow an inferior education on them. The idea was also later propounded by both Armstrong's Hampton Institute and Hampton alumnus Booker T. Washington's Tuskegee Institute of Alabama, and by racists like Dr. Thomas Jesse Jones.[51] But the principles, underlying Douglass' advocacy were distinct from those which guided Booker T. Washington; as a result, Washington's approach and that of his white supporters led to much bitterness, controversy, and acrimony both during the rest of Washington's lifetime and after. Observing Washington's compromising speech in terms of the concession which he made to prejudices of white racists, Kelly Miller, an African-American writer and once Dean of Howard University, wrote that: "Douglass was like a lion, bold and fearless; Washington is lamblike, meek and submissive... Douglass insisted upon rights; Washington insists upon duty... Douglass spoke what he thought the world should hear; Washington speaks only what he feels it is disposed to listen to."[52]

The National Convention of Colored People was preoccupied with mutual improvement, social elevation,[53] and the destiny of their people. But Douglass went further and urged them to seek the "triumph of freedom over slavery, equality over caste, right over wrong." Here Douglass, though an activist, was using the language of moral suasion.[54] His appeal was not couched in a spirit of self-congratulation because some of the brethren had triumphed over prejudice and enhanced their position in society; rather he aimed at stimulating them to greater and more worthwhile achievements, emphasizing that it was absurd for the so-called free men to think of themselves as "free" while others of their kind languished in bondage. He expressed it thus: "Every one of us should be ashamed to consider himself free, while his brother is a slave. . . .We ask you to devote yourselves to this cause as one of the first, and most successful means of self-improvement."[55] Counselling against undue dependence on whites for the basic necessities of life, he saw the dangers inherent in this dependence and counselled them to be industrious and productive rather than just remain at the receiving end. The dangers of limited operations were quite clear to him as they were not to Booker T. Washington. On the issue of undue dependence, he wanted to know what a large class of black men who concentrated on menial jobs would do should the white man feel that they wanted for economic reasons to blacken their own boots or shave themselves instead of having blacks do so,[56] a theme to which he returned the following year. [57] The brethren were therefore admonished by him thus: "We should therefore press into all the trades, professions and callings, into which honorable white men press."[58] There is a marked difference here between what Douglass was counseling and what Washington advocated. He did not see the colored people as the performers of all the drudgeries for the white folks. By his example he sought to set the pace for others and thus said: "I have made up my mind wherever I go, I shall go as a man, and not as a slave."[59]

Seeing the press as one of the major instruments employed to oppress the blacks, for the media often presented a distorted image of the colored people, Douglass said: "Wit, ridicule, false philosophy, and an impure theology, with a flood of low black-guardian, come through this channel into the public mind, constantly feeding and keeping alive against us, the bitterest hate."[60] The pulpit also came in for severe reproof. He continued: "Men with sanctimonious faces, have talked of our being the descendants of Ham-that we are under a curse, and try to improve our condition, is virtually to counteract the purpose of God."[61]

Having observed that the media (the press and pulpit) that had been used to destroy the black man were vital for his salvation, he argued that the press must be used on behalf of the blacks and the blacks must use it themselves; blacks must take and read newspapers, read books to improve their minds and to silence and shame their opposers and oppressors. As a formidable newspaper editor and proprietor, he had used the pages of his newspapers and speaking platforms to advocate first abolition and later civil rights. On the implications of anti-slavery activity, it was his belief that it helped to enlighten ignorance, combatted error, awakened the conscience, and helped to overcome prejudice; furthermore, apathy would be overcome, "the rise of free speech would be secured, mob violence subdued and a deep radical change to be inwrought in the mind and heart of the whole nation."[62] Thus, Douglass was always a voice of hope and sought to substitute this for despondency or despair.

Arguments Against the American Colonization Society

Douglass' main reason for opposing the American Colonization, Society which sought to transfer free colored people to Africa, was based on the fact that it was fostering hatred against blacks. He argued that no class of people in one country has a right to suggest that another class be removed from it; that the arrival of the blacks (even though enslaved) on the James River in Virginia was contemporaneous with the arrival of the Pilgrim Fathers (whites). He maintained that black men had a claim to American citizenship because they had fought and bled for their country and only asked to be treated with at least as much respect as those who had fought against it.[63] Repudiating the transportation to Africa he said: "We are not only told by Americans to go to our native land to Africa and there enjoy our freedom - for we must go there in order to enjoy it - but Irishmen newly landed on our soil, who know nothing of our institutions, nor of the history of our country, as ours, have the audacity to propose our removal from this, the land of our birth."[64] He indicated that he could easily have opted for the bait offered him in England for a comfortable home but he chose to return to American soil to combat prejudice and all its works and was determined to stay in America as a man and not as a slave, asserting his equal rights.

Having been in slavery for about twenty years, his effusions were not the vain imaginings of a scheming brain or mere fantasies, and so he graphically depicted the experience of slavery so as to impress its reality upon his listeners. The numerous sins of slavery are identified in most of his speeches - the absolutism of the master, the ubiquity of violence as an integral part of the system, the use of numerous instruments of torture; and apart from the physical cruelties there were numerous types of mental and spiritual cruelties, such as the denial of the right to religion and worship, the proliferation and universality of laws barring the slaves' education, and the hounding of the so-called "free Negro"-all these realities were repeatedly revealed by Douglass.

In spite of these observations, Douglass did not abandon his internationalist outlook and feeling for humanity at large. He would argue the cause of the African slave as much as he would argue the oppression of the Irish: "far be it from me to underrate the suffering of the Irish people. They have been long oppressed; and the same heart that prompts me to plead the cause of the American bondman, makes it impossible for me not to sympathize with the oppressed of all lands."[65] The quotation revealed Douglass as an internationalist and a moral suasionist, though in essence an activist.

Evaluation of Douglass as an Activist Leader

Douglass's statements were intended to give a clear direction to a beleaguered and bewildered people, first, while still in bondage; and later, after emancipation was secured. Many of his speeches were full of recommendations, admonishments, as well as counselling the need for self-examination and criticism as well as self-improvement. But while preoccupied with the past of the descendants of Africa in the New World and especially in the United States of America, he was also preoccupied with their destiny. In this respect he tended to opt for assimilationist-integrationist solutions which occasionally brought him in conflict with both blacks and whites. He advocated remaining in the United States and thus totally rejected the "Negro" colonization of Africa. Yet, in his concern for the past, to provide inspiration to his people, he rejected the facile assertion of inferiority of the Negro and, like others after him, was to seek some historical evidence to argue that ancestors of Africans - the Ethiopians and Egyptians - were among the earliest of the civilized. The arguments were later developed and espoused by other black scholars, [66] notable among whom were Dr. Edward Wilmot Blyden (in the same period as Douglass), William Wells Brown and George Washington Williams. But his search for identity and for inspiration through Africa and for inspiration, and his rejection of "Negro" colonization of Africa, represented that dilemma mirrored by successive leadership of the African-Americans and other Africans in the diaspora, which provide a paradoxical tradition of simultaneous acceptance and rejection of Africa throughout the nineteenth century and on into the twentieth. This mode of thought has left the successors with a tradition of ambivalence towards Africa.

But Douglass was primarily concerned to see that the colored people did something tangible for their own elevation and not depend solely on the charity of others. His address of July 14, 1848, is characteristic of this attitude of mind. [67] It was Douglass' belief that the colored people would only be elevated and improved as fast and as far as they should improve and elevate themselves and must rise or fall on their own merits and that rising from degradation could not take place when they were careless or unconcerned about their own rights and interests. Concerned that the blacks labored under more handicaps than even aliens newly admitted to the country - such handicaps as being barred from the school house, workshop, counting house, attorney's office, and numerous other professions - he felt that the blacks would need to build up their character in order to sustain them in the struggles to eliminate those multifarious handicaps. He therefore argued that identification of leaders of merit among the race with personal accomplishments would not of itself provide character for the people, as the talents of those leaders could do little to impart character on the majority. He felt that the majority must strive to forge its own character. Among the elements which would assist in the attainment of character, he listed industry, sobriety, honesty, coupled with intelligence and self-respect. [68]

Visualizing the Negro Church as one of the solid institutions of the blacks, he saw it as a vital agency for imparting character. Referring to the first African churches - Bethel Church of Philadelphia, the Zion Church of New York, and St. Phillip's in New York - he saw in them a great concentration of talent and ruling power, and felt that, were they to speak the right word for progress (by which he meant mental culture), through the encouragement of reading and contributions for the elevation of the downtrodden, a revolution would quickly occur among African-Americans.[69] His address to the National Convention of Colored People in Cleveland, Ohio, September 29, 1848, was again devoted to the subject of mutual improvement and social elevation. It was a speech intended to impart hope to the dejected brethren; but that speech revealed his broad interracial outlook and one of his best admonishments were made on that occasion when he said:

> Never refuse to act with a white society or institution because it is white, or a black one because it is black. But act with all men without distinction of color. By so acting we shall find many opportunities for removing prejudices and establishing the rights of all men.[70]

Although Douglass devoted the rest of his life (in the post-emancipation period) to championing the cause of civil rights,[71] with integration as the ultimate goal, his second marriage was also evidence of his integrationist belief, and he served his country in later life in many useful capacities - as Marshall of the District of Columbia from 1881, as America's Envoy to Haiti from 1889,[72] and as an associate of the Freedman's Bank just before its collapse (a venture in which he lost a good deal of his fortune and for which he condemned its operators for their mismanagement).[73] Nothing, however, sums up Douglass' career more aptly than his own words about struggle. In some situations he was a radical and in others a conservative, but this apt quotation of his continues to be used in the twentieth century by those preoccupied with fundamental change in society. Douglass had observed in a speech in 1857:

> If there is no struggle there is no progress. Those who profess to favor freedom and yet deprecate agitation are men who want crops without ploughing up the ground, they want rain without thunder and lightning. They want the ocean without the awful roar of its many waters. This struggle may be a moral one, or it may be a physical one, and it may be both moral and physical, but it must be a struggle. Power concedes nothing without a demand. It never did and it never will. [74]

The leaders hitherto discussed represent a handful among many outstanding men and women who have been categorized by this writer as physical force leaders, moral suasionists, and activists. They merely represented these categories of leadership and were typical of the outstanding men and women who periodically arose to suggest some direction. They were the forerunners of the later leadership after 1860, of those who were carried away by the integrationist ethos or the emigrationist one, or the separate identitists -tendencies which were to dominate the thoughts of African-American spokesmen and leaders in the second half of the nineteenth century and the first three decades of the twentieth and spilling over beyond. But it was also felt among some of the leaders that those who had achieved liberation from slavery had to set the pace and be guided by certain principles for only through those principles were the struggles, whether for elevation or for civil rights, seen in clear perspective. It also called for organization, which became a feature of the succeeding period, but not before the principles had been clearly articulated, debated, and thrashed out.

In observing this early leadership the discussion has not been confined to the characterizations and beliefs which these leaders had in common but attention has also been paid to differences in their approaches to the alternatives posed by the societies in which they lived. It is, therefore no surprise that their assimilationist aspirations led straight into the Civil Rights agitation, at least in North America, that became prominent in the post-Civil War situation, spilling over into the twentieth century. In the West Indies and Brazil the efforts, though on a more modest scale, settled for integration, which was more or less conceded with the passage of time. But they crystallized class divisions which sometimes expressed themselves in color and shade gradations. In the rest of South America there are numerous variations among the expedients adopted by the authorities, between assimilation, extinction, extermination, as well as segregation to resolve the racial problem[75] posed by the African presence in those societies. But the nature of those societies inhibited the emergence of a leadership of African-derived peoples demanding their rights - with the exception of Brazil, where after the demise of slavery there began a limited exodus of people of African origin from the Bahia region back to West Africa, where they became assimilated into West African societies. [76] Others made their exodus from Cuba to West Africa and became influential there; [77] these returnees emphasized the link between Africa and the Diaspora in the New World. But in terms of a sustained leadership in Brazil once abolition of slavery had been achieved, the record is negative, though there is a sense in which the "African Personality" survives in Bahia in Brazil in its cultural expressions and in religious manifestations and ritual. [78]

Some Challenges

The decade of the 1850s is important and instructive for African descendants in the United States of America. A number of factors and legislative enactments as well as pronouncements created a crisis for Africans in the USA. They were challenged by the circumstances to make definite decisions concerning their destiny as black people in a very hostile social setting. Among the enactments were, first, the Fugitive Slave Act of 1850. It remained ominous for slaves who had escaped to the north as well as "free blacks" who were not slaves but could be abducted as slaves or under one pretext or another find themselves, through legal subterfuge, taken into slavery. Some free blacks left for Canada while others went to Europe. Among them were Frederick Douglass, the Rev. Henry Highland Garnet, the Rev. James W. Pennington, the Rev. Samuel Ringgold Ward, and Henry Bibb.

The second enactment was that of 1854 which repealed the Missouri Compromise, thus making it possible for slavery to be extended into the western United States. That was ominous. But the third, the Supreme Court decision of Justice Tanney in 1857 on Dred Scott - who had petitioned for his freedom and was told in no uncertain terms that he was not a citizen and, therefore, could not sue in a United States court was the last straw in terms of the fate of slaves and freed black people. These challenges were dead serious and it should be no surprise that some African-Americans contemplated leaving the country as they could see no hope for the brethren. But these measures, in a catalytic way, were to precipitate John Brown's desperate raid on Harper's Ferry in Virginia, as Brown was convinced in his mind that the institution of slavery was worsening and the one way to clip the wings of the "slave power" (i.e. slaveholders) was through the instigation of a general uprising of the slaves. It was his hope that the invasion would become the general signal for the uprising of the slaves. It was aborted with the consequences that are well known, although John Brown immortalized his name.

Some of the black leaders took these and other earlier measures and practices of discouragement, prejudice, and racism as a challenge to be more determined in their endeavors to end slavery, secure freedom for their brethren, press on with citizenship, and achieve their destiny in American society. They seemed determined to shape that destiny within the United States. But the Fugitive Slave Act of 1850 was an admission that many slaves were escaping, to the consternation of slaveholders despite their watchfulness, and it was the determination of the slavocracy to arrest these departures.

Furthermore, observing that certain slave states had stipulations such as those of the State of Maryland of 1831 forbidding the manumission of slaves unless those so manumitted left the state, the struggles for emancipation against the slave system intensified and they in turn struck back with brute force, violence, assassinations, attempted assassinations, and kidnappings, while at the same time enlisting the support of the Congress and Courts of the United States. These could hardly be encouraging to those blacks who sought integration. Nevertheless they persisted.

Under the circumstances, it is easy to see why some of the Africans of the Diaspora would have contemplated emigration and how others got caught up in the mesh of the net thrown to them by the American Colonization Society, as that Society's aims were to remove the free African descendants whom they found problematic within the American body politic. But even those among the African-Americans who conceived of emigration rejected the American Colonization Society. However, their own endeavors towards this end simply provided continuity to earlier efforts by the leadership that had preceded them in the period between the 1830s and 1850s.

In their advocacies and organizational efforts, moral suasion was not excluded in their various pronouncements. Their moral suasion combined with activism in the pursuit of their goals. But this element of moral suasion was more preponderating in the integrationist orientation of leadership than among the emigrationist advocates. The struggles for equal enfranchisement for all were relentlessly pursued until the slavocracy reasserted itself after Reconstruction. The issues, whether they related to politics, economics, education, or social and religious matters, were all intricately bound together. Thus, an educational issue was simultaneously economic, political and social, and it even touched on religious sensibilities, as many African-American prelates were in the forefront of those activities.

NOTES

1. The first edition of the book was written by a white friend, Olive Gilbert in 1850, the year of the Fugitive Slave Law. See Olive Gilbert, *Narrative of Sojourner Truth: A Bondswoman of Olden Time with a history of her Labors and Correspondence drawn from Her book of Life,* Michigan, 1878; reprint London, 1968. See also a biographical sketch in J. W. Cromwell, *The Negro in American History,* Washington DC, 1914, reprint 1968, pp. 104-114. Also Hertha Pauli, *Her Name was Sojourner Truth,* New York, 1962 and Camelot Printing, 1971.
2. F. Douglass, *Life and Times of Frederick Douglass,* London, John Hobb (ed.), 1882, p. 240. Also in Introduction to *Narrative of Sojourner Truth* cited above. Also Hertha Pauli, *Her Name was Sojourner Truth,* New York, 1971, p. 196.
3. See J. Saunders Redding, *The Lonesome Road,* p. 67 et seq. See also Benjamin Brawley.
4. J. Saunders Redding, *Ibid.* pp. 79-80.
5. Sarah Bradford, *Harriet: The Moses of Her People,* New York, 1961.
6. There are several versions of this song but the message is the same, Harriet's preliminaries for escape. Sarah H. Bradford, *Scenes in the Life of Harriet Tubman,* New York, 1869, p. 17-18. H. Buckmaster, *Let My People Go,* London, New York, 1941, p. 218.
7. Sarah H. Bradford, *Harriet Tubman: The Moses of Her People,* Corinth Books, New York, 1961, pp. 92-93. Earlier text by the same author was titled: *Scenes in the Life of Harriet Tubman,* New York, W. J. Moses, 1869.
8. Sarah Bradford, *op. cit.*
9. Sarah Bradford, *Scenes in the Life of Harriet Tubman, op. cit.* , p. 5. Also Langston Hughes, *Famous American Negroes,* New York, Dodd, Mead and Co., 1954, p. 35.
10. S. Bradford, *Scenes etc. op. cit.*, p. 6. Wendell Phillips wrote of her: "In my opinion there are few captains, perhaps colonels, who have done more for the loyal cause since the war began, and few men who did before that time more for the colored race, than our fearless and most sagacious friend, Harriet." (Ibid.)
11. Bradford, *Ibid.* , pp. 6-8. Douglass said: "Excepting John Brown of - sacred memory - I know no one who has willingly encountered more perils and hardships to serve our enslaved peoples than your have." (*Ibid.* p. 7)
12. This section of the work has also profited from the article of that distinguished historian, Benjamin Quarles: "Harriet Tubman's Unlikely Leadership," in *Black Leaders of the Nineteenth Century,* Leon Litwack and August Meier (ed.) Ch. 3, pp. 43-57.
13. See *The Liberator,* July 9, 1841. Also in C. G. Woodson, *Negro Orators and their Orations, op. cit.* , pp. 127-130.
14. C. G. Woodson, *Negro Orators and Their Orations,* Washington DC, 1925, p. 126. He also helped in the summer of 1838 to organize two branches in Maine. *The Liberator,* 9 and 13 July, 1838. The *Colored American,* New York, January 27, 1838.
15. *The Liberator,* Vol. 24, No. 25, June 23, 1854, p. 100. Also C. G. Woodson,

op. cit. , above, p. 234, entire speech in Woodson, pp. 229-237.

16. Speech of C. L. Remond delivered before the Hibernian Anti-Slavery Society, No. 19, 1841, in *The Liberator,* Vol. 11, No. 47, November 19, 1841. Also in C. G. Woodson, *Negro Orators and Their Orations, op. cit.*, p. 134.
17. Woodson, *Negro Orators and Their Orations, Ibid.*, p. 138.
18. The plea for opportunity had earlier been the subject of a speech in November 1837 by C. L. Redmond to the Rhode Island Anti-slavery Society. This resulted in the Society voting to aid Negroes to obtain employment as clerks. See B. Quarles, *Black Abolitionists, op. cit.* , p. 50.
19. Woodson, *Negro Orators and Their Orations, Ibid.* , p. 235. Emphasis added that effusion revealed him as close to physical force leaders.
20. *The Liberator*, Vol. 27, No. 28, 10 July 1857; also Woodson, Ibid., p. 239.
21. B. Quarles, *Black Abolitionists*, p. 174.
22. *Ibid.*, p. 181.
23. *Ibid.*, p. 202.
24. *Ibid.*, p. 219 and 221.
25. *The Liberator*, 19 November 1841. Also B. Quarles, *Black Abolitionists,* pp. 131-134. Remond had been selected by the American Anti-Slavery Society in 1840 as one of its official delegates to the first world Anti-Slavery Convention in London. Remond's trip being financed by Women's organizations, Remond was not seated as London voted against the seating of women delegates.
26. *The Liberator*, March 11, 1853. *Frederick Douglass Paper*, 13 May 1852, also B. Quarles, *op. cit.* , p. 230.
27. *The Liberator*, August 13, 1858.
28. Alexander Crummell, "Eulogium on Rev. Henry Highland Garnet, D. D., delivered before the Union Literary and Historical Association, Washington DC, May 4, 1882", in *African and America: Address and Discourses,* Springfield, MA, 1891, pp. 273-74, etc.
29. Rev. William J. Simmons, "Rev. Henry Highland Garnet D.D." in *Men of Mark: Eminent, Progressive and Rising,* 1887, and 1968, pp. 656-661. Also Alexander Crummell, *Africa and America, etc., op. cit.* , above.
30. B. Quarles, *Black Abolitionist,* p. 90.
31. See forthcoming book of documents for full address by Garnet. Also Carter G. Woodson, *Negro Orators and Their Orations*, Washington DC.

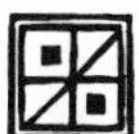

Part 2

The Watershed

Chapter 5

Detractors and the Myths of Humanitarianism

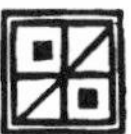

The concept of "humanitarianism" which has been a stock-in-trade of writers from the eighteenth century through the nineteenth and into the twentieth, has prompted this excursion in this work. The British, who founded the colony of Sierra Leone in West Africa in the second half of the eighteenth century, are said to have inspired the promoters of the American Colonization Society which emerged in the early nineteenth century. Both endeavors represented some detraction of the descendants of Africa in a period in which they were evolving leadership for their respective communities. In order to confront these assumptions of humanitarianism and understand the opposition which developed among descendants of Africa in the United States of America against the American Colonization Society it is necessary to examine the motives and preoccupations that gave rise to these pretended humanitarian settlements.

This chapter has two principal aims: first, to assess the claims of humanitarianism in the British and American establishment of the Sierra Leone and Liberian settlements during the late eighteenth and early nineteenth centuries; second, to highlight the fact that the idea of emigrations (often called deportation or transportation or colonization) of African-Americans away from the United States of America was an induced notion, except in a few cases. Through hindsight we become aware of the fact that in the United States of America the idea of transportation to Africa of African-Americans in this period was not popular even with some Euro-Americans as well.

THE CLAIMS OF HUMANITARIANISM

This section of the work is all the more important because for too long the myth of humanitarianism has bedeviled any study of the British Sierra Leone venture as well as that of the American Colonization Society. The claims of humanitarianism continue to surface in the writings of modern and contemporary authors. [1] In order to avoid confusion in terms of usage, an attempt is made here to define humanitarianism. The word is derived from the concept of "humanity." According to Cicero, humanitas signified the qualities, feelings, and inclinations proper to mankind. This in turn came to imply human feelings and conduct towards others, specifically gentleness, consideration, good manners; in short, a gentleman with a "liberal education" would be considered a humanitarian. But Cardinal John Henry Newman suggested that it implied the cultivation of the intellect and the training which produced it (i.e, the goal of a liberal education). Thus, "humanitarian" came to mean a person who devoted himself to the welfare of mankind at large. He was a philanthropist. Thus, humanitarianism came to mean the practice of a humanitarian or humanitarians.

In considering the first settlement of repatriates from the New World, a number of questions arise: Who were the promoters of the first company which resulted in the Sierra Leone Settlement; how generally reflected was humanitarianism in their endeavors; and what caliber of people were brought to Africa? These questions focus on the nature of humanitarianism and the presence or lack of it. It is also necessary to distinguish, as Dr. Eric Williams has,[2] between the professions of faith and the act. From the list of early participants we see an amalgam of people of different persuasions and mixed motives. Broadly, there were three schools of thought, namely: first, the *evangelical* school that was preoccupied with conversions; secondly, the *commercial* school whose preoccupations were with the exigencies of commerce and gain; and third, the *philanthropists*, friends of humanity. One may allow for a fourth school whose interests would be summed up as "selfish" and racially prejudiced. It was among the latter category that one would speak of the racists whose preoccupations were not with charity but with actual removal of persons of African descent in order to ensure that their own society was made up of people of European stock (or what they often termed "homogeneous".

In considering the categorization of the promoters of the Sierra Leone venture in the order indicated above, we find that those of evangelical sentiment derived their inspiration in the eighteenth century from the revival of religious zeal. It gave rise to the missionary zeal of wishing to carry the gospel of Christianity to others in distant lands. Some members of the St. George's Bay Company (which became the Sierra Leone Company) were anxious to proselytize the Sierra Leone and use it as a base for the spread of their activities to other parts of the West African region. Among these enthusiasts were religious prelates, but typical of the group was James Ramsey, formerly a minister in the West Indies for about twenty years, who had first-hand experience of slavery. There was Zachary Macaulay, who is said to have raised anti-slavery to the level of a religion. Later accounts, however, reveal that his motives were not so pure, for, as governor of the Sierra Leone (from 1794) he eventually took advantage of his office to amass wealth.[3]

Among the commercial interests were bankers such as Samuel Whitbread and Henry Thornton who replaced Granville Sharp as chairman when the St. George's Bay Company (formed 1790) became the Sierra Leone Company. Among Africans associated with the venture, who had advocated commerce, were Olaudah Equiano (alias Gustavus Vassa) and Ottobah Cugoano (alias John Stewart). In time, commercial considerations came to supersede any philanthropic motivations.[4] Commercial and economic notions were also implicit and explicit in the thoughts of Dr. Henry Smeathman (botanist), who was to have conveyed the first batch of settlers to Sierra Leone, but died prematurely in 1786. Of the philanthropists and humanitarians the most outstanding were the Rev. Thomas Clarkson, Granville Sharp, William Wilberforce, and Thomas Frazer. Clarkson was very persistent in his efforts for the welfare of the African slaves as well as the liberated Africans. His motivations in the venture were spelled out in a letter to Josiah Wedgewood (M.P.) in 1793. He indicated that he was prepared to sell his shares in the Sierra Leone Company in order to promote "legitimate" commerce with Africa. James Stephens and his son, Sir James Stephens, were others. The elder Stephens knew slavery first hand, having been a lawyer in the West Indies. His son became Permanent Under Secretary at the Colonial Office and urged Wilberforce to greater public exertions on the slave question. He was unimpressed by the planters' arguments (that abolition would ruin them). He was to draft the Emancipation Bill, in which he reluctantly made concessions to the planters in terms of compensation.

But Sharp was even purer in his motivations. He was anxious from the beginning to eschew the profit preoccupations of outsiders. He wished from the beginning to furnish the settlers with a constitution, with a view to creating a viable community. He saw the necessity of providing documentary evidence of freedom for the settlers in a theater in which the slave trade was still prevalent. He was prepared to hire an industrious European to teach crafts to groups of his protégés, who included repatriates from England (1787), Nova Scotia (1792), Jamaican Maroons (1805), and later recaptives from around the coast of West Africa from 1807.

There were those who saw the black poor as the unemployed and black beggars as an "eye-sore" and a blot on British society and many more whose arguments cannot be discussed here. But an examination of the composition of those initially dispatched to Sierra Leone leads to some doubt as to the motives being purely humanitarian. Among the transported were people of African descent hastily collected from London streets, who were in essence beggars and vagrants. The white women of doubtful character (mentioned below) constituted another element which was far from humanitarian.[5] Then, as time went on, it was not only blacks who were brought to the colony but whites also. At this point it would appear that considerations of commerce had gained the upper hand. But implicit in the entire scheme were expediency, philanthropy, commerce, evangelism, and, not least, racism. From the above we can see that the humanitarian principle which has been canvassed for over two centuries is misleading. The motives were mixed because the members of the enterprise constituted people of mixed persuasions.

Humanitarianism Unveiled

Yet, for too long, the humanitarian assertion of these ventures both to Sierra Leone and Liberia have remained the stock-in-trade of textbook writers[6] and these disseminations have created a myth which does not fit the facts. Since Sierra Leone preceded Liberia, it is to this colony that we must first address ourselves. We are not here preoccupied with the history of Sierra Leone,[7] but are more concerned with re-examining the settlement with reference to the claims of humanitarianism and its implication for leadership in the African Diaspora. Among members of the humanitarian school of authors were names such as Coupland, [8] Mathieson, [9] H.A. Wyndham (later Lord Leconsfield), [10] C.M. MacInnes, [11] and G.R. Mellor. [12] There are many others. But skeptical to the humanitarian schools was Dr. Eric E. Williams in whose *Capitalism and Slavery* we find socio-economic arguments for British action in terminating the slave trade and consequently advancing the settlement of Sierra Leone. While the British in the longterm established a colony, the Americans established a "free republic" which, in some respects, in the light of the latter's experiences, might be called a "neo-colony". The chief promoters of the Sierra Leone settlement and the inspiration were in the main those derisively referred as the "Saints" or the "Clapham Sect" or Evangelicals. Notable among them were names celebrated in the annals of abolitionism already mentioned. These stand apart from other members of the "Clapham Sect." Even Dr. Eric Williams saw them as irreproachable.[13] Of the others, doubt is cast as to the purity of their motives. It is here that we come upon the many mixed motives, which influenced their thoughts and actions with regard to the settlement.

From the official quarter, the dominant factor in official minds in Whitehall was the economic motive. This was made possible by a combination of factors. First, the decline of mercantilism made action against the slave trade and slavery possible.[14] Second, between the years of 1783 and 1807 commercial expansion and the American Revolution had altered the British economy to such an extent as to permit action against slavery and the trade. Third, what appeared to be the rising tide of British humanitarianism in 1834 ebbed away when the British restored or reverted to the use of forced or indentured labor (after 1838) in order to save the West Indian plantations, the sugar industry, and sugar capital from being blighted.[15]

No doubt, there were humanitarians among the promoters of the Sierra Leone venture. There were believers in the so-called "civilizing mission" to the African. Evangelization was the motive for others while, for some, commercial considerations still were paramount. Thus, the Sierra Leone Settlement begun in 1787 had agents for Christianity and for commerce, as well as agencies and advocates for European cultural dissemination; furthermore, there were those who considered it necessary to dispatch liberated Africans to the West Indies.

A notable figure in the West African venture was Dr. Henry Smeathman, a botanist who had lived on the west coast of Africa for about four years. He emphasized the commercial advantages which would accrue from the venture. He felt that through settlement the initial outlay could be met by the opening of channels of trade. He had hoped that the Sierra Leone settlement would lead to the cultivation of rice, cotton, sugar, indigo, and tobacco—almost all staples of the planters of the west. He also felt that good brandy could be distilled from sweet potatoes. His plan of settlement was passed on to the British Treasury by the Committee for the Relief of the Black

Poor[16] which seemed enthusiastic about the scheme (bearing in mind that that committee was paying a subsidy to the "Black Poor Hospital" which had been established by private effort through the agency of the "Saints"). But Smeathman had not honestly represented the climatic conditions and the health hazards that prevailed on the Sierra Leone coast-hazards that included malaria, yellow fever, dysentery, and typhoid, diseases which regularly took their toll among visitors to the coast. Nevertheless, at least one modern writer has suggested that, while Smeathman's motives were unclear, Jonas Hanway, the founding Chairman of the Committee for the Relief of the Black Poor, founded in 1781, suspected that Smeathman had plans to traffic in slaves.[17]

Granville Sharp had other fundamental considerations. He wanted Sierra Leone to be more than a settlement for unwanted vagrants or castaways. But Sharp was disheartened and disappointed when many of the Europeans and Africans dispatched to Sierra Leone embarked on slave trading. Sharp's work for the St. George's Bay Company (which founded the first settlement) was not based on a self-interested capitalism, although many of the adherents of the company were still preoccupied with commerce and gain. Among those who might be considered humanitarians in the venture, apart from those named above (Clarkson, Sharp, Stephens and Wilberforce), were those with sterling qualities who manifested scrupulous honesty, were candid and appealed to Christian principles and the Christian conscience. Many of them had been allied to the anti-slavery crusade, which, in the nineteenth century, became elevated to the status of a religion. Nevertheless, the establishment of the Freetown settlement in Sierra Leone gave Britain an opportunity to pursue a more "positive" African policy, which she followed for almost half a century.[18] This policy was later to engulf all West Africa. The policy had the greatest impact between 1787 and 1840. But the influence waned after the suppression of the slave trade, the liberation of Africans, and the pursuit of the "civilizing mission." Prior to their arrival in the colony, the African "settlers" had been slaves, ex-slaves, and domestic servants in English society. Their freedom after the Mansfield Judgement of 1772 (which set the slave James Sommersett free and facilitated the freedom of some and not others) also brought certain social problems in its train. Some of these unfortunate people, turned out of their dwellings, sought employment while others took to roaming about and begging.[19] This begging offended the "respectability" of British high society. From about 1784, certain students had come under the influence of Dr. Peckard, Master of Magdalene College, Cambridge. Dr. Peckard's sermon on humanitarianism influenced a young Thomas Clarkson, who was then a student at St. John's College, Cambridge. This influence was further demonstrated when Clarkson won the first prize for an essay competition. His thesis was An Essay on the Slavery and Commerce of the Human Species, Particularly the Africans. Later Clarkson was to throw his efforts into the work of abolitionists as well as the Committee for the Relief of the Black Poor.

This advancement was the work of the "Saints" in order to evoke the public conscience and consciousness about the excesses of the slave trade. The Committee in 1787 merged with the Society for Effecting the Abolition of the Slave Trade, of which William Wilberforce was a member. The Committee, which undertook to disburse private charity, was soon financially strained, hence the merger, and it was out of this that the Sierra Leone settlement idea was born. One of its leading lights was Dr. Smeathman, who did not live to see the venture get off the ground. What seems to have been paramount in the thoughts of the organizers was how to rid London of the nuisance of black beggars.[20] While the committee arranged for the departure of these "wretched people," the government was to assist by financing the venture. In spite of these factors, Sharp was concerned with the success of the venture as well as the happiness of his protégés. In forming a company, Sharp was concerned that the settlers be aided and, accordingly, he eschewed the profit motive as a factor in returning the descendants of Africa to Sierra Leone. But he was also concerned that the British government should be sufficiently interested to forestall the designs of rival powers who might wish to take over the area. He was concerned furthermore that the Sierra Leone settlement should be opposed to the slave trade and that educational opportunities should be made available for the natives. But the strength of the slave lobby in the British Parliament, the so-called West Indian Interests, prevented the St. George's Bay Company from receiving a Royal Charter. It was therefore dissolved and was replaced by the Sierra Leone Company in 1791.

Granville Sharp was replaced as Chairman by the banker Henry Thornton. The implication was that the philanthropic objectives of the settlement were highly visionary. Thus some of the ideas of Sharp were discarded and, thereafter, it was white settlers who were sent to the colony rather than Africans or people of African origin. Thus, in order that the philanthropy of the new company might be palatable to commercial interests, stress was laid on commercial considerations and less on philanthropic considerations. This Joint Stock Company was to establish factories or stores for marketing of goods. But the influence of Sharp still weighed on the venture and so the company was urged to discourage the amassing of huge profits although most of its adherents pinned their hopes on commerce which was not necessarily humanitarian. Thomas Clarkson, when offering shares of the company, had written:

> I should not permit anyone to become a purchaser, who would not be better pleased with the good resulting to Africa than from great commercial profits to himself; not that the latter may not be expected; but in case of a disappointment, I should wish his mind to be made easy by the assurance that he has been instrumental in introducing light and happiness into a country where the mind was kept in darkness and the body nourished only for European chains.[21]

The directors of the new Company included those of the former company, including Granville Sharp (and two of his brothers), Wilberforce, Henry Thorton (the banker and member of Parliament), and Samuel Whitbread (the liberal brewer who gave money as well as casks of beer for the settlers). Yet one modern writer has observed that "it would be unfair to suggest that philanthropy was merely a cover for business interests." [22] He argued that, if anything, the reverse was true. According to him, the directors were all enemies of the slave trade and desired to prove that "honest commerce was possible in Africa. They were all astute businessmen." [23]

What is clear is that, although the original motives had strong humanitarian components, apart from other motives, as the settlement of the colonists proceeded with changes of leadership on the spot and other developments at home, the philanthropic considerations began to recede into the background while motives of personal aggrandizement came increasingly to the fore. The case of Zachary Mucaulay (one of the "Saints") and his brothers is evidence of this. These men, it is alleged, profited from efforts to terminate the slave trade, especially as prize money offered for the capture of slave ships which went towards the servicing and supplying of the Royal Navy vessels and the recaptured slaves with provisions and clothing) all left room for irregularities. Thus this Governor of Sierra Leone, Zachary Mucaulay, later editor of the *Christian Observer*, became the principal London agent for those Royal Navy captains who claimed prize money. His cousins George and Kenneth Mulcaulay were in charge of the Freetown end of Zachary's firm, known as "Mucaulay and Babington." [24] Thus Zachary Mucaulay came to be referred to in certain quarters as the "great shopkeeper in the colony." [25]

One aspect of the Sierra Leone venture which casts doubts on humanitarianism was the inclusion of about seventy white women of "doubtful character"[26] along with the first settlers, women supposed to have been hastily collected from the "red light districts of London" and allegedly drugged and forced to marry some of the advance party of black colonists. The story appears in many accounts, but one doubted the authenticity of the original story- which, it is suggested, originated from Anna Falconbridge, the wife of Captain Alexander Falconbridge, whom the author Richard West regarded as a "highly sensational" writer. Richard West also argued that during the time in which the ship was moored in Britain, any irregularities amounting to enforced colonization would have been easily detected and dealt with. But some accounts gave the impression of women who were hastily gathered from the streets of London rather than those awaiting transportation. [27] If the story were true, it would certainly cast doubts on the nature of British humanitarianism, for although the ex-slaves were poor the gift of women of doubtful character was hardly in keeping with the avowed intentions of humanitarians. But it seemed consistent with erstwhile policies pursued and advocated during the first period of colonization of the Americas by Europeans, notably the English, that removal of "vagrants," the poor, unemployed and others regarded as a blot on the landscape to the colonies was deemed desirable. In fact, the "ne'er-do-wells," as they were called, sometimes were crimped and did not reach the colonies of their own volition. The incident of the women of doubtful character in terms of the Sierra Leone venture, reveals that the mentality still pervaded official thinking and the thoughts of those who formulated or advised on policy. It was also contrary to the much vaunted "liberal" instincts claimed for English society at the time of the emancipation of slaves, even if this liberalism was thought to be in keeping with humanitarianism. Now let us consider the North American venture to Liberia in terms of this alleged humanitarianism.

Antecedents of the Colonization Idea in Mainland North America

Earlier notions of colonization or "repartriation" of people of African descent as well as later ones from the United States of America or mainland North America were based on the assumption that Africa was a "dark pagan continent" in need of the enlightenment of Christianity at a time when slave owners in the Americas were denying the descendants of Africa in their midst the message of Christianity. There were those like the Rev. Samuel Hopkins of Rhode Island in the eighteenth century who sought an outlet for his theological theories. He obtained financial assistance from the Society for the Promotion of Christian Knowledge, in Edinburgh, Scotland, and although his plan was opposed from certain quarters he was able to send two prospective missionaries to Princeton College for theological training. But the outbreak of the American Revolutionary War soon after cut short the plan. One of Samuel Hopkins' disciples, John Quamine, had been identified in a study by Dr. Horace Mann Bond as one of the earliest Gold Coasters (Ghanaians) to register in an American College.[28] Quamine, however, lost his life in combat during the revolution.[29]

But the roots of colonization predate this organization although most of the earlier suggestions were unorganized, prior to the emergence of the American Colonization Society after 1816. These forerunners seemed to have provided the basis on which the Colonization Society advanced itself so that at the time of its formation the notion of colonization was carried out in a crusading spirit. The foundations of racial separatism and antipathies are replete in the earlier writings of Thomas Jefferson (a former president of the United States of America), who, among others, had signed the Preamble to the Declaration of Independence from England. In those declarations it ought to be remembered that the signatories believed that "all men are created equal." Jefferson was later to write that as a suspicion the blacks "whether originally a distinct race, or made distinct by time and circumstances, are inferior to the whites in the endowments of both body and mind."[30] Feeling that color had drawn a sharp line of division between races, and noting anatomical differences of skin glands, that of the black supposed to exude an offensive and disagreeable odor, and being himself a slave owner, Jefferson expressed the many prejudices of his age and consequently advocated a limited emancipation scheme which would lead to colonization in a distant land of people of African origin. He extended this plea to the Virginia Assembly, in which he advocated a scheme for the emancipation of all slaves when they attained maturity. Jefferson had become convinced that advocacy for equality would convulse the nation to its very foundations. As a prerequisite for colonization to a "favorable place" and at a very opportune time, he urged the state of Virginia to train the emancipated in tillage, arts, or sciences according to their ability until they attained adulthood before being dispatched to begin new settlements. It can be seen that the element of fear was present in the thoughts of Jefferson and he feared that an increase in the black population might bring on the inevitable collision sooner than expected. This attitude also mirrored a kind of Virginian ambivalence, for, on the one hand, a Virginian was advocating colonization; yet, Virginia sought to increase its stock of slaves through the process of slave breeding for labor on the plantation, especially after the United States government abolished the slave trade in 1808.

Another advocate of colonization was a Virginian known as Ferdinando Fairfax, who in 1790 declared for colonization and, while endorsing Jefferson's program in principle, favored individual manumission instead of the wholesale manumission advocated by Jefferson. His approach, he felt, would ensure the end of slavery. Nevertheless, he shared Jefferson's fear of racial explosion and confrontation. Believing that both races could never live together in peace, harmony, or a state of equality; doubting that legislation could sustain the principles of equal rights against ingrained prejudices, and aware of the fact that intermarriage could produce a homogeneous society (but rejecting this solution as being contrary to the sentiments of most people), Fairfax suggested to Congress that land be acquired in Africa for the purpose of colonizing blacks. He naively believed that such a program would move slaveholders to emancipate their slaves. In advocating this solution to the dangers of the impending racial strife, he ignored the tenacity of economic considerations in the sustenance of the institution of slavery. He was also convinced that repatriates would carry the Christian message to their "rude" brethren. Furthermore, there was also a commercial aspect to his advocacy, in his assertion that American traders and merchants would reap valuable advantages from a tropical colony under American supervision. He felt that such a colony would repay in profits all expenses of transporting colonists and at the same time assure the colony of its eventual independence.[31] There were others whose voices had been raised prior to those of Jefferson and Fairfax. They include university professors such as St. George Tucker of William and Mary College, whose advocacy was expressed earlier in 1786. This academic did not believe in the feasibility of a government-assisted scheme, but he also saw grim consequences for non-implementation of the colonization scheme. Nevertheless, he expressed the hope that the individual freedmen would emigrate on their own account, without mass deportations. Tucker did not favor the Jeffersonian idea of a complete mass transfer unless the technique of genocide were employed, and he eschewed genocide. When the United States purchased Louisiana from Napoleon, he recommended that some colonization of blacks to that area could induce slave states to relax their rigid laws against manumission and also that the territory could be employed for the rehabilitation of criminals.

Jon Parish, a Quaker gentleman, during Jefferson's presidency, advocated emancipation and colonization into the western wilderness of the United States. Between 1801 and 1802 the Virginia House of Delegates discussed the possibility of creating a penal colony for rebellious slaves and free negro criminals. The Gabriel Revolt of 1800 in Richmond, Virginia had on its own triggered schemes for colonization of "Negroes" but no action was taken, in spite of the suggestion that the moves were humanitarian.[32]

An earlier scheme of colonization originating with an English Quaker, William Thornton, is even more interesting. It was to have been in partnership with the Rev. Samuel Hopkins (mentioned above). Thornton in 1785 had inherited some slaves from the West Indies and this gave a boost to his plans for colonization. His intention was to found a self-sustaining plantation either in the West Indies or Africa. Through their labors these colonists would purchase their freedom. The West Indian authorities were not enthusiastic for a free Negro population living close to slaves and discouraged the scheme. Thornton in consultation with Hopkins considered floating the scheme in Africa. Implicit in all these activities and advocacies was the assumption, if not the conclusion, that the Negro had no permanent place in North American society.[33] Furthermore, although considerations of profit were not far from Thornton's mind, he did see the scheme as combining two things which should have been mutually exclusive, namely, "philanthropy and profit." He felt that the scheme would bring direct trade to the United States and establish that valuable commercial link between it and Africa; and goods hitherto purchased from the West Indies (spices, gold dust, ivory, gum, and dyes) would come directly from Africa, where the settlements had been laid. This seemed another of those attempts to beat the restrictions of the mercantilists. There were many more ideas of colonization current at the time including those of James Madison (once a President of the United States): he coupled emancipation with colonization, thinking that without colonization emancipation would involve disaster. Many of these ideas were canvassed with a view to getting rid of the black freedman.

Some Divergent Viewpoints

In the early nineteenth century, the rise of evangelicalism together with the revival of Calvinism stimulated concern for the religious and moral welfare of paupers in society. It was into this evangelical ferment that the Rev. Robert Finley of Basking Ridge, New Jersey (an area with a large number of free blacks), found his zeal for advocating colonization. Finley confessed himself amazed and dismayed by the fact that the free blacks in his parish lacked any knowledge of the Bible.[34] This amazement is all the more surprising since the Rev. Finley does not seem to have been aware of the technique of slave societies in fostering ignorance together via the deliberate policy of prohibiting descendants of Africa from reading, writing, and even assembling for worship where no white persons were present. This bar was enshrined in the legislative enactments of most of the states.[35] But Finley was soon to reach the conclusion, judging from the weight of prejudice around him and against this class of people, that mere distribution of the Bible or knowledge of its contents did not bestow equality on the "Negro," and he, like others before him, came to the conclusion that emigration, i.e. the removal from the United States, was the only solution.[36]

Yet after reaching this conclusion, Finley was still so hypocritical as to speak of establishing a "benevolent society" for colonizing free Negroes in Africa as a means of improving their condition and resolving the larger problem of race in America. He began to peddle the notion that his forefathers had brought the Negroes to America and it was an act of expiation for him and his generation to restore them to Africa.[37] An expiation indeed! The Rev. Finley became one of the architects of the American Colonization Society and one of its first vice-presidents, and believed that colonization would lead eventually to emancipation. He argued that colonization would achieve three main objectives: first, that the U.S. would be rid of blacks; while secondly, Africa would be the recipient of "partially civilized Christianized" settlers, and thirdly, the Negroes would enjoy a "better situation" than in the U.S. But above all, he claimed divine sanction for the scheme. Thus, when it suited the Euro-Americans (alias whites) fancy to regard "negroes" as Africans they did so and when it did not suit their purpose Negroes were not Africans. Thus Finley stressed that Negroes were Africans by color, temperament, and fortune and that God had destined them for Africa. He had even discussed the idea with Paul Cuffee (the Afro-American Bostonian captain and shipowner who had made two visits to Sierra Leone[38] prior to his death) and had observed that contributions for the African school system increased when this was linked with colonization. Finley further assumed that in Africa the "contracted minds" of colored people would expand and this would tend to the general good. He saw the Sierra Leone scheme of the British as divinely inspired. Moving to Washington, D.C., he sought congressional support for a U.S.-government financed emigration with American warships as the means of transportation. His scheme was in no way divorced from commercial profit, for he argued that profit would accrue if the colony were wisely established. He also saw the colony as a channel through which missionary work could be advanced and argued that the scheme itself in the long run would achieve painless emancipation. In December 1816 he published his *Thoughts on Colonization* with a view to enlisting the support of influential men in public life, among whom were clergymen such as the Rt. Rev. William Meade, as well as politicians such as Henry Clay, Daniel Webster, and many more.

The Founding of the American Colonization Society

At the time of the inception of the American Colonization Society (1817) earlier ideas on colonization had become intermingled with the propaganda and advocacy for colonization of free blacks. But the point was stressed again and again that colonization was for free negroes and not slaves.[39] Free Negroes were portrayed in a bad light, in fact, as tainted with every sin that had a name.[40] They were "wretched," "promoters of mischief," "miserable"-all this in spite of efforts that were being made to cultivate their minds. They were considered "vicious and unhappy," dangerous to the social interests of the whites; they were "ignorant"; they were "wicked and reckless." When the assemblage of notable personnel met in the Hall of the House of Representatives on December 28, 1816, it adopted a Constitution and took the title "American Society for Colonizing the Free People of Color in the United States." It elected a president and thirteen vice-presidents.[41] The work of the Society devolved on a Board of Managers and an Executive Security.[42]

It must be remembered that the American Society for Colonizing the Free People of Color in the United States consisted of a disparate group, with slave owners preponderating and forming the hard core and the pillars of the Society. Disregarding the evidence that the Society, as composed, was made up of slave owners, and bearing in mind the assumptions and attitudes of slave owners, Phillip Staudenraus, one of the authorities on the Colonization Society, asserted that it is not true to say that the Society was intent on securing or maintaining slavery. The inference is drawn by Staudenraus that the scheme was philanthropic. It is not enough, however, for Staudenraus to assert this without providing the evidence for his assumption. Staudenraus ignores the fact that most of the members were anxious to manipulate the leadership of the free blacks, whose presence in the North American body politic provided a cause for slave restiveness implied through a conscious or unconscious racism, opined that the scheme was well considered and proper. In describing the African element in America as "alien," Staudenraus ignored the fact that the European element was just as alien. The flood of impoverished refugees from Europe whether Anglo-Saxon, Huguenots, Irish, Scots, Jews, Poles, Hungarian revolutionaries and others were, in fact, alien to the "American" environment, yet this alien element did not cease to flow into the United States of America even at the turn of the twentieth century. Yet the alien nature of these European infusions was not made an argument for their deportation or exclusion. Furthermore, the suggestion that the African element constituted an "inferior race"[43] to the original white settler element of the latter arrivals is not borne out by genuine diagnosis, but is rather the adoption of assumptions fashioned out of rationalizations of those times in order to salve the consciences of those who inflicted misery on others. These explanations are too glib to be the stock-in-trade of any respectable modern scholar. The European element, having degraded the African-American through centuries of unrequited toil, sought to remove the "eyesore" which they themselves had created to a different environment. But in answer to the assertion of the inferiority of the African element, it is essential to be reminded of the views of West Indian historian C.L.R. James, recently deceased, who studied the slave trade and, armed with the facts of history, remarked that: "It was on a peasantry in many ways superior to the serfs of Europe that the slave trade fell."[44]

Bearing in mind that serfdom still prevailed in large parts of Eastern and Central Europe even after the formation of the American Colonization Society in the nineteenth century, it is not easy to give credence to the assertion of an "inferior race" in the midst of others. Furthermore, in answer to this charge of inferiority, it was the white abolitionist, William Lloyd Garrison, who rose to the charge. He insisted in his campaign against the American Colonization Society that the free blacks "are superior in their habits to the host of foreign emigrants who are crowding our shores, and poisoning our moral atmosphere."[45] Be that as it may, an examination of some of the assumptions of the American Colonization Society will illustrate the nature of this "hypocrisy."

Aims and Objects

Although the Colonization Society defined its aims and expectations in its Constitution to be exclusively directed to promoting the voluntary colonization of free Negroes in Africa or some other place that the United States Congress would consider expedient, it is not only from this declaration of intention that we must search for the aims and objectives of this Society. Its members' opinions about people of African descent residing among them are of extreme importance in illuminating the real motives of its most ardent activists. It is impossible to encompass this mass of repetitive information in a work of this scope. We shall therefore content ourselves with a some representative citations, which, even if they did not reflect the views of all the members, at least reflected the views of a vocal wing within the Colonization Society.

The slave owners who could not accept readily the idea of emancipation and the elevation of the slave automatically or gradually to the same status of equality could conceive of no other solution, if they were persuaded about manumission than that the liberated persons of African descent should quit the state within a specified period of time. Thus we recall a law of Virginia of 1806 which permitted manumission only on condition that the manumitted blacks left the state within a year. But the Colonization Society sought to overcome this obstacle to emancipation by accepting responsibility for all manumitted slaves on the condition that they would be deported. There was the case of Kosciusko, who, after helping the United States to win its independence, liberated the serfs on his Polish estate leaving a bequest of $20,000 in Jefferson's charge for the purpose and the education of young female slaves. But the laws of Virginia made strict compliance with the bequest impossible. It was then envisaged that the difficulties could be transcended by incorporating the bequest with the funds of the American Colonization Society. The bequest finally went to the "African Education Society" of New Jersey, which aimed to combine literacy and manual education and prepare the free colored youths for service in Africa and this arrangement earned the commendation of the American Colonization Society. [46] This incident alone illustrates the difficulty in pressing the emancipation question on an aristocracy that was obdurate and determined to ensure that its paradise created out of the servitude of Africans remained undisturbed.

Some Tenets and Beliefs of Colonizationists

Briefly stated, the following were the general principles to which members of the Society subscribed:

1) colonization of the free blacks who constituted an "unwanted" element in US society would eliminate the dangers of racial strife;
2) the presence of these blacks was not conducive to peace and good order within a society which was hell bent on maintaining slavery;
3) the scheme of colonization was itself a "benevolent" gesture for which the black man ought to be thankful, as the alternative was worse;
4) it was held by some of its adherents that, if colonization commenced, slavery would disappear;
5) among those with a religious persuasion, there was the assertion that divine providence guided the conduct and destiny of the nations and that providence was behind the scheme which would

make for the happiness of U.S. society;

6) it was believed that American society would eradicate a social cancer by the transfer of people of African origin to Africa and this would be an act of expiation in which the deportees would also play the major part in the "civilization" of their brethren;
7) this in turn, would accelerate the arrival of the American millennium, as the land of America would then consist of one "happy, united, homogeneous race" of people (but this latter assumption failed to take into consideration the enforced miscegenation which had pervaded the entire history of slavery in the Americas and which had produced its outcrop of a mixed pedigree);
8) it was a major assumption of the Society that the establishment of a settlement in Liberia would become the advance base for "civilizing" activity and so it sought governmental patronage for its scheme.

But above all, the major factor animating the scheme was the assumption that both races could never live together in peace and harmony. These were by no means all the beliefs of the members. It is thus appropriate to consider some of the reactions of the opponents of the Society, including the free blacks.

Criticisms and Reactions to the Society

Within U.S. society, the Colonization Society came in for a good deal of censure. A study of the U.S. newspapers for the first thirty years of the Society's existence is quite instructive. Some assailed the Society on its premises while others questioned its good faith, arguing that if the Society were really genuine in promoting the welfare of the blacks as equal human beings, why did it fail to advocate their amalgamation as a solution to the race problem? The criticisms emanated from both black and white. In fact, the African-Americans were in the forefront of the objections raised against the colonization program. Accordingly, it is essential that we consider their response first.

Black Reactions to Colonizations

Besides individual expressions of opposition or approval, there were organized protests as well. We have observed, in another context, that under the leadership of Richard Allen, supported by James Forten, Absalom Jones, Robert Douglas, and the Rev. Peter Williams, a meeting of the colored citizens was convened in Bethel African Methodist Episcopal Church in the city of Philadelphia and their resolutions declared in unequivocal terms against the attitude of the promoters of the Colonization Society. Not only did those assembled defend themselves against vilification from certain quarters, but they declared: "We will never separate ourselves voluntarily from the slave population of this country."[47] They castigated the Society for wishing to plunge them back into bondage by a circuitous route and lamented the plan to dump Negroes "into the savage wilds of Africa."[48]

The Colonization Society seemed surprised, as during the previous year some of the same leaders of the blacks in Philadelphia had endorsed Paul Cuffee's emigration scheme and had commended his efforts. James Forten, for instance, was known to have assisted Cuffee and praised his endeavors. As a result of this protest activity, the Rev. Robert Finley hastened to Philadelphia to placate the Negroes and came away with the illusion that many of the "enlightened ones had accepted the notion of colonization as the only way out" of the United States' racial crisis. Finley died shortly after he had assumed duties at the University of Georgia, but until the end of his life he maintained that colonization was the way to terminate North American slavery, while his opponent, Henry Clay, continued to assert that colonization was only for free negroes.

In the summer of 1817, James Forten called another protest meeting, attended by 3,000 free Negroes, and addressed a plea entitled: "An Address to the Humane and Benevolent Inhabitants of the City and County of Philadelphia." In this address "Negro" complaints were articulated. First, colonization would deny the benefits of civil and religious instructions to freed slaves. Second, Forten, arguing that removal would raise the price of slaves and inhibit further manumission, counselled: "Let not a purpose be assisted which would stay the cause of the entire abolition of slavery."[49] Protests also came from other quarters. For instance, the Quakers of Philadelphia rejected the colonization plan as intrusion on Negro welfare projects. The Pennsylvania Abolition Society since 1790 had instituted schemes for the welfare of free negroes in Philadelphia, through the medium of committees (notably the "apprenticing committee") which supervised education, work, and activities among the poor blacks. Robert Vaux, one distinguished Quaker abolitionist, informed Thomas Clarkson, the English abolitionist, that the Colonization Society "originated in the bosom of the Slave States."[50] Some free Negroes of Richmond, Virginia accepted colonization as tending to the mutual advantage of blacks and whites, but rejected colonization to Africa and instead opted for colonization on the Missouri or any place considered conducive by Congress to the public good and Negro future welfare.[51] The Colonization Society, which sought congressional support, received none of this congressional assistance, but it was suggested that the scheme could be amalgamated with the British Sierra Leone endeavor. The British, however, who had lately fought the Americans as the "enemy," could hardly be expected to open the Sierra Leone to the Americans. While Congress was hesitant in supporting the Colonization Society, the latter decided to accumulate on the spot (i.e., in Africa) data which would compel Congress to be more decisive. Thus the Rev. Samuel John Mills who travelled to England and later to Africa on behalf of the American Bible Society) agreed to collect data on the subject. Mills, however, was "less a collector of African data and more an admirer of British benevolence." [52]

He was accompanied by Ebenezer Burgess, Professor of Mathematics and Natural Philosophy in Burlington College, Vermont. The mission could not be said to have been successful and although Mills produced a report urging colonization, he died in June 1818 before delivering it. The task of delivery devolved on Professor Burgess. Burgess in delivering the report argued that colonization was the "best remedy for the scourge of Africa."[53] The Colonization Society seized upon the report to impress upon Congress that colonization was a practical proposition, and the report vindicated them. With a little government assistance (the granting of a pilot and a ship) they were able to convey the first batch of colonists, consisting of about 113 (86 of whom were men, the rest their wives and children), to Liberia. But the scheme was doomed to failure almost from the outset. The Colonization Society came in for more reproof and censure at the Convention of Colored People in the city of Philadelphia in 1830 under the leadership of Richard Allen. At that convention, through the advocacy of the Rev. T. J. Holly, Haiti was considered as a possible place of emigration but the African idea was not accepted. In the meantime, the colony founded at Mesurado, Liberia was saved from collapse by the arrival of Jehudi Asuman, who came out to the colony and took charge and remained there for six years instead of the short period of sojourn he had earlier envisioned. He linked commerce with the spread of Christianity. The hostility of the neighboring African peoples did not give the colonists an easy time, but the colony survived, although efforts to make colonization a national policy were never realized, even after Henry Clay became the Society's president in 1836. [54] Some colonists returned to the United States and this tended to give the impression that the Mesurado venture was unsuccessful. African-American leaders continued to resist the colonization program; but every time free blacks indicated they were a "distinct caste" within the American body politic, this was interpreted by agents of colonization as proof that the blacks had become converted to colonization.

One of the Society's first acts was to attempt to conclude an agreement with the local potentates on the West African Coast, so as to make the island settlement for free slaves of African origin from North America. It sent out a batch of colonists, about 88, who arrived in 1820 during the worst season. The African potentates rescinded their agreements with the Society and the climate was unsatisfactory to the newcomers; these unforseen contingencies led to difficulties and disillusionment and many of the settlers died, including three Euro-American agents. The survivors secured their safety by fleeing to the British colony of Sierra Leone. But in 1822 the Society obtained another piece of land at Mesurado, about two hundred and fifty miles southwest of Sierra Leone and the territory was named Liberia as it purported to be a land of freedom and its capital was named Monrovia in honor of President Monroe of the United States. It was more successful than the initial effort and as it began to thrive the Colonization Society became more inclined to assert that it was proving the practicality of colonization. Between 1820 and 1831 it is estimated that about 2,228 persons of African descent arrived at an average rate of 200 a year and that, of those, 248 had been Africans recovered from slave ships and 388 were slaves who had been liberated with a view to colonizing them in Africa. The new nation of Liberia had begun its existence. It could be held up as an example of the potentiality of the American Colonization Society. Yet, in spite of the interest which the United States government took in the activities of the colonizationists and the aid it gave, the Society failed to persuade the government to assume complete control over Liberia as the British had done in the Sierra Leone.

Blacks Favorable to Colonization

There were certainly some blacks who, after initially opposing colonization, later advocated it and became missionaries to the new colony of Liberia under the auspices of the Colonization Society. Before passing judgement on African-Americans who were initially opposed to colonization and later embraced it with enthusiasm we must observe that there were also Euro-Americans, whose names are also celebrated in the anti-slavery crusade, who had earlier embraced the colonization scheme. Notable among them were William Lloyd Garrison, Arthur Tappan a wealthy New York merchant and many more. [55] Garrison's period of incarceration for publishing a libelous article gave him some insight into the despicable aspect of slavery and turned him into an anti-slavery advocate.

Among the early black critics of colonization was John Russwurm, celebrated as the first black graduate from an American college (in 1826), an alumnus of Bodwin College, Maine, and who, as co-editor with Rev. Samuel E. Cornish, edited the first African-American newspaper, *Freedom's Journal* (1827) in New York. He had not only criticized the Colonization Society but repudiated it; yet, in 1829, he became a convert to colonization and eventually went to Liberia. [56] Later, through the pages of the first Liberian newspaper the *Liberian Herald*, which he revived, Russwurm urged African-Americans to support the colonization scheme. [57] Russwurm came in for some severe censure from the colored community. [58] But thereafter the theme of colonization continued to recur in Colored Peoples' Convention discussions. The Convention of 1830 certainly condemned the plan. At an anti-colonization convention in New York a year later, the colored people affirmed that America was their home because the sweat, blood, and toil as well as the bones of their fathers had enriched America's soil and they were determined to live and die in America. The subject of colonization continued to rankle at Colored Peoples' Conventions until 1853, when, at the inspiration of Dr. Martin Delany, a Colored Peoples' Convention that met in Cleveland, Ohio took the issue more seriously by appointing agents for Haiti, Central America, and the Niger Valley. Their object was to assemble an Emigration Convention the following year.

White Reactions to Colonization

As with the blacks, there were whites who favored colonization and those who denounced the scheme. We had earlier observed that among some of the later anti-slavery stalwarts, some support for colonization had existed (Garrison, Arthur Tappan, Gerrit Smith). But Arthur Tappan in the Spring of 1833 abandoned the Society because of the shock revelation he had received that the Colonization Society was supplying spirituous liquor[59] to Liberia and thus becoming a corrupting influence on the morals of the natives. By January 2nd, 1831, William Lloyd Garrison had joined battle against the Colonization Society. Much of his arguments were based on his reading of the *African Repository*, the organ of the American Colonization Society, which he read at first with perplexity, then with astonishment, and finally with indignation. He then endeavored to expose it as a fraud by slave owners in order to sustain slavery.

He first assailed the Society in the pages of *The Liberator*, which he began to publish from January 1, 1831. Next, he produced, in 1832, a 240-page book entitled *Thoughts on African Colonization, or an Impartial Exhibition of the Doctrines, Principles and Purposes of the American Colonization Society*. In this publication he argued that the Society was guilty of hypocrisy. He recalled and effectively used the speeches and pronouncements of slave owners and their adherents as well as editorials of the Society's friends. He accused them of hoodwinking and deceiving many people who had good intentions. According to Garrison, the Colonization Society encouraged the slave trade, degraded the Negro, was generally detrimental to Africa, and aided the Southern slavocracy in their designs. Garrison asserted that three-quarters of the Society's officers were slaveholders and not one of them had liberated his slaves for transportation to Liberia. He was concerned as to whether the doctrines and principles of the Society were in accord with the gospel and, having directed his attacks on the Society, he was determined to destroy it. Garrison's tirades against the Society produced some dissension within the rank-and- file of the Society and produced some defections. Garrison argued that while the Colonization Society would compromise with slavery, the abolitionists were determined not to; the abolitionists were therefore set on a collision course with the colonizationists as well as the slave owners. These white American views soon filtered into England and leading abolitionists in England were also encouraged to repudiate the American Colonization Society. Thus, Zachary Macaulay expressed his views on the Society to William Lloyd Garrison in 1833 in the following manner:

> I can have no objection, indeed to the plan of colonizing in Africa, with a view to its civilization, and to the extension of Christianity in that deeply injured quarter of the globe.... But the Colonization Society appears to me to adopt, as the basis for its schemes, not the love but the hatred and contempt of the negro race, and to regard everyone tinged with their blood as an object not of kindness and brotherhood, but of abhorrence.... [60]

After the relevations in the *African Repository* that 1,857 gallons of whiskey, [61] brandy, and rum had been sold in Liberia by the colonial agent of the American Colonization Society, the Society became more odious and further alienated British public opinion. These strictures and attacks created internal problems for the Society, which contributed to its adoption of a new Constitution in 1838 by which it conceded more control to the branches of the Society in the respective States of the American Union. Even speeches in England by the executive secretary, Mr. Gurley, to appease public opinion in England failed to impress those who would otherwise have rallied to the support of the colonization program.

In 1834 William Jay, son of the famous John Jay, in the United States of America, taking an anti-slavery platform produced his *Inquiry into the Character and Tendency of the American Colonization and American Anti-Slavery Societies*. According to him, colonization "vitiated the moral sense of the community, by reconciling public opinion to the continuance of slavery, and by aggravating those sinful prejudices against the free blacks." [62] This work had the effect of producing more defections from the Society's adherents. But there was a further nail in the coffin of the American Colonization Society with the formation of the American Union for the Relief and Improvement of the Colored Race. The aim was to uplift their race and Arthur Tappan made a contribution of $5,000 to its funds. Thus, by 1834, reports were rife that colonization as a project was dead. [63]

As the Society refused to be vigorously anti-slavery it lost some friends, but in 1834 the Maryland Colonization Society took an anti-slavery stand.[64] This came as an embarrassment to Garrison. It resulted in heart-searching throughout the Society. In New York the Society acknowledged the waste of money in the colony and now sought to concentrate its efforts in Liberia to agriculture and also temperance. Some within the movement were alarmed at the new development. Soon the Philadelphia and New York branches of the Society openly declared that their scheme included emancipation and that "Ten thousand slaves would at this moment be released from thraldom, if they could be transported from the country." [65] Through the adopted new constitution in 1838, the Colonization Society was compelled to become a federation of state auxiliaries, with each state entitled to representation on the new board of directors in proportion to its contributions and the size of its colony. Thus the new constitution revolutionized the Society and only the national president and vice-presidents were elected. Thereafter the Society was plagued with internal bickerings and financial problems and it failed to recapture its original dynamism. "Ironically, the idea of colonization as a solution to the race question was still popular, but the American Colonization Society and its friends were not."[66] Throughout the 1850s there was a false hope raised of the Society regaining its former vitality, while in the 1860s the Society was fighting for its existence. Many forces were ranged against it. Among these were the following:

1) Anti-slavery forces took away its friends, confused others.
2) Debt and mismanagement diminished its credit.
3) It lacked vitality as an effective movement for African colonization. Among those who sought to revive it were Anson G. Phelps (founder of the Phelps-Stoke foundations).
4) Liberia too was one of its problems, as the settlement had attained a figure of 3,000 (excluding Africans). The cry for genuine inde-

pendence was advanced while Africans also reacted against exploitation by immigrant Americans.

The problem of political jurisdiction (between independent settlements and the Government of Monrovia) loomed large. Eventually, in 1839, the Commonwealth of Liberia was proclaimed, uniting all the independent settlements except the Maryland settlement. In 1841 Joseph Jenkins Roberts, an emigree from Virginia, became governor.

Problems with British merchants loomed large and British merchants from Sierra Leone flouted Liberia's commercial laws. Liberia was experiencing a power struggle. There were even threats of Britain seizing Liberia. Since the U.S. government was not claiming sovereignty over Liberia, Liberia's independence was proclaimed by 1846. The Society formulated a Constitution which excluded the majority of the African population. In 1848 Joseph Jenkins Roberts was elected first president. Maryland in Liberia imitated Monrovia in Liberia's example but as it was almost wiped out in 1857 by confrontation with Africans it had to unite with the bigger Liberia to form one country. Britain and France recognized Liberian independence but the U.S. recognition came only in 1862.

From 1847 the American Colonization Society became an emigration agency. Their future efforts were directed towards sending emigrants to help build the republic of Liberia. Between 1848 and 1854 they chartered 41 ships and sent nearly 4,000 people to Liberia. State Societies also gathered emigrants. The Society's debts were eliminated through gifts from large bequests and legacies. Large sums were being made available by some southern states, notably Virginia, Maryland, and New Jersey, for the colonization of people to Liberia in the 1850s. The policy was deliberately fostered by those legislatures. The free Negroes were aware of the growth of the sentiment for their expulsion from the United States. But during the 1840s and 1850s they were still suspicious of the intentions of the American Colonization Society and of those of Liberia. [67] The Society manifested interest elsewhere. Planters' agents recruited negroes for Trinidad, Jamaica, and British Guiana from New York, Philadelphia, Boston, and Baltimore.

The Dred Scott decision of Chief Justice Tanney in 1857 (which cast doubts on Negro citizenship in the United States of America) and Lincoln's sentiments[68] in 1858 (closer to those of Jefferson, casting doubts about Negro equality and on whether the black and white races would ever be able to live harmoniously in the United States of America) gave colonization a shot in the arm. It became the occasion for stepping up their activities and they called for congressional help. Prior to that (in 1855) Congress had agreed to install a squadron in Monrovia to ensure that the ban on the slave trade was being observed. It also appeared to some colonizationists that the Civil War and the prospect of mass emancipation of slaves would provide the opportunity for implementing the colonization scheme. Lincoln's Government seemed preoccupied with the scheme for the colonization of Central America. The American Congress in 1862 appropriated a sum of $600,000 for the colonization of freed men, but their preoccupations were with areas such as the Dutch West Indies, Dutch Guiana, British Guiana, British Honduras, Guadeloupe, and Ecuador; neither Liberia nor Africa were included in the program. It was alleged that the government was swindled and this compelled Secretary of State William Seward to terminate the scheme.[69] But this projected scheme of colonization—in essence, deportation-evoked the resentment of the Central American governments, which saw the effort of the United States as encroachment on their respective sovereignties.[70] Leaders of the Colonization Society continued to hope for government aid. But the intervention of the Civil War dashed the hopes of colonizationists, who then began to turn their attention to Barbados[71] as an area from which they could recruit emigrants to Liberia. The Fourteenth Amendment to the U.S. Constitution, which came with the end of the Civil War conferred citizenship on freedmen and so put the emigration idea "on hold" for a while. At the celebration of its fiftieth anniversary in 1867, the Society under its Secretary William Coppinger (who had been with the association since he was ten years old) exhibited a flare of its past dynamism. But Coppinger's death in 1892 left the Society in a state of nominal existence, with its aims limited to promoting "African civilization" and strengthening Liberia. In the meantime, the confrontations between Liberia and Britain and France led to the limiting of the area of Liberia[72] in 1900. But until the 1950s the American Colonization Society continued to exhibit some skeletal existence.

Assessment of the Colonization Program

Summarizing the sentiments of those who favored and advocated the transportation of the freed African slave in America, it can be stated that they had reached the conclusion that the deportees were the most degraded of any society and were therefore unfit for improvement and incorporation in American society. Yet the same advocates of colonization felt that these people, if educated, even in a rudimentary way, could be useful instruments for the civilization of the "savages" of Africa and so saw this "return" of liberated slaves to Africa as the atonement for the sins committed by the abduction of their forefathers from Africa. The reasoning was paradoxical and often was the open expression of veiled racism in a sophisticated form. Thus, by this line of reasoning, the degraded liberated slave was perpetually condemned to a position of inferiority. It was not inferiority by natural endowment, but by virtue of which opportunities for advancement were more often than not denied; it was inferiority by declaration and that declaration had the force of both convention and law. It also had the force of practice. Accordingly, a resolution of the General Assembly of the Presbyterian Church observed that "an insurmountable obstacle has been placed to the execution of any plan for elevating their character and placing them on a footing with their brethren of the same common family." [73]

Thus, by the line of reasoning of the most prejudiced minds, there was nothing for the African-Americans in the United States but there was everything for them in Africa, an absurdity which did not fit the facts of the African-American's contributions to the foundations of the United States society. The attitude was reflected in the praise which the Right Reverend William Meade was prepared to bestow on African-Americans in Charleston, South Carolina who appeared ready to depart for Africa while he had no word of praise for those who were determined to remain in the country of their birth. [74] The American historian George F. Bancroft himself expressed it thus: "Serve the white man or depart, was what was meant. Without our bountiful good riddance the free Negro was to have the blessed opportunity to become an inspired missionary, perfectly suited to spread, in the benighted land of his savage forefathers, what he had learned in spite of our ungenerous treatment and unsympathetic civilization."[75]

Although the Colonization Society sought under a camouflage to present free Negroes as agents and missionaries of the Christian faith in Africa, they could not have been ignorant of the fact that the removal of these free Negroes could make the slaves less discontented and the institution of slavery in the United States more secure. Thus confident that their object commended itself to every class of society, one of their editorials took pains to emphasize that "The landed proprietor may enhance the value of his property by assisting the enterprise. The patriot may contribute to the immortal honor of his country by generously relieving those whose degradation and misery in the midst of us, though a reproach, seems inevitable.... And what is more in character with the Christian profession than to enlighten dark minds-to labor for the substantial interests and renown of one's country, and by deeds of noblest and most extensive charity, to break the shackles of superstition, and by conferring on uncivilized nations the freedom which is in Christ, prepare them for an eternity with the perfect God." [76] The declarations of prominent members of the Society, often repetitive, were an amalgam of lofty idealism and intolerance, hypocrisy and religious fanaticism, blindness and much vaunted enlightenment. Thus we find that one of the most prominent slavocrats, Henry Clay, was a mastermind at churning out these confounded sentiments. In one of them he is reported to have said, "Of all classes of our population, the most vicious is that of the free colored. It is the inevitable result of their moral, political and civil degradation. Contaminated themselves, they extend their vices to all around them, to the slaves and to the whites.... Every emigrant to Africa is a missionary carrying with him the credentials in the holy cause of civilization, religion and real institutions." [77]

But the desire to steer a middle course between those who advocated the retention of slavery in the Colonization Society and those who sought complete and unequivocal emancipation made the Society even more suspect. It was later to become the target for both sides. Henry Clay's[78] address to the Society at its annual meeting in 1835 did nothing to dispel the image of the Colonization Society. He said: "The partisans of interminable, inexorable slavery, have pronounced us mad, and our scheme infuriates.... The partisans of immediate abolition have pronounced it a scheme to protect slavery.... It is because it disclaims alike all the interference with slave property, and all connection with immediate emancipation, that it is the object of common attack from both parties." [79] But the Society was far from satisfactory in using the argument of one of the extremes to refute that of the other. Thus, from the early 1830s, the Society found itself on the defensive continuously endeavoring to refute the attacks of its assailants and striving by veiled language to defend itself against the accusations of the anti-slavery movement that it was an apologist for slavery and at the same time trying to placate the pro-slavery regions' suspicions that it was a mischiefmaker. The Secretary of the Society, on August 30, 1832, wrote to the leading colonizationists in Mississippi asserting that the aims of the organization were to unite the wise and virtuous of the nation, North and South, in a common purpose and hoped that within a short time it would be realized and appreciated that the plan of the organization aimed at lessening the existing prejudices between the North and the South and added: "The great questions in regard to the perpetuity or gradual abolition of slavery we believe must be decided by the Southern States themselves, yet we do hope that our plan will exert a *moral influence favorable to voluntary emancipation*. "[80] But his masterpiece of evasiveness did not convince those who saw the insidious nature of the Colonization Society. Yet it is impossible to deny that there were among the colonizationists of the southern states some religious members or some with deeply religious convictions who had more than a faint hope that colonization could be an instrument of emancipation. But much as the Society sought to convince cynics that its scheme was in the best interests of all and should naturally commend itself to reasonable people, in essence it was designed to eliminate the free African-Americans and its references to emancipation were rare.

In his assessment of the Colonization Society, G. F. Bancroft wrote: "It is commonly charged by extremists that the American Colonization Society 'carried water on both shoulders,'-made one kind of an appeal to the South and another to the North. That was true, without being as inconsistent as the figure of speech implied. The aim was to appear to the North as a missionary enterprise that would be helpful to all who wished to emancipate the slaves, and to the South as a missionary enterprise that would remove the free Negroes, who were believed to be injurious to slave property. A large proportion of the southern members wished the Society to serve a pro-slavery interest; that failing, they called it anti-slavery. Because it wished the co-operation of slave-owners who were opposed to slavery, aggressive anti-slavery men called it pro-slavery." [81]

The Colonization Society's Achievements

It is necessary to consider this topic in the short-term as well as the long. The American Colonization Society's achievements can be considered not only in terms of the physical transplantation to Africa, but also in terms of the impact it had on the minds of Americans. In terms of transplantation it was a failure, for even after its activities had come to an end the number which had been voluntarily persuaded to quit for Africa or had been aided by this organization was negligible. But perhaps it might be said that the foundation of the settlement of Monrovia (Liberia) is a testimony to its contributions.

Nevertheless, the organizers of the Society were certainly skilled masters of equivocation and geniuses at evading issues. But they had the foresight to realize that unless they enlisted the support of top dignitaries in the nation, the seat of national government, as well as those of the local governments (the states), success seemed elusive. While stressing the necessity for voluntary colonization, it strove to secure the co-operation of the government of the United States while it made membership easy by admitting any one who subscribed to the organization's constitution and contributed one dollar annually. Since the foreign slave trade had been prohibited and yet flourished by default, the United States government by the law of March 3, 1819 had hoped to suppress that trade. Thus, in one part of the law the President of the United States was authorized to provide "for the safekeeping and removal from the United States of all Negroes captured from foreign slave traders and to appoint agents to receive them on the coast of Africa." [82] The sum of $100,000 was appropriated for the execution of the plan. The President was induced to appoint an agent of the Colonization Society to take charge of the money to secure the repatriation of some slaves to Africa recently smuggled into the country. This enhanced the prestige of the Society at home, for the Society and the government were seen to be unofficially cooperating and by this means the Society gained a foothold in Africa. The idea began to gain currency that the best way to suppress the slave trade in West Africa would be through the establishment of a few colonies on that coast peopled by African-Americans. [83]

In its long life, the Colonization Society had succeeded in touching the sensibilities of several State Legislatures who seemed not to have been favorably inclined towards it. Observing this measure of the success of the Society, William Jay, an ardent critic of the Society, wrote:

> Men of all parties and of all religion and of no religion have zealously espoused its cause.. On the roll of its officers, are emblazoned the names of the most popular leaders of rival political parties. The Legislatures of fourteen States have passed resolutions in its favor. The highest ecclesiastical judicatories, or almost every religious denomination, have recommended it to the patronage of their churches. Politicians have declaimed, ministers have preached, and Christians have prayed in its behalf. To promote its objects, liberal contributions have been made from the coffers of the nation, and the pockets of individuals. [84]

But their success with donations and contributions and the establishment of Liberia did not succeed in removing any sizable section of the African-American population from the country. Its activities, like those of the abolitionists in the United States, had induced a kind of rethinking and a realignment of forces both from within and without the anti-slavery movements, so that for a time even distinguished abolitionists like Benjamin Lundy, Gerrit Smith, Mr. Knapp of the Garrison and Knapp fame, were initially taken in by the professions of the Colonization Society. Most of them were later to reject the Society. Gerrit Smith was a convert to abolition from colonization, whereas Lundy was an abolitionist who later regarded the activities of the Colonization Society as having been harmful to the country.[85] But southern rethinking beginning with Virginia in 1828. Fear of an anti-slavery or emancipation trend gaining ascendancy because of the colonization idea of the Society began a reaction which by about the 1830s was to deprive the Colonization Society of much of its power and success in achieving its originally proclaimed plan. The Society was more successful with the evangelicals who were keen on sending missionaries to Africa and on appearing to spearhead a missionary venture by its colonization idea. And although Bancroft reveals that for nearly two decades the Society was the chief means of co-operation between North and South.[86] that activity merely postponed the evil day when hostilities between both parts of the country were to break out essentially over the question of slavery which was linked up with the preservation of the American Union.

Tactics of the American Colonization Society

In its endeavors the American Colonization Society, unlike abolitionists, considered the goodwill of both northerners and southerners vital for its success. Clearly it saw that its scheme would not be realized if it opposed the South vigorously, for at the time of the Society's formation the South was not only determined to maintain slavery but was clamoring for the reopening of the foreign slave trade abolished by the United States government in 1808. [87] Viewed in this light, the Colonization Society tacitly acquiesced in the maintenance of slavery and this was far from being a humanitarian advancement. But some sections of the South, preoccupied with the economic advantage, opposed the notion of colonization. [88] Yet southern attitudes manifested ambivalence. Some southerners saw that a removal of the free colored people from the country could ensure the continuance of the institution of slavery. Yet others saw what could be the natural consequence of the success of this kind of venture, as it might lead to a further demand for emancipation, thereby depriving the slaveholders of the property which sustained their wealth. The Society's existence depended on the contributions and support of southern states like Virginia and Maryland. Furthermore, at its inception, leadership and financial support were all but exclusively southern. [89] Clearly the goodwill of southern slave owners was vital to the Society's success. It was Garrison's contention that three quarters of the Society's officers were slaveholders, none of whom had liberated their slaves for transportation to Liberia. [90] But the Society sought very early in its existence to obtain the patronage of rich southerners; and rich southerners were, in the main, slaveholders. Even the Society's first president, Chief Justice Bushrod Washington, speaking on the occasion of the celebration of its first anniversary, indicated that the South was one major source of financial assistance. He said: "Among a small but opulent society of slaveholders in Virginia, a subscription has been raised... of such magnitude as to illustrate the extent of the funds which we may hope thereafter to command.... [91]

From the above citation it is not difficult to see how southern support would have been forthcoming initially, since the Society had openly declared its support for the right of property- a euphemism for the right to own slaves and perpetuate slavery. A notable southern Churchman, a Virginian, Bishop William Meade, campaigned for the Society in the South. He also solicited funds as well as assisted in formation of branches of the Society in the South. He revealed that while engaged in this labor of love, he frequently came upon slaveowners who accepted emancipation on condition that it was followed by colonization. Colonization, therefore, became a *sine qua non*. Bishop Meade himself being a colonizationist often praised those African-Americans who accepted colonization in principle as "sensible" or "intelligent," regarding opponents as "worthless." The motives for seeking to remove the free colored population from the United States of America were often subtler than could be inferred from the glib statements asserting that Afro-Americans and Euro-Americans could never live together peacefully as vast differences separated their mental horizons. Considering the credentials of some of those drawn into the movement, it is difficult to attribute humanitarianism to the Society. Doubtless it had humanitarians and even ministers of religion of the Christian denominations, but this will hardly earn the entire movement the label of humanitarianism. If being a minister of religion was the criterion for deciding that an activity is humanitarian or not, we might as well regard slavery as humanitarian (which it was not), since most of the Christian denominations participated in the slave trade and the fostering of slavery and many of their members were slave owners; while others, on dubious biblical authority, asserted that the enslavement of the African had divine sanction. Those who did not own slaves were owners in principle by being its apologists. [92]

The veteran scholar Dr. W. E. B. DuBois had suggested that the American Colonization Society "meant different things to different people." [93] But even from the Society's annual reports and other publications, it is easy to see how much southern influence pervaded the working of the Society. It had been ushered into existence by the encouragement and approbation of a congressional committee of the legislatures of Maryland, Virginia, Georgia, and Tennessee, as well as by various ecclesiastical synods and conventions and a host of friends of every profession, no less distinguished for their wisdom than their virtue and from every section of the United States, to erect a refuge for "suffering humanity." [94]

Most of its adherents believed they were taking part in a good cause;[95] and if they were not genuine they, at least, believed their own propaganda. But the Society was often on the defensive; so too its annual reports tended to be justificatory. But from its own publications we learn that the "plan of colonizing the free people of color, in some place beyond the United States," was first conceived in the South. According to one report it originated from the Legislature of Virginia (one of the largest slave holding states) about 1810. The report reveals that earlier attempts to procure through the agency of the U.S. government territory in Portuguese South America proved abortive.[96] Attention was then turned to Africa. In response to those who accused the Society of aiming to manipulate the leadership of the free colored people in order to perpetuate slavery, the Society's first president, Chief Justice Bushrod Washington, observed: "If, as is most confidently believed, the colonization of the free people of color, will render the slave who remains in America more obedient, more faithful, more honest, and consequently, more useful to his master, is it proper to regard this happy consequence to both as the sole object which the Society hopes to attain?"[97]

At the root of most of the sophisticated and equivocal arguments advanced for endeavoring to colonize the free colored population of the United States was race prejudice. As Charles Foster argues: "Slavery was not its true target because slavery was after all, a solution; emancipation created a problem."[98] Or as another author puts it: "Most white southerners did not want negroes as freemen and most white Northerners did not want freemen as Negroes." [99] Foster further developed the argument with evidence and reached the conclusion that the "object (of colonization) was not to remove the prejudice but to remove the Negro."[100] But even the officers of the Colonization Society as well as their records are explicit on their motivations. Ralph Gurley, the Society's first secretary, had argued that elevating and instructing the free negro in America would contribute to the restiveness of slaves.[101]

The fear of accelerating black-white competition was another consideration. Accordingly, it was considered politic that a black man should make room for a white man. [102] The numerous pronouncements of members of the Society showed that there was too much hate generated in their program. It led Gerrit Smith, who abandoned them for the abolitionist cause, to suggest that the Society's greatest sin was lack of love for the Negro and the absence of concern for his difficulties. But much of the arguments amounted to little more than "mere prejudice glossed over with piety"[103] as one author suggested.

In fact, it appears as more than mere prejudice, for the advocates of colonization at various times spelled out their xenophobia. If the language of piety or expiation was used, it provided a palliative for the real intentions, which were far from humanitarian-the removal of free men of color from the United States in order to consolidate the institution of slavery. But it proved unworkable as a solution to the problems of race contact and conflicts in society in the Americas. It also amply demonstrated that solutions had to be found elsewhere, by means other than removal to another clime.

The founding of the American Colonization Society (hereafter ACS) has been associated with the name of Robert Finley, a Presbyterian Minister in Somerset County, New Jersey. His principal aim, which was stressed in the aims of the new society, was the colonization of the free (black) colored population in the United States in Africa. He succeeded in obtaining the support of faculty members at Princeton University. Later he drew support from Washington, D.C., to which he repaired, and was given a letter of support by the Princeton Faculty for President James Madison, a former graduate of Princeton. When the supporters of the Society held their inaugural meeting in December 1816 they also had a stalwart supporter in the person of a wealthy and prominent member of Georgetown known as Francis Scott Key.

Although Finley was impressed by the British founding of a colony for free blacks of London in Sierra Leone, he also consulted the black Bostonian shipowner, Captain Paul Cuffee, who had earlier conveyed some African-American families to Sierra Leone and intended settling there himself, until his death in 1817. This latter consultation was supposed to have given gravity to Finley's scheme, [104] yet it is believed that prior to his death, Cuffee had warned his brethren against the American Colonization Society. But Finley continued to be the chief driving force for the American Colonization Society.

White Attitudes at Inception of the American Colonization Society

At its inception and during its early years, the American Colonization Society seemed to have had massive southern support and some prominent northern support as well in the United States of America. The slavocrats of the South were exhilarated by the fact that the Society's plans constituted the best solution to the presence of free black people in Southern society and of resolving the racial problems which existed and which they imagined would convulse the nation, if that class of people were allowed to remain in the South, in particular, and in American society, generally. The presence of these free blacks remained an embarrassment to the slavocracy, especially with its potential for making slaves restive and with possible consequences of inciting slave disorders, escapes, and eventually securing their liberty. Such a development, it was felt, would inhibit northern investments and undermine southern wealth and power. Besides, the southern laws for the immediate departure of free negroes, once manumitted, could mean the flooding of northern cities, a fact which also made some northerners nervous. This, then, became their inducement to the American Colonization Society program. Some abolitionists who supported the American Colonization Society were later to recoil and even denounce it. But some of them were misguided into believing the propagandists of the American Colonization Society that colonizing the free people to Africa was the fastest way of implanting "Christian civilization" in Africa. [105] Yet we must not lose sight of the fact that these freed people had not been given sufficient training in Christianity for them to become teachers and disseminators of Christian doctrine; the doors for the acquisition of such knowledge that had been closed to slaves were still closed to them.

The American Colonization Society scheme also had plans for certain slaves to receive manumission by accepting a direct passage to Africa, hardly to be regarded as sufficient training for them to become religious missionaries in Africa. But the American Colonization Society was caught up in the web of contradictions of its own making which were evident in its publications and in the pronouncements of its principal spokesmen as well as in its own pretensions, which were highlighted from time to time. It might or might not have crossed the minds of those with this evangelical vision how these newly emancipated slaves with the proviso for their direct transshipment to Africa could have assumed the role of effective missionaries. But the various conventions of the American Colonization Society were replete with those contradictions as were their public posturings. The African Repository, their principal organ of dissemination of their propaganda, deserves study in this regard.

African-American Countermeasures against the American Colonization Society

Not only were the majority of African-Americans (especially the freed) astonished by the audacity of the American Colonization Society proclamations and protestations, but they were also dismayed by the fact that some stalwart anti-slavery white people were deluded into expressing themselves as satisfied with the projections of the

American Colonization Society. But as usual, it was only by their articulating their own opposition that African-Americans could generate sufficient awareness of the sinister nature of the scheme that had been contrived for them without their own input. Protest began slowly, such as the two protest assemblies that were mounted at Bethel African Methodist Episcopal Church in the city of Philadelphia[106] in 1817 under the leadership of Bishop Richard Allen, Rev. Absalom Jones, and other prominent African-Americans such as James T. Forten. One of those assemblages saw as many as 3,000 protesters determined that the United States would remain their country and rejecting absolutely any attempts to sever their relations with the country of their birth or with their brethren still enslaved. It was the curtain raiser to the vehemence of the opposition that the American Colonization Society was to experience, despite the support it obtained from wealthy slavocrats and northern men of affairs. Nowhere was this more evident than in the activities of black religious prelates who were among the few in the forefront of leadership of the black people at the time. It must not be forgotten that the leadership of religious prelates, which was already manifest in the late eighteenth century, became more prominent throughout the nineteenth century and into the twentieth. A comprehensive work on this leadership has yet to be undertaken, although fragments of the activities of that leadership have continued to appear since the nineteenth century.[107]

However, one source through which the budding leadership could express the sentiments and objections of their brethren was the press. The founding of a newspaper provided at least an opportunity for them to counter the propaganda of the American Colonization Society. Thus, African-Americans instinctively decided after a small gathering of enthusiasts to establish a newspaper in 1827 for that purpose. Among them were Pastor Nathaniel Paul of the First Baptist Church in Albany, William Hamilton, a trustee of the AME Zion Church, the Rev. Peter Williams of St. Philip African Episcopal Church, the Rev. Samuel Cornish and John B. Russwurm, recently graduated from Bowdoin College in Maine. It was this assembly that inspired the emergence in March 1827 of the weekly *Freedom's Journal*, edited by Cornish and Russwurm. Here was an organ through which they could disseminate their abolitionist viewpoints and expose the American Colonization Society and its adverse propaganda against free African-Americans. It was also an organ for the dissemination of good advice to their brethren, encouraging such things as sobriety, temperance, honesty, hard work, and ideas for elevation and improvement through education and industry.

Freedom's Journal, one of the first publications in the abolitionist line, circulated initially on the eastern seaboard, including New England. That initiative continued to emphasize the leadership of prelates which had been manifest since the eighteenth century. Both editors were clear as to their duty, and the *Journal* was to be concerned with the needs and predicament of their people. Through their untiring efforts and their spiritual defense (and offense) against their detractors in the pages of their journal, they became the mouthpiece for their brethren, reflecting the moral, political, and social considerations of those times with regard to their elevation in United States society. But ill-health forced Cornish to yield the editorship solely to Russwurm. But within fifteen months of Cornish's departure, however, Russwurm himself decided to move to Liberia (in 1829), to serve as an administrator in the Liberian school system. It resulted in the collapse of the *Journal.* This collapse touched the sensibilities of some enthusiasts of Cornish and prompted the floating of another journal, titled *Rights of All,* with Cornish as editor. Its objectives were not far different from those which had inspired the erstwhile *Freedom's Journal.* The intention was to organize a weekly journal along the same lines as its predecessor, but circumstances were such that the *Rights of All* came out as a monthly and only six issues appeared before it folded up in October 1829. Yet the *Rights of All* in its short life had provided the vitality and sparkle of its predecessor. But in the meantime, in the same year as the collapse of the *Rights of All,* a free colored man of Boston, David Walker published a pamphlet titled *Appeal to the Colored Citizens of the World,*[108] in which he issued a condemnation of the American Colonization Society. Walker also suggested that slaves should rise and throw off the shackles of their oppressors by the same violent methods that were used by their oppressors against them. While it was not the only publication of that year that was to have profound impact on the thinking of blacks, Walker's *Appeal* was certainly the most radical and the one that set the tone of the ensuing debate. The second publication from the pen of a black man in that year (1829) was one titled *Hope for Liberty,* [109] containing the poems of a slave, George Moses Horton of North Carolina, and his reflections on the condition itself. A third publication of that year was William Young's *The Ethiopian Manifesto,* [110] in which its author expressed the hope that a leader of consequence would arise to liberate his people from the excesses they were enduring in the United States. Some sense of the furor and consternation provoked by David Walker's publication can be gleaned by looking at the newspapers of the time and those of the succeeding years following the Nat Turner revolt in Southhampton County Virginia in

1831.

However, eight years after the collapse of the journal *Rights of All*, the Rev. Cornish found himself installed as the editor of a new paper entitled *The Colored American*. Cornish used the paper to enlighten his brethren (and others) on such issues as the denial to free blacks of opportunities in education, business, and employment, and to expose the propaganda of the American Colonization Society against the abilities and achievements of free blacks. Here too Cornish acquitted himself well and the paper met the expectations and received the approbation of the brethren. His consummate skill in handling so deftly the issues of the day and championing his people produced a greater awakening and consciousness in the black opposition to the American Colonization Society. Even a modern historian has observed that *The Colored American* "generally furnished an accurate barometer of Negro thought." [111] But a reading of the pages and editorials of its predecessors reveals a consistency in the standards that the editors of the earlier papers had set. But all the papers were run in a crusading spirit to attract the attention of both white and black, to focus them more concretely on the problems which plagued those times, and to convert both the skeptics and faint-hearted. Cornish and others after him pursued their objectives with a singular attitude of mind.[112] Issues such as general welfare and the relief of distress, fraternal organizations, literary activities, marriages and deaths, education, boarding houses, commercial activities of blacks, and admonishments were featured in the pages of those papers. They also carried biographical sketches and historical material as well as the current and past achievements of black people in order to inspire their endeavors, and the editorials were very effective in this regard. But they were also vehicles of protest against the treatment of blacks by whites as well as some of the failings of blacks in their own cause. Furthermore, their topics ranged beyond the confines of New York in an endeavor to attain both a regional and national perspective. But, in the main, they dealt with the black community in the northern United States.

These literary excursions by the leadership provided the mouthpiece for the black people against their exclusion by the white-controlled papers and became useful instruments for refuting their dissemination of falsehoods, distortions, and calumnies. [113] Thus, apart from stressing the need for prudence, industry, sobriety, temperance, and prosperity, Cornish stressed the value of self-discipline as a prerequisite for the group's enhancement and elevation through education as a vital channel. His religious persuasion impelled him to conceive of his activities as a "religious mission."[114]

Cornish also used the pages of his papers to castigate white Presbyterians for excluding blacks from quality education in church-sponsored academies, the type of exclusion that was experienced by the Rev. Henry Highland Garnet and Alexander Crummell at Dartmouth. [115] He also continued to assail the American Colonization Society by insisting that colonization was regression not progression and that rather than take such retrograde steps blacks were demanding equal privileges in America. [116]

These censures touched the sensibilities of white Presbyterians who, though supporters of the American Colonization Society, were also benefactors to black Presbyterians and especially to the New York First Colored Presbyterian Church, of which Cornish was pastor. They seemed to have perceived his censorious searchlight on them as an act of ingratitude on the part of blacks. An example of such ingratitude, in their eyes, would have been Cornish himself, who owed much of his education and his pulpit to the white Presbyterians of New York and Philadelphia. Some of them showed their umbrage by issuing threats. For instance, two ministers on the faculty of Princeton Theological Seminary lashed out at Cornish and the blacks, perceiving him as their spokesman. The ministers were Archibald Alexander and Samuel Miller, professors of ecclesiastical history; both of them had been in the forefront of support for Finley's scheme for colonization of free blacks. While Alexander was more measured in his effusions, Miller was less restrained; demanded that Cornish moderate his open hostility to the American Colonization Society or lose the support of white subscribers[117] to *Freedom's Journal*. As students and faculty of the seminary had acted as agents in the distribution of the journal, Miller's warnings were soon put into effect. In modern parlance this would be called intimidation. But Miller, feeling that he was "entirely dissatisfied with the spirit and apparent tendency of the paper," discontinued his subscription; the faculty and students of Princeton soon followed suit. [118] The general attitude is reflected in the following statement of Miller's colleague, Archibald Alexander:

> It behooves those who industriously sow prejudice against Colonization in the minds of free people of colour, to consider what injury they may be inflicting on them and their posterity.... If I were a coloured man, I would not hesitate a moment to relinquish a country where a black skin and the lowest degree of degradation are so identified, that scarcely any manifestation of talent, scarcely any course of good conduct can entirely overcome the contempt which exists. [119]

This mental blockage of white ministers of religion and adherents of the American Colonization Society was quite pervasive. But intimidatory tactics of this kind, no matter how passionately felt. did not deter the black leaders from continuing their vehement opposition to the American Colonization Society and its activities. Cornish, like some of his contemporaries, was not inclined to compromise his principles because of past or present material assistance. He went on to resign his post as Pastor from the black (though white-supporteded) Presbyterian Church.

The African-American prelates of this period were fighters even for the most basic things, such as blacks seeking licenses to operate street carts as peddlers. Even in the 1820s and 1830s there were restrictions on this, amounting to blatant discrimination, when even white immigrants were being allowed to acquire such licenses. But the many ramifications of such discrimination against his brethren incensed Cornish, evoking his denunciation especially as he considered these tendencies incompatible with the much vaunted "civilization" of the Christians.[120] He assailed the contradictions in the actions of the American Colonization Society and its Christian supporters in their determination to export free African-Americans to Liberia while at the same time opening their shores to immigrants from Europe. The riots in Cincinnati (Ohio), provoked by whites against blacks, which occurred in July 1829, because of that city's attempt to re-invoke the customary imposition of $500 bond on free blacks entering the state. The bond had been in abeyance, but was re-instated to render the status of blacks within the State untenable and force them to accept colonization; the move produced the opposition that it was designed to provoke. But the riots themselves resulted in some blacks departing for Upper Canada where, at last, they found that land was available for settlement.[121] The incident received ample space in the *Rights of All*. But the *Rights of All*[122] was unrelenting in its strictures on the prominent spokesmen and promoters of the American Colonization Society. Cornish was no less scathing, and spoke for the majority of his people against detractors of the African-Americans and their leadership as he had done in the preceding decade. But, as had been observed above, it was David Walker's *Appeal to the Colored Citizens of the World* that provided a voice for the voiceless, muzzled by the prevailing propagandists and their negative activities. It was a period which experienced the visitation of violence on those outspoken for abolition of slavery and against the machinations of the American Colonization Society. It also saw a spate of black Church burnings in New York. But despite Cornish's arguments against the ACS and against discriminatory practices, he remained through and through a moral suasionist, who anticipated change through argument as well as legal and constitutional processes. These, of course, proved elusive for a long time.

His leadership was to be followed by others in succeeding years. The way things stood, the Colonization Society stood little chance of colonizing the majority of free African-Americans to Africa. Despite its transfer of a few thousand, it was a dismal failure. The leadership of African-Americans in their opposition to the scheme had triumphed against the gigantic scheme of subterfuge ranged against them by the colonizationists. But the vehement opposition to it had brought the antislavery movement to a radical threshold, for, when the antislavery movement split in 1840, the new body which became the American Foreign Antislavery Society, which, unlike Garrison's American Antislavery Society, believed in political action. Many African-Americans went over to the new organization, including Frederick Douglass, while a few remained with Garrison in the original body.

Some Setbacks

Even before the split in the American Antislavery Movement, the American Colonization Society had already witnessed the repudiation of its aims and the decimation of its ranks. One prominent defector in 1834 was the Rev. Samuel Cox, a white Presbyterian minister. In his abjuration of the Society, he declared that the majority of free African-Americans were opposed to the American Colonization Society.[123] Some black ministers like the Rev. J. W. Pennington had complained that the American Colonization Society by its activities had aided the intensification of racism. But even a meeting of slave holders in Baltimore, Maryland in 1859 found itself at variance with the Maryland law of 1831 which forbade the freeing of slaves unless they were sent out of the state. The convention of slave holders, known also as the "Slave Power", concluded that the proposal for removing free blacks, a principal stipulation of the American Colonization Society, was ill-founded. The slavocrats expressed the indispensability of those African-Americans to American agriculture, industry, and urban domestic services.[124]

Yet despite the opposition of African-Americans to the American Colonization Society there were three prominent African-Americans who supported the society in the hope that they might use its assistance to realize their own notions of "providential design." These three were Edward Wilmot Blyden, the Rev. Alexander Crummell, and Bishop Henry McNeal Turner. The first, after being refused entry to an American College on discriminatory grounds, departed for Liberia under the auspices of the American Colonization Society and became one of the most prominent and formidable spokesmen for the African personality. Alexander Crummell after completing his theological studies at Cambridge University in England went out to Liberia as a missionary and educator and remained there for twenty years before finally returning to the United States. Bishop Henry McNeal Turner visited Liberia, but on behalf of his church, the African Methodist Episcopal Church, of which he was bishop. But the one thing all three shared in common was that they each had the position of vice-president (of which there were many) of the American Colonization Society.

In reflecting on the leadership which Cornish had provided to the black community through his newspapers and his ministry, it must be stated that he kept moral suasion in perspective for the attainment of the goals which his people sought, despite attempts by white ministers to confuse his perception as to what was politic and what was not. As a victim of their wrath he suffered their ostracism, which, for a time, closed the doors of opportunity to him, as was usual with vocal professions of faith in those times. But he bore each buffeting with fortitude and equanimity. Many of the advocates of antislavery at the time, both black and white, suffered periodic violence and intimidation and those who adhered to that faith were bold indeed.

The issue at the time revolved round designating the black people either as "African" (and so, fit for deportation) or as "black" or "colored" (and still to be colonized). It is this kind of Hobson's choice which they were asked to endorse without consultation because the organizers of the American Colonization Society thought they knew what was best for them. Yet, by their origins, they could be Africans or African-Americans with the option to become citizens in America or voluntarily emigrate. But American Colonization Society activities, despite protestations to the contrary, were hell bent on removal by coercion on the assumption that whites and blacks could never live together harmoniously in one society. In essence, they spread the gospel of hate, based on an assumed reason for antipathy for a particular color. It also needs to be borne in mind that the American Colonization Society was peddling its propaganda at the very time the anti-slavery endeavors were gathering momentum and so tended to detract from those activities while at the same time spreading confusion in thought and perception.

The discussion now leads us to consider the crises generated among African-Americans in the United States in the face of growing hostilities to their existence as free citizens in the country. These crises produced two broad cleavages, with other opinions oscillating between the two polarities. Of the polarities, the one urged the necessity to remove themselves from slave societies of the U.S. to seemingly more favorable environments in a new land. Of the second polarity were those who advocated the necessity to stand firm, despite provocations, in their endeavors to achieve integration and full citizenship together with its accompanying benefits. With the battle lines drawn, the controversy sharpened and the antagonisms and acrimony between them deepened. Thus, the crises in the objectives of leadership came increasingly to the fore in their deliberations and persisted from the second half of the nineteenth century into the end of the second decade of the twentieth century. The crises in those objectives now need a brief examination.

NOTES

1. See Hollis Lynch, "Sierra Leone and Liberia" in *A Thousand Years of West African History*, J. F. Ajayi and I. Espie (ed.) Ibadan and Edinburgh, 1965, p. 327. Almost immediately Lynch speaks of `other motives,' pp. 327-28, section by A. E. Afigbo. Also, Omer-Cooper, J. D., etc., *The Making of Modern Africa*, London and Harlow, 1968, pp. 85-86, Porter, Arthur, *Creoledom: A Study of Development of Freetown Society*, London, 1963, p. 20, et. seq.
2. Williams, Eric E., *Capitalism and Slavery*, Ch. 11, pp. 175-196 (titled `The "Saints" and Slavery' for his distinction between kinds of humanitarians genuine and otherwise.
3. West, Richard, *Back to Africa*, pp. 78-80. Macaulay himself came to be described as the "greatest shopkeeper of the colony." p. 80. See also pp. 81-82, *Ibid*.
4. Asiegbu, *Slavery and the Politics of Liberation 1787-1861*, London and Harlow, 1969, p. 10.
5. The number of white women has never been consistent. R. L. Buell, *The Native Problem in Africa* referred to 51; Richard West puts the figure at seventy, *op. cit.*, pp. 25-26. In Johnson Asiegbu, *op. cit.*, the figure is stated as "some seventy," p. 6. But they were in general agreement that the white women were prostitutes of "low character." See also C. B. Wadstrom, *Essay on Colonization*, London, 1794, Part II, p. 220. He described the women as 'strumpets.'
6. See below for references.
7. There are many good histories of the Sierra Leone and one which approximates a reference book is that of C. Fyfe, *A History of Sierra Leone*, Oxford, 1962.
8. Coupland, R., *The British Anti-Slavery Movement*, London, 1933.
9. Mathieson, W. L., *Great Britain and the Slave Trade 1839-1865*, London, Longman, Green & Co. (preface) et seq., Ch. 1., 1929; *British Slave Emancipation 1838-1849*.
10. Wyndham, H. A., *The Atlantic and Emancipation*, London, 1937, pp. x-xi, also Chs. 1& 2, et seq.
11. MacInnes, C. M., *England and Slavery*, Arrowsmith, Bristol, 1934, pp. 197-98, also Chs. 9-12.
12. Mellor, G. R., *British Imperial Trusteeship 1783-1850*, London, Faber and

Faber, pp. 25, 27, Chs. 1 & 2, esp. pp. 41-43; 414 et seq.
13. Asiegbu, J. U. J., *op. cit.*, pp. xv-xvi, E. E. Williams, *Capitalism and Slavery*, Chapel Hill, N. Carolina, 1944, pp. 179-86.
14. Asiegbu, *Ibid.*, p. xv.
15. Asiegbu, *op. cit.*, p. xvi.
16. Asiegbu, *Ibid.*, Appendix I, pp. 160-62 for Smeathman's *Manifesto*. The Committee for the Relief of the Black Poor was headed by Jonas Hanway, a merchant.
17. West, Richard, *Back to Africa*, London, 1970, pp. 23-23.
18. Asiegbu, *op. cit.*, p. 1.
19. See Fyfe, C., *A History of Sierra Leone*, London, 1962, pp. 13-14.
20. Fyfe, Christopher, Ibid., pp. 14-16. Also Prince Hoare, *Memoirs of Granville Sharp*, London, 1820, p. 268.
21. Quoted in West, Richard, *op. cit.*, pp. 33-34, esp. 33.
22. West, Richard, *Ibid.*, pp. 33-34.
23. *Ibid.*, p. 33.
24. *Ibid.*, p. 79-80, *et seq.*
25. *Ibid.*, p. 80.
26. The figures vary. See C. Fyfe, *History of the Sierra Leone*, *op. cit.* See R. L. Buell, *The Native Problem in Africa*, Vol. 1, p. 859; West, *op. cit.*, pp. 24-26 in his *Memoirs of Granville Sharp*, p. 270. Prince Hoare referred to sixty Europeans, mainly women but is silent on their character and status in English society. Some put it as low as 51.
27. Staudenraus, P., *op. Cit.*, p. 8. Also R. L. Buell, *The Native Problem in Africa*, New York, 1928, 2 Vols., Vol. 1. *loc. cit.* Others which take a contrary viewpoint include: R. July, *The Origins of Modern African Thought*, p. 48-49.
28. H. M. Bond, "African-American Relations see through African Students Enrolled in American Negro Colleges: A Progress Report of a Historical Study?" Atlanta University, 1960. Unpublished manuscript delivered as a lecture to Third AMSAC Conference, 1960. Quoted by permission of the late Dr. Horace Mann Bond. Quamine may have been Kwamina. See Staudenras, *op. cit.*, pp. 4-5.
29. P. Staudenraus, *The African Colonization Movement 1816-1865*, New York, Columbia University Press, 1961, p. 5. See also, pp. 2-4.
30. Thomas Jefferson, *Notes on the State of Virginia*, London, 1787, p. 239 for preliminaries revealing his racial slurs and prejudices see *Ibid.*, pp. 228-30.
31. Ferdinando Fairfax, "Plea for liberating the Negroes within the U.S..., "*American Museum, or Universal Magazine*, Vol VIII, December 1790, pp. 285-87. Also P. Staundenraus, *op. cit.*, p. 3.
32. Stanislaus M. Hamilton (ed.), *The Writings of James Monroe*, New York, 1900, VOl. III, pp. 292-95, 336-38.
33. P. Staudenraus, *op. cit.*, p. 6.
34. *Ibid.*, p. 15.
35. For a development on this thought see Thompson, V. B., *The Making of the African Diaspora in the Americas, Longman, Harlow, 1987, Ch. 8, entitled "Conflict between Darkness and Light."*
36. *Staudenraus,* op. cit., *p. 17.*
37. Ibid., *p. 17.*
38. *See Memories of Captain Paul Cuffee: A Man of Color,* also Rev. Peter Williams. (Rev.) A Discourse Delivered on the Death of Captain Paul Cuffee; A Man

of Color, New York, 1818.

39. Information in *National Intelligence,* December 24, 1816.
40. For the absurd way in which the free negro was treated see Franklin, J. H., *From Slavery to Freedom,* 1956, Chapter headed: "The Anomaly of the Free Negro" or for a more contemporary assessment of the plight of the "free negro" see George M. Fredrickson, *The Black Image in the White Mind: The Debate on Afro-American Character and Destiny, 1814-1914,* New York, Harper, 1971.
41. Its first president was Chief Justice Bushrod Washington, a nephew of George Washington (first president of the United States). Among its thirteen Vice-presidents were the Rt. Rev. Robert Finley (in acknowledgement of his services), Henry Clay (Southerner and Speaker of the House of Representatives, later Secretary of State, Presidential aspirant and also President of the Colonization Society from 1836 to 1849), William Crawford, Secretary of the Treasury, General Andrew Jackson (later president of the United States).
42. William Thornton was also on the Board of Management.
43. Staudenraus, P., *The African Colonization Movement,* pp. vii-viii.
44. James, C. L. R., *Black Jacobins,* London, 1938, p. 2.
45. Garrison, William Lloyd, *Thoughts on African Colonization, op. cit.,* p. 129.
46. Bancroft, F., *op. cit.,* above, p. 158.
47. Staudenraus, P., *op. cit.,* p. 32. A. Meier and E. Rudwick, from *Plantation to Ghetto.* Revised edition, 1966, 1970, p. 106.
48. *Ibid.,* p. 32. But even in these sentiments we must observe some of the induced Negro prejudices. He is significant in mirroring the nature of ambivalence to Africa. These same people had commended Cuffe's efforts.
49. Woodson, C. G., *Negro Orators and their Orations,* Washington D.C., 1935, p. 57, et. seq.
50. "Robert Vaux to Thomas Clarkson," Philadelphia, May 13, 1819 in *Moorland Collections,* Howard University. Also quoted in P. Staudenraus, *op. cit.,* p. 33.
51. *Boston Recorder,* February 18, 1817.
52. Staudenraus, P., *op. cit.,* p. 43.
53. *Ibid.*
54. Clay became President of the Colonization Society in 1836 in succession to James Madison and remained President until 1849.
55. West, Richard, *Back to Africa,* London, Jonathan Cape, 1970, pp. 141-42.
56. Woodson, C. G., *The Mind of the Negro as Reflected in Letters Written During the Crisis 1800-1861.* Washington D.C., The Association for the Study of Negro Life and History, 1926, p. 3, et. seq. also pp. 16-163.
57. *The Liberator,* (Boston) in C. G. Woodson, *The Mind of the Negro, op. cit.*
58. Woodson, *The Mind of the Negro, etc., op. cit.,* in n. 55 above, *loc. cit.,* pp. 161 ff.
59. See Tappan, Lewis, *Life of Arthur Tappan,* New York, Hurd and Houghton, Cambridge, Riverside Press, 1871, Appendix 4, p. 419.
60. West, Richard, *op. cit.,* p. 148.
61. See Tappan, Lewis, *Life of Arthur Tappan, op. cit.,* above. His figures were higher.
62. See below n. 84.
63. P. J. Staudenraus, *op. cit.,* pp. 231-32. It seemed as if colonization was serv-

ing, as suggested by G. J. Birney, as "an opiate to consciences."

64. *Ibid.*, p. 233.
65. *Ibid.*, p. 235.
66. *Ibid.*, p. 239.
67. See F. Douglass' strictures on the colonization scheme in H. Brotz, *op. cit.* above, pp. 213-215.
68. See Roy P. Bastered, *The Collected Works of Abraham Lincoln*, New Brunswick, New Jersey, 1953, Vol. III, pp. 145-146. Also p. 179.
69. Staudenraus, *op. cit.*, p. 247.
70. *Ibid.*, p. 247.
71. *Ibid.*, p. 248.
72. See N. N. Azikiwe, *Liberia in World Politics*, London, 1934, pp. 15-16, *et. seq.* Also R. L. Buell, *Liberia: A Century of Survival*, Philadelphia, 1947, pp. 21-29 *et. seq.* and his *The Native Problem in Africa*, New York, 1928, 2 Vols., esp. Vol. II.
73. Bancroft, *op. cit.*, p. 161.
74. *Ibid.*, pp. 161-162. In *Third Annual Report of the American Colonization Society*, Vol. I, p. 67.
75. *Ibid.*, P. 162.
76. Bancroft, *Ibid.*, p. 162. Cited from *The African Repository*, Vol. I, p. 67.
77. Bancroft, *Ibid.*, pp. 162-163. From Society's *Tenth Annual Report*, pp. 21-22. See speech of Henry Clay on 1st January, 1818 to the Society in *Second Annual Report of the American Society for Colonizing the Free People of Color in the United States*, Washington, 1819, p. 110.
78. An American Secretary of State and a Southerner.
79. Bancroft, *op. cit.*, p. 180. From *The African Repository*, Vol. XII, p. 10.
80. *Ibid.*, p. 181. Italics in Bancroft. From Publications of the *Mississippi Valley History Society*, Vol. IX, p. 364.
81. *Ibid.*, p. 190.
82. *Ibid.*, p. 164.
83. See Charles Francis Adams, *Memoirs of John Quincy Adams*, Vol. IV, pp. 292-294. This theme was stressed from the beginning of the Society's operations. See also *Second Annual Report of the American Colonization Society*, Washington, 1819.
84. Jay, William, *Miscellaneous Writings on Slavery*, Boston, John P. Jewett & Co., Cleveland, Ohio, Jewett, Proctor, and Worthington, London, Sampson, Low., 1853, p. 79. Also Jay, *Inquiry into the Character of the American Colonization and American Anti-Slavery*, New York, R. G. Williams for the American Anti-Slavery Society, 6th edition, 1838, p. 77.
85. See Jay, W., *Miscellaneous, etc.*, pp. 75-77. Also *New Haven Christian Spectator*, March 1833 (for speech of Knapp). Also *Life, Travels and Opinions of Benjamin Lundy*, pp. 306-307. See Garrison, *op. cit.*, pp. 3-4.
86. Bancroft, *op. cit.*, p. 191.
87. For the abolitionist act of 1808 see *The Public Statutes at Large of The United States of America*, Vol. III, pp. 426-430. For reassurance to the south see *First Annual Report: American Colonization Society*, 1818, p. 33.
88. Professor Thomas Roderick Dew of William and Mary College warned against this. See my chapter on slave-rearing in respect of Virginia in case the wealth of Virginia vanished overnight by implementation of the urge for colonization of Negroes, in V. B. Thompson, *Making of the African*

Diaspora, p. 201.
89. See *Second Annual Report of the American Colonization Society*, p. 147. Also J. E. Cooker, (ed.) *The Early Anti-Slavery Movement and African Colonization*, Norman, Oklahoma, 1957, pp. 61-65, *et. seq.* 157.
90. Garrison, W. L., *Thoughts on African Colonization*, or *An Impartial Exhibition of the Doctrine, Principles and Purposes of the American Colonization Society*, Garrison and Knapp, Boston, 1832.
91. *First Annual Report of the American Colonization Society*, 1818, Washington DC, p. 6. Also quoted in F. Bancroft, *op. cit.* above, p. 160.
92. See Ann Maury (ed.), *Memoirs of a Huguenot Family*, New York, 1853, pp. 348-53 for a letter dated 30th March 1757 by the Reverend Peter Fontaine of Westover, Virginia addressed to his brother Moses in which he defends the institution of slavery. He even asserted that to live in Virginia without slaves was morally impossible.
93. W. E. B. DuBois, *The Suppression of the African Slave Trade to America*, Cambridge, Mass., 1896.
94. *Fourth Annual Report of the American Colonization Society*, 1821, p. 59. South Carolina also signified approval of the Society.
95. *Eighth Annual Report*, Washington, 1825.
96. *Fourteenth Annual Report of the American Colonization Society*, 1831, December 1, 1830.
97. *Second Annual Report*, 1819, p. 9. The President of the Society developed the argument a year later. See *The Third Annual Report*. 1820.
98. C. I. Foster, "`The Colonization of Free Negroes in Liberia, 1816-1835,'" in *Journal of Negro History*, Vol. 19, p. 47.
99. Theodore Draper, *The Rediscovery of Black Nationalism*, p. 9.
100. Foster, *op. cit.*, p. 48.
101. Letter of the Reverend Ralph R. Gurley on the *American Colonization Society*, addressed to Henry Ibbottson, Esq. of Sheffield, England (Washington, 1833), p. 5. Also Foster, *op. cit.* above, p. 48.
102. *Colonization of Free Colored Population of Maryland*, and such slaves as may *hereafter become free*. Published by managers appointed by the state of Maryland, (Baltimore, 1832), p. 3.
103. *American Colonization Society: Seventeenth Annual Report*, 1834. Also Foster, *op. cit.*, p. 65.
104. Staudenraus, P. J., *The African Colonization Movement 1816-1865*, New York, 1961, pp. 17-21, 26-31; also Henry N. Sherwood, "Paul Cuffee," *Journal of Negro History (JNH)*, VII (1923), pp. 153-229. Sheldon H. Harris, Paul Cuffee: Black America and the African Return, New York, 1972, pp. 24-34, 38-41, 50-54.
105. Curry, Leonard P., *The Free Black in Urban America, 1800-1850: The Shadow of the Dream*, Chicago, 1981, p. 244.
106. Staudenraus, P. J., *op. cit.*, pp. 32-33; also C. H. Wesley, *Richard Allen: Apostle of Freedom*.
107. See for instance, William J. Simmons (Rev.), *Men of Mark: Eminent, Progressive and Rising*, 1887. Reprint New York, 1968.
108. Aptheker, H. (ed.) 'One Continual Cry', David Walker's Appeal to the *Colored Citizens of the World in Four Parts*, Humanities Press.
109. The poems were republished in 1837 with the title: *Poems of a Slave.*
110. The full title of this text was: *The Ethiopian Manifesto in Defence of the Black*

Man's Right in the Scale of Universal Freedom.

111. Quarles, Benjamin, *Black Abolitionists,* London, 1969, p. 184.
112. See *Freedom's Journal,* March 16, 1827.
113. See for instance *Freedom's Journal,* March, 30 and April 1, 1827.
114. *Ibid.,* May 18, June 1, 1827.
115. See Alexander Crummell (Rev.) "Eulogium on Henry Highland Garnet, D.D.," Crummell in *Africa and America: Addresses and Discourses,* May 4, 1882, Springfield, Mass, Willey & Co., 1891.
116. *Freedom's Journal,* June 8, 1827.
117. *Ibid.* Sept. 7 and 21, 1827; also *The Colored American,* Oct. 14, 1837.
118. *Ibid.*
119. See James W. Alexander, *The Life of Achibald Alexander, D.D., L.L.K.,* Philadelphia, 1857, pp. 395-97.
120. See *Rights of All,* July 17, 1829.
121. Litwack, Leon F., *North of Slavery, The Negro in the Free States, 1790-1860,* Chicago, 1963, pp. 70-73. *Rights of All,* Sept. 18, 1829.
122. See *Rights of All,* July 17 and Oct. 9, 1829.
123. see *The Liberator,* May 3, 1834.
124. That was not the first Convention of slaveholders. They held this first Convention at Annapolis, Maryland, in January 1842. *The National Anti-Slavery Standard. The Liberator*

Part 3

Later Leadership

CHAPTER 6

CRISES IN THE OBJECTIVES OF LEADERSHIP, 1860-1920

BACKGROUND TO THE CRISES

The foregoing chapters should by now have shed sufficient light on the factors responsible for the crises of this phase in the study of the evolution of leadership among Africans of the Diaspora in the Americas, principally in the United States, where that leadership was more articulate than elsewhere. It is essential to summarize these factors, as they also illuminate the conflicting tendencies in the crisis situations that were to persist into the twentieth century, especially the first two decades. Handicaps against which Africans had fought in the Americas from the time of their enslavement until the time of their emancipation did not diminish; rather they increased and further strained their relations with the Euro-Americans and among themselves, based on their perceptions of the problems and their possible solutioning. Some of these handicaps which had engaged the thoughts and activities of the free and freed Africans in the United States at a time when their numbers were negligible and had been the preoccupations of the organizers of the National Convention movements as well as the various State Conventions of the Africans of the Diaspora in the Americas, which survived into the post-emancipation period, emphasized a continuity of the struggles in which they had employed activism and the language of moral suasion to transcend. Yet it seemed, to paraphrase the cliché, "the more they seemed to advance the more things remained the same." What had therefore seemed promising came back to haunt their waking moments as deceptive. Their energies were undiminished in seeking to move forward despite acute discouragement. Prior to the Civil War and emancipation, the aims among the free and freed Africans had been to achieve not only emancipation for all their brethren but to attain civil rights and their own elevation through education and vocational opportunities. But the freedom which they achieved proved ephemeral, illusory, and nominal in its import. Indeed, it was much worse, for it seemed in some respects not to have moved beyond the slave experiences of the majority of the brethren, even for those among them who had never been slaves. The Euro-American society into which they sought to be integrated became even more hostile to the existence of free blacks than it had been in the earlier period. Even in that earlier period these free people had been unwelcome to say the least and the increase in their numbers after emancipation was deemed to be more problematic. Even their friends, former adherents of the anti-slavery movement, had become ambivalent and unwilling to exert themselves further in securing the next stage of freedom. Thus, seemingly forsaken and abandoned in the midst of what appeared to be a conspiracy of white racial supremacy, the leaders of the African Diaspora had to rely increasingly on their own resources and ingenuity and capacity in order to remove the many obstacles which piled on layer upon layer, especially during the last two decades of the nineteenth century, when their status had reached its lowest ebb. These handicaps, to sum up, were juridical (stipulated in numerous enactments), political (involving disfranchisement), economic (in the institution of peonage, the closing of the doors of economic opportunity, and the violent prevention of individual and group efforts among African-Americans), social (through enforced and violent segregation measures and methods), cultural (by closing the doors to meaningful contact and intercourse and by stifling efforts to acquire education and religious association), and psychological (through violent, intimidatory, and discouragement tactics). All of these were designed to keep the "Negro in his place." Such was the existing climate when the crisis dawned on these beleaguered descendants of Africa in the United States of America.

In observing earlier leadership prior to 1850, we categorize the leaders for convenience and precision (physical force, moral suasionist, and activist) according to the circumstances surrounding them from their enslavement in the Americas until just before the outbreak of the Civil War (1861-1865) in the United States. The character of leadership altered drastically, especially after the Civil War, but each of the categories mentioned above could still be discerned, except that a greater preponderance was to be found among the latter two categories than the first. The objectives changed as the circumstances changed in the United States after the emancipation de facto at the start of the Civil War and *de jure* after President Lincoln's Emancipation Proclamation of 1863, although the war persisted until 1865.

In the British territories of the Americas, and principally in the West Indies, the proclamation of 1834 signaled the beginning of the end of slavery, but not until the abolition of the apprenticeship system, which came to an end in 1838, sooner than had been intended by the British enactment of 1833, because the apprenticeship system (a continuation of slavery by another name) proved most inconvenient and unworkable. Slaves became free in the West Indies, except in the French colonies, a generation before they were "emancipated" in the United States of America. Their struggles in both theaters of slavery revolved around how to sustain that freedom without its deteriorating into peonage, which it later became. There were conflicts and the most serious in the West Indies occurred in Jamaica in 1865 and was described by officialdom as the "Morant Bay Rebellion" (which was, in essence, a riot), in which two of the principal leaders, George William Gordon and Paul Bogle, were executed by the British authorities. Modern scholarship[1] has helped to correct the impression of a "rebellion" instead of a riot and has helped to correct the distortions of those times for enlarging our understanding of the events which led up to the tragedies of those times. But as the British government had no intention of enfranchising the descendants of the Africans, they remained disenfranchised until about the middle of the twentieth century, in an era when gunboat diplomacy could be employed to silence them. What was conceded was tokenism[2] towards the "colored people" in a highly color-conscious Jamaica and the West Indies but where these enfranchised colored people rubberstamped the intentions of officialdom rather than being the leaders of the downtrodden descendants of Africa. Descendants of Africa were not to make their presence felt until the twentieth century. Not even the formation of the Universal Negro Improvement Association in Jamaica in 1914 made the desired impact until the outbreak of rebellion throughout much of the West Indies in the 1930s, almost a century after the termination of the apprenticeship system. Only then did the British government begin to take cognizance of the aspirations of the descendants of Africa and others in the West Indies. But those developments do not fall within the scope of this work. What is important to state is that the events of 1865 in Jamaica, even in official circles, showed how the fervor of the St. Domingue (Haiti) revolution continued to haunt the Americas, as the leadership of that revolution was, in the main, one of the physical force leaders. Some, like Toussaint L'Ouverture, were also moral suasionists, for which they paid with their lives when they became trusting of their sworn enemies, who tried (unsuccessfully) to undermine the burgeoning revolution. Thus, periodic pleas and upheavals centered around economic and social conditions such as those which swept the West Indies in 1938 and produced the Moyne Commission, an inquiry instituted by the British government under Lord Moyne. This need not detain us. However, racism, racial and color discrimination, and economic exploitation did not vanish from these British colonies, and it was reinforced by color discrimination which had become commonplace in the West Indies and much of South America since slavery times and now pervaded the social system.[3]

The British West Indies had their own peculiarities of color gradation which had been nurtured from the days of slavery and which continued to manifest themselves in the struggles for power, for representation, and for a voice in society. In time these became minimized, except in social and economic relations, but the entire process resolved itself by mid-twentieth century.

Yet, it was in North America, and especially the United States, that the leadership of the African Diaspora manifested the greatest movement, activity, and thought, helping to shape the ideology for advancement of their people in the "American" socio-economic setting. Prior to their emancipation the question had already begun to agitate the minds of citizens, both Euro-Americans (alias whites) and African-Americans (alias blacks and colored). The nagging question was, what should be done with the emancipated African-Americans? Those who dreaded the prospect of African-American neighbors alongside Euro-Americans (even among some who had championed the cause of antislavery) began to conceive and revive schemes of their colonization, the most ardent being the American Society for the Colonization of Free Colored People (an organizational name shortened to the American Colonization Society), already discussed above in terms of its detraction and claims to humanitarianism. There were others who opted for the alternative of integrating "free colored people" into society by conferring citizenship on them and elevating them through education and moral instruction, two things (among many others) which slavery had denied them. There were, of course, those who had no immediate solution and foresaw impending conflict between ex-slaves and ex-slave owners who had per force lost their slaves but were adopting a wait-and-see attitude. These were also to affect the perceptions of African-Americans in the succeeding years, as they also had differing aspirations. Some African-American freedmen had already left the country, on their own initiative, for such places as Canada, Haiti, or Liberia (through the auspices of the American Colonization Society), believing that they might secure their manhood and dignity as well as advancement elsewhere than in a racist United States of America.

As Reconstruction after the war became radical, the hopes of integration were raised and the desire to move away became less pronounced. But after the Federal Government struck the Compromise of 1877 and proceeded to withdraw troops from the South, leaving the South to its own devices, the status of the African-Americans deteriorated. Draconian measures which contributed piecemeal to wholesale disfranchisement were enacted, coupled with the use of violence and other intimidatory tactics and the use of clandestine organizations such as the Ku Klux Klan; all these events contributed to a negation of the gains which the newly emancipated and the veteran freedman had achieved. Thus a second notion was induced into the thought processes of African-Americans, namely, that of migration and emigration, the former being within the confines of the U.S.A. to a more congenial political and social climate, the latter, away from the U.S.A. to a place where people might be assessed on their own merit rather than on the basis of their color.

The "New South", as it was called, was desirous of keeping the African-Americans on the lower rungs of the societal ladder, blocking their aspiration to any social advancement. The majority of southerners were of this viewpoint; some, however, felt the need for integration. The North, which had earlier championed their cause in the antislavery period, not only became fatigued but also quickly assimilated the outlook of the South and felt that the migration of African-Americans northwards should be discouraged and resisted. Thus, it was no surprise that what essentially was an initial crisis became compounded to become a series of crises. Even the South was ambivalent concerning the retention or expatriation of African-Americans, conscious of the fact that their departure would not only leave menial tasks to whites but that production problems would arise for the South in general, which was still largely agricultural. Yet, many die-hard firebrands continued to advocate African-American expulsion from the South, insisting after three amendments (XIII,

XIV, and XV) to the Constitution of the United States, that their removal would only contribute to harmony in the South, as "the Negro was not a citizen." As a result, even African-Americans who wished to remain in the South found things bewildering and their existence there becoming intolerable because of the menacing activities of whites. Some southerners, however, hoped to cow the African-Americans through the use of terror tactics into submission and accepting their lot without protest or organized resistance. It was into this situation later in the century that Booker T. Washington came to become "the Negro leader" by 1895, who not only openly acquiesced and sanctioned segregation and disfranchisement of the mass of African-American people but also explained away the excesses of the South, thus becoming the most admired spokesman of the anti-integrationists. Accordingly, African-Americans, not only in the south but elsewhere in the country, found themselves facing conflicting alternatives, hovering between [A integration (which sometimes meant assimilation)], [B segregation and subservience], or [C migration and emigration] (the latter incorporating more-or -less notions of a "separate identity" which was to become more pronounced as the century progressed). These issues, which had begun to surface in the first phase of leadership (pre-1860) in the African-American Convention Movement, assumed an urgency after the promises of Reconstruction had failed. Not only was the period seen as one in which African-Americans constituted the "villains of the piece" but antagonisms welled up in the minds of southerners, spilling out as hatred and hostility for African-Americans. It arose first from the emancipation and second from the inevitable rivalry for power in political, economic, and social spheres. The controversy over Reconstruction need not detain us here, as that subject has been assessed and reassessed. Our main concern here is the aftermath of the failure of Reconstruction in terms of the way it shaped the perceptions of leadership to meet the challenge of a rapidly deteriorating situation in which African-Americans fared badly, even by comparison with later emigrants from Europe. By the end of the nineteenth century, the African-Americans had plumbed the lowest depths of degradation, due to an unholy trinity of legislation, customary practice, and new terror tactics - such as intimidation, physical battery, mutilation, and murder. This state of affairs which African-American historian Professor Rayford Logan, aptly described as the "nadir" of race relations in the U.S.A, persisted into the first two decades of the twentieth century.

Despite the continuity in African-American rank-and-file before and after the Civil War, a new leadership emerged to deal with the changed and changing circumstances, counseling and urging a new approach to the question of the destiny of African-Americans. While the type of moral suasion and activism that had characterized the pre-1860 leadership was still discernible in the statements and activities of the emerging post war leaders, there were also periodic manifestations of "physical force" style (although all three of these terms were rapidly becoming inadequate). [4]The two dominant issues at this time can rather be summed up in two terms- integration versus emigration and in time a third ["separate identity"] was to emerge out of the rejection of the implications of the first. The term "integration" implied possible assimilation, the conceding of 'civil rights', enfranchisement and citizenship rights, not just citizenship in a nominal sense. As progress towards integration stalled, however, some African-American leaders again advocated emigration. But other individualists concerned with the plight of the brethren came to the fore. Their activity became sub-divided between (1) the internal emigrationists (led by Benjamin Singleton, the "Moses of the Colored Exodus" and Henry Adams) (2) the external emigrationists led by M. R. Delany in 1877 until his death in 1885, and then Bishop Henry McNeal Turner of the A.M.E. Church to the end of his life in 1915.

The leadership of the African Diaspora broadly split two ways and in time three ways by the emergence expressed with greater intensity of the separate identitists who rejected the implications of integration or felt it was synonymous with total assimilation instead of co-existence. The debates were sometimes acrimonious. But each had weighty arguments for the positions they held and the outcome of their arguments reveal genuine preoccupations with their plight and pariah status in the United States of America.

Women Activists

This leadership crisis cannot be properly appreciated without at least a passing mention of the leadership role of certain women, often of the elitist and middle-class camp, either by origin, persuasion, or upbringing. They also fell within the integrationist camp and lived and operated in the "Age" of either Douglass or Washington. The three most outstanding were Mary Ann Shadd (1823-1893), Ida B. Wells-Barnett (1862-1934), and Mary Church Terrell (1863-1954). The first had been born in (and had begun to operate in) the *ante-bellum* period, whereas the other two were born during the Civil War and continued their activities into the twentieth century. There were many points of similarity between them as well as many divergent points, but this is not a biographical study but rather one intended to capture the essential advocacies of leadership in an age dominated by men and also by the personalities of two male stalwarts. Their lives recalled those of their predecessors, Harriet Tubman and Sojourner Truth; the former lived until 1914, while the latter died before the turn of the century. Although both these women survived into this phase of later leadership and continued their activities on a more modest scale, they had become spent forces by the time of the ascendancy of Ida B. Wells-Barnett and Mary Church-Terrell, though they remained inspirational to their successors. It is also important to observe another common characteristic between Mary Ann Shadd and Ida B. Wells-Barnett: both of them founded and edited newspapers. Shadd was the forerunner and, in fact, the first African-American woman editor of a newspaper in North America since the early 1850s. Her paper, *The Provincial Freeman*, came up against the prejudice of black men who did not approve of a paper run solely by women. She later made a concession appointing a Reverend gentleman by the name of William P. Newman, who was really nominal editor, while Shadd (and her sister Amelia) kept a tight rein on their paper. Mary Ann, the daughter of black abolitionist Abraham Shadd, later became one of the early members and founders of the Convention Movement and was to participate at one such Convention in Philadelphia in which she demonstrated her oratorical powers (another feature common to these three women) and received the commendation and approval of Frederick Douglass. Douglass himself, the most ardent opponent of emigration from the United States, was able to say of her speech that it was "one of the most convincing and telling speeches in favor of Canadian emigration" he had ever heard. [5]

Like Mary Church Terrell and Ida Wells-Barnett, Mary Ann Shadd was both an educator and a critical leader as well as a believer in the importance of education for elevation of their people. But she came early to the emigrationist idea, after the passing of the Fugitive Slave Act of 1850, which compelled her to publish a pamphlet titled *A Plea for Emigration, or Notes of Canada West - Its Moral, Social and Political Aspects (1851)* . But she envisaged this emigration to Canada as a prerequisite for integration with "all free people under the protection of British law".[6] Like her father she was fortified in the belief that integration and racial parity could eventually be achieved based on the principles of education, thrift, and hard work. Even in this belief she seemed to have anticipated Booker T. Washington, although unlike him she did not limit such education to the vocational-technical level, as is amply demonstrated by her own life; for, after the Civil War, despite her earlier achievements as a teacher and organizer of schools in Wilmington (Delaware), West Chester and Norristown (Pennsylvania), and New York City, she obtained an American teaching certificate in 1869 and later taught in Detroit and Washington D.C. Furthermore, at the age of forty-six she enrolled for evening courses in Law at Howard University (the first woman to do so), and graduated in 1883; and despite the onerous nature of the studies she found time to write articles on issues that affected her people and society generally.

She remained an indefatigable fighter against racism during her time in Canada, where she edited her paper, and later when she returned to the United States following the conclusion of the Civil War. In fact, her anti-slavery activities so impressed Dr. M. R. Delany (a major at the time of the war) that he invited her back to the United States to assist in the war effort. [7] She worked enthusiastically and after the war, instead of returning to Canada, decided to remain in the country of her birth. She became a frequent participant at conventions and conferences of women's rights held around Washington D.C., in which the participants were black and white women, apart from men. [8] In fact, in the 1870s, she became a confidant to Susan B. Anthony, the renowned suffragist for women's rights. Shadd was invited to address the National Women's Suffrage Convention in 1878, after which she went on to found the Colored Women's Progressive Franchise Association.

Shadd had been critical of Reconstruction politics, especially for dividing and exploiting the black community. She continued to the end of her life to speak, write, and campaign on issues affecting African-Americans, including matters such as the Ku Klux Klan, and was an unrelenting champion for the causes she espoused - suffrage, anti-racism, emigration, and integration - but in essence she was an assimilationist-integrationist, although in an earlier period (in her 1848 pamphlet, Hints to Colored People of the North) she had reproved African-Americans to be less imitative of white materialism and urged them to take their own initiatives without waiting for white support. In short, she counseled both the spirit of independence and self-help (reminiscent of the activities of Richard Allen, the Free Africa Society, and the A.M.E. Church). Her admonishment that they work for a national identity (manifested in the 1840s) was to re-echo among successor leaders. Here too she was expressing the same sentiments as her contemporary, Lewis Woodson, an African-American prelate, who had also reached the conclusion that integration was unworkable in the United States of America and counseled choosing between emigration or the establishment of black communities to be called "Africanas."[9] Thus, this idea of a black national identity - urged by Woodson, supported by emigrationists like M. R. Delany and Henry Bibb in the 1850s, and strongly advocated by Mary

Ann Shadd - was to find more forcible expression as the century wore on.

Mary Ann Shadd distinguished herself as a leader of consequence both in terms of ideas and in her many varied activities and also as a role model. She died two years before Frederick Douglass (in 1893) and two years before the "Age of Booker T. Washington" began. Although her life's work received a eulogy by Douglass, she had immortalized her own name as one of the worthy spirits of the "Age of Frederick Douglass" and her memory remains inspirational to many who study her life's work.

Ida B. Wells-Barnett's career, which began two generations after that of Miss Shadd, as far as she was concerned, ended on a note of personal failure. She was relentless in her assault on racism and became an outspoken opponent of lynching, against which she waged unrelenting war in a Baptist weekly in Memphis (Tennessee) known as *Free Speech and Head Light*, of which she became partner and editor in 1889.

With the destruction of the Press and with mounting Klan pressure she left the South for New York, where immediately the African-American owner-proprietor and editor of the *New York Age*, Thomas T. Fortune, invited her to work with the paper. Here again, she went on to produce anti-lynching pamphlets such as *Southern Horrors* (1892) and *A Red Record* (1895). She continued to lecture in the North and Northeast and, sometimes, in the West and parts of the South. She extended her activities beyond the U.S.A. into Britain and organized anti-lynching societies in both countries. Apart from her work on the newspapers, she wrote for other papers as well and took part in activities on racial matters, became active in the short-lived Afro-American Council (almost the successor to the Afro-American League, which had been formed in 1890, the Council being a product of a revival of the League in 1898). Struggling against racism was an abiding passion to the end of her life and the struggle for racial justice a clear goal which she pursued unflinchingly. In the course of this struggle she fell afoul of the Tuskegeean through her criticisms of him, while the latter and his associates employed the "Tuskegee Machine" to prevent her from ever achieving any office in the Women's Club movement-which, ironically, she had been so instrumental in founding.

Wells-Barnett was a civil rights champion and was one of the founding members of the National Association for the Advancement of Colored People (N.A.A.C.P.) when it emerged in 1909. She was a believer in research and the gathering of facts as the necessary prerequisite to preparing the ground for causes she championed. Having become disillusioned with the nature of justice dispensed in the United States and convinced that issues must be argued and thrashed out, she sometimes advocated boycotts and pressure group tactics. She was a radical of the William Monroe Trotter and DuBoisian type and, sometimes, tended to surpass them on what were, for her, matters of principle. She never hesitated to criticize them. She was sometimes so radical that she became a one-person show and it is no surprise that one contemporary writer has described her as a "loner."[10] Even within the N.A.A.C.P. she often disagreed with both black and white and was regarded within the movement as possessing the potential of a wrecker. As an anti-lynching campaigner she could hardly endure Mr. Washington's justification of the atrocities of the 1890s and she attacked him unhesitatingly. Despite her feeling of personal failure at the end of her life, it was her tactics that the N.A.A.C.P. adopted in the fight against lynching.

The third woman under consideration in this work, Mary Church Terrell (wife of Judge Terrell), had towards the end of the nineteenth century distinguished herself as a leader of black women's clubs. But she also fought for enfranchisement and used the public platform to agitate the issues that preoccupied her contemporaries. Even before she was thirty years of age (in 1892) she had helped to organize the Black Women's Secular Society in the United States of America and four years later was elected President of the newly formed National Association of Colored Women (1896). She intruded herself in white women's suffrage and reform circles but she was a fighter for racial justice and equality for women. She was quite successful in the nineteenth century and carried her activities into the twentieth century, well beyond the period that this work is concerned with. Her leadership role continued to be exercised into the third phase of the evolution of African-American leadership on the American continent. Like the two other women already discussed, she manifested great oratorical powers which enhanced her reputation in certain public circles.

Terrell had begun her career by teaching in (1885) at Wilberforce (Ohio) and two years later was on the faculty of the Preparatory School for Colored Youth in Washington, D.C. and taught in the foreign languages department headed by Robert Herberton Terrell, who was to become her future husband. A year later, financed by her father, she left for Europe for further study (foreign languages) and was abroad from 1888 to 1890. These experiences were to constitute a kind of apprenticeship for the task she was later to undertake in the U.S.A. She taught for a year on her return and then married Mr. Terrell in October 1891. Encouraged by her husband she embarked on a career as a paid lecturer, suffrage activist, civic worker, organizer, and leader in the early black women's club movement.[11] Although she was deemed a middle-of-the-roader falling between the "radicals" (as represented by Monroe Trotter, W. E. B. DuBois, and Ida B. Wells-Barnett) on the one hand and the "accomodationists" (as represented by Booker T. Washington and his coterie of admirers and protegés) on the other, she sometimes caused Mr. Washington distress by her pronouncements on some subjects affecting the African-Americans. Even though her husband had received his appointment as a municipal judge for the District of Columbia on Mr. Washington's recommendation (as one of the many patronages which the latter exercised as the confidant of U.S. Presidents), yet the judge could not restrain his headstrong wife. Characteristically, the Tuskegeean warned the judge that if his wife continued criticizing Washington, then the judge could not continue to expect his friends to help him. Her views on the suffrage, for instance, differed from those of the Tuskegeean, and her association with the N.A.A.C.P. (which Washington considered hostile to him) also made him feel that she was fundamentally against him. But, being a middle- of-the-roader, she tried to please both sides, treating Washington and his wife as her dear friends, often entertaining them at her home in the District of Columbia.[12] Despite the warnings, however, there were times when she spoke out on issues, such as oppression, which she loathed, heedless of whether or not she endeared herself to the Tuskegeean. Although she had since the 1880s committed herself to activities that she felt would enhance the welfare of the majority of her fellow African-Americans, yet her principles were molded on white middle class values, and though she might speak of the poor among her brethren, she was very distant from them and, in fact, like her other associates, was not a leader of the masses in an age when the plight of the masses was desperate.

Whether from the female or male quarters, however, this emerging leadership did not include any leaders from the rank and file of the masses, nor directly address them. They constituted the "talented tenth" which DuBois came to believe should, in fact, lead the rest. Thus, by the 1890s there were a handful of leaders peddling the people's causes through their embracing of "socialistic" ideas, but they were still elitist and were subsumed by the majority of socialists who were white. They still did not make any significant contribution to enhancing the African-American masses. But there was one prelate and man of the cloth who, apart from his activism, wrote socialist tracts (now largely forgotten). George Washington Woodbey was a drawer of crowds but nothing came of this association with white socialists, as racism plagued their ranks as well as their thoughts. Although the elite tended to claim (or left it to be implied) that they were acting on behalf of the masses, yet it was not until the twentieth century that the African-American masses began to produce leaders who represented some of their sentiments and only then did the plight of the masses begin to emerge among issues that needed to be confronted. The Urban League for instance, which purported to struggle on behalf of the masses, was thoroughly elitist. Even those who joined black labor unions did not begin to have any practical effect on the plight of the masses before the emergence of Garvey's U.N.I.A.

EMERGENCE OF THE CRISIS

At the close of the American Civil War, with Lincoln's emancipation proclamation having determined the end of official slavery in the land, African-Americans, those previously free as well as the newly liberated, envisaged a new dispensation. Accordingly, the leadership which had thrown its energies into the anti-slavery crusade and the war effort now found itself with a task quite different from that which had preoccupied it in the preceding period. The issue was no longer freedom and emancipation, but the exercise of that freedom under the law—in short, the conferral of citizenship and the rights appertaining to that status. So the leaders had to re-fashion their weapons for the legal and societal battles of securing these goals. With the formal close of Reconstruction in 1877 the white South returned to power and began to pass discriminatory measures against those who had enjoyed enfranchisement in the Reconstruction period. For a new generation of African-American leaders as well as some of the old guard, this new state of affairs constituted a crisis. What attitude were they to adopt towards the larger "American" society, which seemed to have acquiesced in the re-empowering of the white South, especially when the voices of protest in that society were growing fainter and fainter? What alternatives were open to them in a society in which they were rapidly losing their rights and were being thrown back into an arena from which they had fought so hard to escape? The major concern which exacerbated the crises of leadership had preoccupied them in the earlier phase prior to the Civil War but the coming of the war seemed to have resolved it. With the benefits of the war evaporating, however, some began to revive the old plan of migrating, either to other parts of the Americas or to other regions of the United States itself, or completely outside it - even unto the continent of their forebears. Accordingly, while believers in the society pinned their faith on integration, assimilation, and obtaining civil rights within the U.S. itself, others despaired of this as the century wore on and once again embraced the notion of emigration. The battle had been joined between these two opposing camps, with arguments aplenty on both sides - acrimonious and bitter, to be sure, but also sincerely held by each of the opposing camps. Those debates and actions would influence the perceptions of African-Americans far into the twentieth century.

Emigration resurfaced periodically, especially in times of depression, economic distress, suppression of political rights, and legislative "promotion" of segregation and murder. In such times, the African-American leadership tended to focus on such fundamental issues as the dignity of the person and how to secure it under such menacing, threatening, and intimidatory conditions which seemed to have the force of law and custom. In time, this idea of migration and emigration was referred to as "nationalism" by some and as "separation" by others and for those who still felt something could be worked out within north American society their activities came to be referred to as "nationalism" and "separate identity." Even from the integrationist quarter, the notion that integration implied assimilation began to be discounted because of the unfavorable construction put on the idea (as if African-Americans wished only to get their hands on white women), and "integration" began to mean more what it had always implied-i.e., full citizenship and the rights appertaining there to and complete enfranchisement without any reservations. In time, it came to mean coexistence - provided of course, that full citizenship rights were conceded and enjoyed by all without reservation. The issues continued to be clarified through such debates. But the African-Americans were not without their detractors, who sought to see them only partially integrated, excluding those who stood for full citizenship; there were also those who felt they should be removed from the country, otherwise disfranchised and segregated. The nineteenth century saw the development of many theories to justify one point of view or another. But the persistence of the migration idea reflected the malaise of society and the perception by some that they were being unfairly treated. The polarization of positions between African-Americans at this time was personified in the domination of single personalities; our reflections on the polarized views of these leaders, who typified the rest, forms the bulk of this chapter.

In the period between 1860 and 1895 the arguments of Douglass for integration as against the arguments of the emigrationists led by Delany and Bishop Turner and some others dominated the era. From the latter date Booker T. Washington's accomodationist views and acceptance of disfranchisement, segregation, and gradualism dominated the scene that the voices of his opponents were treated with scant regard. Nonetheless, they found spokesmen in some personalities, and their chief spokesman was Dr. W. E. B. DuBois. He was assisted by William Monroe Trotter of the *Boston Guardian* as well as some white advocates of integration, who preempted the activities of the Niagara Movement when they formed the National Association for the Advancement of Colored People (N.A.A.C.P.). Much of the following discussion will focus on DuBois' alternative approaches to the position taken by Washington, whose views received wide coverage in the press. But it is not easy to understand the controversy without indicating the essential position taken by Booker T. Washington on vital issues which affected the African-Americans. For it is these which exacerbated the crisis and the conflicting positions taken by DuBois in dealing with the destiny of the African-Americans on American soil.

Booker T. Washington, the Compromise and Methods of Operation

Washington's autobiography, *Up From Slavery* (1899), showed the rising leader as a remarkable and resourceful man. His training at Hampton Institute under General Armstrong provided the foundation for that leader's life work. Later, with the same support and those of other white southerners, he embraced the kind of education he had received at Hampton (Virginia) and moved on to Alabama to establish Tuskegee Institute on the same model as that of Armstrong in Hampton. The emphasis of both institutions was industrial education. No one could doubt the value of education that was practical, provided it did not result in a narrow outlook and vision of life and provided it kept abreast of developments in the realms of science and technology. When it essentially glorified manual labor and disregarded any other method of mental elevation, then it was bound to encounter the opposition of others who felt that all opportunities should be made available, without limitations on the capacities of people on the basis of their color or origin. It was around such matters that controversy was to center as the crisis progressed.

Despite the background training of Washington that was to prepare him for his career, it was his 1895 speech that rocketed him to the level of national leader. Under the circumstances, it is appropriate to begin with that event, for it set the pace and the tone for the black South, which would in turn influence the North and the policies of the Federal and southern governments. The 1895 speech was a remarkable construction, revealing diplomacy, some sound common sense, some criticisms of what he considered to be past mistakes, some admonishments to white southerners, a preference for capitalism, some advice to his black brethren, and even suggestions that they begin at the bottom instead of the top; but it left a wide gap as to when worthy benefits would be attained and here he left this to the discretion of the white South in effect, resigning the destiny of the blacks to the moods and fancies of the South.

Atlanta Cotton Exposition Speech

Mr. Washington's speech at the Atlanta Cotton Exposition was delivered on September 18, 1895. Its effect was electrical and reverberated through the entire U.S.A. Washington had, at last, sprung onto the pedestal of a national leader. The speech needs to be read in its entirety because it set him on a course that he intended to pursue to the end of his life, involving accommodation with white southern racists, who insisted on holding down the "Negro" or as the saying went, "keeping him in his place" - which meant denying him any rights whatsoever, be they political, economic, or social. This meant that Mr. Washington was only saying the things the white racist South wished to hear, provided they did not elevate the African-Americans beyond their groveling stage. Washington's approach thus was tantamount to fawning flattery of the South. By stressing "duties" instead of "rights," Mr. Washington was condemning African-Americans to a passive role in the evolution of the "New South" and asking them to accept an indefinite period of tutelage subject to the whims and caprices of the exalted white South. Since that South was forced by circumstances to conceded emancipation of slaves, it seemed curious that given the mood of the South after the Civil War and after the end of Reconstruction, he could be so trusting as to do what Douglass before him had rejected, that is, placing the brethren in the jaws of the lion. Indications of the New South's tendencies were in the use of bullying tactics against the blacks, and the activities of terrorist organizations like the Ku Klux Klan, and the lynching of blacks either through this or other lunatic fringe organizations, or by enactments that whittled down the gains made after the Civil War. These lynchings, which had become sadistic pastimes, increased in number and frequency, attaining epidemic proportions. These were the men to whom the African-Americans of the South were to resign their destinies by being meek and humble and undemanding of their political rights of citizenship, men whose slogan was that "the Negro is not a citizen." Furthermore, Mr. Washington by his emphasis on "service" was condoning peonage practiced by the South through which many African-Americans suffered economic hardships and by his undue emphasis on "industrial education" and his jibes at higher education he tended to deflate the value of higher education and restrict the prospects of higher education for African-Americans by implying that it had no practical value. Such behavior may well reflect an inferiority complex, Washington not having had university education himself. Using many half truths or falsehoods, he was in effect, laying down the law and the path along which black people were to travel thereafter. He emphasized the importance of earning money, even if that money was a pittance. In his statement on education he was pandering to the South and northern philanthropists who supplied money for his brand of education at Tuskegee, often at the expense of other black institutions not favored and not run on Tuskegeean lines.

But the Atlanta speech, by making all these concessions, earned the label of "The Compromise" by the content of its concessions to southern bigotry. Mr. Washington might have been prudent in minimizing the intensity of racial conflict in the South, but he only relegated the blacks to a position of subservience. While many of them acquiesced, others sought to leave the South. The implications extended beyond the South and mirrored governmental acquiescence in the plight of African-Americans nationwide. Mr. Washington also expressed his acquiescence to segregation in this extract from his speech:

> In all things that are purely social we can be as separate as the fingers, yet one as the hand in all things essential to mutual progress.[13]

He renounced social equality in the following term:

> The wisest among my race understand that the agitation of questions of social equality is the extremist folly, and that progress in the enjoyment of all the privileges that will come to us must be the result of severe constant struggle rather than of artificial forcing.[14]

He went on to promise the future South all the patience, faith-fullness, law-abiding, unresentful, and sympathetic help of the "colored people" which he anticipated would usher in "a new heaven and a new earth" for the South in general[15] The rhetoric was, no doubt, pleasing to their ears. For not only had he built up an illusion for the future but he had accepted the subordination of African-Americans in the South quite at variance with the position forthrightly advocated for equality of citizenship by Frederick Douglass in 1889. [16] Furthermore, Washington over-dramatized his belief in commerce as a passage to salvation, for the doors were barred to most black people by the organizational policies of the south. His remarks, in one fell swoop, turned back the clock from the gains envisioned by his predecessors in leadership of the "colored" community.

The press, North and South, acclaimed Washington "the leader" and wholeheartedly supported him. These eulogies hardly made the distinction, as Professor Rayford Logan reminds us, between "Washington's fancies and the facts."[17] Some papers declined to report or comment on the speech; the *Chicago Tribune*, for instance, neither condemned nor approved this speech while the *Detroit Tribune* was straightforwardly critical.[18]

The Tuskegeean's speech had created the impression in some newspaper circles that he had renounced social equality and black suffrage temporarily and that he emphasized industrial education and the opportunity to gain a livelihood and that black people could find many manifestations of friendship in the New South.[19] Yet, following the speech up to the end of the century and into the first decade of the twentieth century, the conditions of black Americans in the south deteriorated and they were inferiorized. Absurd situations arose when colored men could be murdered by their white farmer employers for arguing about money. Yet Mr. Washington continued to give the impression that conditions in the South were improving and race relations were advancing when the contrary was actually the case - an untruth which Washington carried abroad on his European tours. Often these repetitive patterns of summary and arbitrary justice disgraced the name of "democracy" and did not lend credence to Washington's effusions and illusions about southern "friendship" for members of his race. The extent of the subterfuge practiced by southern whites may be gleaned from their espousal of women's suffrage for purposes of offsetting black votes (which outnumbered those of whites), the advocates hoping that colored women would not bother to vote.[20] There were others who expected the use of residence qualification to deny a sizeable proportion of the black vote because of what they deemed to be the "migratory habits" of blacks.[21]

As far as the disfranchisement of the blacks, went not even northern newspapers in places like Boston and Pittsburgh came to their rescue; the general chorus of their effusions were "The White Man Must Rule." Even the acceptance of black men into the United States Army, which was construed by others (even people of Washington's ilk) as a sign of equality, manifested more cynicism than fact; the poem: "Sambo as a Soldier" expressed the principle at work (which probably survives in our day):

:...But as for me, upon my sowl,
So liberal are we here,
I'll let Sambo be murdered in place of myself
On every day of the year.

So hear me all, boys, darlings
Don't think I'm tipping you chaff,
The right to be kilt, I'll divided wid him,
And give him the largest half. [22]

Yet in terms of the vote, precautionary measures were being taken to prevent the disfranchisement of poor whites so that the professional and "intelligent" colored people might not exercise their vote significantly.

The imagery and vilification of blacks went on piling up in ever more and more lurid fashion. This imagery was harnessed to discredit them as unfit for citizenship, civil rights, or any humane consideration whatsoever. Observing one serious implication of the Washington speech, the late Professor Rayford Logan of Howard University wrote:

> The author of this book hazards the guess that Washington's Atlanta Compromise address constituted the consciences of the judges of the Supreme Court who in Plessy v Ferguson, the following year, wrote into American Jurisprudence one of the least defensive doctrines, the constitutionality of equal but separate accommodations.[23]

As a consequence, Thomas T. Fortune, the "fiery editor" of the *New York Age*, who had earlier supported Mr. Washington, came full circle to urge a "revolution" at a meeting in Brooklyn to celebrate the one hundredth anniversary of the birth of John Brown. His disillusionment with black "progress" had led him to write:

> It took tons of blood to put the fifteenth amendment into the constitution and it will take tons to put it out. You want to organize and keep your powder dry, and be ready to demand an eye for an eye and a tooth for a tooth, for there is coming a great crisis for the Negro in this country.[24]

Although he is said to have incurred the odium of the press, his sentiments (shared by a good many) must have chagrined Washington, who must have observed that public sentiment was moving away from his kind of approach to the predicament of African-Americans. Furthermore, Fortune himself had veered towards Pan-African sentiments at this time, when Henry-Sylvester Williams of Trinidad was bringing into being the Pan-African Association, which prepared the Pan-African Conference in London of 1900. Fortune was later able to assert that the West Indian barrister of Afro-Caribbean origin had stolen his ideas of Pan-Africanism. [25]

One of the active participants at the 1900 London Pan-African conference was Dr. W. E. B. DuBois, who helped in writing the

"Address to the Nations of the World," in which his now famous statement was reiterated that "the problem of the twentieth century is the problem of the color line." DuBois himself was not drawn into controversy with Mr. Washington until some time after the "Compromise Speech" of 1895. Years were to elapse before he directed his searchlight on the speech and the consequences flowing from it. He had spent the first years after obtaining his doctorate degree in History from Harvard University doing research, publishing, and teaching, first at Wilberforce University and later at Atlanta University. The publication of his doctoral thesis on the Suppression of the African Slave Trade to America in 1896 by Harvard enhanced his stature and was a source of pride to some members of the African-American elite who knew him or knew of him. His other researches resulted in the publication of *The Philadelphia Negro* (1897), which was to be followed by a series of published works, especially from the Atlanta University Studies on the Negro from which several publications emerged. In addition to that, he had written quite a number of articles. Then there emerged in 1903 his collection of essays titled *The Souls of Black Folk*, about which more shall be said presently. He also engaged in other intellectual pursuits, many of which were concerned with the shaping of the "Talented Tenth" of the African-American community, whom he believed would eventually uplift the rest of their brethren. Accordingly, he threw his energies into the American Negro Academy, founded in 1896 with Alexander Crummell as its first president; then, at the death of Crummell, DuBois became its president for a period of five years. The Academy published what were styled *Occasional Papers* of the American Negro Academy, in which matters relating to the elevation and the achievements of African-Americans were discussed. It was an intellectual exercise which suited DuBois' training and temperament, but from which he hoped benefits would accrue because he believed that the race problem in the United States was due, in the main, to ignorance; once this ignorance was dispelled by study and the dissemination of information he thought, this racial problem would vanish. It was too simplistic and optimistic a viewpoint at the time, but experience was to show the complexities of racism about which DuBois's studies would enlighten him with the passage of time. In 1915 he produced *The Negro*, which dealt with some aspects of African achievements. Yet long before DuBois had undertaken these series of studies (including his very competent *Black Folk Then and Now*), he had been unsure of any African contributions to civilizations; but study, maturity, and time were to enlighten his understanding, and he himself was to correct distorted views which he had assimilated from the not-so-well informed society which had nurtured him and even openly challenge those distortions. But the most significant publication in terms of the controversies that became sharper in this period of the deterioration of the stature of African-Americans in the United States was the *Souls of Black Folk*. It was not a sudden conversion, but rather one which was slowly building up inside him. By 1902 the battle lines against the Washington position (on the franchise, education and citizenship rights, anti-racism and anti-lynching, and the indiscriminate murders of African-Americans) were being drawn. With the publication of the book in 1903, DuBois had thrown down the gauntlet by devoting a whole chapter to Booker T. Washington. [26]

William Monroe Trotter of the *Boston Guardian*, another vitriolic African-American writer had, already shown his disenchantment with Mr. Washington's compromise and seemed the unofficial leader of a group that was emerging whose views diverged radically from those of Mr. Washington. In time, DuBois was to become the unofficial leader of these radicals. as his criticism of Mr. Washington had placed him at the head of the opposition. This began the mutual disenchantment between Washington and DuBois, disenchantment which was to last (despite a number of futile attempts at reconciliation) until the death of Mr. Washington in 1915. Allowing for the fact that their differences were fundamental, reconciliation, even for temporary gain, would not have worked, especially as so many of Washington's disbursed patronages came from his white backers and philanthropists. The demand for universal suffrage now was quite at variance with Washington's "no suffrage" or "gradual suffrage" in an indefinite future. Nor in terms of education would DuBois and Washington have agreed, because Washington insisted on industrial education whereas DuBois felt that all fields should be opened to African-Americans (among others). DuBois' initial advocacy for integration diverged considerably from the segregation which the South wished to foster and which Booker T. Washington by his Atlanta Exposition speech had accepted and had emphasized in his famous "separate as the fingers" speech.

DuBois versus Washington

The controversy which ensued between African-Americans and Euro-Americans subdivided and polarized African-American opinion in the United States of America. The issues revolved around the participation of African-Americans as members of the society which had passed three amendments to the constitution of the United States specifically with a view to conferring citizenship on them. With Reconstruction "closed" and systematic disfranchisement of people who had been enfranchised and the ascendancy of the South over the entire nation, there emerged a crisis of confidence in the capacity of the Federal government to protect African-Americans, raising grave doubts as to whether life was possible in the "New South" or even in the whole of the country. The mentality of disfranchisement which pervaded the South had prospects of that mentality affecting the North's perception of African-Americans in their midst. The second issue of contention between Washiongton and DuBois was education. For a while Booker T. Washington, through the influence of his alma mater, Hampton Institute, had extolled "industrial education" exclusively at the expense of higher education of the university kind and making snide remarks about those African-Americans such as DuBois and his associates who had been recipients of such education. These radicals insisted on all forms of education and rejected the limitations being imposed by Mr. Washington on the freedom of choice of individuals and their communities.

Once DuBois went on the attack, he criticized Washington for apologizing for wrongs done to African-Americans by Euro-Americans and blaming the victims of injustice instead of a system which allowed for these excesses. From a reading of the documents, it may reasonably be inferred that the Tuskegeean desired to be pre-eminent and the dominant one to whom others, including DuBois, were subordinated. There might have been an inferiority complex on Washington's part in relation to DuBois, who enjoyed the benefits of higher education and would, periodically, attempt to distort the real issue in their controversy by accusing DuBois and his associates of seeking to become white. It was a red herring thrown in for good measure and he had an array of newspapers which helped to boost up his propaganda against the radicals. But DuBois was too much of a free and independent spirit to be contained for any length of time by anyone—especially Washington—whose views and methods struck DuBois as dictatorial and condescending as well as subservient to white views. Criticism of Washington continued to emanate from the *Boston Guardian*. Appearing at the height of the controversy, early in the century, it was said to be the most critical paper of Washington's regressive methods, tactics, and ideas. The editor of the paper, William Monroe Trotter, accused Washington of having fashioned a political machine with himself as the political boss while pretending to be an educator.[27]

In the early stages of their controversy, DuBois had tried to avoid open controversy with Washington, conscious of the fact that the man wielded immense influence and had the backing of many whites - especially those who had more money to donate to Washington's schemes, enabling him to disburse patronage and influence the employment by the Federal government to certain posts designated as "Negro posts"; or even through inducing employers to dismiss his critics from their employment or denying them opportunities for further advancement, or denying them status in societies and clubs. Many, who later fell afoul of the Tuskegean and his "machine" learned the high price of such criticisms. But DuBois had reached the conviction that silence alone would not resolve the issue and preferred to see issues discussed openly so that people could follow the arguments and the contents of the debates. But Washington was also backed by newspapers; many of the African-American ones had his financial support, even the outstanding *New York Age* of Thomas T. Fortune. Fortune was to learn the bitter lesson of departing from the Washington rank-and- file even after he had sold his *New York Age* to the Tuskegean. Fortune himself never recovered from this breach with the Tuskegean and died a broken man and in tragic circumstances. But all this is hindsight. The DuBoisian approach was cautious at the beginning but later it had become bolder. When he eventually became editor of *The Crisis*, which he edited for the N.A.A.C.P. from 1910, he left no stone unturned in his assault on the Tuskegean; but more about that later.

At the commencement of the twentieth century, DuBois - who had not been opposed to Hampton and Tuskegee, which he had described as "great institutions" began to doubt the wisdom of Washington's pronouncements, activities, and methods. This machine was used by Mr. Washington to browbeat dissident voices into conformity and unquestioning acceptance of his leadership and limited goals. It was used to disburse patronage and deny people opportunities for governmental employment. As a result, only the most courageous could be critical of the views of the Tuskegeean; often, to do so was to court disaster, penury, and unemployment or a diminished status from which one could not ascend. Underhanded methods were employed whereby people found themselves dismissed from their posts without finding out the real reasons for such dismissals. Washington used spies to infiltrate organizations that he felt were hostile to him and which he wished to undermine, as he did with the Niagara Movement (1905-1909) and the National Association for the Advancement of Colored People (1910); or by placing his appointees inside key positions as he did with some of the African-American women's organizations and made sure that those he considered his enemies, like Ida B. Wells-Barnett, were denied the opportunity for office.

When Washington stressed economics as the basis for power and discounted the importance of politics, DuBois, in contrast, (but like Douglass before him), saw politics as the proper vehicle for helping to define rights and remove discriminatory legislation which prevented opportunities in education, employment, and economic enhancement. There were often glaring contradictions in the Tuskegeean's methods, for despite his disavowal of political activity, he was the confidant of Presidents, who periodically and often sought his advice and to whom he sent favorable or unfavorable information about African-Americans to secure or deny them appointments. While pretending openly to eschew politics, his opponents saw through his pretense and the techniques he used as very consistent with the political acts of a political boss. Furthermore, because the leading voices in the white South saw him as a non-believer in the franchise and one who discounted higher education, he often obtained financial grants while many "Negro Colleges and Universities" were starved for funds. Washington denied on several occasions that he was against higher education. [28] But these denials cannot be taken at face value, nor were they believed by his critics.

His often uncomplimentary remarks about recipients and dispensers of higher education[29] to the African-Americans did not inspire confidence in his pretended position on higher education, as his actual emphasis was exclusively vocational. It was also true that as long as the white philanthropists and donors hailed the Tuskegeean as "the Negro leader," his critics were often ignored or explained away as acting out of frustration because they had not attained his exalted status.

Another point of divergence between Washington and his critics was his emphasis on the need to secure the goodwill of the white upper class rather than expecting legislation to raise the status of African-Americans, yet it cannot be gainsaid that legislation to offset existing racial laws could have beneficial effects.

Although DuBois, during this period of confrontation with Washington, has been portrayed by some writers as a "protest leader and propagandist" and his writings described as journalistic rather than scholarly,[30] this viewpoint is a matter of opinion. His first book, originally submitted as a doctoral dissertation, still finds publishers today, almost a century after it first appeared. Other works like some of those mentioned above - *Black Folk Then and Now, Dusk of Dawn,* and *The World and Africa* - are scholarly works and venerated by those scholars whose opinions differ from these prejudiced observers. Yet it is a sad commentary on American society that a man so well schooled, a university graduate with a doctorate from one of the best and brightest of American institutions of higher learning, (Harvard), could not find acceptance to work in any of America's best institutions of learning; that in those early days he had to exercise leadership in the only sphere left open to him and which he had to cultivate in order to combat injustice and the handicaps inflicted on African-Americans. In such a struggle a drowning person must tread even sliding stones in order to obtain momentary footing. It is a credit to his tenacity, resilience, and determination as well as perception and perspicacity that he remained standing in the struggle. In the circumstances of those times, no one could have done better. Nevertheless, his views were given prominence in many magazines, journals, and newspapers; among them were the *Atlantic Monthly* (which still publishes today), the *Independent*, and the *World's Work*; and they were views that could not be ignored, as they touched on the state of society and the plight of suffering African-Americans, despite all the techniques, tactics, propaganda, trickery, and vilification which Washington and his supporters, both black and white, employed to undermine DuBois' criticisms, advocacies, and organizational efforts.

Divergences and Convergences

The views of DuBois and Washington, [31] as those of Douglass and Washington, [32] have been contrasted by various writers. DuBois (and Douglass by his earlier advocacies) both disapproved of the way Washington appropriated and monopolized funds for African-American education from philanthropists who preferred Washington's version of education. African-American Colleges and Universities who saw the value of higher education as DuBois perceived it were ignored financially. DuBois and Washington also differed on the suffrage, with DuBois, like Douglass before him, seeing the necessity for its being conceded immediately in order to protect the civil rights of African-Americans, while Washington's public posture was that voting rights were not the most important issue, thus giving the impression that he was against it. Yet, his private posture revealed him to be a gradualist as far as the suffrage was concerned. His stances, whether public or private, generated much controversy, criticism, opposition, and vitriol from his adversaries, most notable among them being William Monroe Trotter, founder and owner of the *Boston Guardian*, and seen as leader of the "radicals." Among these radicals were graduates from colleges and universities throughout New England. A study of Monroe Trotter through the pages of the *Boston Guardian* is sorely needed.

Washington's pronouncements and methods (including intimidation, abuse, and accusations of those who disagreed with him, as well as his so-called "diplomacy", and covert hostilities towards those

African-Americans who did not share his views) were repeatedly censured. Once DuBois had published his *Souls of Black Folk* in 1903 (one of the chapters of which was titled "Of Mr. Booker T. Washington and Others") it was clear that the cleavage between the opposing viewpoints was complete.

Yet from the white press in the same period, noxious material was spewing forth which characterized the "Negro as Beast"[33] and projected the most appalling consequences for American society if the pandora's box of integration were opened. What is even more interesting is that the book which carried this image of the African-Americans was published by a religious publishing house. The proponents of this idea of the Negro as beast employed the exaggerated picture of "Negro" sexuality to alarm the white population into directing their energies, ire, and viciousness towards subjugating black Americans and to justify the brutalities meted out to African-Americans. African-Americans saw their hope for integration and equity evaporating by default, due to the intensity of the vicious propaganda unleashed against them. Integration was interpreted in some white circles as the quest of licentiousness, as a license to cohabit with white women - a distortion that aroused passions well orchestrated by the forces of chicanery and skulduggery.

There were times in this long saga when DuBois, despairing of obtaining opportunities for education for African-Americans, urged them to create their own social services, unions, and industrial enterprises under their own direction, for he had come to feel that under existing situations the education advocated and fostered on them by Euro-American society was more an instrument of their own exploitation than a channel for social mobility and race advancement. There were also times when he felt that their patience and perseverance would earn African-Americans the cooperation of whites-believing that it was ignorance that produced a negative and hostile white attitude to their education. At other times, DuBois was not so sanguine about patience and calm in order to persuade a hostile white society to approve of meaningful schemes and educational integration for both races.

The many "Atlanta Studies" on "Negro Problems" DuBois undertook and supervised (in order that sufficient information would accrue for the social enhancement of the blacks) belongs to this period from just before the end of the nineteenth century to the first decade of the twentieth. Numerous problems occupied him in this period and a later generation marvels at the tremendous energy he expended on such social betterment, the *Negro Artisan* the *Negro Church* and many more. It was a period when his earlier jaundiced views of Africa as a "cultural vacuum" were undergoing radical modification and assuming a more favorable outlook, a far cry from his erstwhile expression of the "primitive." [34]

The persistence of lynchings in the South and Midwest compelled DuBois' continuation of protest activity. He had, in 1897, joined with other African-Americas of the "Talented Tenth" to found the American Negro Academy. It was a time in which he implicitly believed in the value of ideas and information in enlightening the ignorance of the whites and society at large for the purpose of achieving his objectives of civil rights and racial harmony. It was his doubts about the efficacy of intellect alone that led him, with other African-American intellectuals, to form the Niagara Movement between 1905 and 1906. At the inception of this movement, Mr. Washington's power was at its apogee. Ironically, it was only the failure to achieve a rapprochement between the supporters of Washington and DuBoisian viewpoints concerning status and the unification of forces against their white adversaries and detractors that propelled them into the formation of the Niagara Movement.

THE NIAGARA MOVEMENT AND ITS DETRACTORS

There are many accounts of the formation of the Niagara Movement.[35] The venue of the meeting of July 1905, Fort Erie, Ontario, with its vista of Niagara Falls, provided the movement with its name. DuBois, as one of the principal founders of the movement, had also given some account of it in his *Dusk of Dawn*,[36] so that these details should not further trouble the work. It is essential now to consider some of its principles declared at the time of its founding and how it exacerbated the crises of the African-American leadership in the succeeding years. These declaration of principles issued forth in the form of demands, as follows:

1) Freedom of Speech and criticism
2) An unfettered and unsubsidized press
3) Manhood suffrage
4) The abolition of all caste distinctions based simply on race and color
5) The recognition of the principles of human brotherhood as a practical present creed
6) Recognition of the highest and best human training as a monopoly of no class or race
7) A belief in the dignity of labor
8) United efforts to realize these ideals under wise and courageous leadership[37]

From the last declaration, leadership continued to be a serious preoccupation in shaping the destiny of the Africans of the Diaspora in the Americas.

The Niagara Movement founders (here-in-after the Niagarans) were not without their critics, some of whom denied that racial prejudice was in the ascendant and rejected the anti-segregationist stance of the Niagarans. Yet race relations were still at their "nadir" as far as ordinary African-Americans were concerned, as the following representative incidents will illustrate: violence against blacks and race riots punctuated the cities such as the Atlanta race riots (1906) and the Springfield race riots (1908) and these continued even after the return of African-American soldiers from the First World War. It was unrealistic to deny that racial prejudices and injustices were increasing in the face of the evidence that is now ubiquitous. Either those who denied them were supporters of Booker T. Washington seeking to confound and discredit the Niagarans as "agitators and troublemakers" or they were blinkered. The positions of Booker T. Washington and DuBois and Trotter, on the other hand, were too entrenched and irreconcilable despite the many tactics and threats made to achieve compliance and conformity with Washington's perspectives in what was being touted as "reconciliation." For Washington it was all or nothing; either they capitulated to his wishes and dictates or faced the consequences. That was hardly an inducement for reconciliation to people of such considerable intellectual stature, convictions and dignity.

But the detractors of the Niagarans were soon at work to attempt to discredit them. They were featured in certain publications as not inclined to accept "race integrity" because of their disinclination to accept the separate or segregated status for the blacks and, by implication, were said to be opting for inferiority. They were therefore not considered the "real leaders" of African-Americans, that distinction being reserved for Booker T. Washington.[38] Yet the *Chicago Law Register* almost restated the sentiments of Frederick Douglass a generation earlier that human rights were never achieved without aggressive protest. [39]

The proclamation of principles by the Niagarans was good as it stood but the movement had no headquarters and no organizational officials who acted as a clearinghouse for information. DuBois' implicit faith in the "Talented Tenth" of the black race conditioned the formation of the movement, which was still remote from the masses of African-Americans or their aspirations. It was this belief in "the leadership of the best" (and for this, read intellectual and elitist) elements of his race that accounts for his ineffectiveness against the mass movement of the Jamaican, Marcus Garvey, about a decade and a half later.

Washington's emphasis on economic enhancement for African-Americans failed to take cognizance of the fact that political power for his brethren and help to enhance this by his emphasis on industrial education was seen by DuBois to be linked with the enhancement of the southern economy at the expense of African-Americans who were relegated to the bottom of the pile. This was a serious point of departure between both leaders of the African-Americans. An essential element in their inability to cooperate, apart from these divergences of viewpoints, lay, as one author has suggested, in their respective "personalities." [40] Although many whites continued to visualize Mr. Washington as the only interpreter of African-American aspirations and life, yet the emergence of the Niagara Movement presented them with a determined opposing viewpoint and, although they might choose to ignore DuBois, yet he and his views and those of his associates could not be wished away, despite the heavy-handedness of the "Tuskegee Machine" and despite Booker T. Washington's secret endeavors to undermine Niagara. [41]

The controversies which arose in both the black and the white press show how the cleavage between both tendencies and leadership became more pronounced. But the Niagara Movement was handicapped by a lack of finance to conduct its campaigns. Money still "talked" and southern and northern white philanthropists, among whom were Andrew Carnegie and Nathaniel Peabody, continued to support the Tuskegeean. Even some of the men with whom DuBois was to be associated in the founding of the National Association for the Advancement of Colored Peoples in 1910, such as Oswald Garrison Villiard and others, who were themselves admirers of Mr. Washington and, periodically, during those years of conflict with the Tuskagean, were concerned that DuBois not say or do anything that would incense the Tuskegeean lest some of the sources of N.A.A.C.P. funding dry up. Such fears showed how powerful the "Tuskegee Machine" had become that it compelled even white "liberals" to continue to look over their shoulders to ensure that they were not being undermined. It was an incredible situation which must surprise a contemporary observer and showed how the dead hand of Booker T. Washington tainted everything he touched. Yet, despite this attempt by some of the white "liberals" to please both camps, in the long term Washington perceived them as his adversaries.

The Niagara Movement was a natural response as a counterweight to the Tuskegeean's monopoly of "Negro" opinion. That monopoly, while it satisfied Mr. Washington's white financial backers, inhibited

African-American efforts to secure higher education because of Washington's determination to circumscribe them within the rigid walls of "industrial education" and by the virtue of the fact the he strove to dampen enthusiasm for the ballot, thus preventing African-Americans from having a voice in the affairs of the nation. They were unable to accept disfranchisement after the three amendments to the constitution guaranteeing them this had been in existence for some time. It was not just sheer frustration, contrary to the views of some writers, [42] but the need to see integration implemented and in place that drove them on. They were also actuated by the conviction that they were entitled to their civil rights, which were being denied them by manipulatory and dilatory tactics, by intimidation, by references to misguided and false theories of race, by subterfuge (such as the so-called "grandfather clause" and many others) and which sometimes hid behind a mild-mannered man in the person of Mr. Washington to frustrate these aspirations by his portrayal as the only authentic voice among African-Americans.

By the time the Niagara Movement was officially disbanded it had organized and sponsored five annual conferences between 1909 and 1910. Booker T. Washington was invited but did not attend (and it would have been surprising if he had been willing to see the initiative wrenched from him and judging from the man's character he could not have participated in such a movement in which he was not the controller and leader). The initial assembly, in July of 1905, had focused its attention on a number of issues and the committees it constituted are revealing. It established the following committees: Finance, Interstate Conditions and Needs, Organization, Civil and Political Rights, Legal Defence, Crime, Rescue and Reform, Economic Opportunity, Health, Education, Press and Public Opinion. Its major weakness at the end of the period of its existence could be seen to be principally, apart from financial resources, its elitist orientation and failure to harness the support of the masses of the African Diaspora. It was a movement of the elite, by the elite, for the elite, based on its assumption that its own preoccupations were in fact those of the mass of African-Americans. Its emergence sharpened the polarization of African-American camps, the Washingtonians and the DuBoisian.

From its inception, Booker T. Washington conspired to destroy the Niagra Movement, and even made suggestions that some of its adherents should be caused to lose their employment. Such high-handed tactics showed how the "Tuskegee Machine" had overgrown itself and was doing things which, if practiced in the open, would be treated as breaches of the law and infringements on the rights of citizens. Washington sent out agents to spy and report on the movement and its proceedings. He had many agents, some of them prominent African-Americans who, were willing to play the role of "Uncle Toms." The activities of Mr. Washington's spies inside the Niagara movement have already been discussed elsewhere[43] and so will not detain us here. The proceedings he encouraged and directed were sickening and insidious to say the least. One of his spies, Charles W. Anderson, who spied at the conference in order to report back to Mr. Washington, remarked that when at the conference those who were loyal to Niagara were asked to stand up, "practically, all who stood were either women or boys!"[44] It would seem from this report that he, as well as his initiator and mentor, Mr. Washington, had no regard for women and obviously did not take them seriously. A case could be made out that even the "women and boys" so disparaged by the Washingtonians were wiser than the "old fools" in the Washingtonian rank-and-file and that they showed a better understanding of what was at stake than their detractors and were clearer on the principles at stake. By his pusillanimous and covert activities, it was obvious that Washington feared the influence of the Niagara Movement.

The Niagara Movement had been preceded by the founding of an organization by white people known as the Constitution League in 1904 at the inspiration of John Milholland. The Constitution League and the Niagarans, an all-black organization, had identity of views on many subjects and especially those dealing with the enfranchisement of African-Americans and others. They both were in favor of the Platt Bill, which was to reduce Congressional representation for states which disfranchised African-Americans. Booker T. Washington, an opponent of the Bill, saw the possibility of a uniting of forces between the Constitution League and the Niagara Movement and was determined to prevent this. Washington emphasized that the southerners would be prepared to surrender Congressional seats rather than concede the vote to blacks.[45] Even from that expression of sentiment, it is difficult to reach any other conclusion than that he himself could not be in favor of the vote despite the assertion of later writers that privately he believed in the suffrage. If his public policy and pronouncements portrayed him otherwise, it must have been a kind of strategy which did not enhance the political, social, and economic status of the people he claimed to lead. But the hoped-for unity between the Constitution League and the Niagara Movement did not occur; there probably were some finer points of operation which made this impossible even if it did not inhibit their cooperation. The Constitution League believed that a grassroots movement of African-Americans could influence Congress. The Niagara Movement published a paper known as the *Voice of the*

Negro and its publication mirrored its admiration for the Constitution League. This certainly struck terror into the Washingtonians who, at the instigation of their leader, were bent on preventing either a merger or cooperation between the two organizations. They also saw another possibility in such a combination. New England had its own Boston Suffrage League under the leadership of the other radical and ardent critic of Washington, William Monroe Trotter. Both the Boston League and Niagara were black organizations while the Constitution League was a white one. A fusion of these three organizations would have proved an unbeatable combination against the Washingtonians. However, the fusion was not favored by some and even DuBois seemed ambivalent. The failure to come together organizationally, however, did not prevent them from working together, and universal suffrage was still their principal preoccupation, and this identity of principle paved the way years later for the emergence of the N.A.A.C.P.

The Niagara Movement was, in fact, the precursor of the N.A.A.C.P. in fighting cases through the Courts in order to undermine racist laws and seek their abrogation. In 1907, the Niagara Movement sponsored a (test case) involving a Miss Barbara Pope, who was fined for refusing to enter a "Jim Crow" car when the train on which she was traveling crossed the state line into Virginia. They were successful in appealing her case but were saddled by debt approximating $240.[46] The case was also reported in a monthly magazine, the *Horizon*, which DuBois and two associates, F. H. M. Murray and L. M. Hershaw, founded in order to air the views of the Niagara Movement.[47] But the movement kept its perspective clear on civil rights and violence against blacks and the suffrage issue continued to be agitated. Its limited financial resources limited its ability to act in many of the cases that came to its attention. It was also struggling against the tide of congressional refusal or reluctance to see to the enforcement of the Fourteenth and Fifteenth Amendments to the Constitution.[48]

Nothing came of the suggestions that the Niagara Movement should align its forces with Socialists and the working class in order to broaden its mass base.[49] DuBois is said to have been favorable to the idea because at the time he had begun to regard himself as a "Socialist of the Path."[50] Yet he remained somewhat skeptical because he was aware of the fact that white workers and white socialists discriminated against blacks. But what confounded and compounded the problems of the Niagara Movement and in time was to hasten its demise was the ascendancy of internal dissension and conflict. Not disregarding the tendencies from Washington's agents to infiltrate and undermine the movement, it is not clear at this point how much of this infiltration or wooing from the Tuskegeean quarter contributed to the increase of these internal dissensions which were ultimately to result in the movement's demise. It was able to hold its fifth conference in August 1909, but it was already on its last legs by 1908, torn asunder by internal dissension and external buffeting.

The demise of the Niagara Movement also coincided with a time when African-Americans, who had always voted for the Party of Lincoln, the Republican Party, were becoming increasingly disenchanted with it due to the lack of progress in their status; yet they hardly found the alternative, the Democratic Party, deserving of their votes. At the time of the 1908 election between Bryan, a Southern Democrat and racist and Republican William Taft (more favorable to many African-Americans), DuBois (unsuccessfully) tried to persuade them to vote for Bryan, but was opposed by the Niagarans and Washington. Taft in the end won the election but this did not enhance either DuBois' judgment or prestige. Internal wrangling and external barraging put the ultimate sledge hammer on the movement, so while the Niagara Movement fizzled out the N.A.A.C.P. rose from its ashes. Efforts to sustain the *Horizon* did not succeed and by 1910 it too had gone out of existence.The new organization, the N.A.A.C.P., was to become the premier movement for the pursuit of the principles advocated by the Niagarans, many of whom in cooperation with "liberal whites" came together to form the new organization.

Reflections on Niagara

Despite its demise, a movement like Niagara was not just a flash in the pan. It arose in its own milieu by the circumstances which dogged the aspirations of Africans of the diaspora in a hostile social milieu in the United States. Nonetheless, it was a pioneer and trail blazer and its contributions to the issue of higher education for blacks did much for legal redress; it also tried to organize a political lobby consisting of "informed, independent and articulate citizens." [51] By their protest activities they provided the alternative to Booker T. Washington's accommodation policy and by subscribing to similar causes produced blueprints that were to guide African-Americans and the inheritors of the mantle in the N.A.A.C.P. For the new organization was to profit from the experience of the pioneer Niagara Movement and organize their tactics and their pursuit of civil rights through the Courts of the United States, winning some spectacular successes in those endeavors.

EVALUATION OF NIAGARA

As the first national organization of African-Americans which insistently and unreservedly demanded the same civil rights for their people which other Americans enjoyed, the Niagara Movement merits some evaluation. Elliot Rudwick[52] has made this pertinent assessment which mirrors success in terms of legacies or what it bequeathed to a later generation and also in terms of failure largely resulting from the circumstances of the time and those internal and external to the movement.

In terms of success, the Niagarans had helped to educate their brethren to a policy of protest and generated some awareness among whites that there were "colored men" dissatisfied with the prevailing pattern of race relations. Secondly, they had hewn a path for the younger people to follow and helped to lay the foundations for the emergence of the N.A.A.C.P. Despite these, a number of factors contributed to its failure. First, its program was a radical advancement for the era in which Mr. Washington had been designated leader by ruling circles. Second, Washington's devious and obstructive tactics as operated through the "Tuskegee Machine" took their toll with the subterfuges and importuning as well as employment inducements for support and denials for non-support all had ways of securing compliance for the faint-hearted, some would say "realists" but the inducement of money also had its own pull on those who might have been tempted to take an opposition posture, against this, the Niagarans were impecunious.

A third weakness of the movement was that it lacked any mass support; in fact, it was isolated from the masses, but this was based on the perception of the Niagarans as to the inferiority of the unlettered masses. Being filled with their own exalted intellectual achievements and social prestige made any approach on their part extremely difficult. They were, in fact, a minuscule minority of a minority. Fourth, their perception of human rights was not easily translatable to the mass of their people and nothing they said reached the masses to galvanize them into action. Fifth, in making the ballot their paramount concern seemingly neglected the economic dimension, both of which were vital to the elevation of the masses. The Niagarans apparently hoped that the ballot would facilitate the passing of measures to enhance the economic opportunities and status of African-Americans. Sixth, DuBois was said to be aloof and "aristocratic in outlook" and, by contrast, lacked Washington's diplomacy, political acumen, and tactics. He never fully realized the role of social action in a leader. He was an intellectual who sought to drive home some essential ideas, leaving it to the practitioners to effect the changes or implement the suggested policy. Seventh, despite his assumptions about the "Talented Tenth," they were not the leaders. Eighth, the organization was further weakened by internal idiosyncracies such as "individualism" and "egotism" of the kind attributed to members such as William Monroe Trotter. With his choleric temperament and combative tendencies, many internal conflicts were generated and evoked external hostilities from their opportunistic opponents.

The N.A.A.C.P. and Leadership

The formation of the National Association for the Advancement of Colored People was not without controversy, both internally and externally, for here was an interracial organization which sought to champion the rights of blacks in an era when some black leaders like the Tuskegeeans had accepted rigid segregation. While some of the whites had their reservations on how far they might go in championing the "Negro" cause, there were ardent believers in interracial linkages and coexistence. Nevertheless, although much of the funds for the functioning of the organization came from the whites, blacks were still suspicious of their motives because the entire Board of Management was controlled by whites.[53] DuBois was the only black person on that Board. DuBois was made Director of Research and Publications for the mouthpiece of the organization, The *Crisis*, which he edited. He demanded and was given a free hand in the operation of the journal and many of the ideas in the editorials corresponded to his own. His arguments with those who supplied the funds are not relevant to this work. It is sufficient that the members of the organization were agreed that theirs, like Niagara, was a civil rights movement and seriously preoccupied with the enfranchisement of blacks and the securing of their full citizenship rights. Some of the white members were admirers of Mr. Washington and sometimes, this brought them into conflict with DuBois whenever they felt that DuBois had overreached himself in attacking Mr. Washington. This divergence of views in terms of tactics came quite early in their relations but were never fully resolved. There were times when they persuaded DuBois that he should not attack the Tuskegeean, but it was not possible to restrain DuBois when he felt that principle was at stake. Some of the whites favored his attacks while those like Oswald Villiard Garrison did not, conscious of Mr. Washington's power machine and his manipulatory abilities and tactics which could deprive the N.A.A.C.P. of the support of white members either materially or morally.

Integration as conceived for those times included assimilation although in time this was to be modified to mean coexistence without its being total assimilation of African-Americans by Euro-Americans. Since Washington's views on integration were contrary to the views of the new organization, conflict was bound to arise. DuBois was to insist that he had no intention of attacking Mr. Washington and wished to praise him for good work but also to criticize him for any failures which were harmful to the cause of blacks.[54]

From its inception, the N.A.A.C.P. had chosen the path of caution in the hope of placating Mr. Washington and so attracting financial support from whites, and especially, those favorable to the Tuskegeean, such as Andrew Carnegie. Accordingly, in constituting the steering committee, those regarded as "extremist" (such as Trotter and Ida B. Wells-Barnett) were excluded, while middle-roaders like Mary Church Terrell and Leslie Pickney Hill were included. Later Wells-Barnett was also coopted. All these mirrored the sensibilities which dogged the movement at its inception, during the lifetime of Mr. Washington, and during its long existence.

Some gleanings from one of the earliest editorials in *The Crisis* would reveal why the struggles against the Tuskegeean's rejection of the ballot would cause much controversy as the years progressed. DuBois said of the N.A.A.C.P. that it "is a union of those who believe that earnest, active opposition is the only effective way of meeting the forces of evil.... They believe that the growth of race prejudice in the United States is evil. It is not always consciously evil. Much of it is born of ignorance and misapprehension, honest mistake and misguided zeal.... For this reason it must be combated. It is neither safe nor sane to sit down dumbly before such human error or to seek to combat it with smiles and hushed whispers."[55] Such images were oblique references to Mr. Washington, who outwardly cowtowed to the whites ("smiles") while expressing privately views in favor of the ballot ("hushed whispers"). Washington for his part did not see the organizers of the N.A.A.C.P. as his friends no matter their professions of friendship. Besides, the presence of DuBois in the organization gave Washington all the excuse he needed for distancing himself from it.

The N.A.A.C.P. first emerged as the National Negro Committee, founded on the initiative of influential and articulate whites namely, Oswald Garrison Villiard (grandson of the great abolitionist William Lloyd Garrison), Lilian Wald, Jane Addams, John Milholland, Mary White Ovington, William Walling, Arthur and Joel Spingarn, and approved by stalwarts of the Niagara Movement, DuBois, J. Max Barber, J. Milton Waldron, and L. M. Hershaw. The foundations of this organization were laid both by the earlier organizations like the Constitution League led by Milholland, the Niagara Movement and Monroe Trotter's civil rights organization in Boston.

It is not the task of this writer to tell the story of the N.A.A.C.P., for more competent hands and some of its founders have already done so. Our consideration of it is related to how Africans of the Diaspora used their leadership position to fight for one or other of the competing alternatives which they saw in terms of their destiny in American society -integration (with or without assimilation) which confined their activities to the United States and elevation within it, or emigration and separate identity.

Since the N.A.A.C.P. was concerned with the first of these goals, its energies were directed towards securing this through legal test cases and court pronouncements, despite detractors both north and south who continued to advocate from a racist standpoint the segregation of whites from blacks with all the implications in residence, occupation, employment opportunities and even in terms of health and other social matters. Such views were sometimes shared by white "liberals" both north and south. In its long life the N.A.A.C.P. has had some notable successes, often the successes were not followed with implementation but the successes constituted landmarks which were to galvanize and inspire further endeavors and hopefully success.

Despite his editorship of *The Crisis* and the management of its publication and circulation, DuBois never lost sight of the fact of the need to forge a leadership among African-Americans. While observing that the "Souls of White Folk" were "filled with hatred for black folk," he wrote that instead of being led and defended by others, as in the past, "the [Negroes] are gaining their own voices, their own ideals."[56] From the flow of DuBois' thoughts, it was clear, not only that leadership remained a major preoccupation at the end of the second decade of the twentieth century, but that he still perceived this leadership to be that of the "Talented Tenth."

With the death of Booker T. Washington in 1915, DuBois' leadership, which had become manifest by the end of the nineteenth century, came into its own. A few years later he met his match in one of the most formidable of propagandists - Marcus Garvey.

The Crisis Journal

DuBois' management of *The Crisis* journal in its earlier years manifested some qualities of leadership which merit some comment. In terms of organizing the paper, editing it, securing its wider circulation and subscription, and getting many African-Americans to be its subscribers, all these reflected credit on him. True, when the recession of 1929/30 descended on the world, the circulation fell as people were preoccupied with bread and butter issues to survive.

The first issue of *Crisis* appeared in November 1910, after DuBois transferred from Atlanta University to take up his new responsibilities. The journal was a monthly. It began with a circulation of a thousand and in less than one year it had reached a circulation of 16,000 and by 1913 the circulation was 30,000 and three quarters of its subscribers were African-Americans. As a result DuBois was able to exercise his independence in the handling of the *Crisis* journal, principally because he did not insist on having his way on the Board of Management. Two issues on which DuBois remained uncompromising were the vote and higher education. However, he sometimes faltered on segregation, at times rejecting it and, other times advocating and approving it. His advocacy of it was that it was a temporary expedient in order that the blacks might build power and excellence and thus provide the race with the leverage to achieve ultimate integration. While advocating this for a constituency which resisted the limiting of educational possibilities for African-Americans, he echoed their sentiments in a manner which irritated their detractors, even if they were racists and sought to limit opportunities. The *Crisis* was to experience hard times with the coming of the great depression of the 1930s but it continued to publish even after DuBois took leave of absence and returned to teach at Atlanta University, by which time he was already sixty-five years of age; but he made his final departure from the N.A.A.C.P. in 1939 and in the same year at Atlanta University he founded another journal, *Phylon*. His departure from the N.A.A.C.P. was not without controversy, for the period from Booker T. Washington's death to DuBois' departure was dogged by controversy within the N.A.A.C.P. itself.

DuBois up to 1920

In exercising his leadership at the commencement of the First World War, DuBois' plan was that the nation should close ranks and that African-Americans make the sacrifice for the United States' war efforts in order to demonstrate that they would make the supreme sacrifice for their citizenship rights. His acceptance of segregated regiments for blacks all seemed contrary to his earlier views on integration and exposed him to much censure and ridicule from the blacks and some whites. But he saw the sacrifice as one that would present the case starkly for their integration into American society as citizens. The frustrated hopes which resulted in the post-world war situation, with African-American soldiers returning home with distinction after their heroism on the war front to be confronted with racial violence, murders, and lynchings, all these subjected DuBois to ridicule for his advocacies in the war period. It turned out to be a very lonely period for him, but while his views on issues raised doubts in certain quarters, especially from the radical printers of the paper *The Messenger*, nonetheless DuBois held his ground and expressed ideas which, at the time, appeared to him appropriate. By 1920 integration had suffered a severe setback and the idea itself was to come into conflict with a resurgence of the emigrationist idea that emerged with the Afro-Jamaican, Marcus Mosiah Garvey, and his establishment of the Universal Negro Improvement Association (U.N.I.A.), headquartered in New York. The issues of these conflicting perspectives belong to another period in visualizing the evolution of leadership in the African diaspora in the Americas. But by the close of the year 1920, African-Americans supported one or another of three alternative views - integration, emigration, or separate identity. The latter two seemed consistent with nationalism, the former outside the United States and more prominently in Africa, and the other within the United States with advocates for territory acquired for the purpose. These ideas had periodically surfaced among African-Americans during the nineteenth century while the major clamor was for integration, but the same ideas were also to re-emerge in the politico-religious movements of the early twentieth century known in our day as the "Nation of Islam."

While Garvey's movement was the greatest mammoth emigration movement ever to emerge and galvanized the mass of African-Americans with branches in several parts of the country, the migrationist idea never completely vanished from the contemplations of some Africans-Americans. In fact, prior to 1920 and Garvey's organization, another African in the Diaspora with the name of Chief Alfred Sam had raised enthusiasm for emigration and even organized a trip to the coast of West Africa in 1916, but nothing came of the endeavor. Even earlier, at the end of Douglass' life, the fervor for emigration was as undiminished as the advocacy of those who preferred integration. But the most vocal were those locked in combat for citizenship rights in the United States, the Washingtonians and the DuBoisians. The voices of the migrationists led by Delany and Bishop Turner were not stilled, but reconciliation between the conflicting views remained elusive.

Booker T. Washington's accommodation postures had fuelled the conflict, but with Washington's departure from the stage and the death of Bishop Turner in the same year, 1916 proved an opportune moment for new experiments and the discarding of old antagonisms. For the African-American elite it resulted in the Amenia Conference at Troutbeck in 1916 resulting in a reconciliation of the Washingtonians and DuBoisians in the African-American rank-and - file. The principles on which they proclaimed themselves in general agreement formed the basis of their tactics for the future. [57] The N.A.A.C.P. was to pursue its own efforts through the courts and by lobbying Congress to remove all handicaps that were preventing African-Americans from becoming full citizens of the United States. The year 1916 was also important as the year of Garvey's founding of his own U.N.I.A. and his arrival in the United States hoping to meet Booker T. Washington, without realizing the Tuskegeean had died the previous year. Since Garvey claimed to have been influenced by reading Mr. Washington's *Up From Slavery* (though not the only influence, as he had worked in London at the office of the Nubian-Egyptian Duse Mohammed Ali, who published the *African Times and Orient Review* and later settled in Nigeria to produce a paper known as the *Comet* in Lagos until the latter's death in 1944 at the age of eighty. It would be interesting to speculate on what Garvey would have thought of Washington as an "accomodationist," especially as Washington discouraged any kind of emigration, whether internal within the U.S.A. or external to Africa or anywhere else. Yet, Garvey was to become the greatest propagandist, popularizer, and organizer for emigration away from the United States. It appears that Garvey, like Thomas Fortune before him, would have embraced the Tuskegeean for his program of education for the masses but despised him for his accomodationist and subservient stances. Garvey might also have crossed swords with him had they ever met, as Fortune later found to his cost; for, although Washington and Fortune admired each other and Fortune approved of many good things that Washington did, yet he was not equivocal on the question of the vote for African-Americans. Washington used Fortune while it suited Washington but once he had no further use for the man, he came down heavily against what he must have considered Fortune's antics. In the end Fortune lost to a wily politician who in his public pronouncements eschewed politics and discouraged his people's participation in it. Yet, he was the organizer of one of the most vicious political machines ranged against a people who only sought their basic human rights in a society that was hostile. Garvey might indeed, in fact, have found himself embattled with Mr. Washington had they every met, but this must remain in the realm of conjecture.

But by the time DuBois was buckling down to exercise his leadership, which had already been evident since he took head-on the confrontation with Mr. Washington at the beginning of the century and from 1903, a new generation was coming to the fore that seemed anxious to exercise leadership as well or contend with the older generation of leaders. This generation was already beginning to perceive the earlier leaders as old fashioned. DuBois experienced challenges from the mammoth mass movement of Marcus Garvey and from those who generated the artistic activity of the 1920s which came to be known as "The Harlem Renaissance," The latter, while acknowledging DuBois as among the pioneer leaders, used the foibles of youth to see whether their own alternative approach to the race problems in the United States could arrive at better results than their predecessors. [58] They were to be disillusioned, as they thought they could achieve stature without the burden of politics and political action. But their endeavors belong to a later period in this evolution of leadership, which will be examined in another text. But this new generation, some of them newly graduated from college and university, were given a chance to see how they would deal with issues when Joel Spingarn called into being another Amenia Conference at which the older generation leaders agreed to take a back seat and see what the youth were capable of. [59] But these were mere dress rehearsals for the time when the issues of integration, civil rights, and alternative nationalisms would agitate the minds of a later generation of leaders in the 1950s and 1960s, and once again bring them to the fore of discussion by mass leaders, whose actions (with or without their compatriot Euro-Americans) would galvanize the United States into frenzied activities. But these fall well outside the scope of this work.

So, in 1920, when Garvey's African emigration scheme was very much alive and had awakened a hitherto silent African-American mass into action, marches, and further organization, the means of seeing their dreams realized in another land - Africa, the land of their forebears - were stalled for many reasons: not least, the hostilities they generated from the civil authorities within the U.S.A.; but also the European colonial powers who then dominated Africa. But there was also the hostility of the "Talented Tenth" (though not all of them), led by DuBois, who clearly saw a challenge to his leadership in Garvey and seemed overwhelmed by Garvey's capacity and genius for organization. Other factors that beset the Garvey movement might be attributed to inexperience, but there was also the infiltration of enemies into their rank-and-file, as had happened to organizations in which DuBois was involved when the Tuskegeean sent his men to spy and report on the activities of both the Niagara Movement and the N.A.A.C.P. These infiltrations by adversaries also wreaked havoc on the management of the U.N.I.A.'s affairs and finances and also reported back to its enemies. But the major point in apparent failure, because failure is a matter of opinion and perception, considered in the short and long terms, is the failure by Europeans and Euro-Americans to support or uphold what was in essence Garvey's own "Zionist movement" in an era in which the Jewish Zionist movement was being supported through the "Balfour Declarations." [60] It is a factor to be taken into account in comparing the two movements, that the one movement was supported and the other opposed. It will require deep and extensive studies to unravel the reasons why one was staunchly supported while the other was opposed with ridicule and much hostility. It is a good point at which to take our leave of the crises of leadership objectives and proceed to examine the African diaspora's ambivalence to Africa prior to 1920. Before we embark on this subject, however, it is well to make passing mention of another kind of leadership among African-Americans which has not received much mention in this work. It is less well studied and needs to be studied more. It concerns the leadership of African-Americans who joined their Euro-Americans associates in socialist movements of one kind or another.

One striking feature of U.S. society was the exclusion for a long time of African-Americans from white controlled and dominated labor or working class unions. [61] Blacks, in due course, formed theirs and still for a considerable time such affiliation was not possible, mainly due to the racism of the white unions. This need not detain us here. Many tracts and works on these experiences abound. [62] But in the second half of the nineteenth century there were socialists like the African-American Marxist and Reverend gentleman, George Washington Woodbey. Some of his thoughts were developed and written down before the those of the Soviet Leader Vladimir Illiach Lenin, and some of the ideas which were sometimes credited to Lenin had been evolved by the Rev. George Washington Woodbey. His works are not easy to find today and one would be grateful for sources. It remains curious that during this period of DuBois' own publications and numerous writings, not once did he mention George Washington Woodbey. Such an omission cannot be treated as amnesia and must, at this point, appear as a deliberate omission. For at some point in DuBois' career, when he regarded himself as a "Socialist of the Path," he must have encountered the Rev. Woodbey, who was also very active just as DuBois was beginning his activities with the American Negro Academy. Woodbey was, in fact, a remarkable orator and a man who drew large crowds, sometimes was harassed by the police, and sometimes imprisoned, but remained an ardent spokesman for the socialist cause. A study of Woodbey's career might help to shed light on why many African-Americans later recoiled from socialism and from their association with communism. It is also revealing that at a time when many African-Americans were recoiling from socialism, the veteran DuBois, in the evening of his life, publicly announced his joining of the Communist Party. This step was more an act of defiance of the society which had denied him so many opportunities and which had arraigned him for "un-American" activities in the Marcathyite era, and induced him in the end to spend his last days in Africa until his death in 1963, on the eve of the Great Civil Rights March on Washington.

The leadership of those Africans who were associated with the socialist movement did not become prominent, except those of people like A. Philip Randolph and Chandler Owens. They still belonged to the "Talented Tenth" whether by origin, adoption, or inclination. We need to know more of this kind of leadership, especially as being submerged within movements that were dominated by whites, they did not become household names like those of some members of the "Talented Tenth" and mass leaders like Marcus Garvey, or (at a later time, in a later generation) like Malcolm X (Al Hajj Shebaz Al Malik) and the Rev. Martin Luther King, Jr. We must now turn our attention to the tradition of acceptance and rejection of Africa by African-Americans, which was also a tradition of ambivalence towards Africa.

NOTES

1. Ansell Hart, Jr., *The Life of George William Gordon*, Kingston, Ja., Institute of Jamaica, 1972.
2. The term here does not coincide with its usage in the U.S.A. where it was synonymous with Negro. In Jamaica and the West Indies it relates to pigmentation that is differentiated from Negro. It was employed for other studies of color excluding white that could be described as `yellow', `brown', `red', or even `quadroon' and many more.
3. For the background to these developments see Eric Williams, *From Columbus to Castro*, Chs. 26 & 27 and especially pp. 461, 471-75; also p. 554 for his list of the series of reports on various colonies during the 1930s. For a specific example of one South American territory see Abdias Do Nascimiento, Brazil; *Mixture or Massacre,* The Majority Press, Dover, Mass., 1989 (first publication in 1979) see preface pp. xii-xvi., pp. 57-90; 179-202. Also Abdias Do Nascimento and Elisa Larkin Nascimento, *Africans in Brazil,* African World Press, Trenton, N. J., 1992, pp. 147-167.
4. See, for instance, the effusions of Thomas T. Fortune of the *New York Age* when lynchings were so much in the ascendant in which he advised his brethren to gird themselves for `revolution' in R. W. Logan, *The Betrayal of the Negro*, etc., p. 312. The statement was made in 1900 at a meeting in Brooklyn to celebrate the one hundredth anniversary of the birth of John Brown.
5. Jason H. Silverman, "Mary Ann Shadd and the Search for Equality", in *Black Leaders of the Nineteenth Century*" (Leon Litwick and August Meier eds.), Urbana and Chicago, 1988, p. 94. Much of the information on Mary Ann Shadd in this work is gleaned from Jason Silverman's article, appearing in pp. 87-100 of the above-mentioned text.
6. *Ibid.*, p. 81.
7. *Ibid.*, p. 97.

8. *Ibid.*, pp. 98-99.
9. *Ibid.*, p. 88. Lewis Woodson, a lesser know advocate of emigration who had also nurtured a better know advocate, Dr. Martin Robinson Delany, has had the contours of his thoughts and advocacies discussed in a very admirable and competently executed recent article. It is well adverting to. See Gayle T. Tate, "Prophesy and Transformation: The Contours of Lewis Woodson's Nationalism", *Journal of Black Studies,* Sage Publications, Inc. Vol. 29, No. 2, (November 1998), pp. 209-233.
10. Thomas C. Holt, "The Lonely Warrior: Ida B. Wells-Barnett and the Struggle for Black Leadership", in *Black Leaders of the Twentieth Century,* (John Hope Franklin and August Meier eds.) pp. 39-61.
11. Sharon Harley, "Mary Church Terrell: Genteel Militant", in *Black Leaders of the Nineteenth Century,* Leon Litwick and August Meier eds. p. 310.
12. *Ibid*.
13. See C. G. Woodson, *Negro Orators and their Orations,* Washington, D.C., 1925, p. 582; pp. 580-83 for entire speech of Booker T. Washington.
14. *Ibid*., p. 583.
15. *Ibid*., p. 583.
16. See Douglass, F., *Life and Times, op. cit*., pp. 332-344; also H. Brotz, *Negro Social and Political Thought, op. cit*., pp. 277-284 headed: "What the Black Man Wants". In that speech Douglass said: "I am for the `immediate, unconditional, and universal" enfranchisement of the black man, in every state in the Union." (p. 278) *et. seq*. also his speech on "The Civil Rights Case ", pp. 298-306.
17. See Rayford W. Logan, *The Betrayal of the Negro,* p. 283-86 also 308-312.
18. *Ibid*., p. 286.
19. *Ibid*., p. 286.
20. *Ibid*., p. 290.
21. *Ibid*. loc cit.
22. *Ibid*., pp. 293-294.
23. *Ibid*., p. 312.
24. *Ibid*., p. 312.
25. See Thompson, V. B., *Africa and Unity: The Evolution of Pan-Africanism,* 1969, p. 56, also, *New York Age,* 12 March, 1906; Elliot Rudwick, *W. E. B. DuBois: Propagandist of the Negro-Protest,* New York, 1972, p. 209; also George Shepperson, "The African Abroad or the African Diaspora", in *Emerging Themes of African History,* (T. O. Ranger (ed.)), 1968, Heinemann, Nairobi, EAPH, London, p. 169.
26. See DuBois, W. E. B., *Souls of Black Folk,* Chicago, A. C. McClurg & Co., 1903, 2nd edition, pp. 41-59. See also his `Talented Tenth' in *The Negro Problem,* James Potts & Co., New York, 1903, Ch. 2. pp. 31-74.
27. Rudwick, Elliot M., *W.E.B. DuBois, Propagandist of the Negro Protest,* Athenum, New York, 1972, p. 65 et seq.
28. see for instance Booker T. Washington, *The Future of the American Negro,* Boston, 1900, p. 79. See also Booker T. Washington and W. E. B. DuBois, *The American Negro (Southern States)* , T. Fisher Urwin, London, 1909, for the views of both men.
29. See *The Negro Problem,* (Contributions by B. T. Washington, W. E. B. DuBois and others), James Pott & Co., New York, pp. 12-16, 22.
30. See for instance Elliot Rudwick, *op. cit.* The author's entire irritation with

DuBois pervades this book.

31. *Ibid.*, p. 64 et seq.
32. Miller, Kelly, *Race Adjustment* loc. cit., The Neale Publishing Company, New York & Washington, 1908, pp. 17-25.
33. Carroll, Charles, *"The Negro A Beast" or "In the Image of God,"* St. Louis, MO, 1900; for an extension of this notion and its consequences in U. S. society see George M. Frederickson, *The Black Image in The White Mind*, Hanover, New Hampshire, Weselyan University Press, 1971, Wesleyan Paperback, 1987, Ch. 9; see especially pp. 275-82. The content of this book is that the Negro is a beast, but created with articulate speech, and hands that he may be of service to his master - the white man. The author of this book also produced others in which he deflated the "Negro" and made many absurd inferences. The books themselves need to be read. The following are instructive: *The Negro: The Tempter of Eve or the Criminality of Man's Social, Political and Religious Equality with the Negro, and the Amalgamation to which these Crimes Inevitably Lead*, Adamic Library, St. Louis, MO, 1902, also *The Negro Not the Son of Ham or Man Not a Species Divisible Into Races*, (a lecture) Washington, 1898.
34. DuBois, W.E.B., "Talented Tenth," in A. Meier, E. Rudwick and F. L. Broderick (eds.) *Black Protest Thought in the Twentieth Century*, Indianapolis, Bobbs-Merril, 1965, pp. 51-52.
35. Barber, J. Max, "The Niagara Movement," *Voice of the Negro*, (1905), p. 522, *What's the Niagara Movement?* (Pamphlet), 1905, Howard University Library, also Niagara Movement Declaration of Principles (pamphlet), 1905, Howard University Library.
36. DuBois, W. E. B., *Dusk of Dawn*, pp. 88-95.
37. *Niagara Movement Declaration of Principles*, (pamphlet 1905), Howard University Library, Also Dubois, *Dusk of Dawn*, *op. cit.*, pp. 88-89.
38. *Outlook*, LXXX (1905), p. 796.
39. *Chicago Law Register* reprinted in the *Washington Bee*, Aug., 12, 1905.
40. Ferris, William, *The African Abroad*, Vol. 1. pp. 276-77. E. M. Rudwick *op. cit.*, pp. 59-62, 64-71, 75-77, 82-83, 85-88, 89-93, 103-104, 141. The issues were much more than personalities, though their egos were involved in what was essentially a fundamental cleavage.
41. See Mary White Ovington, *The Walls Came Tumbling Down*, New York, 1947, pp. 76-77 et seq.; also August Meier, "Booker T. Washington and the Rise of the N.A.A.C.P.," *Crisis*, LXI (1954), p. 70; see also same author, "Booker T. Washington and the Negro Press," *Journal of Negro History*, XXXVIII (1953), pp. 67-90.
    Also Redwick, *op. cit.* pp. 98-100, 115-116.
42. Rudwick, E. M., *op. cit.*, p. 104. Someone described them as 'an agregation of sore heads'; also pp. 92-93.
43. Rudwick, *op. cit.*, pp. 98-116 *et seq.* also p. 330 n. 22 et seq.
44. *Ibid*, p. 99.
45. *Ibid*.
46. See "Abstracts of Minutes, Niagara Movement," August 15-18, 1906, Howard University Library; see also *Washington Bee*, Aug., 25 1906, also L. M. Hershaw, "Pope Case," *Horizon*, (May 1907), p. 17.
47. See L. M. Hershaw, "Pope Case," *Horizon* (May 1907), p. 17.
48. Quoted in Rudwick, *op. cit.*, p. 110 from Minutes of Third Niagara

Conference, DuBois Papers.
49. Rudwick, *Ibid.*, p. 110.
50. August Meier, *Negro Thought in America 1880-1915*, Ann Arbor Paper Backs, University of Michigan Press, 1966, p. 185.
51. *Ibid.*, p. 119.
52. *Ibid.*, pp. 117-118.
53. See *The Crisis*, Vol. 1, no. 2, December 1910 for a list of the Board of Management.
54. See W. E. B. DuBois, *Dusk of Dawn*, New York, 1935, pp. 224-25. See also DuBois' tribute to Booker T. Washington at his death in *The Crisis* (Christmas edn.) Dec. 1915, p. 82. He also offered his goodwill to Booker T.'s successor Robert Russa Moton.
55. The *Crisis*, Vol. 1, No. 2, December 1910, p. 16.
56. W. E. B. DuBois, "The Souls of White Folk," *Independent, LXLX* (1910), p. 339; also "The College-Bred Negro Communities," (pamphlet) Atlanta University, 1910; also DuBois, "Forty Years of Freedom," *Missionary Review of the World*, XXXIV (1971), pp. 460-61.
57. See W. E. B. DuBois, *The Amenia Conference: An Historical Negro Gathering*, Troutbeck Leaflets, No. 8. (privately printed) Sept. 1925. For summary of principles see pp. 14-15, also *Dusk of Dawn*, pp. 243-45.
58. This is competently examined in David Lewis, *When Harlem was in Vogue*.
59. In DuBois, *Dusk of Dawn, op. cit.*, pp. 299-302.
60. The Declarations were made in 1917. For a brief observation of the preliminaries leading up to the Declarations see Howard Morley Sachar, *The Course of Modern Jewish History*, A Delta Book, New York, 1958, 1977, pp. 372-376, especially p. 375.
61. see for instance Charles H. Wesley, *Negro Labor in the United States 1850-1925*, Vanguard Press, New York, 1927. Bernard Mandel, "Samuel Gompers and the Negro Workers, 1886-1914," *Journal of Negro History*, XL (Jan. 1955), pp. 234-60.
62. see reference to this in the 'opinion' column of *Crisis*, Vol. 1, No. 6, (April 1911), p. 15 headed 'socialism again', also Harold Gruse, *The Crisis of the Negro Intellectual*, New York, William Morrow and Co. Inc., 1967, 1971 (fifth printing), pp. 147-170, 171-180.

CHAPTER 7

TRADITION OF AMBIVALENCE

REJECTION AND ACCEPTANCE OF AFRICA

This chapter seeks to explore, briefly, the emergence of a tradition among Africans of the Diaspora in the Americas (here the term is used to be all-inclusive of those classified as Negroes in the Americas and being descendants of ancestors and ancestresses who had first been taken out of Africa and brought to the Americas) which produced its own paradox, that is, the acceptance and rejection of Africa at the same time. Viewing the group as a totality, this acceptance and rejection of African were so intertwined that they evolved with the societal evolution of the Africans in the Americas and as slavery progressed on to emancipation. But the contradictions and ambivalence which were bred by this attitude of mind continued to plague African-American thinking concerning their destiny - whether it was to be in the Americas or elsewhere, including Africa. As observed in the preceding chapter, a crisis arose in the leadership of the Africans of the Diaspora in the United States concerning the issues of integration and emigration, and, these issues were hotly debated and at the turn of the nineteenth century/twentieth century, these two tendencies continued to influence thought and debate, although to it was added that of a "separate identity" (alias "nationalism"), which became increasingly articulated in the twentieth century, even by those who had previously advocated integration and later recoiled from it.

In observing African Americans of this era (from the eighteenth into the twentieth centuries), many patterns of ambivalence are apparent. There were those who would have been inclined to forget Africa as the slave-owners preferred, and there were those who could not forget. In between these polarities there were numerous tendencies and out of these tendencies contradictions were bred. There is a history to this evolution and it is necessary to at least sketch this briefly. But it is still essential to emphasize that the African debate which became so very pronounced in the second half of the nineteenth century had antecedents in the eighteenth and also was to spill over into the twentieth century. The African revival re-emerged when conditions in the United States became miserable either politically, economically, or socially, and sometimes when all three factors were in play at the same time and circumstances surrounding the downtrodden descendants of Africa became intolerable.

Some Background

Africans enslaved in the Americas for the first two centuries and more of their existence, and principally in the United States of America, tended to describe themselves and were described as "Africans." This is not surprising, for the stubborn determination of some Africans not to forget was often reinforced by the fresh supply of enslaved Africans into the Americas. It was obvious from experiences on board slave ships, the melancholy songs, forms of resistance to enslavement by Africans, both violent (in terms of slave revolts) and passive (such as refusal of food or pining away until death carried them off), that these consistently mirrored the acceptance not rejection of Africa by the enslaved, who had not yet become acculturated to the new world of the Americas. There was no record of any enslaved Africans or those designated as slaves who rejoiced because they were being taken out of Africa. [1] Some even thought worse of the fate that would befall them in the Americas than actually happened. They felt they were being brought to be eaten, a fact which appears in the writings of so many slave traders that one need not belabor the point. [2] Visualizing it thus, the vast majority of the enslaved sentimentally accepted the land from which they were taken which was in the continent of Africa and so logically accepted Africa.

The problems of rejection only began to manifest themselves once they had been beached on the soil of the Americas as conflicting values and modes of perception intruded into their consciousness and misrepresentations of facts confused their perspectives. The harsh treatment of the slave system, serious attempts to undermine the cohesiveness of those who had a common language and cultural background, and the sustained erosion of their languages - all these factors conspired to compound the ambivalence which was to emerge. The tradition which later grew of some acceptance and some rejection of Africa seen in a broader perspective is indeed a tradition of ambivalence which has persisted to this day. The veteran and distinguished African-American scholar and leader of the late nineteenth and early twentieth centuries, Dr. W. E. B. DuBois, expressed it in his concept of a "double consciousness" or the dual man. [3]

If the problem loomed of itself among the most educated descendants of Africa in the Americas, it must have been all the more puzzling for the unlettered Africans in the Diaspora who were confronted with numerous conflicting ideas, values, stories, histories, and experiences, apart from the active propaganda of white America, which sometimes called them Africans and at other times Americans, sometimes neither, consequently placing them in a state of "betwixt and between." This was further compounded by their enslavers, who sometimes suggested that they were Africans and at other times a new breed, if not sub-human altogether. They were "Negroes" or "niggers" and many other pejorative names that were spun out of their experience in bondage and after; and if not Americans, then just mere objects. This ambivalence of their enslavers passed on to the enslaved modes of thought and perception which gradually became assimilated into their own thought processes and psychological make-up.

But ideas of a return to Africa, the so-called "Back to Africa" tendencies or movements, whichever is preferred, existed from the first enslavement of the Africans. Slaves drowning themselves in the sea in the belief that death translated them back to Africa, their land of origin, was a common phenomenon which slave trading ship captains dreaded and sought to guard against. Their songs expressed the desires and hopes of return, even though on the plantations they were often not made too explicit in order not to alert the owners or masters to the state of acute discontent among their wards. [4]

Those endeavors to achieve a transplantation of their kind to Africa at various times from the eighteenth to the twentieth centuries, apart from expressing their frustrations with the Americas, principally the United States, were positive expressions of that acceptance of Africa as home of origin of their forebears and home of destiny for realization in the future. But, as has been observed elsewhere in this work, advocacy of this African aspiration was much more in the ascendant during periods of acute economic and social distress than during periods of relative calm. The thoughts, preoccupations, and endeavors of descendants of Africa towards those ends must be distinguished from the "repatriation" or "transportation" or "colonization" plans of their racist detractors. The American Colonization Society and the colonization of Liberia and the Sierra Leone colonization of the British Sierra Leone Company emerged from these racist preoccupations, despite the claims to humanitarianism. (This point has already been discussed above and need not detain us here). The schemes of the Colonization Society and those that created Sierra Leone repatriates had other motives and so do not belong to the genre of ideas and movements expressing a positive acceptance of Africa. Those were mere schemes of repatriation of free descendants of Africa in the Americas and Britain for reasons other than benevolence as Europeans and Euro-Americans sought their own solutions to the "race problem" of their own making by repatriation or exclusion of African descendants through transportation. Yet those schemes influenced the self-perceptions of some of these African-derived people in the Americas and contributed to the cleavages, especially in the nineteenth century. But Africans in the Americas manifested their own initiative in this direction from as far back as the eighteenth century.

Some Early Attempts at Reconnection with Africa

Africans in the American colonies which became the United States of America had from time to time since the second half of the eighteenth century manifested interest in emigrating to Africa. These advocates first manifested themselves in New England in contiguous states like Massachusetts and Rhode Island (a hive-off from Massachusetts) and as far south as Maryland. An early expression of this was in 1773 when free Africans in Massachusetts submitted a petition to the Massachusetts Legislature expressing their desire to emigrate to Africa (where they proposed to establish a settlement) and seeking assistance to facilitate this move. Late in that century, between 1780 and 1790, African populations resident in Providence and Newport, Rhode Island, (two ports which had seen the arrival of Africans through the slave trade connections with the West Indies and Africa) expressed a similar interest in Africa. In 1780 they founded in Newport the *African Union Society*, in fact the first "free African" voluntary and welfare organization. This Society was earlier in time than the Free African Society of Philadelphia founded by Richard Allen, Absalom Jones, and other enthusiasts in 1787. The latter organization was not concerned with the notion of an African return. But despite this rejection of Africa, it still called itself "African" and the churches which later emerged from its exertions were also designated "African."

The Newport society, however, apart from its concerns with matters pertaining to the welfare of its people in such matters as births, deaths, marriages, providing for widows of deceased members, and assisting the poor, aimed at assisting the apprenticing of young people in certain trades; but above all, it aimed at the economic and social enhancement which became a general obsession in the United States. It sought to persuade the Free African Society of Philadelphia and the Societies in Boston and Rhode Island to evolve a national policy towards the African emigration issue, but was unsuccessful with Philadelphia. But its chief promoters in their African excursion felt that transfer to Africa would hasten the emancipation of slaves in the Americas and that their Christian knowledge would make them suitable as instruments for the "uplifting and civilizing" [5] of their African brethren in the parent continent. Here they were thinking in terms that were to be re-echoed through the nineteenth century by other black prelates in the United States. Thus, their views in this respect were nuanced reflecting the Euro-American bias of the time and of succeeding generations and so prevalent in the reflections of the Rev. Alexander Crummell in the nineteenth century.

But they did help some of their members who chose to return to West Africa, [6] even if in the long-term their dreams were not realized; their activities manifested the acceptance of Africa. Their interest in West Africa had been heightened by the British establishment of the Sierra Leone settlement, but once it became obvious to them that the British had established a colony, they made it clear that their aim was for a "free settlement" without the necessity to be subservient to whites. [7]

The Newport Society went on to issue circular letters to assemble meetings with the African descendants of Boston, Providence, and Philadelphia, but its efforts to crystallize a policy on Africa national in scope by its contacts through the northern seaboard, sadly failed.

However, on January 4, 1787, the Boston free African community petitioned the General Court to aid their transfer to Africa. One of the signatories of this petition (which was signed by seventy-five African-Americans) was the celebrated founder of the Black Masonic Order among African-Americans, Prince Hall. As early as those times they had expressed pessimism about the prospects of attaining equality in the United States.

But the African community of Philadelphia and some in Virginia (who sought settlement along the Mississippi River, instead of Africa) provided the leadership in the rejection of Africa as a place for settlement, despite using the name of Africa for the various organizations they had founded. Then came Paul Cuffee in the early nineteenth century with a revival of the idea of emigration to Africa.

Paul Cuffee of Boston was among the pioneers of those stressing their solidarity with Africa. But despite his two separate trips to Sierra

Leone in 1811 and 1815 and the transfer of some descendants of Africa there on the second trip, his scheme was not realized, as his demise in 1817 terminated his own hopes of ever settling there. But his endeavors had been kindled, we are informed, by his father's admonishments to do something positive and practical for Africa. [8]

Among other individuals who accepted Africa and later settled or died there was the Rev. Daniel Coker of the African Methodist Episcopal Church of Bishop Richard Allen, who accepted the sponsorship of the American Colonization Society and, in February 1820, went to Sierra Leone. His departure for Africa, it is said, paved the way for Richard Allen to become the first bishop of the A.M.E. Church as Coker was earlier in the forefront of the contest for Bishop. Nathaniel Peck, who accompanied Coker, on arrival in Freetown (Sierra Leone) in March 1820 gave thanks to God for "now treading the soil of my mother country." [9] Lott Cary from Richmond, Virginia, who went to West Africa in 1821 as a Baptist preacher, was another of those who accepted Africa. His intention, in departing from the United States, was to go to a country of his forebears where he might be respected and evaluated on his merits rather than, as was the case in America, by his pigmentation. [10] Another was Newport Gardner, who, as an octogenarian in 1825, sailed from Boston to Africa. His example, he hoped, would inspire the youth, as he felt he would never be elevated in the United States. He died in Africa within half a year of his arrival. Another was John B. Russwurm, a graduate of Bowdin College, Maine, and the first African-American to earn a degree from a U.S. college. He was joint editor with the Rev. Samuel B. Cornish of *Freedom's Journal* in the United States in 1827, but he still departed for Africa (Liberia) in 1829 under the auspices of the American Colonization Society and served as a Superintendent of Schools and editor of the *Liberian Herald*. At his death in 1851 he was Governor of the Cape Palmas colony sponsored by the Maryland State Colonization Society. Russwurm, who had initially opposed African colonization of the American Colonization Society, later became converted to the idea and by 1829 had gone to Liberia. In affirming that conversion he stressed that he knew no "other home for the man of color, or of republican principles, than Africa." [11]

In the 1830s and 1840s it was another ex-Virginian liberated person (and later a teacher and minister of religion) who ran a school for blacks in Pittsburgh, Pennsylvania. He was the Rev. Lewis Woodson (reputed to have been a teacher of Martin Robinson Delany when he was nineteen), who championed emigration. Woodson saw the need for organization and advocated racial solidarity and in expressing his nationalistic sentiments urged that the organization so formed be named African. The acceptance and rejection of Africa went on, however, in the various arguments of the African-American community throughout the nineteenth century.

Thus, among the earliest of the advocates of acceptance of an identity with Africa were Paul Cuffee, John Russwurm, Daniel Coker, Lott Cary, Newport Gardner, and Nathaniel Peck. These were some of the representatives of the "free" blacks. But they evoked equally vehement hostility and opposition from other free blacks who saw the advocacy as pernicious and misguided, insisting that they were already a permanent feature of American society. Their chief and celebrated spokesman was none other than Frederick Douglass. He used his newspaper, the *North Star*, to assail the idea and carried it into his subsequent publication, The *Frederick Douglass Paper*. The debate that went on was conducted with much bitterness on both sides of the divide, with Euro-Americans (white people) taking sides with one or other of the factions. There was reasoned argument on both sides. Those who argued for staying at home (in the U.S.A.) saw the transference to Africa as capitulation to the bigots and implied complicity with the American Colonization Society. Transportation seemed like "apostasy," seeing that their forefathers' blood and their own had "watered" the soil of America. Their anti-colonization refrain continued to be heard at the annual Conventions of Colored (Negro) People from 1830 onwards. But even Douglass was prepared to make a distinction between individual departure as opposed to a mass exodus. He remained the opponent of the latter kind. Yet the position between emigrationists and the "stay-at-homes" (integrationists) was sharply polarized and punctuated with bitterness. Yet, periodically, Douglass in referring to his people called them African-Americans.

The Fugitive Slave Law of 1850 mirrored Federal government acquiescence in the status of slavery and the repatriation of fugitive slaves to the State of their origin. So prior to 1850 among African-Americans, apart from individual endeavors, as Weisbord aptly concluded, there was no emigrationist groundswell.[12] Emigrationists at this time were stigmatized as "traitors."[13] But the law raised once again the specter of danger to free descendants of Africa in North America as well as freedom-loving slaves, and the emigration idea was again canvassed. The advocacy for this, as has been mentioned above, reached its apogee at the Emigration Convention championed by Dr. M. R. Delany at the Convention in Cleveland, Ohio, in 1858 (following two earlier conventions in 1854 and 1856). The initial call for the emigration convention had gone out in 1853, following Dr. Delany's publication in 1852 of his *Condition, Elevation and Emigration and Destiny of the Colored People of the United States,*

Politically Considered. At the Third Emigration Convention three possibilities of places for emigration emerged. The Rev. James Theodore Holly was the chief advocate of emigration to Haiti, the first independent black nation of the modern New World after Palmares. James Redpath championed Central America or Canada, and Martin R. Delany championed Africa. Out of that Convention emerged Delany's trip to West Africa and his *Official Report*, as well as that of his associate Co-Commissioner Robert Campbell, already mentioned. These, among others, were to keep the hope of Africa burning in the hearts of some of its descendants in the United States of America.

But the notion of rejection of Africa was so strong that when at a Negro National Convention in 1869 a proposal was made to confer honorary membership on Liberia's President J. J. Roberts, there was opposition. A cleavage emerged, as the Pennsylvania delegation not only ridiculed the idea but was clearly incensed that Jenkins Roberts "ran away to Liberia in the time of our need, and hid himself in swamps of Liberia and cried Colonization." [14]Another cause of objection to Jenkins was that the conferment of such an honor after Jenkins connections and sympathies with the American Colonization Society would be interpreted as acceptance (tantamount to an endorsement) of the aims and objectives of the Society. [15]

It is out of the tradition of rejection and acceptance of Africa that we see the emergence of a Pan-African tradition. At first this might seem contradictory, but the circumstances of the milieu in which the African Diaspora developed its ethos and codes of conduct and the hostilities of the environments as well as their fluctuating prejudices helped to fashion this tradition. Nowhere does this appear more clearly than among the prominent leaders of the African Diaspora, who have left their mark on the struggles for civil rights in the United States and the other parts of the New World Diaspora. Among the leaders it is difficult to pinpoint one who totally rejected Africa or who accepted Africa without some reservations, but all of them were an amalgam of rejection and acceptance of Africa, more or less in proportion to their convictions, circumstances, and prejudices - or perhaps their current interests. Some of the prejudices were induced, as we have earlier noted, for example, with the American Colonization Society. The conception of "primitive" Africa, which was so widespread in European and Euro-American thought and writing, filtered into the consciousness of these descendants of Africa to make some of them recoil from the notion of any link with Africa. Yet, there were those who felt this affinity and tried to pass it on to their progeny. The example of John Cuffee, father of the celebrated Captain Paul Cuffee, is a case in point. Prior to his death, he had called Paul, the most successful of his sons, and reminded him to do something practical for Africa. Apart from the many reasons usually cited for Cuffee's ventures towards the Sierra Leone, this factor is never mentioned. Information relating to it occurs in an obscure corner of the Memoir of Paul Cuffee. [16]

There were others like John Russwurm, the first Afro-American to graduate from an American college and founder of the anti-slavery newspaper *Freedom's Journal* (1827), who at the inception of the American Colonization Society rejected the idea of emigration to Africa and who in time emigrated to Africa and to Liberia under the auspices of the same organization and founded the first (and very successful) Liberian newspaper, the *Liberia Herald*. There were others like him, the Rev. Henry Highland Garnet, for instance, who had resisted the idea initially and was against the principle, yet later formed the "African Civilization Society" (1858) with a view to promoting this aspect of the African link. [17] Late in 1881 Garnet, among others, arrived in Liberia and a few months later he died. The Rev. Alexander Crummell, who delivered the Eloguim on the death of Henry Highland Garnet, [18] was an advocate of this movement to Africa and remained in West Africa for twenty years as a Minister of Religion and educationist from 1853 and promoter of African-American emigration to Africa. He later returned to the United States of America (in 1873) and became the first President of the American Negro Academy, founded in 1897. As a clergyman in America he continued to influence black congregations about Africa. It might be observed that this particular advocate of a move to Africa was both an American and African by sentiment. Many of the African-American leaders were in this respect dual personalities. Even the greatest African-American leader of the last century, Frederick Douglass, while he was a staunch opponent of the emigration to Africa, periodically spoke of the descendants of Africa in the Americas as the African-Americans and was a patron of the African Methodist Episcopal Zion Church. There was rejection and acceptance in his activities, but these seeming contradictions of acceptance and rejection of Africa were each supported by strong arguments.

Such a tradition of acceptance and rejection of an ancestral homeland was not peculiar to the African Diaspora. Some Jews still express their opposition to and support of Zionism and are not seen as peculiar. Irish-Americans are similarly divided *vis-a-vis* the Irish Republican Army. Euro-Americans like William Lloyd Garrison, who later became one of the most ardent opponents of the Colonization Society, was said to have been, at an early stage in his career, a believer in the idea of emigration for the colored people from the U.S.A.

There were also among anti-slavery advocates Euro-Americans who also believed in colonization and later recoiled from it while others became converted to colonization. This also occurred in the rank-and-file of the blacks themselves.

The chief protagonists of emigration to Africa and the exponent of a return to Africa after 1850 were Martin Robinson Delany and his West Indian associate, Robert Campbell. Both men reported on their visit to Africa; in fact, the title of Campbell's book showed the importance he attached to it: called it a *A Pilgrimage to my Motherland*. He is said to have later been the founder of the Lagos newspaper *The Anglo-African*. Yet at the outbreak of the American Civil War, Delany himself threw his energies into the Civil War effort in North America. He became a Major in the Union Army and, with the prospects of integration being raised, the notion of return to Africa lost its glamour. Moreover, it is necessary to observe that one of the factors in the preoccupation with Africa was frustrated hopes and aspirations. For it was evident in Delany's own views that having made a heart-searching examination of the situation in North America, he had arrived at the conclusion that the descendants of Africa would need to remove themselves in order to flourish and find a proper outlet for their talents. William Lloyd Garrison, the white abolitionist, reviewing Delany's book in 1852 in the pages of *The Liberator* implied that the publication was a cry of despair and that what was needed at that time was hope. But the publication came out only two years after the passing of the Fugitive Slave Law by Congress and this made even the African-American freedman unsafe, as any impostor from the slave states could claim a freedman - and one who had never experienced slavery or had long escaped from the citadel of slavery and had been living as a free person for years. Those fears led a number of African-Americans to emigrate from the U.S. to Canada, and one such person was the Rev. Samuel Ringgold Ward, who eventually published his autobiography, *The Autobiography of a Fugitive Negro*, in which he appended some information about his anti-slavery labors. Delany was to return periodically to the emigration idea a number of times before his death in 1885 in Xenia, Ohio. He and some Charleston African-Americans, in 1877, floated the Liberian Exodus Joint Stock Steamship Company. In spite of this state of ambivalence towards Africa among African-Americans and other Africans of the West, the cleavage about their hopes for their people was real and Douglass became, in time, the spokesman for the "stay at homes" (Americans) while Delany became the spokesman for the "let us all go home" (to Africa) contingent. These conflicting tendencies pervaded the nineteenth and twentieth centuries and remain strong to this day. The arguments between Douglass and Delany, which appeared in the pages of newspapers which they each edited, still beg for more serious research. Nothing will be done here but to distill the basic considerations in their respective advocacies. They were succeeded by others later in the century and in the early years of the twentieth century. Their successors included Bishop Henry McNeal Turner (1880s), Chief Alfred Sam (1914), Alexander Crummell, Edward Blyden, Marcus Garvey (1920), and the Rastafarian (Jamaica in the 1960s). These are the direct successors of the Delany tradition of acceptance of Africa. DuBois for a while, as opponent of Garvey, was an advocate of integration, at times an Africanist even by his intellectual pursuits and his Pan-African activities; yet at other times he advocated separate identity. DuBois had been integrationist, segregationist, nationalist, and emigrationist at different points in his long life. In the evening of his life it would appear that Pan-Africanism had won and he had accepted Africa. Not only did he become a citizen of Ghana, become associated with the ill-fated *Encyclopaedia Africana* project, but wrote a poem about a United States of Africa and lived in the domain of one of the greatest African advocates of Pan-African unity in the twentieth century. In spite of what people have said of DuBois' Communist Party affiliation, the President of Ghana, Dr. Kwame Kkrumah, in his obituary on DuBois, spoke of him as "a great African." But his vision of history was also a Pan-African one, as evidenced in his publications *The Negro* (1900), *The World and Africa* (1946), and *Black Folk Then and Now* (1939). Yet when contemplating the African-American within the context of America, he was American and Pan-Negroid. His studies of blacks *The Philadelphia Negro* (1897), *Souls of Black Folk* (1903), *Black Reconstruction* (1935), *The Gift of Black Folk* (1924), and his monumental first work, *The Suppression of the African Slave Trade to America* (1896), are again expressions of this Americaness.

That frustration which was the common experience of the African-derived peoples in the U.S.A. has continued to run through these advocacies for a return to Africa and is evident in the activities of Delany's successors. It appeared in Bishop Henry McNeal Turner, disappointed with the disfranchisement of the blacks and himself after the failure of Reconstruction; and with Garvey, whose statements and writings make these frustrations explicit. The Rastafarian, though belonging to the plebeian side of the protest activity of the Diaspora, mirror this same complex of frustrations of hopes and aspirations. But this is not to say that the advocacies did not carry conviction. Their reasons for the desire to be reconnected to Africa have respectable intellectual foundations as well as emotional ones.

When Lott Cary, one of the African-Americans to emigrate to West Africa, expressed his intention to go to Africa, he expressed sentiments which arose out of the frustration which many people of African descent felt in the U.S.A. In 1820 he said:

> I am an African, and in this country [America] however meritorious my conduct and respectable my character, I cannot receive the credit due to either. I wish to go to a country where I shall be estimated by my merits, not by my complexion, and I feel bound to labor for my suffering race. [19]

He was expressing the sentiments of many who tenaciously clung to the emigrationist ideal. A few years after this a free African-American, David Walker, published his *Appeal to the Colored Citizens of the United States* (1829) and expressed the frustrations even more forcefully thus:

> My beloved brethren: The Indians of North and South America - the Greeks - the Irish, subjected under the king of Great Britain - the Jews, that ancient people of the Lord - the inhabitants of the Island of the Sea - in fine, all inhabitants of the Earth, (except, however, the sons of Africa) are called men and of course are and ought to be free. - But we, (colored people) and our children are brutes and of course are and ought to be slaves to the American people and their children forever - to dig mines and work their farms; and thus go on enriching them from one generation to another with our blood and our tears!!! [20]

But in spite of the venting of this frustration, Walker did not seek his solution in Africa. He felt that it could be realized there in America and called for an overthrow of the slave system. Decidedly, he recognized his Africanness but insisted that he and his brethren were Americans, as they had by their sweat and tears and blood helped to fashion America as it then was. But the Africanness further surfaced when he exhorted the brethren that God would give them a Hannibal who would then enable them to overthrow the slave system. [21] In his disapproval of the colonization proposal of the American Colonization Society, he rejected their scheme absolutely and asserted that the wretchedness of the blacks was aggravated by the American Colonization Society.

In the West Indies also can be traced the tradition of acceptance and rejection of Africa. Henry Sylvester-Williams, who was instrumental in the founding of the First Pan-African Association in London (1897) and Secretary to the Association and organizer of the first Pan-

African meeting in London in 1900, demonstrated this acceptance of Africa that apart from the "Appeal to the Nations of the World," which he signed and which was offered to Chamberlain as Colonial Secretary, his activities for a while related to the welfare of Africans in Africa. He later went to live in South Africa and worked there under very trying conditions (1903-1904). Eventually, he returned to his home in Trinidad (1908) and died there in 1911. But he had demonstrated more fully that acceptance of Africa, although his eventual return to the West (London) and then to the West Indies not only showed that Africa was under the colonial yoke but that the white colonists disbarred the infiltration or settlement there of descendants of Africa from the Americas. A study of Henry Sylvester-Williams by the late Professor H. R. Hooker indicated that, in spite of the return to Trinidad,

> Not all pan-African sentiment was gone, though 'improvement' bodies were much more fashionable in the island now. The *Mirror* printed an account of the formation of an Ethiopian Association at Princess Town, which would `encourage unity in the negro race... make them see the evils of being dependent and to instill in them the spirit of independence.' To the extent that the word `Ethiopian' was used, one might argue that some of William's earlier preachments had taken effect. To the extent that the body was concerned with the here and now of Trinidad, one is forced to conclude that Africa was only vestigially significant. [22]

What remained towards the end of his life was a flicker of his previous Pan-African strength and enthusiasm. But at his death at the age of 42, one Trinidadian paper, the *Mole*, recalled Williams' contributions to Pan-Africanism thus:

> ...undoubtedly his name will longest be remembered and cherished by his own people for his great interest in their behalf, which culminated in the well-known Pan-African Congress [sic]. [23]

What is interesting about this commentary is that it signified a Trinidadian acceptance and recognition of Sylvester-Williams' Pan-African activities, whereas a later Trinidadian descendant of the same name and later Prime Minister of Trinidad and Tobago, Dr. Eric Williams, could lament the fact that George Padmore, another great Pan-Africanist from Trinidad (who gave much of his life to the African struggle for independence and to exposing the abuses of British colonialism in Africa), had preoccupied himself too much with Africa and less with the West Indies. [24] We see there the rejection of the same Africa that the activities of earlier protagonists had made acceptable. In the light of the above-cited remarks of Eric Williams, we see the ambivalence expressed again in his thought of castigating Padmore, despite Williams' own preoccupation with "African Solidarity." This ambivalence has been more recently popularized in one of the Calypsos of the *Mighty Chalk Dust*, the latter himself being a teacher and educationist. But Hooker suggests that only the *Mole* was interested in Henry Sylvester-Williams as "champion exponent of Pan-Africanism" while to others in Trinidad "he went to his grave as a Trinidad barrister, remembered more for his speech against alcohol than for his advocacy of black dignity on three continents." [25] That may not be the last word on Sylvester-Williams; a latter assessment may yet recall his valuable contributions to the Pan-African tradition.

Although people of African descent or the African-derived peoples in the United States of America had called themselves Africans during the first two centuries of their existence in a strange new land, and had been identified as such, the situation began to alter in the early part of the nineteenth century. A factor was the danger of their deportation to Africa instead of being allowed to remain in the United States. Part of it was induced by the emergence of the American Colonization Society (1816-1817) although there were previously conceived schemes for the removal of people of African origin away from the country in order to achieve, as they thought, racial harmony, as the people of African origin were seen as the source of conflict (a debatable point). Some of the schemes for emancipation and expatriation occurred in the eighteenth century and in his *Notes on Virginia*, Thomas Jefferson considered that possibility. Since many descendants of Africa opposed the schemes that were being devised by the American Colonization Society, who sought to remove those free from among the enslaved descendants of Africa, protest activities and meetings began to be held against the schemes. The other factor which contributed to a change of name was the emergence of the Convention Movement among descendants of Africa and other (both National and State) Conventions adopted the term "colored people." So the term was preferred by the Convention of Colored People and this was very much in the ascendant between 1830 and 1860. At the National Convention of Colored People in 1835 it was suggested that the term "African" be dropped and "colored" be substituted or adopted. [26] Many churches founded by descendants of Africa which had proliferated in the eighteenth century employed the term "African", one of the foremost of them being the African Methodist Episcopal Church which began in Philadelphia under the leadership of Richard Allen. So there were to be African Methodists, African Baptists (such as the Churches in Savannah and African Presbyterians) and later members of the African Orthodox Church. That the nomenclature African was very much in vogue is shown by the many Churches in the U.S.A. which continued to refer to themselves as African.

Despite these usages, the fear of expatriation and exclusion from the United States persisted in the pre-Civil War period, and not only the American Colonization Society but some so-called Euro-American "friends of Africa" advocated this expatriation. So, in changing the nomenclature to "colored," African descendants were proclaiming their intention not only to stay in the country but also to claim their rights in a country which their toil and blood had helped to build. Professor St. Clair Drake's assertion - that this "repudiation of the term African" did not necessarily imply a gesture of psychological rejection of Africa nor a lack of interest in the fate of the people of the continent who were still regarded as "kinsmen" [27]-is hardly convincing. Those who opted for the integrationist and amalgamationist position were clear as far as this was concerned and their chief spokesman, Frederick Douglass, emphasized it time out of number. Those who opted for the emigration option did so, in the first instance, to other regions rather than Africa, and Africa was for some of them only an afterthought. But there were also ardent believers in Africa, although their numbers were negligible. Yet in the next sentence, St. Clair Drake asserts that:

> However an image was in the making throughout the nineteenth century which stressed the deadly character of Africa's climate, the menace of its fauna, and the `savagery' of its people. This image, did, eventually, have a negative effect upon American Negro attitudes toward Africa, but it also spurred some Negroes to try to change the image to what they conceived of as the African Reality." [28]

The statement was clearly representative of one of the factors which had helped to fashion the negative attitude towards Africa, which many African descendants in the U.S.A. came to feel it would be a liability to identify with. The rejection of Africa or the attitude of ambivalence towards Africa which some of these people mirrored had been distilled to them through the psychological warfare that the slavocracy had waged against African values, concepts, and personalities since their first arrival. It worked its way through their consciousness into their subconscious mind and it was to generate controversy in the rank-and-file between those who had a favorable image and those who did not, an attitude of mind which has persisted into our day so late in the twentieth century.

Thus, St. Clair Drake's later point is a valid one and does imply some psychological rejection of Africa, especially the image of "savage" Africa, contrary to that of the minority who strove to fashion a different image of Africa from that expounded by the Euro-Americans and their European associates. We are not overlooking the valuable contributions which their efforts made to the fashioning of some bond of union, albeit spiritual in the main, with Africa. But these descendants of Africa in the Americas or Africans of the Diaspora, even in conceiving evangelistic schemes, tended to assimilate and express the prejudices of the Europeans and Euro-Americans and used the same expressions coined from the former in visualizing the Africans—terms like "benighted land," "uncivilized man," and "heathen" [29] belong to this genre of thought.

Question of Destiny

The question of destiny loomed large in this initial rejection of Africa, for it was clear at the time that the vast majority of African-derived peoples in North America had psychologically sought to tie their destiny to that of the European-derived peoples of the U.S.A. This preoccupation was never foolproof, for there were those who were concerned with the fate of Africa and succeeding generations inherited this mantle of defenders, vindicators, and protectors of the African image. But people of African origin in the U.S.A., apart from their physical characteristics, have never been allowed to forget their African origins (and why should they?). The African consciousness on the parent continent of the fate of its dispersed brethren is more recent in origin than that of the dispersed children of Africa in the New World for Africa, but whether at home or abroad consciousness has been confined to a minority. Apart from individual contacts with Africa either at a student level, missionary level, or as emissaries on behalf of the U.S. government or nongovernmental organizations (NGO's) the increase in the contact has been more persistent in the post-Second World War era and has been greatly enhanced by the emergence of certain formerly colonized states to sovereign status since the 1960s, commencing with the independence of the Sudan and Ghana in 1956 and 1957, respectively. But one area, since the early nineteenth century, where the contact between North America, the Caribbean, and Africa has been frequent is the Republic of Liberia,[30] the offspring of the American Colonization and the Maryland Colonization Societies. But there was another area from which West Africa had contact with its descendants from the Americas and that was Brazil (and Cuba to a very limited extent), a movement which had begun as a trickle in the late eighteenth century but which also bloomed between the second half of the nineteenth century and the early twentieth century. [31] These Africans from Brazil have left their imprint in parts of West Africa (especially in Nigeria) in places such as Campos Square in Lagos.

The question of destiny for Africans at home and those abroad never completely left the thoughts of certain Africans in the Diaspora in the Americas and elsewhere in the West and was preserved by intellectual, religious, and some quasi-political movements. Today more than ever, the question is more vehemently emphasized on both sides of the Atlantic and there is the promotion of a greater awareness, especially with the emergence of the Afrocentric movement following in the footsteps of those who, in the immediate post-Second World War period, organized writers and artist's assemblies such as the First and Second Congresses of Negro Writers and Artists in Paris and Rome in 1956 and 1959, respectively, and later leading up to the Africana or Pan-African Festival in Dakar and Lagos years after. The late Professor St. Clair Drake reminds us in this book *The Redemption of Africa and Black Religion* that these post-war manifestations and activities have themselves emerged from two traditions which had fashioned the attitudes of African-Americans towards Africa, namely, the missionary tradition and a race-conscious Pan-Africanism.

But despite the detractors, organizations continued to be formed in the United States with a definite reference to Africa or with an African orientation during the nineteenth century into the twentieth. Some of the more recent examples would be Malcolm X's Organization of African American Unity, but that falls outside the scope of this work. The persistence of this African connection since the eighteenth century from the formation of Richard Allen and Absalom Jones' Free African Society in Philadelphia (1786) followed by the founding of the African Churches in that city both of the Methodist and Baptist persuasion, and the recognition of the African in David Walker's *Appeal to the Colored Citizens of the World* (first published in 1829) and the production of the *Ethiopian Manifesto* in the same year by another descendant of Africa, Robert Young, all reflect the long tradition of this African connection in the Americas.

At the beginning of the twentieth century we can still see the leadership of prelates in this acceptance of Africa, with Bishop Alexander Walters of the A.M.E. Zion Church (who was President of the Pan-African Association formed in 1897) officiating at the first in the series of Pan-African Conferences, held in London in 1900. Apart from it being a historic conference, he was one among three others who became signatories to the appeal the conference issued to the great powers, titled "Address to the Nations of the World," in which the solidarity with Africa was expressed and they urged that the independence of Liberia, Ethiopia and Haiti be upheld. [32]

When Dr. W. E. B DuBois attempted to extend the conferences after the First World War, although he received a nodding approval from the National Association for the Advancement of Colored People, he observed that they saw his obsession with Africa as "quixotic." [33] But the conferences which followed testified to the African Diaspora's acceptance of Africa, a fact which was more vehemently expressed after Benito Mussolini, the Facist Italian leader, invaded Ethiopia (Abyssinia) in 1935. The attitude was demonstrative of a growing consciousness of Africa in an era in which the masses in the United States knew and cared little for her.

In summarizing this tradition of acceptance and rejection of Africa, we see the acceptance expressed in the formation of organizations and institutions—the churches and friendly and other beneficent societies; the Historical Societies such as the Negro Society for Historical Research, Garvey's Universal Negro Improvement Association (with Africa as the focus), and the World Ethiopian Federation. It has been expressed in publications and literature and embedded in the speeches of leaders. One recalls the Ethiopian Anthem of the Universal Negro Improvement Association. It has surfaced in the folklore and songs of people in the Americas, e.g. the song "A Long Way From Home." There have been organizational efforts to assemble facts on Africa through research and publications and the establishment of libraries and now museums (such as the National African-American Museum at Wilberfore, Ohio and the African-American Museum in Savannah, Georgia) and contact with African dignitaries and scholars and people in other walks of life (beginning with the founding of the American Negro Academy in 1897, whose first President was Alexander Crummell, who had before that spent twenty years of ministration in Africa to be succeeded by Dr. DuBois who was to write copiously on Africa). But there were the founders of the Negro Society for Historical Research at Yonkers, New York, among whom were Arthur Schomburg, an African of the diaspora whose place of birth was Puerto Rico and who began the task of collecting books relating to Africa and people of African descent and has immortalized his name in the archives bearing his name - the Schomburg Collections in New York. He represents only one in that endeavor. It was also done by the admission of African students into institutions founded for and by African-Americans; this in itself was to emphasize and reinforce the linkage with Africa, especially from students from Africa who returned after studying in America. The names are too numerous and do invite many more studies. Some of these were imbued with knowledge and enthusiasm for Africa and the need to forge that solidarity with their kith and kin in the Americas. Added to these are the organization of conferences from the outset of the Convention Movement in the nineteenth century into the twentieth, and although most of the convention sessions were concerned with destiny within the United States and other parts of the Americas those activities and other circumstances generated the Emigration Conventions, which were also to focus attention on Africa. But we see that those first and second "Congresses of Negro Writers and Artists" (1956 and 1959, respectively) also helped to foster a Pan-African perspective among African descendants at home and abroad and, even earlier, on descendants of Africa in the Americas who had in earlier times fashioned the Pan-African movement and were also in attendance at the immediate post- Second World War Pan-African meetings.

Although the tradition of ambivalence derived from induced notions of African "savagery" and assumed "heathenism" and many such expressions and modes of thought projected by the Europeans and Euro-Americans from whom enslaved descendants of Africa in the Americas took their cue, that tradition produced numerous conflicts in the leadership and rank-and-file alike and has continued to influence debates, if not conflict, even into our day. It is an area that deserves indepth study.

We must now consider the African Diaspora in comparison with the Jewish Diaspora in the next chapter. This can be only briefly discussed, in the hope that it will inspire further research on the subject.

NOTES

1. The sole exception was that retrospectively stated by Phyllis Wheatley in her poem quoted above. See Ch. 3 above.
2. See also Davidson, Basil, *Black Mother*, London, Victor Gollanez, 1961, pp. 100-101.
3. DuBois, W. E. B., *Souls of Black Folk*, Forum Series edited by C. L. R. James, London, Longman, 1965, pp. 2-3. See also DuBois, *Dusk of Dawn*, New York, Chicago, 1903; also 1935, ch. 7 esp. pp. 173-74.
4. Weisbord, Robert G., *Ebony Kinship: Africa, Africans and the African-Americans*, (Chapter on pre-Garvey era), p. 12.
5. Miller, Floyd J., *The Search for a Black Nationality: Black Emigration and Colonization 1787-1863*, Urbana, Illinois, University of Illinois Press, 1975, pp. 4-5.
6. Harris, Robert L., Jr., "Early Black Benevolent Societies, 1780-1830," *T-M-R* 20-23, Autumn, 1979, pp. 608-609.
7. F. J. Miller, *op. cit.*, p. 9.

8. Quoted in *Memoirs of Captain Paul Cuffee, etc.* on aspects of the life of Paul Cuffee. See Thomas, Lamont, D., *Paul Cuffee: Black Entrepreneur and Pan-Africanist*, Urbana and Chicago, 1988.
9. Weisbord, *Ebony Kinship*, p. 15.
10. *Ibid.*, p. 16.
11. Quoted in Weisbord, *op. cit.*, p. 17.
12. *Ibid.*, p. 17.
13. *Ibid.*, p. 18.
14. *Ibid.*
15. *Ibid.*
16. See *Memoirs of Captain Paul Cuffee, op. cit.*,
17. For the principles quiding the 'African Civilization Society' see H. Brotz, (ed.) *Negro Social and Political Thought*, pp. 191-195.
18. Delivered before the Union Literary and Historical Association, Washington, DC., May 4, 1881, reprinted in *Africa and America: Addresses and Discourses*, Springfield, MA, Wiley and Co., 1891.
19. Kilson, M. and Hill, A. C., *Apropos of Africa*, Frank Cass and Co., London, 1969, p. 79, (hardback).
20. Walker, David, *The Appeal in Four Articles to the Coloured Citizens of the United States*, 1829, Reprint H. Aptheker (ed.), 1968, Humanities Press, New York. The leadership of David Walker and the ideas he expressed are currently being reevaluated by a Professor at Howard University so we should not dwell too much on this as a comprehensive assessment is very much in the offing.
21. *Ibid.*
22. Hooker, H. R., *Henry Sylvester Williams: Imperial Pan-Africanist*, London, 1975, pp. 114-15.
23. *Ibid.*, p. 118, quoted from the *Mole*, (Port of Spain).
24. Williams, E. E., *British Historians and the West Indies*, London, Andre Deutsch, 1966, p. 210.
25. Hooker, *op. cit.*, p. 118.
26. The term 'negro' (later capitalized) was later adopted and in the era of Booker T. Washington's leadership which began seriously from 1895 after his Atlanta 'Compromise' Speech (1895), the term began to be spelled with a capital N.
27. See St. Clair Drake, "Negro Americans and the African Interest", in John P. Davis (ed.), *The American Negro Reference Book*, New York, 2 Vols., Vol. 2, 1966, p. 663, total article in pp. 629-66.
28. *Ibid.*, p. 663.
29. Alexander Crummell, *Hope of Africa.*
30. Another contact point was that involving the British colonial government's transfer of labor from the Sierra Leone-Liberian Axis to the West Indies - the so-called "Kru migrations." See J. U. J. Asiegbu, *Slavery and the Politics of Liberation*, and for a much more indepth study see Monica Schuler, `*Alas Alas Congo!*'
31. Richard D. Ralston, "The Return of Brazilians to West Africa in the 18th and 19th Centuries," *Canadian Journal of African Studies*, Vol. 3., No. 3, Fall, 1970, pp. 577-92.
32. see Walters, Bishop Alexander, *My Life and Work.*
33. DuBois, W. E. B., *Dusk of Dawn*

Part 4

Two Diasporas—
Symbols and Experience

CHAPTER 8

CONCEPT OF THE AFRICAN DIASPORA *VIS-À-VIS* THE JEWISH DIASPORA

INTRODUCTION

This study has arrived at a point at which the comparative perspective becomes imperative; imperative because the original concept of a diaspora (Greek for "dispersion") was related to the Jews of the Hellenistic Period. By extension it has come to be used for some experiences which appear similar in the historical evolution of other peoples. The African Diaspora, as a concept, is more recent and belongs to the nineteenth century in conception and the twentieth in persistent usage. In order to unravel points of similarity and contrast, some examination of the history of the African-Hebraic (Jewish) connections is necessary. This means a brief background history of this linkage, as narrated through the books of the Old and New Testaments, as these are the principal sources from which prelates of African descent in the dispersion in the United States and, to a limited extent, in the British West Indies, deduced parallels between their predicament and that of the Jews. Then there is the need for a brief statement of the diaspora as has been represented by religious and secular Jews. Some of the symbolic assimilations by those prelates of African descent in the American African Diaspora deduced from Judaic or the Judeo-Christian experiences are examined. These they felt coincided with their own experiences, especially because of the fundamentalist orientation of their thought. Sometimes, these thoughts have been taken verbatim and given the aura of prophecy with respect to the African-derived people. It is also necessary to sketch, briefly, some points of convergence and divergence between both diasporas and the inferences that may be made as to the validity of an African diaspora in comparison with that of the Jews. But to arrive at this validation it is essential to begin from the perspectives of a Jewish critic of the conventional view of the Jewish Diaspora, as this will provide not only a different perspective from the conventionally accepted notion of the Jewish Diaspora, but because it provides an alternative viewpoint that is rooted in historical and economic analysis.

A Critic of the Conventional View of the Jewish Diaspora

The African-Hebraic connection goes back to antiquity, as one Jewish writer, himself a victim of Nazi atrocities at Auschwitz (1944), Abram Leon, informs us. This African-Hebraic connection as well as the Jewish Diaspora itself can be seen in many forms of interrelationships with other peoples, but an essential element of that Jewish diaspora could be seen in trade and the commerce of those times and their extension into other periods of contact. It is also Leon's contention that the diaspora of the Jews had long been in existence, even before the specific historical landmarks of those specific experiences generally associated with the Jewish Diaspora, even by its own ardent spokesmen.

Generally, we are accustomed to think of the Jewish Diaspora in terms of shorter or prolonged periods of exile of the Jews from Israel or Palestine. Among these major landmarks are the period of "captivity in Egypt," [1] the Assyrian invasion of Israel under Sargon in the seventh century before the common era (BCE) and the peopling of parts of the country of Israel with the invaders, whose progeny in their union with the surviving Jews produced the Samaritans. Then there was the "Babylonian Captivity," which occurred about the fifth century BCE, and finally the destruction of the Temple of Jerusalem by the Romans (70 CE) under the Roman Emperor Titus, which, it is generally believed, created the longest diaspora of the Jews, encompassing two thousands years.

Abram Leone himself does not agree with these landmarks of the Jewish Diaspora, arguing that the diaspora of the Jews belongs to antiquity, and though agreeing that it occurred at different times, does not believe that the Roman destruction of Jerusalem was the major factor in the Diaspora of the Jews—nor that of the Persian period nor even the Babylonian captivity. He recognized that even after the latter, it was only a handful of Jews who returned to Jerusalem for the purpose of rebuilding their Temple, but the vast majority of Jews by this date were living in the diaspora. Leon's point, although controversial and contrary to the Orthodox Judaic religious conception of the Diaspora, is an attempt at correction of the commonly held belief that the Diaspora only occurred on three or four occasions (as indicated above), with the major one occurring in 70 CE. It is his contention that long before 70 CE, a larger proportion of Jews dwelt outside than inside Palestine: in short, they were in the Diaspora before the actual events commonly said to define it and before the dates often credited to the Jewish Diaspora.

Leon argues that "the preservation of the Jews is explained by all historians as the produce of their devotion through the centuries to their religion or their nationality." [2] But he insists that "differences among these historians begin to appear only when it comes to defining the `goal' for which the Jews preserved themselves, the reason for their resistance to assimilation." He argued that some taking the religious point of view tended to speak of the "sacred trust of their faith"; others, like Dubnow, defended the theory of "attachment to national idea." Leon, while rejecting both positions, suggested that the attention by idealistic historians to the causes for the historical phenomenon of the preservation of the Jewish people in their "national spiritual strength, in their ethical basis and in the monotheistic principle" must be found elsewhere, that is: in a study of the economic role played by the Jews, for only this could contribute to elucidating the causes for the "miracle of the Jew". [3]

While Leon was, in fact, correct in asserting that "without a thorough study of Jewish history, it is difficult to understand the Jewish question in modern times," he had insisted that the "plight of the Jews in the Twentieth century is intimately bound up with their historical past." [4] It is for this reason that he argued against starting with religion in order to explain Jewish history. He felt that, on the contrary, "the preservation of the Jewish religion or nationality can be explained only by the `real Jew,' that is to say, by the Jew in his economic and social role," [5] as that preservation contained nothing miraculous, arguing that "Judaism has survived not in spite of history, but by virtue of history."[6] He felt that this could be done only by the study of the historical function of Judaism, and that the struggles between Judaism and Christianity in society, despite their religious guises were in essence social struggles. He could not bring himself to agree with the general pattern of Jewish history which emphasized that "the wars between the Romans and the Jews resulted in dispersing the Jewish nation to the four corners of the world; and that in the dispersion, the Jews fiercely resisted national and religious assimilation."[7] He rejects this position, arguing that Jews in the dispersion at various times were rejectionists depending on their circumstances - which, he emphasizes were largely economic and social. Thus, he stated that:

> The dispersal of the Jews does not at all date from the fall of Jerusalem. Several centuries before this event, the great majority of Jews were already spread over the four corners of the world. It is certain that well before the fall of Jerusalem, more than three-fourths of the Jews no longer lived in Palestine.[8]

Leon further argued that "the Diaspora was consequently not at all an accidental thing, a produce of acts of violence." He felt that the fundamental reason for Jewish emigration must be sought in the geographical conditions of Palestine and went on to observe that:

> The Jews in Palestine were the possessors of a mountainous country which at a certain time no longer sufficed for assuring its inhabitants as tolerable an existence as that among their neighbors. Such a people is driven to chose between brigandage and emigration. The Scots for example, alternately engaged in each of these pursuits. The Jews, after numerous struggles with their neighbors, also took the second road... People living under such conditions do not go to foreign countries as agriculturists. They go there rather in the role of mercenaries, like the Arcadians of Antiquity, the Swiss in the Middle Ages, the Albanians in our day; or in the role of merchants, like the Jews, the Scots and the Armenians. We see here that a similar environment tends to produce similar characteristics among peoples of different races.[9]

He went on to contend and demonstrate that "The overwhelming majority of Jews of the Diaspora unquestionably engaged in trade." Furthermore, that Palestine itself from very remote times "constituted a passageway for merchandise, a bridge between the valleys of the Euphrates and the Nile," with Syria as the "inevitable highway of the conquerors.... Trade and ideas followed the same route. It is easy to see that from a very early date these regions were thickly populated, and possessed great cities whose very situation lent itself to commerce."[10]

In light of Leon's study of the Jewish experience from antiquity and observing the hostility to the Jewish people from antiquity to our own times, he was able to say that: "It is not the loyalty of the Jews to their faith which explains their preservation as a distinct social group; on the contrary, it is their preservation as a distinct social group which explains their attachment to their faith." But be this as it may, from the perspective of the prelates in the African Diaspora in the Americas, it is from their perception of the preservation of the faith of the Jews that they in turn drew their examples and symbolisms in order to explain the predicament of the Africans of the diaspora in the Americas. Accordingly, we shall advert to the Biblical texts, be they doctored or altered or rendered verbatim, as it is from those texts and the interpretations of them that those African-American prelates took their cue.

But Leon, who did not see the Jews as a national group, referred to them as "a people-class,"[11] based on their economic role in the various societies in which they dwelt; and to reinforce his denial of their being a nation - whether in antiquity, in the Middle Ages, or in modern times - he explained that the language of nationality which was claimed for them, Hebrew, had disappeared very early as a living language. He also observed that "The Jews everywhere adopted the languages of the peoples among whom they lived. But this linguistic adoption generally occurred in the form of a new dialect in which we find some Hebraic expressions. There existed at various times in history Judaeo-Arabic, Judaeo-Persian, Judaeo-Provencal, Judaeo-Portuguese, Judaeo-Spanish and other dialects, including, of course, Judaeo-German, which has become present-day Yiddish. The dialect thus expresses the two contradictory tendencies which have characterized Jewish life - the tendency to integration in the surrounding society and the tendency to isolation, deriving from the socio-economic situation of Judaism. It is where the Jews cease constituting a special social group that they became completely assimilated in the surrounding society. "Assimilation is no new phenomenon in Jewish history."[12] he insisted, quoting the Zionist sociologist Ruppin.

He observed that during the Persian epoch of the Jewish Diaspora, the principal colonies of the Diaspora were situated in Mesopotamia, in Chaldea, and in Egypt; and from the documents found at Elephantine in Egypt dating from the fifth century BCE, some useful light is thrown on the condition of the Jewish colonies of the Diaspora. Thus, from the archives belonging to a Jewish family it was revealed that the "Jews engaged in trade, bought and sold houses and land, loaned money, acted as depositaries, and were well versed in matters of law." Furthermore, he observed, "It is very interesting to note that even the songs and chronicles are in Aramaic which shows that as early as the Fifth Century B.C. Hebrew was no longer a customary language for the Jews. Aramaic was the great Asiatic language of the period, the commercial language." [13] Furthermore, he argued, the religion of the Jews of Elephantine was not as developed as the official religion codified during the Ezra-Nehemiah era, the era in which the Jews had petitioned the Persian governor in order to rebuild their temple in Jerusalem. He insisted that the reform of the Ezra-Nehemiah era was not aimed precisely at "concentrating all the Jews of the Diaspora around the single temple of Jerusalem." But it was, in fact, to Jerusalem that the gifts of the Jews dispersed throughout the world continued to flow up to the year 70 A.D. He argued that it was more to get at this wealth that Antiochus Epiphanes made his offensive against the Jews, having been advised that the public treasury at Jerusalem was full of large sums and that there were "enormous public riches." [14]

In further extending his thought to the Hellenistic period in Egypt and especially during the Christian era, he observed that there was a huge community of Jews at Alexandria forming a separate community which governed itself and was not subject to the jurisdiction of the Greek courts. Also from the cultural standpoint, these Alexandrine Jews "were completely assimilated and no longer spoke anything but Greek. It was on their account that the Hebrew religious books had to be translated into that language." Although the Jews spread to other regions such as Italy, Gaul and Spain, Jerusalem, he admitted, "continued to be the religious center of Diaspora Judaism." [15]

Leon did not discount the belief that when conditions proved unfavorable the Jews suffered and became victims of hostility and that when conditions were good they constituted privileged people in the societies in which they dwelt, whether in Persia in Hellenic times and in their colonies or during Roman times in Roman colonies and in other times and places. Thus he wrote:

> The situation which the Jews had acquired for themselves in the Hellenistic epoch appears to have undergone no fundamental transformation after the Roman conquest. The privileges conferred upon the Jews by Hellenistic laws were confirmed by the Roman emperors. "The Jews enjoyed a privileged position in the Roman Empire." The fact that nearly a million Jews lived in Alexandria alone is sufficient evidence

> of their primarily commercial role in the Dispersion, which embraced three and a half million Jews several centuries before the seizure of Jerusalem, whereas hardly a million continued to live in Palestine. "Alexandria in Egypt, under the Roman Emperors, was what Tyre had been in the epoch of the Phoenician commercial glory.... Under the reign of the Ptolemies, a direct trade between Egypt and India had been established. From Thebes, caravans went to Merowe in Upper Nubia, whose markets were also frequented by caravans from the interior of Africa... A Roman fleet went to the mouth of the Nile to receive the precious objects and distribute them in the Empire." Two out of the five sections of Alexandra were inhabited by Jews. The role of the Jews at Alexandria was so important that a Jew, Tiberius Julius Alexander, was appointed Roman governor of this city. [16]

Leon went on to observe that "From the cultural standpoint, these Alexandrine Jews were completely assimilated and no longer spoke anything but Greek. It was on their account that the Hebrew religious books had to be translated into that language" and that communities similar to that of Alexandria were located in all the commercial centers of the Empire. [17] However, it was his contention that "It was solely the economic and social position of the Jews in the Diaspora which, even before the fall of Jerusalem, make possible their religious and national cohesion."[18] But he cautioned against the assumption, despite Jerusalem as the focal point for Jewish religion (quoting Strabo), that it would be "erroneous to think that Palestine was entirely inhabited by Jews." For in the north were to be found several Greek cities while almost all of the west was "inhabited generally, as each place in particular, by mixed tribes of Egyptians, Arabians, and Phoenicians...."[19] In the time of Strabo, Jerusalem was a great city of wealth, consisting of 200,000 inhabitants, with the Temple as the major reason for its importance.

Leon, who saw the assimilationst orientation of Jewish "tribes" of Arabia or Jewish farmers of North Africa, asserts that nothing remained of them but "legends" in contrast to the commercial colonies which flourished elsewhere in places like Gaul, Spain, and Germany. It was, therefore, his contention that:

> ...if the Jews have been preserved, it was not *despite* their dispersion but *because* of it. If there had been no Dispersion prior to the fall of Jerusalem, if the Jews had remained in Palestine, there is no reason to believe that their faith would have been different from that of all the others nations of

> Antiquity. The Jews, like the Romans, the Greeks, the Egyptians, would have mixed up with the conquering nations, would have adopted their religion and their customs. Even if the present inhabitants of Palestine would have continued to bear the name of Jews, they would have had as little in common with the ancient Hebrews as the inhabitants of Egypt, Syria and Greece have with their ancestors of Antiquity. All the peoples of the Roman Empire were carried away in its fall. Only the Jews have been preserved because they brought into the barbarian world, which followed upon the Roman, vestiges of the commercial development which had characterized the ancient world. after the Mediterranean world was dismembered, they continued, among themselves, to link its scattered parts together.[20]

In keeping with this thought he insisted that, as a result, for many centuries, "the Jews continued to be the sole commercial intermediaries between the East and the West. Spain and France progressively became the centers of Jewish life."[21] He also recounted their fabled prosperity in numerous lands, including what would today be regarded as Eastern Europe in places like Poland and Russia and the rise of the Rothschilds of Cracow and Levko, the banker to three Polish kings and Bochnia and also the administratòr of the mint of Cracow. The essential point of his contention was that as long as a natural economy reigned, the Jews were "indispensable to it; it was economic decline that provided the "signal for persecution against the Jews" and for a protracted period continued to exert an adverse influence on their situation.[22]

But the assimilationist orientation of these prosperous Jews was expressed in their insistence that they were nationals of the countries in which they dwelt; thus, in the nineteenth century when this orientation was at its apogee, German Jews would insist that they were Germans and Germans only in whatever concerned nationality and their intellectuals often took that position, even during the second half of the same century.[23] He believed that it was the inflow of Jews from Eastern Europe that gave a new lease on life to what he termed the "moribund body of Judaism."[24] By that time Judaism had undergone another transformation and with the increase of anti-Judaism (anti-Semitism) it also produced Jewish nationalism and, consequently, "the renaissance of the Jewish nation," the formation of a modern Jewish culture, elaboration of the Yiddish language, Zionism, all accompanying the process of emigration and concentration of Jewish masses in the cities. This concentration in urban centers, he continued, also fuelled modern anti-Semitism.[25] These anti-Semitic activities reared their ugly heads at universities in the attempt to bar Jews from entering the intellectual professions. [26] With such tendencies emerged the assertions that what Europe chose to describe as the "Jewish question" defied any solution. [27]

Soon pogroms were organized against Jews, culminating in the pre-World War II excesses against them and those which accompanied the war, as shameful an episode in human history as the African slave trade. By this time, the "Jewish question" was as much an issue for concern in Eastern Europe (from which Jews were emigrating to the west) as it was in western countries (the recipients of the immigrants). The antagonisms manifested towards them soon assumed the garb of "racism" often led by fanatics. Jews began to be perceived as the harbingers of every sin that had a name. Out of these experiences in the nineteenth century emerged the idea of Zionism, with Dr. Leo Pinsker as its inspirer in the second half of the nineteenth century and Theodore Herzl as its champion and chief proponent, as elaborated in his book *The Jewish State*. Although Pinsker had advocated a return to Palestine for the "Lovers of Zion," the conviction and resourcefulness of Herzl helped to give it substance until out of the preoccupation emerged the Jewish National Congress in the late nineteenth century. The idea was not without critics and opponents, but these would become minimized as the Jews suffered further persecution, pogroms, ostracism and all the devilry human beings were capable of unleashing. The formulations which came with organization and intellectual as well as religious revivals and the revival of the Hebrew language and other modes of cultural evolution all contributed to giving it direction, and with it came again to the fore the notion of the "Return" as emphasized in the Biblical prophecy of "restoration".

Jews in influential positions in the Western world were able to influence the opinions of governments and, in time, with power to exercise leverage, which compelled governments in the Western world to hearken to the plight of the Jews. It was during the First World War that the Balfour Declaration (named after the British Prime Minister Lord Arthur J. Balfour) was issued with its commitment to a "National Home" for the Jews in Palestine. The notion of the two-thousand-year-old exile was fed into Zionism by the religious authorities and their adherents. From that moment the notion of the "Promised Land" became an obsession of the Jewish masses.

The Judaic derivative as consistent with the Christian perception of the Biblical derivative became the religious arm of Zionism. But it also satisfied some emotional yearnings of those non-religious Jews in terms of a "national home," even if it has not resolved the "Jewish Problem".

BACKGROUND OF AFRICAN-JEWISH CONNECTION

A comparative perspective between the Jewish Diaspora and that of the Africans (especially in the Americas) may seem, at first sight, far-fetched. But we need to take account of some factors which made this comparison plausible and necessary. The first is that Africa, as a continent, has always remained contiguous with that land that was traditionally known as Palestine or the Land of the Hebrews, the forebears of the Jews. The contact between both communities of Africans and Hebrews has existed since ancient times and there had been movements of persons on both sides of what today is an apparent divide. In ancient times movement from one part into the other was uninhibited or unrestricted; the current geopolitical division only came about in the nineteenth century, after the re-cutting of the Suez Canal. Second, their peoples had shared many religious and cultural experiences from ancient, through medieval, and into modern times. Third, Africa had, at various times, provided refuge to the ancestors of the Jews, the Habiru (alias Hebrews), fleeing from famine and/or persecution. Even the patriarchs and some of the earliest leaders of the Jews found sanctuary in Africa. The Book of Genesis, one of the five Books of the Law (*Torah*), told us about the journeys and exploits of Abraham and that famine had driven Abraham into Egypt to sojourn there "for the famine was grievous in the land" (Genesis 12:10). According to the story he concealed the identity of his wife Sarai [Sarah] so that she would appear [as] his sister in order that he might not be killed by the Egyptians[28] (Genesis 12:11-20).

Again, in Chapter 16 of Genesis, we are told that Sarai, having failed to bear Abraham any children but having an Egyptian maidservant, whose name was Hagar, urged him to take Hagar to wife and bear a son through her so that Sarai herself might be blessed with a son. The passage reads:

> And Sarai said unto Abram, [`]Behold, now, the Lord hath restrained me from bearing. I pray thee, go in unto my maid; it may be that I may obtain children by her.['] And Abram hearkened to the voice of Sarai.And Sarai Abram's wife took Hagar her maid, the Egyptian, after Abram had dwelt ten years in the land of Canaan, and gave her to her husband to be his wife. And he went in unto Hagar, and she conceived: and when she saw that she had conceived her mistress was despised in her eyes. (*Genesis*, Ch. 16, vs. 1-4)

Subsequent verses tell of how Sarai's anger was kindled against Hagar and the latter fled from home and was advised by an angel to return home to her mistress and there was promised that her seed would multiply into numberless multitudes (Genesis 16:1-4) Hagar bore Ishmael. This too was a promise of God (Genesis 16:11). The birth of Ishmael is mentioned in verse 15. Through this good fortune Sarai too conceived and bore a son called Isaac. While according to the Hebrew version the covenant was made with Abraham about the descendants of Issac to become a great nation, God also promised to make Ishmael the begetter of a great nation (Genesis 17:20). The passage for Ishmael reads:

> And as for Ismael, I have heard thee: Behold I have blessed him, and will make him fruitful, and will multiply him exceedingly; twelve princes shall he beget, and I will make him a great nation.

Hagar the Egyptian had given birth to a child for Abraham, thus, the linkage in blood had been established between the *Habiru* (Hebrews) and Africans. But the Arabs claim their descent from Ishmael and Ishmaelites; and, if this claim be accepted, the Hebrews, Arabs, and Egyptians (Africans) are related by blood. But other incidents were to establish consanguinity.

In this ancient linkage between Africans and the Jews we find that Moses was brought up by Pharaoh's daughter as an Egyptian Prince and was learned in all the arts of the Egyptians. It was Pharaoh's daughter who named Moses because she drew him out of the water (Genesis 2:10 and Acts 7:22-23). The passage from the Acts of the Apostles reads:

> And Moses was learned in all the wisdom of the Egyptians, and was mighty in words and in deeds. And when he was full forty years old, it came into his heart to visit his brethren the children of Israel.

Yet, prior to Moses, it was Joseph, the son of Jacob (Israel), who, through the envy by his brothers, had been sold into Egypt. But it was Joseph who rescued them from famine and brought his father Jacob (Israel) and all his brethren to Egypt until Jacob's death (Genesis 42-47). According to the Acts of the Apostles, the brethren that came with Jacob to dwell in Egypt in (Goshen) were "three scores and fifteen" (seventy-five persons), but at the time of the Exodus from Egypt they were numbered in thousands and their numbers could only have increased through intermarriage with Egyptians and other Africans in the vicinity. Those who left Egypt were regarded as a "mixed multitude." [29]

But we must return to Moses, who also married Zipporah, the daughter of Jethro, Priest of Midian, who bore him two sons (Exodus

18:3-4) after his escape from Egypt into the land of Midian, which was also Africa (Exodus 4:20). Again we find Aaron and Miriam, the brother and sister of Moses, murmuring against Moses because he had married an "Ethiopian woman" (Numbers 13:1-2) and as a punishment Miriam was struck with leprosy for seven days (Numbers 13:10). All these emphasized the linkage in blood with Africans.

During the first millennium before the establishment of Christianity, Jewish communities were living in Egypt. They formed a large community in Alexandria after the conquest of Egypt by Alexander the Great and were in large numbers at the coming of Christianity. After the dispersion which followed the destruction of Jerusalem and the second Temple, many spread to other parts of the Near East and many communities of Jews formed on the North African coast and elsewhere in Asia Minor.

Furthermore, at the time of Jesus Christ's birth, when Herod the Great sought to destroy the child because of the fear of the rise of a rival king, the parents of Jesus found sanctuary again in Egypt. Because of these many associations, it was God's injunctions to the Jews that "Thou shall not abhor an Egyptian because thou was a stranger in his land." An appropriate paraphrase would be "this land and people gave you sanctuary during your sojourn and in times of distress."

In the two thousand years since 70 CE, Jews and Africans have coexisted and intermarried in North Africa and in the Iberian Peninsula, especially during the seven centuries of Moorish hegemony in Spain. After the fall of Granada in 1492, they were expelled together and many returned to Africa. The African-Jewish connection is, therefore, longstanding. But these apart, as has been indicated elsewhere, the word "Diaspora" itself is Greek for "dispersion" and derives from the Septuagint translation of the Bible in the Book of Deuteronomy, the fifth book of the Jewish Torah or what the Christians call the Pentateuch, the fifth of the five Books of Moses. It relates to prophecy and its fulfillment, as therein stated in Deuteronomy:

> The Lord shall cause thee to be smitten before thine enemies; thou shalt go out one way against them, and flee seven ways before them; and shall be removed into all the Kingdoms of the earth. [30]

Despite this dispersion for transgression, in time, it was to be followed by a return and restoration, as had occurred, though minimally, in the "Babylonian Captivity." [31] In Deuteronomy it is thus stated:

> And it shall come to pass, when all these things are come upon thee, the blessing and the curse, which I have set before thee, and though shalt call them to mind among all the nations, whither the Lord thy God had driven thee..
>
> And shall return unto the Lord thy God, and shall obey his voice according to all that I command thee this day, thou and thy children, with all thine heart, and with all thy soul.
>
> That then the Lord thy God will turn thy captivity, and have compassion upon thee, and will return and gather three from all the nations, whither the Lord thy God hath scattered thee...
>
> And the Lord thy God will bring thee into the land which they fathers possessed, and thou shall possess it; and he will do thee good, and multiply thee above they fathers. [32]

The above quotation relates to escatological considerations and is expressed in explicit terms as to destiny, hence the "return." With these, we may assert that the Jewish Diaspora is the original Diaspora, while the African Diaspora is the secondary Diaspora; and those who have perceived the various dispersions of Africans from their original homeland as diaspora have drawn their inspiration from the Jewish experience. The term diaspora has continued to be used for other forms of dispersion with a secular rather than religious connotation, and is now very much in vogue. But it is instructive to study the African Diaspora in the Americas in comparison with that of the Jews; by hindsight, there are many points of convergence as well as some qualitative differences.

Nonetheless, in the Americas, many aspects of Jewish symbolism came to be deeply meaningful to Africans in their own diaspora. It was also the result of inculcation by their ministers, who saw parallels. Thus, the names of Moses, Joshua, David, Daniel, Jeremiah—the names of the prophets, priests, and kings of the ancient Hebrews—found expression in song—songs of sorrow, songs of protest, of defiance, liberty, sarcasm, denunciation, and hope: the Spirituals, the blues, the calypsos, which the Africans in the Americas forged from the time of their transfer from Africa to the nineteenth and twentieth centuries. The River Jordan might have had its equivalent in the Mississippi in the United States, or (in the perception of the African-American prelate, Alexander Crummell), the Atlantic Ocean. [33] The objectives—liberation, redemption, freedom - were the same for the Jews and the Africans, although the latter naturally would have likened the Mississippi to the Jordan in their hope of redemption from their enslavers and securing the freedom to operate as free people.

Central Thesis of the Jewish Diaspora

In order to comprehend the points of convergence and divergence between the Jewish and the African diasporas, it is essential to state briefly what is the central thesis and theme of the Jewish Diaspora. It involved A) dispersion, B) sojourn in foreign lands (as punishment for transgressions against God and in fulfillment of prophecy) and, eventually, C) a return as a result of divine pardon when the Jews had mended their ways. Their restoration after dispersion into all the kingdoms of the earth implies the emergence of a national identity in a land promised to them in the covenant which God made with their patriarchs. All of these ideas fed into the Zionist return movements when determined efforts began to be made by dispersed Jews in the European world. It also implied escatological features essentially concerned with their destiny. In terms of Jewish perception, on this earth this destiny was coated with the veneer of spirituality.

Jews themselves have employed two terms in relation to their diaspora, the word *galut* to mean dispersion and *tetuzot* to mean exile. This diaspora has its basis in the Biblical prophecy which condemns them to dispersion into "all kingdoms of the earth." By observing the features of this dispersion and exile more in terms of its implications, which later translated itself into Zionism in the nineteenth century, we are able to comprehend the ethos of the "return" which became very persistent in their preoccupations in the second half of the nineteenth century and the first four decades of the twentieth.

The Jews of the diaspora had a variety of experiences ranging from good to bad, from success and prosperity to persecution, pogroms, vilification, and victimization to expulsion in certain cases and even violent death in many situations. These experiences were to generate an awareness of what Jews and non-Jews tended to describe as "the Jewish question" consistent in the minds of other people with the "Jewish problem." Its African equivalent in the African Diaspora was called "the Negro problem." These experiences in time not only created the ethos for the "return" but later became an obsession after a long period of incubation until it evolved into modern Jewish nationalism and later Zionism. The latter in the time of high advocacy had a religious perception of the return, a political conception of it, and a cultural version as well. There were others among these Jews, and especially those who had prospered in the Western world in Europe and America, who had assimilated and adjusted themselves to their societies, and who initially rejected the notion of a return to what the enthusiasts would refer to as Erez Israel ("the land of Israel"). While the religious leaders saw events in terms of prophecy and divine providence, political zionists de-emphasized the religious conception, while the cultural exponents also saw it in terms of their history and the possible loss of their culture while sojourning in foreign, often hostile, lands. So whether conceived in terms of dispersion or exile (and both pertain to the Jewish concept of diaspora), these perceptions are equally applicable to the African experience.

By the late nineteenth century the leaders of the Zionist movement had adopted policies which enabled them to organize; and organization was vital to the success of their aspirations, as only through organization did the prospect of transfer of people to the designated homeland in Palestine appear realizable. Secondly, they aimed, through political and diplomatic channels, to have their cause represented with a view to winning support for the overall objective of diaspora Jewry. Thirdly, as part of what was conceived of as "cultural revival," they saw the necessity for the revival of the Hebrew language and education. This also gave gravity to the concept of a distinct nationality.

But the opponents of these endeavors among the Jews had misgivings, believing that these activities would only create more problems for diaspora Jewry than it would resolve. Many seemed contented to remain in the societies in which their lives had taken root and did not wish to have them disrupted. But the advocates (Pinsker, Herzl and many more celebrated in the records of Zionism) were outstanding men. Soon, many professional people, intellectuals, and, in time, business people lent their hands and minds to the effort. The persecutions which they had endured and experienced, including the atrocities which broke out with the rise of Hitler in Nazi Germany, were to convince more and more Jews in the Jewish Diaspora that a national homeland was a vital prerequisite to both the resolution of their problems and the ensurance of their survival. By 1897, the Jews had attained the culmination point in terms of their organization through the emergence of the Jewish National Congress. Significantly, that too was the year of the founding in the United States of the American Negro Academy, an organization dedicated to the mental and material emancipation of the African-Americans as well as their intellectual growth.

Because of their dispersion of the Jews through the centuries, much of Jewish history is perforce diaspora history. The same cannot be said for African history, as the bulk of the African population remained on the parent continent, unlike the Jews, for whom, despite the "return" in modern times, the majority of Jews are still in the diaspora. Despite the buffettings which African societies endured from antiquity through medieval times and into the modern era, especially the slave trade which racked their continent for four centuries, African societies have survived in such a way that their diasporan history is but a small arm of their total history. But the diaspora established an extension of Africa nonetheless, although Africans suffered another century of domination (under European imperialism) after the termination of the slave trade and the slavery system. Only a small fraction of the African population in the diaspora had sought return, just as with the Jews, emphasizing a similarity in their experiences. For despite the realization of a "national home," the majority of Jews are still in the diaspora. But Israel—for the Jews in the dispersion and those at home—remains a focal point in their perception of an original homeland. For the Africans in the Americas, recent heightened consciousness of Africa (principally in the twentieth century) has only lately made for a sense of identity which was ever-present in the emotional considerations of the Jews. There were, of course, in the African Diaspora always a number of African descendants, who always thought of it as the original homeland; but the thought was not as consistent and sustained as the Jewish perception of Israel.

Opponents of Jewish Zionism would argue that this sentimental attachment to the original homeland did not exist, except among a minority, and did not begin to manifest itself before the late nineteenth century. Be this as it may, the Jews from the nineteenth century onwards had evolved a leadership of thinkers, idealists (in short, a leadership of ideas) that took the initiative in organizing conferences, balanced by a moral, financial, and organizational leadership which eventually made the idea of a "national homeland" (alias "Zion") a reality. This leadership intensified the activities of the faithful in this objective; for leadership was hardly meaningful if it did not inspire and enthuse and galvanize the Jewish "masses" into action. Through contact with powerful personalities in some of the States of Europe and in the United States, their endeavors received the boost which they needed through the intervention of powerful forces from these Euro-American quarters, which enabled them to exact the Balfour Declaration of 1917, to which British Prime Ministers, A. J. Balfour, Lloyd George, and Lord Milne (Colonial Secretary and Foreign) subscribed their names and lent the weight of their authority.

Leadership which emerged in the nineteenth century among the Jews of the Jewish Diaspora took the form of political and economic assistance to achieve effective organization. By contrast, the leadership of the African Diaspora in the Americas that evolved with a vision of Africa was negligible and not very significant for those times. They were thus lone voices "crying out in the wilderness" of American race prejudice and disdain. Accordingly, their advocacies did not attain the same level of organizational success that the Jews in the Jewish Diaspora had achieved. An essential point in the evolution of Jewish leadership in the Diaspora needs to be stressed in comparison with that of Africans in America. It was that the Jews, regardless of their handicaps, were free people, whereas for African-Americans (even among their leaders and others nominally "free"), the danger of being re-enslaved was ever-present; moreover their deportation was being actively canvassed. Any one of these expedients would have vitiated their efforts and prevented cohesion and effective action.

It must not be assumed, though, that many Jews did not oppose the Zionist revival of the notion of the "return." In fact, the Jews in the Western world rejected it initially; it was the Eastern European Jews —many of them victims of persecution, pogroms and belonging to the lower "class" strata of society—who were to tip the scales in favor of Zionism and improve the prospects for its realization. Once the concept of the national home had been formulated, it was difficult to dampen the fervor for it. Once they had come to believe and assert that only the creation of a Jewish State could provide the real cure for anti-Jewishness and resolve the so-called Jewish question, the notion took on a life and momentum of its own.

The African Diaspora, by contrast, lacked an African Chaim Weizemann to press its case with a powerful nation and to charm them with careful artistry to secure an African equivalent of the Balfour Declaration. They also lacked the African equivalent of the Moses Mendellsshons, Rothschilds, and Montefiores who exercised leverage in the societies of Europe and the Americas and who lent the weight of their wealth and influence to sustain the organizational efforts. The spokesmen for an African nationality, led by Delany and McNeal Turner and some other prelates, lacked the influence as well as the financial strength and societal standing for the powers of the West (especially the European powers who were then imperialists in Africa with their own and designs for African exploitation) to make their influences felt. They could hardly gain audiences. We should recall the Petition from West Africa of the National Congress of British West Africa in 1920 to Lord Milne (as Colonial Secretary) and the delegation which they sent to London. The delegation was not received and they were totally ignored by the Colonial Office. They merely had the audience of a private organization, the League of Nations Union, under Professor Gilbert Murray, which they naively thought was an organization of some gravity in the Western World.

That meeting produced no tangible results.

When it gathered momentum, the Jewish preoccupation with Zion was insistent, while that of Africans in America ebbed and flowed, lacking any consistency and perseverance for this advocacy. In America the African Diaspora was always faced with the ever-present danger of deportation, despite the contributions Africans had made to the society. For instance, as late as April 1863, President Lincoln had spoken thus to General Butler:

> But what shall we do with the Negroes after they are free? I can hardly believe that the South and North can live in peace unless we get rid of the Negroes. Certainly they cannot, if we don't get rid of the Negroes whom we have armed and disciplined and who have fought with us, to the amount, I believe of some 150,000 men. I believe that it would be better to export them all to some fertile country with a good climate, which they could have to themselves. You have been a staunch friend of the race from the time you first advised me to enlist them at New Orleans. You have a great deal of experience in moving bodies of men by water—your movement up the James was a magnificent one. Now we shall have no use for our very large navy. What then are our difficulties in sending the blacks away? [34]

In his reply, after spending the night considering the matter, General Butler replied:

> Mr. President, I have gone very carefully over my calculations as to the power of the country to export the Negroes of the South and I assure you that using all your naval vessels and all the merchant marine fit to cross the seas with safety, it will be impossible for you to transport to the nearest place that can be found fit for them-and that is the Island of San Domingo, half as fast as Negro children will be born here.

As a complement to this thought, shortly after, the Secretary of the Interior was reporting that the "Negroes" were no longer willing to leave the United States and they were needed in the army and thought for those reasons that they should not forcibly be deported. Thus, on July 2, 1864, all laws relating to the colonization of the "Negro" were repealed. [35]

Butler's reply implied more. He implied that it was morally reprehensible and financially unsound. Indeed, it was unethical to deny the relevance of the African-Americans' contributions to the nation. By advising against their forcible removal from the country, Butler was perceptive in terms of the morality involved in exploiting their prowess and then despatching them as if they were mercenaries. It even went against the principles which had guided the manumission of the slaves in an earlier period, when service in the army or militia was one criterion for obtaining freedom. All these factors bedeviled the diaspora of the Africans in the Americas. These were a people who had amply earned their emancipation, yet, due to the forces ranged against them, the tirades and calumnies heaped on them, and the doubts about their capacity for improvement, there was a stubborn refusal to recognize their contribution to society, while that of the Jews was acknowledged throughout the world. We shall return to this presently.

The Jews and their Contributions

In the appropriation of the term "Diaspora" we need to reemphasize how the world has been influenced by Jewish people, concepts, symbolisms, and inventions. We may refer to four important figures of history who were Jewish and whose influences have been fundamental: they were Jesus Christ, Karl Marx, Sigmund Freud, and Albert Einstein, all of whom make their mark in the realm of ideas. There are enough examples in other spheres to emphasize the weight of Jewish contributions to humanity, as well as techniques in fields such as the foundations of banking which still sustain economic life in modern societies. But their history, which has largely been diasporan history, has vindicated them. While the contributions of the Jews have been acknowledged, those of Africans and their descendants are ignored and for this reason we intend to recall, albeit briefly, some of their worthy contributions in the United States,—concrete, material inventions which have also benefitted mankind, and this despite their long enslavement. DuBois' *The Gift of Black Folk* was an early attempt to indentify some of their contributors.

The Myth of Being Worthless

While the Jews played prominent roles in many spheres in the growth of ideas, in business and banking, in the growth of movements and even in the so-called "lowly trades," the Africans in the American dispersion produced only a few affluent and prominent representatives. Some of these had inherited their wealth from their white or mulatto parents; while others had themselves owned slaves in Louisiana and Savannah (Georgia). A few, by their perseverance and hard work, had also improved their economic status. But the majority continued to fight discrimination, violence, and detraction and other destructive attempts at preventing their growth mentally, spiritually, and materially. The records are replete with the destruction of efforts by these unfortunate people, often unprotected by the law and given no redress. But despite the odds against them, the Africans in the United States produced some outstanding people of quality and ability, some of whom contributed and piloted some worthy inventions from which mankind has benefitted. Yet the world remains oblivious to the fact that the initial experiments which produced these inventions were, in fact, due to the ingenuity, the persistence, and the exertions of these African-derived people. It is, therefore, necessary to recall some of them in this work, despite the obstacles put in their paths and attempts to discourage them.

As we approach the inventiveness of some Africans in the Diaspora, the question raised by my editor as to whether Booker T. Washington knew something more than his critics such as Dr. DuBois and others which the latter were oblivious to deserves a reply. The issue related to the creative genius of the African people. My editor referred to the controversy which has arisen between Wole Soyinka and three critics of his in a matter which revolved around the content and nature of African writing and poetry in which the Yoruba deity, Ogun, a creative deity, featured prominently in Soyinka's reply to his critics which first appeared in *Transition* #48 (1975), Essay titled: "Neo-Tarzanism: The Poetics of Pseudo-Tradition" reprinted in: pp. 293-305 of his book, *Art, Dialogue, and Outrage: Essays on Literature and Culture.* (N.Y., Pantheon Books, 1993). The question raises a very fundamental issue that cannot be fully addressed in this work without its consuming more space than the size of this book would further allow. But it is a very pertinent question in the re-evaluation of Booker T. Washington and the controversy which dogged his time.

Booker T. Washington as a southerner who knew the white southerners well, understood their preoccupations, tendencies, attitudes to their African wards as well as their perceptions of the blacks, also knew of their capacity to commit excesses when provoked. His language was nuanced to maintain as much tranquility in placating that south while moving to advance his people individually and collectively in a very hostile milieu and charged atmosphere. He was certainly a diplomat and a proponent of the concept that: "half a loaf is better than none". For rather than see it all taken away and the doors of opportunity totally barred to them, he preferred to create his own opportunities undisturbed, while, at the same time, engaging the language of fawning flattery which boosted the egos of white supremacist southerners so as not to act in more nugatory and destructive ways than they were wont to do. This did not mean that some of his open proclamations, advocacies, and activities, were not retrogressive and open to censure, especially those concerning the franchise which implied political power. His openly expressed sentiments on that issue had certainly departed from those of Frederick Douglass two generations earlier. So, also, was his style of conduct with the intrusion of spies into the rank and file of his black critics and his endeavors to undermine and silence them. In that connection he manifested the contradictions of one who overtly eschewed politics but built up a "political machine". It was no surprise that with the influence he exerted, even as the confidant of American Presidents, he alarmed his critics and opponents by his machiavellian techniques of conduct.

While it is difficult to be accurate on the working of Booker T. Washington's methods, much less interpret with any precision the workings of his mind set, the issue raised by the questioner's point is bound to resurface in a subsequent excursion, even if not by this writer. The issue is a larger undertaking than prudence will allow in this work.

African Inventors of the Diaspora

We here recall some of those inventions and their inventors, to remind those who already know and to inform those unaware of their contributions. It must not be forgotten that as slavery defined the African in the Americas as a thing instead of a person, his personal achievements customarily went unmentioned and his endeavors at inventing automatically became the property of his master or owner. Yet there is abundant evidence that slaves routinely invented a variety of useful devices, from household appliances to agricultural devices. So, since they did not exist as persons in law, they could not patent their inventions, as a patent was (by definition) a contract between the citizen and the state and slaves were not citizens. But even the free African-Americans were treated as non-citizens, sometimes as subhuman. Nevertheless, their genius could not be repressed and African-Americans can be justly proud that in a period in which the United States was gravitating from an agricultural to an industrial economy, from the middle of the nineteenth century into the twentieth century, African-Americans made contributions which issued forth in spheres such as transportation, electricity, industrial machinery and, by 1913, had actually patented approximately one thousand inventions—and, moreover, some of those inventors were women.

The first among these distinguished individuals was Henry Blair, who in 1834 had registered a seed planter, and then in 1836 a corn harvester. The next patented invention was an outstanding achievement by Nobert Rillieux: a multiple-effect vacuum evaporation process for refining sugar; it was not only revolutionary for its time but *continues* to be used in manufacturing sugar as well as in the production of condensed milk, gelatin, glue, soap, and many other products. Other inventors followed in the post-Civil War period. Lewis Latimer invented the first electric lamp with a carbon filament, having perfected an inexpensive production technique for the making of carbon filaments for lamps; his cotton thread filament made electric light bulbs practical and inexpensive. Although Thomas Edison is credited with inventing the light bulb, Edison's initial bulb continued to burn out, and it was Latimer's inventions that gave Edison his breakthrough and made the electric lightbulb a fact of life. Furthermore, Latimer is also known to have drawn designs for Alexander Bell's telephone patent, worked for Thomas Edison, [36] General Electric, and Westinghouse and, in 1890, produced the first book on the electrical lighting system. Similarly, Jan Matzeliger, by inventing the shoe-lasting machine, revolutionized shoe production and gave a real boost to the shoe industry: the result was that not only were better quality shoes produced, but the production costs had been cut as well and shoes were cheaper for purchase; but above all, the shoe industry within a short period of time doubled its revenue, so that it stood at over 400 million dollars. Another inventor of note was Elijah McCoy, who invented the automatic lubricator for locomotive engines in 1872. His drip cup eliminated the necessity of stopping and starting engines in order to lubricate them. Out of that invention and because of its effectiveness emerged the expression "the real McCoy" as a shorthand way of emphasizing the superiority of an original invention over its counterfeits.

Then there was Granville T. Woods, who in 1884 patented an improved steam boiler furnace, three years later came the Induction Telegraphy System which allowed communications between moving trains and between manned stations, thus making rail travel safer. It was said that twice Thomas Edison attempted to claim priority over this invention but Woods won in both cases and was certified by the U.S. patent office as the real inventor. He also invented a telephone transmitter in 1884, followed by an apparatus for the transmission of telephone and electric messages in 1885, which was bought by the American Bell Telephone Company. Then he evolved an electromechanical brake and apparatus in 1904-1905, both sold to Westinghouse Electric Company. He also invented an electric railway in 1901, which was sold to Thomas Edison's General Electric Company. Although Edison tried to hire his services, he remained independent and formed his own company, known as Woods Electric Company. Granville T. Woods was reputed to have been the most productive of the inventors, having in his lifetime patented no less than one hundred inventions.

Following on his heels was Garret Morgan, who invented a belt fastener for sewing machines in 1921, and before that (in 1914) the smoke inhalator, followed by his automatic traffic light in 1923. His smoke inhalator became a life-saver used by fire departments and was transformed into a gas mask used by soldiers in the First World War. His automatic traffic light was sold to General Electric for $40,000. Other inventors included John Parker, who invented a screw for tobacco presses in 1884; William Purvis, who had over a dozen inventions in machinery for making paper bags; J. A. Burr invented a lawnmower in 1899; G. Grant produced the Guld tree in 1899; and J. Winters, a fire escape ladder in 1887. Then, of course, there were the numerous inventions of George Washington Carver: he produced no less than three hundred synthetic products from the peanut, over a hundred from the sweet potato, and seventy-five from the pecan. Among those products were adhesives, axle grease, bleach, facial cream, dyes, fuel briquettes, ink, insulating board, linoleum, metal polish, mucilage paper, rubbing oils, soil conditioner, shampoo, shoe polish, shaving cream, synthetic rubber, wood stain, wood filler, buttermilk, cheese, flour, instant coffee, mayonnaise, meal, meat tenderizer, milk flakes, sugar, and worcester sauce. He also produced dehydrated foods, and his sweet potato flour was used by the United States Army during the First World War. Being a selfless and altruistic person, Dr. Carver refused to be drawn away from his work at Tuskegee Institute to work for either Thomas Edison or Henry Ford, both of whom tried to entice him by huge monetary inducements. [37]

African-Americans made contributions in other spheres, such as the arts and music, and many more too numerous to discuss in this text. Despite these achievements, the bulk of African-Americans, first in slavery and then after emancipation, like their Native American compatriots, carried the burdens of the society and yet were deliberately relegated to the bottom of the societal arrangement and in this social arrangement knew full well the discipline of starvation and arduous and often unpleasant toil. Even before emancipation, a few who were not slaves (because of the definition of the "womb law" [38]) and others who had secured manumission (through one of many channels) had difficulty exercising their right to freedom. Moreover, the position of these "free people" before the emancipation of all the slaves was anomalous, many of them existing in a betwixt-and-between state. One eminent historian has described them as "Quasi-Free Negroes." [39]

The anomalous situation which tended to leave them neither slave nor citizen accounted for the growth of the Convention Movement among African-Americans, often described as the National

Convention of Colored People in the United States, and resulted in the many petitions they addressed from Convention to Convention to the American people with periodic declarations of "Rights and Wrongs" in which they continued to claim or assert the rights to the benefits of citizenship in the country of their birth. These petitions and declarations and resolutions were so recurrent and were again made in the National Convention of Colored People in Syracuse, New York, in 1864, just as the Civil War was entering its final throes, only to stress the same identical points before "Reconstruction" evan began.[40] The "Address..." of 1864, as with previous ones in the 1850s, revealed the Convention leaders as still preoccupied with the following related themes: "complete emancipation," enfranchisement, and "elevation of the race." The language of these "Addresses" was the language of moral suasion, since it was couched as a petition and reasoned argument pleading with the society to recoil from injustice and right the wrongs hitherto done to their black brethren. They also added, for good measure, in order to bolster up their argument, the progress they had made despite these obstacles to their elevation. For instance, in the Syracuse Address, they argued:

> No where in the annals of mankind is there recorded an instance of an oppressed people rising more rapidly than ourselves in the favorable estimation of their oppressors.[41]

They further added in recalling grievances that:

> When the *Anti-slavery Standard*, representing the American Anti-slavery Society, denies that society asks for the enfranchisement of colored men, and the *Liberator* apologizes for excluding the colored men of Louisiana from the ballot-box, they injure us more vitally than all the ribald jests of the whole pro-slavery press.[42]

In appealing to the nation to adhere to the cause of justice, they realized that the prerequisites for achieving this were, in the first instance, the complete abolition of slavery, and, second, the realization of political equality through the elective franchise in all the States of the Union and the States coming thereafter.[43] The argument emanating from the Syracuse National Convention of Colored People was the most comprehensive thus far. They observed that previously their petitions for the elective franchise had been denied on the grounds that while colored men were protected in person and property, they were not required to perform military duty. They saw this as a palliative, arguing that they were subject to any call the government was pleased to make upon them and they could not properly be made to suffer because the government did not see fit to impose military duties on them, insisting that the fault was the government's and not theirs. But they then went on to argue that in the Civil War they had contributed numbers to the war effort in the army and navy and that they came as volunteers and patriots who saw their country imperiled.[44] But the Convention further appealed to their emotions by insisting that:

> Your fathers laid down the principle, long ago that universal suffrage is the best foundation of government.[45]

They insisted that the colored people shared this view of government, and added:

> May we defend right in time of war, and yet be denied the exercise of these rights in time of peace? Are we citizens when the nation is in peril, and aliens when the nation is in safety?[46]

They entreated their fellow citizens to have faith in their own proclaimed principles, arguing that if freedom is good for any, it is good for all, and insisting:

> If you need the elective franchise, we need it even more. You are strong, we are weak; you are many, we are few; you are protected, we are exposed. Clothe us with this safeguard of our liberty...[47]

These pleas and protestations were not just idle exercises, for their plight was much worse than they had explained or were prepared to say. Discriminatory laws ranged against them, forbade their entering cities, States, and attaining certain status in society. In some States, there were stipulations for their sudden departure from those States, failing which they were or could be sold into slavery. [48] Attempts to rise in society were more uncertain and slow in the case of these descendants of Africa in the Americas. The efficacy of their organizations was ephemeral, being chronically starved for funds. Sometimes, they aped only what they saw since, through the conspiratorial manipulatory tactics of slave societies, much of what they knew of Africa or remembered of it including their languages and other forms of communication had been purged out of them. Already deprived of their names early in slavery, they experienced a consistent and persistent onslaught on their African personality, beginning with the conferring of a new name and with policies preventing the speaking of their so-called "barbarous" languages. Their religious beliefs and rituals were downgraded to the status of superstitions and sorcery; the resulting incomprehension led them into seeking to embrace Christianity, which was only allowed if and when it suited the slavocracy. This embracing of Christianity was the case for some and not for others (like the Muslims of Brazil, who carried out many revolts in the guise of *jihads*). Their being visualized as heathens and practitioners of superstitions was not dissimilar to the treatment of the Jews, who, because of their adherence to Judaism, were branded as "heretics." At the time of the Inquisition in Spain, which spread elsewhere, Jews were expelled together with the Moors (Africans) or, if they refused, were compelled to adopt Christianity under threat of fire and the sword. In other areas, as free people, the Jews adopted other beliefs: some became Muslims, others became Christians of one denomination or another, and others stayed with Judaism (some Orthodox, others Liberal, or members of Reformed Judaism). But here they were exercising the liberties of free people. In the long period of their dispersion the Jews, through persecution, were not allowed to forget that they were different and "odious." The Africans in the American Diaspora suffered no less. They continued to be treated as scums of the earth and beasts of burden; even after emancipation they continued to be so regarded and they were said to be no part of the "divine plan" for man's "salvation." [49]

Whether in slavery or "freedom" they were vilified. They were "odious" and brutish and nasty; in fact, every wicked epithet was used for them. The derogatory comments made about Jews were not dissimilar to those used for Africans (and for others such as the American Indians and the Irish in other times and places). An example of this ubiquitous attitude of mind and pronouncement may be cited by reference to the statement in the 1900s of Sir Cyril Butt, the British founder of Educational Psychology, who asserted that racial differences in intelligence test scores were the result of heredity. He proceeded in his conclusion to assert that Jews and Irish were less intelligent than the English and that men were smarter than women. His assertions were, of course, rebutted by other competent researchers, who found his statistical computations to be fabricated.[50]

The Jews, however, whether Orthodox or not, were allowed in most cases to retain their memory of their history, their vision of their destiny, and, importantly, the hope of "The Return." There were, of course, Jews in the Jewish Diaspora who wished to integrate and settle where they were, and many did. But the persecution, oppression, and pogroms against them led some of them back to the path of "the return" as the only hopeful path. The Judaic religion nonetheless was a sustaining element and it became a rallying factor in times of persecution and extreme frustration, despite their many efforts to integrate or coexist within the society in which they resided. As with the Jews, the oppression of centuries unabating periodically evoked the thought of an African "Return" with the notions of an "African Redemption," couched in religious terms by descendants of Africa, who had not been allowed (through policies, sustained onslaughts, and strong-arm tactics) to retain their religion or even a semblance of it, except where by ingenuity and evasive tactics (as in Brazil, Cuba, Haiti, and a few other places), they maintained their beliefs and practices away from public gaze. The system forced on them a version of Christianity when it suited the slavocracy but also disallowed it if it suited the authorities, (except the Latin colonies, which stipulated it as necessary in their slave codes such as the *Siete Partidas* of Alfonso the Wise and the French *Code Noir*).[51] That was due not to any benevolence but rather to the desire to uproot and eliminate African religions and belief systems, which could become valuable instruments in slave revolts, quite apart from the solidarity of the enslaved. This attempt at cultural genocide was pervasive and persistent.

Slavocrats in the Americas kept a close watch on the religious activities of the enslaved Africans, including those of the free blacks. Their reactions to the Denmark Vesey revolt of Charleston, South Carolina, in 1822, and the policies thereafter imposed, are instructive. In the course of time, Africans in the diaspora in the Americas came to adopt Jewish symbols, which also became symbols of their struggles in their confrontation with the slavocracy; and, after slavery, symbols of their oppression. The importance of the Old Testament prophets in their perceptions and their assumption of some significance has been observed elsewhere in this work. Although the possession of the Jews, these symbols were appropriated by the Africans of the African Diaspora for their own purposes. Those symbols loomed large in their songs, especially the "Spirituals." They might have been used for living persons in times of stress, such as Moses for Harriet Tubman, in the song "Go Down Moses." Nonetheless, in those early days their prelates took the Bible literally and so adopted the exploits of Moses, Joshua, Daniel, and many others as their own and saw them as deliverers of one kind or another. From this kind of thinking, it was a short step to the notion of God's hand in their history and His intervention on behalf of His longsuffering people. Furthermore, since many of the earlier leaders of the African-Americans were prelates (a form of leadership that flourishes even today), the imagery derived from both Jewish and Christian symbols continued to preoccupy their thoughts.

While some of the early and later emigrationists outside the United States (like the Rev. Theodore J. Holly, Rev. Samuel Ringgold

Ward, Rev. Henry Highland Garnet), and later, inside the United States (Bishop Henry McNeal Turner), were prelates, others were from religious arms of the African return movement. Significantly, the A.M.E. Church, which in the early days of the Convention Movement in the 1830s and 1840s did not advocate emigration to Africa. However, one of its first prelates to settle in Africa in 1820 was the Rev. Daniel Coker, who began missionary work in the Sierra Leone (West Africa) until his death in 1846. After Coker's death, it took forty years for the A.M.E. Church to revive his missionary efforts through the Rev. H. John Fredericks in 1886, an endeavor urged on by Dr. Daniel Payne, an eminent black educationist and himself a Bishop of the A.M.E. Church. It was one of his last acts prior to his demise. Fredericks himself trained three West Africans for the task of evangelism in Sierra Leone.

In 1891, a determined effort was made. Bishop Henry McNeal Turner, on his visit to West Africa, ordained H. M. Steady, D. B. Roach and G. D. Decker for this purpose. The African Mission in West Africa maintained its contact with the home mission in the United States. Bishop Turner, during that visit, organized the first Annual Conference of the A.M.E. Church in Africa in October 1891.[52] He later visited Liberia. His efforts, thereafter, may be gleaned in the A.M.E. publication, *The Voice of Missions*.

Turner visited South Africa in 1897, where the efforts of a Sotho woman from Basutoland (currently Lesotho), Charlottee Mayne, herself a graduate of Wilberforce University, Ohio, run by the A.M.E. Church, encouraged a linkage between the A.M.E. Church at home with the fledgling effort in Southern Africa. A first session of the A.M.E. Church was held in South Africa, at Pretoria in the Transvaal, as a protest against racial discrimination. Bishop Turner was at the first session of the A.M.E. Conference in South Africa, where he consecrated the Rev. James Dwane as Bishop in March 1898. But the relationship between the Ethiopianist movement of Dwane and the A.M.E. Church was not sustained. Then, in 1900, Bishop Levi Coffin of the A.M.E. Church was appointed to the General Conference of the South African Church. His efforts to organize a Church and enhance education were frustrated by the white racist regime in the South, who churlishly sought to keep out African-American missionaries, especially those of the A.M.E. Church and of the Baptist variety. The fate of Bishop W. T. Vernon and his party when they attempted to land in South Africa is instructive. They were detained aboard their ship with a view to deportation and only through the diplomatic interventions of the American Consul-General with the Minister of the Interior were they allowed to land. Other Bishops of the A.M.E. Church in later years were to experience the same difficulties.[53] Attempts to extend their endeavors to Central and Eastern Africa were unsuccessful because racist regimes, espousing white supremacy, were being inaugurated there.[54]

At home in the United States, the early prelates of the A.M.E. Church (beginning with Richard Allen, founder of the Church and first bishop), were more often than not fundamentalist in their close adherence to the Bible, assimilating it both literally and figuratively. Allen himself drew his own lessons and preached his sermons drawing and inferring from the Judaic experience. He had even argued that in the enslavement of the Jews in Egypt God himself had pleaded the cause of the slave, inferring that God would plead the cause of the enslaved Africans in the Americas. Bishop Allen still looked and hoped for divine intervention and, when responding to criticisms of the newly liberated Africans and their inadequacies, he argued that the Jews, released from enslavement, had mirrored the same mentality, which persisted for a while, and that time and inculcation would remove that mentality and its lingering blemishes from African-Americans.[55]

An examination of the thoughts of many of these prelates would reveal many examples of such translation of the experiences of Jewish history from the Bible into the African experience in the African Diaspora.[56] But it was in the nineteenth century that many of these symbolisms were elevated into actual correspondences with the Jewish experiences, and no one stressed this more in the nineteenth century than the Rev. Alexander Crummell. Even Bishop H. M. Turner, a later successor for emigration to African, although he expressed Ethiopianist ideas, did not adopt the Crummellian thought process that slavery was due to divine providence and that there was divine purpose to the enslavement of the Africans in the Americas. McNeal Turner differed from Crummell because, for him, the oppression of African-Americans and the racism of the society imposed such handicaps that they made emigration imperative and the only viable alternative for the bulk of African-Americans. Both men rose to prominence from divergent backgrounds. Crummell emerged as an intellectual after obtaining his degree from Cambridge University in England. Turner epitomized the hard-working person from a lowly background, who, according to W. E. B. DuBois, at the time of Turner's death in 1915, was described as "a man of tremendous force and indomitable courage... In a sense Turner was the last of his clan; mighty men, physically and mentally, men who started at the bottom and hammered their way to the top by sheer brute strength; they were the spiritual progeny of the ancient African Chieftains and they built the African Church in America."[57]

Though Turner himself on his visits to Africa was assiduous in making converts to Christianity, yet he did not characterize these as "civilizing" Africa (as Crummell and Edward Wilmot Blyden had), nor did he stress divine providence. He rather emphasized the secular and political aspects of the African return in terms of nationality—not dissimilar to the political aspects of Jewish Zionism, despite his being a religious prelate. However, the A.M.E. project in Africa coupled evangelism with education and saw both as inseparable.

The Received Tradition of the Jewish Diaspora

Despite Abram Leon's critique of the received Jewish tradition of the Diaspora and the emphases of the Zionists, it was that version and interpretation of the Jewish Diaspora which was perceived by the African Diaspora prelates in the United States and from which they drew their own inspiration and formulated their version of the African Diaspora.

Points of Convergence and Divergence

The Assyrian invasion of Israel and deportation in the seventh century BCE[58] and the Babylonian Captivity[59] a century later (586-538 BCE) resemble (in many ways) the African enslavement in the Americas between the fifteenth and nineteenth centuries, but the dispersion which resulted from the destruction of Jerusalem and the second Temple under the Roman Emperor Titus in 70 CE, although contributing to the prolonged exile of the Jews,[60] has no real parallel with anything that could have occurred in Africa before the twentieth century. Both features of individual and group dispersion for improvement have a similarity; but the core period of the African diaspora spans four centuries, while that of the Jews, after A.D. 70 CE, approximates twenty centuries (and elsewhere has been stated as commencing so early as to approximate thirty centuries). [61]

But, as David Vital reminds us, the Jewish diaspora involved the following: first, dispersion and exile as a fulfillment of prophecy for transgression against divine injunctions and stipulations; second, a long sojourn in foreign lands; and third, the Return and Restoration, with escatological implications in terms of destiny all bound up in religious faith. But to point out one divergence the African Ddiaspora does not result from a transgression of divine will, although some fundamentalist prelates in the eighteenth and nineteenth centuries of the Christian era in America tended to imply this. Seeing slavery as hideous, they observed God's hand in the way they conceived of their return to Africa as redemptive both for them and Africa. [62]

The Return and Restoration among those prelates derived largely from the perception, adoption, and interpretation of the Jewish experience as consistent with the African experience; from implied escatological considerations in terms of destiny; and from the symbolic use of the African Diaspora for facilitating the redemption (in religious terms), regeneration, and "civilization" [63] of Africa. These African prelates in the African Diaspora, therefore, saw their missionary proclivities in Africa as part of that necessary participation in the evangelization of their parent continent. Thus, in perceiving themselves as a "chosen people," [64] this notion coincided with the Jewish notion of being a "chosen people"[65] to regenerate some sections of humanity. It is not so stated explicitly in the Old and the New Testaments, but the prelates of the African Diaspora were adroit in their interpretations in a manner that seemed plausible and convincing to their flock. In both diasporas, the Jewish and the African, returns were sustained by religious orthodoxy.

While the Jewish return notion gained momentum in the late nineteenth century after the pogroms and persecution against the Jews in both Eastern and Western Europe, but especially in the East, the African conception gained momentum by the middle of the 19th century. It was stated as a call to duty and service and through the extrapolation of apt quotations in the Bible appertaining to the Jews, but seemingly consistent with providential design and made to apply to Africans of the diaspora in the Americas.

The difference remained that, despite some periodic persecutions, Jews all through nineteen centuries of the diaspora since 70 CE were free, whereas nominal freedom only came to the Africans in the diaspora in the Americas in the late 19th century.

For divergence the period of African enslavement is longer than that of the Jews in the Babylonian captivity and the dispersion of 70 CE was a dispersion of free people and despite the disabilities suffered by some of them in different societies and at different times, their lot was better than the not so idyllic enslavement of the African people, whether in bondage or "quasi-free".

While the African diaspora lasted longer than the first two of the Jewish diaspora, the third Jewish diaspora has lasted more than nineteen centuries, longer than that of the Africans which lasted four centuries and since their emancipation they have continued to be in the diaspora for another century and a half. Nevertheless, that third diaspora of the Jews, although was forced on them, yet they departed not as slaves but as free people. It is an essential point of departure between both people's diasporas and the Jews dwelt among other communities as free people. By contrast in more modern times, the African diaspora was a condition of abject and strenuous servitude and this factor represents a qualitative difference between both.

Thus, as free people, the Jews were not discouraged from evolving their leadership whether in Europe or in the Americas, despite their repeated persecution and the periodic pogroms that were visited on them. They had their religion (except at the time of the Inquisition[66] in Spain but Africans who were Muslims were also equally persecuted there). The conspiracy and methods of the slavocracy did much to deprive Africans in the American diaspora of their leaders. Despite this, many efforts were made to evolve leadership, many of them cut down by brutal techniques of the slave regimes and other excesses even after the dethronement of the Slave Power. Here again their experiences would coincide with those of the Jews as both groups were victims of violence, persecution and unwarranted excesses.

While this experience produced a leadership fervor, this helped the Jews to harness their energies into organizational activities in Europe and in the Americas to become worldwide. By contrast, the Africans in the Americas were weakened by techniques of "divide and rule," which had been fostered among them from earliest times by their enslavers and which had conditioned their outlook that when the African issue came to the fore of their considerations, they either shied away from it or suffered from a failure to harness, co-ordinate and energize their efforts into a channel for achieving unanimity or even a singular attitude of mind. The result is that they found their energies vitiated by cleavages and acrimonious disputations.

While the Jews encouraged an awareness of their history and went on to foster the teaching of the Hebrew language and even evolved Yiddish in the context of the societies in which they dwelt, the Africans had been shorn of their language, except in a few places. The nature of propaganda against Africans from their first landing until the nineteenth century of European colonization of Africa, and their domination of African lives, and the persistence of Euro-American propaganda against Africa. often far from edifying, but sustained by inculcation, Africans in the American diaspora, except for a very few, sought to distance themselves from Africa.

The Return and Eschatology

The Jews, at least, experienced the "return" in terms of the first and second diaspora. The third diaspora "return" was realized in 1948 with the creation of the Zionist State of Israel. But before this was realized, the "return" was long in gestation not only in Europe but in many parts of the world including the United States of America. This is part of the received-tradition.

With the African diaspora, there were examples of individual and symbolic returns. These had begun, even as Africans were being drawn away from the African shores. Those who were unchained or undid their chains or who began an insurrection on board slave ships, sometimes, had the satisfaction of clearing the vessels and drowning in the belief that death translated them back to Africa. That was symbolic. Those who resisted and died or pined away on the plantations until death claimed them were fortified in the same belief that death took them back to Africa. Even during funeral ceremonies in slavery, those Africans who participated in the ceremonies often used expressions such as "remember me to them at home" to the deceased.

Slave revolts such as those led by Joseph Cinque in 1839 off Cuba, ordered the captain to steer the vessel (*La Amistad*) towards Africa though, eventually, it landed in ports of New England (New London, Hartford, and New Haven [Connecticut]). The slaves had return to African in mind, and, in the end, they were returned to Africa. But this "return" was not as concerted as the Jewish returns and does not accord with the Jewish prophetic conception of return. It assumed concrete form in the advocacies of Prelates such as Alexander Crummell and Dr. Edward Wilmot Blyden, who saw their missionary efforts and persuasions as in keeping with this prophetic vision. Here they translated the prophetic vision of the Jewish diaspora as extending to them. But prior to the inauguration of the State of Israel individual Jews, not in significant numbers, had through the centuries trickled back into Palestine and even after the establishment of the State. European domination of Africa forestalled any such trickle back to Africa. Some came but not in significant numbers and some later returned to their places of origin. But, of course, there were African returnees from Brazil and Cuba between the 1850s and the end of the nineteenth century even before slavery was abolished in both countries. These spread themselves along the West African coast and many of those who settled in Lagos (modern Nigeria) and their descendants continued to be known as Brazilians, some of them with relations in both Brazil and Cuba. But among the Jews the vision of the return was first sustained by religious orthodoxy, an idea which gained momentum after several European persecutions of the Jews through many centuries in Europe but which became catalytic from the second half of the nineteenth century. The Jewish National Congress helped to give it direction.

The Africans of the diaspora, who escaped upon landing in slave societies and established more or less durable Maroon communities such as those of Palmares in Brazil, Surinam in Dutch Guiana and the *Ranchairos* and *Palenque* of Cuba, and, to some extent, the Maroon communities of Jamaica, St. Vincent, Grenada, were symbolic expressions of the return where physical returns proved daunting. but most of their communities were destroyed by determined slavocrats, except in a few cases. The Aluku of Surinam, the so-called Boni Maroons (now residing in Cayenne, French Guiana), are examples of this survival under difficult conditions.

Another point of departure which had points of convergence is that in their longest diaspora compared to that of the Africans, the Jews though free, suffered many handicaps, discrimination, vilification, periodic persecutions, pogroms and violence as well as calumnies against them. Though Africans were enslaved, apart from a handful, slave or free, all suffered the kinds of indignities listed above and experienced by Jews. In fact, both communities were seen as expendable and their lives counted for nothing. The laws of the society rather than protect them for most of the period contributed to summarily mishandling them with so much loss of lives. Jewish emancipation in many parts of Europe secured them as free people and assisted their ability to operate as free people. "Negro" emancipation, when it was pronounced by Lincoln on January 1, 1863, did create free persons but only nominally. Long before their emancipation the position of the "free" Africans in the United States was anomalous and they were kept in a state of between and betwixt, being half-slave and half-free and hedged by all the constraints imposed on them by law and customary practice.

They experienced a short period of freedom in the years of Reconstruction only to see all this taken away from them by murders, lynchings, intimidation, pillage and undemocratic laws which resulted in their total disfranchisement in the south. Such attitudes of discrimination for which the South was famous extended to the Northern states of the United States. These made the position of the "free" blacks precarious. The cards were stacked against them. By contrast, the Jews moved freely in society and were able to form organizations, which could inveigh against discriminatory practices but not without much struggle and effort. In this respect they did better than Africans in the diaspora who, up to the 1920s, were still faced with the prospects of their deportation from the United States of America. In other theaters of the Americas laws and customs were used to undermine them and brutality was harnessed to inhibit an African consciousness. The Afro-Cuban revolt of 1912, for instance, intended to secure the benefits of full citizenship for which they had fought together with their Euro-Cuban compatriots, is one example of that severity of handling that was tantamount to intolerance. But it mirrored the obsessions in Euro-Cuban thoughts concerning the prospects of an Afro-Cuban domination of the island through numerical strength. It was an illusion generated and fostered by the triumph of the St. Domingue (Haitian) revolution of African descendants over the slaveholders at the beginning of the nineteenth century. The spectre of *St. Domingue* remained the obsession of many slave societies in much of the Americas.

African Prelates' Perceptions and Emphases

In the United States among the African-derived prelates, no one expressed the hand of God in the experiences of the African people more than the Rev. Alexander Crummell. His writings are replete with the notion, nay doctrine, of "Providential Design". It, therefore, is essential to bring in some of his reflections and thoughts through his conversion of citations and prophecy appertaining to the Jews into becoming relevant for the African diaspora. While deducing much from the Biblical texts in terms of the Jewish experience to serve his perceptions of the importance of the African diaspora for Africa regeneration, some of his thoughts were earlier in time but find parallels in Jewish Zionist thought while it was in gestation in the late 19th century and when it gathered momentum.

In a sermon delivered before an assembly of women in Chelthenam, Bath (England) in 1853, solicitations for the welfare of Africans of the diaspora in the West Indies were expressed. Prior to his departure for Africa to take up his duties there for the next twenty years, he revealed that he had puzzled over the slave trade and the enslavement of Africans for over three centuries but had come to the realization concerning this onslaught on one race that the question was being answered and saw its outcome as arising from "Providential Design." He being convinced that it was through Christianity that the regeneration and elevation of Africa would be achieved felt the sudden "irresistible desire to return to their land of birth" by the newly Christianized descendants of Africa. He felt great admiration for those who were assiduously engaged in this task of evangelism in Africa and others contemplating it. In order to cap his perception, in the light of Jewish experience, he said:

> And yet again; the children of Africa have been sojourning nigh three centuries in America; and in the course of time large numbers of them have become free. The free blacks of America are a disturbing element in the midst of the white inhabitants of the paradoxical republic; and hence by the force of the oppression principle, thousands of them had been forced, by cruel laws to exile themselves to the coast of Africa. There they have formed the Republic of Liberia, with free

> institutions with schools and churches, and missions of their heathen kin. [67]

While in his effusive sentiments he paints an idyllic picture of Liberia, which was far from being the case, nonetheless, Liberia as it was then did imply promise. His notions of "civilized Christians" returning to the continent of their forebears to spread enlightenment to a "vast benighted continent," [68] as he termed it, not only assumed a perception from the Eurocentric quarter but savored of prejudice which was to be assimilated into the idiom of some African-American prelates of the time.

The three directions from which these missionary efforts by Africans of the diaspora were emerging, which he observed, were the United States, the Antilles and Brazil[69] parallel those of the later proponents and advocates of Jewish Zionism. They perceived the three areas as being Western Europe, with its "powerful Jewish Community," often not enthusiastic about the in-gatherings but providing substantial financial and technical aid and support that was vital to the success of the scheme. The second related to Jews uprooted in Europe, Africa, Asia which, in the long-term, made the ingathering to Israel. Finally, the "great Russian Jewry" which had been kept apart for a generation from fellowship with other Jewry,[70] constituted the third wave. It was Crummell's belief that with such dedicated servants in the missionary field in order to reclaim the African continent for Christ, he hoped then that "Ethiopia, from the Mediterranean to the Cape, from the Atlantic Ocean to the Indian, 'shall soon stretch forth her hands unto God.'"[71] He saw all these occurring "under the immediate direction of the Almighty."[72]

The model of the diaspora which he employed was the Israelite sojourn in Egypt near four hundred years and from that experience he made his own inferences. He insisted that achieving the return for the Jews was no easy matter, judged by the manner in which they rebelled against their leader—criticizing him for their failure to have victuals they had eaten in Egypt and criticizing the manna which was bestowed on them as food. But Crummell saw God's hands in all their trials, adding "and when His hand is upon a people, it is destiny, and they cannot resist it. His hand was upon them, His hand guided them through the terrible journey—this was symbolic of the terrible experiences Africans had endured in the land of bondage in America and the difficult crossing to reach Africa all due to providential design, as "He had a great work for them to do" and "this process of migration was the passage, through which they were to enter upon and do that work." [73]

In that quotation he implied or stressed they were a "chosen people" as the Jews had been and the eschatological content of that thought pervaded much of his writings in the nineteenth century. The crossing of the Atlantic was equivalent to the crossing by the children of Israel of the Jordan. For him those who crossed over had come to participate in what he termed "God's great work of evangelization" through accepting the colonization principle. He rejected the colonization principle advanced by the American Colonization Society because, as he saw it, it was a manifestation of the "oppression principle" even if a "free Liberia emerged" through the process.[74]

In terms of the "return," a very important peg in Jewish diasporan thinking, Crummell not only stressed this but again took his cue from the Biblical texts. Thus, in likening the Euro-African connection with that of Joseph and his brothers who sold him Crummell said: "As for you, ye though evil against us, but God meant it unto good, to save much people alive." He continued: "For that, I maintain, that is, 'to save much people alive', that is the great mission of our race to this coast [West Africa] to turn this heathen population from darkness to light, and from the power of Satan unto God, that they may receive forgiveness of sins, and inheritance among them who are sanctified by faith."[75]

Thus in keeping with this perception of the Divine will he wrote:

> The day of preparation of our race is well nigh ended; the day of duty and responsibility on our part, to suffering, benighted, Africa, is at hand. In much sorrow, pain, and deepest anguish, God has been preparing the race, in foreign lands, for a great work of Grace on this continent. The hand of God is on the black man, in all the lands of his distant sojourn, for the good of Africa.[76]

The above quoted thought is reflected by the religious wing of Zionism in the ninteenth century and in the same manner in which the Jews were later to reflect that they had to take a hand to achieve their salvation Crummell was to say:

> I add still further that the redemption of Africa cannot be brought about there by one single agency of foreign missionaries... The great principle which lies at the base of all successful propagation of the Gospel is this, namely, the employment of all indigenous agency.[77]

From the Jewish quarter here is the viewpoint of an ardent Zionist as he contemplated the Jewish question and its solution. He said:

> But our preparedness, the state of our leadership and our ability to muster the necessary forces in times of emergency - these depend upon us. No one can give us these things, and no one can take them away from us. [78]

One final quotation of Crummell will suffice to emphasize how his fundamentalist outlook adapted the Jewish experience in the period of exile in Egypt to advance similarities in the African diaspora. Thus, the sojourn in Egypt near four hundred years seemed to have had a parallel in the African enslavement four centuries as Crummell not only intended it to be implied but understood as being consistent with God's purpose. For, he continued:

> Their Fathers during their sojourn in that land, had suffered the keenest miseries and afflictions. But God had never suffered their bondage to be, entirely, at anytime, unmixed and absolute evil. Large providential favors were mingled with their sore trials in all their tribulations, they were still God's people, much temporal prosperity, yea, even miraculous increases had been given to them; the spectacle of high civilization was continually set before their eyes. Thus, in various ways, they were going through a system of mental and moral training, God was preparing them for another land, and far distant duties. Generations passed away; and many a soul sank, and many a spirit fainted and many a despairing man laid down and died; but the work went on.
>
> By and by when God was ready for his own large ends and purposes, then He commenced the processes and policies for that noble work which tells, even in our day, in every Christian Church and household in the world. The two special expedients to that end were, First, colonization, at God's bidding, from Egypt; and secondly, a re-settlement in the land of Canaan, *under the immediate direction of the Almighty.* [79]

Although some of these thoughts or variations on them exist in the writings of Dr. Edward Wilmot Blyden in the same era and he too was an advocate of African diasporan emigration to Africa, Crummell epitomized this mode of thought which some African-American prelates and missionaries expressed. Their aim, as in the case of Zionism later, was for a national homeland or as Martin Delany expressed it: "Africa for the Africans." While many continental Africans of the time and today would have agreed with his goal of a nationality in Africa, in essence Pan-Africanism, they would have rejected his prejudices, derived from the Eurocentric source, and his assumptions about Africans, as members of a "benighted continent" with no religion, which is false. But his very premises and some of his perceptions of African history being jaundiced and the product of acquired misrepresentation, much of it largely discredited, such as the "Ham theory," and his conception of Kushite (alias Nubian) history, would have exposed him to much censure. But Crummell was a man of his times and perceived according to his own lights and experiences. Nonetheless, he still defended the African and rejected the assertions prevalent in slavery times that the African family was not part of humanity, did not possess a soul, and was under a curse. [80]

This is the point at which to let the subject drop, except to infer from the experiences so far recounted, the void that leadership had filled in the African diaspora in the Americas and, especially, in the United States of America during the protracted period of its evolution despite divergent perspectives. A modern scholar[81] has argued at a conference of the African Diaspora that the term should be abandoned because as he said, "Africans are not Jews." The implication in this admonishment is that Africans in the Americas still have a problem of conceptualization. The argument for abandonment has still to be made convincingly. However, the scholar in question seems to have a valid reason for the shedding of this vocabulary from African deliberations because the term, like others such as "Black Zionist," "black Titan," "black revolutionary" harnessed by some historical writings, tends to perceive the history of the African people "always in terms parallel in white history." While not disagreeing with the fact that parallels exist between black and white history, but Africans, he felt must see their history in "its own right" and they do not need parallels in the experience of other peoples to shape or recount their history. He rejects this approach as those who tended to do this were previously detractors to African history having formerly insisted that the Africans had no history. He felt that the term "African dispersion" would suffice. [82] It is an emphasis on the autonomy of African history.

While this writer sympathizes with the point of view represented above, the diasporic element was an idea absorbed into the perceptions of eighteenth and nineteenth century African-descended prelates in the Americas, principally in the United States. They had employed their own understanding of the Biblical texts rooted in the Judeo-Christian tradition to deduce language and symbolisms derived from the Old Testament Jewish experience to interpret their own experience in the Americas. As has been shown with quotations above, they, sometimes misguidedly, sometimes by conscious adoption or absorbtion, appropriated the Jewish experience to their own.

One cannot examine the thoughts of many of these prelates without recognizing the sources of their perceptions in relation to the plight of their people. Yet they constituted the early as well as ongoing leadership and it is not possible to examine the evolution of leadership without a consideration of their own weighty perspectives. But they were essentially people of their age, and a later generation is within its rights in visualizing them differently. In this respect it will be appropriate to view them as leaders of the African dispersion in the Americas. But this will hardly deter those who have a preference for the term "diaspora" to continue to employ it.

NOTES

1. If Sigmund Freud is to be believed or taken seriously, then what he said of the Egyptian episode needs to be taken cognisance of with the skepticism that he implied. See his *Moses and Monotheism*. The entire text needs to be read to understand the Freudian position on the Egyptian episode.
2. Abram Leon, *The Jewish Question: A Marxist Interpretation*, Pathfinder Press, Inc. New York, 1970, 2nd edn. 1950, p. 65.
3. *Ibid.*, pp. 65-66. See also his pp. 115-22 where he observes the revolt of A.D. 70 was not as a national offensive but class based, and other such manifestations.
4. *Ibid.*, p. 66.
5. *Ibid.*
6. *Ibid.*, p. 67.
7. *Ibid.*, p. 67.
8. *Ibid.*, p. 68.
9. *Ibid.*, pp. 68-9.
10. *Ibid.*, p. 69.
11. *Ibid.*, p. 74.
12. *Ibid.*, pp. 79-80.
13. *Ibid.*, pp. 96-7.
14. *Ibid.*, p. 97. His reference here is gleaned from the Second Book of the Maccabees, III, 6.
15. *Ibid.*, pp. 98-99 & 113.
16. *Ibid.*, pp. 112-13.
17. *Ibid.*, p. 115.
18. *Ibid.*, p. 114.
19. *Ibid.*
20. *Ibid.*, p. 122.
21. *Ibid.*, p. 123. et seq. for his expansion of this thought with evidence of its nature.22. *Ibid.*, p. 132.
23. *Ibid.*, p. 214.
24. *Ibid.*, pp. 214-224, Ch. VI.
25. *Ibid.*, pp. 221-222.
26. *Ibid.*, p. 229.
27. *Ibid.*, p. 228.
28. The reasons why he might be killed are unclear and are dubious, but remain as part of the received tradition.

29. *Exodus*, Ch. 12, v. 37-38. The figure quoted was 600,000 footmen beside children. *Numbers*, Ch. 11, v. 21.
30. *Deuteronomy*, Ch. 28, v. 25.
31. *2 Chronicles*, CH. 36.
32. *Deuteronomy*, Ch. 30, v. 1-3, & 5.
33. Crummell, Alexander, *African and America*, p. 408.
34. W. E. B. DuBois, *Black Reconstruction*, p. 149.
35. *Ibid.*
36. Gleanings of these inventors and others' achivements could be had in the following texts:
    C. G. Woodson, *The Negro in our History*, Washington DC, The Associate Publishers, pp. 461-67.
    Maulana Karenga, *Introduction to Black Studies*, Los Angeles, 1984, 3rd print, pp. 120-23.
    Diggs, Irene, *Black Inventors*, Chicago, Third World press, 1975.
    Haber, Louis, *Black Pioneers of Science and Invention*, New York, Harcourt Brace and World, Inc., 1970.
    Klein, Aaron E., *The Hidden Contriubtors: Black Scientists and Inventors in America*, New York, Doubleday and Co., 1971.
    Robert C. Hayden, *Eight Black American Inventors*, Reading, MA, Addision-Wesley Co., 1972.
    Carwell, Hattie, *Blacks in Science*, Hicksville, NY, Exposition Press, 1977.
    Adams, Russell L., *Great Negroes Past and Present*, Chicago, Afro-American Publishing Co., 1969.
37. White, Anne Terry, "George Washington Carver" Scholastic Book Services, also C. G. Woodson and C. H. Wesllley, The Negro in our History, Revised 12th edition, 1972, pp. 581 and 709.
38. By this law the status of a child born followed that of the mother. Thus if the mother was a slave the child automatically became a slave.
39. See Franklin, J. H. and Moss, Alfred, *From Slavery to Freedom*, McGraw Hill, 6th edition, 1988, ch. 9; also J. W. Blassingame and Mary Berry, *Long Memory*, Ch.1.
40. See for instance 'The Address to the People of the United States' in *Minutes and Proceedings of the National Colored Convention*, held in Rochester in 1853, p. 8, et. seq., in Howard Bell (ed.) *Minutes and Proceedings of the National Negro Conventions 1830-1864*, New York, Arno Press and the *New York Times*, 1969. In that address they said: "We are Americans, and as Americans, we would speak to Americans. We address you not as aliens nor as exiles, humbly asking to be permitted to dwell among you in peace; but we address you as American citizens asserting their rights on their own native soil." See also the Syracuse Proceedings in Bell, *Ibid.*, pp. 41-43, 44-62.
41. Bell, *op. cit.*, (Syracuse Proceedings), p. 46.
42. *Ibid.*, p. 48.
43. *Ibid.*, pp. 53, 55-56.
44. Bell, *Ibid.*, Syracuse Convention, pp. 56-57.
45. *Ibid.*, p. 57.
46. *Ibid.*, p. 58.
47. *Ibid.*
48. Goodell, William, *The American Slave Code in Theory and Practice.*

49. See Carroll, Charles, *The Negro: A Beast Or In the Image of God*, American Book and Bible House, St. Louis, MO, 1900, p. 166.
50. See Haber, Louis, *Women Pioneers of Science*, New York and London, Harcourt Brace and Javanovich, 1979, foreword.
51. See Thompson, V. B., *The Making of the African Diaspora in the Americas: 1441-1900,* Longman Group, London and Harlow, 1987 (and subsequent issues to 1992), Ch. 8.
52. Bishop Turner made a second visit to West Africa in February 1893. Not only was it for Turner a pilgrimage but he saw it as a response to the African people in the task of evangelism among Africans and for strengthening their churches. See *Voice of Missions*, February 1893; also E. S. Redkey, *Black Exodus*, p. 179.
53. Jordan, Artisha Wilkerson, *The African Methodist Episcopal Church in Africa*, New York, n. d., *pamphlet*. (1973).
54. *Ibid.*
55. Singleton, *The Life Experiences of the Rt. Rev. Richard Allen*; also C. H. Wesley, *Richard Allen: Apostle of Freedom*.
56. Crummell, A., *Hope for Africa*, pp. 1, *Africa and America* (1891), pp. 407-408, 415-20.
57. DuBois, W. E. B., Editorial, *Crisis*, Vol. 10, No. 3, July 1915, p. 120.
58. *Encyclopedia Britannica*.
59. 2 Chronicles, Ch. 36.
60. Cohen, I., *The Zionist Movement*, introduction.
61. Kubowitzkim, A. Leon, *United in Dispersion: A History of the World Jewish Congress*, preface.
62. Crummell, A., *Hope for Africa*, London, 1853, pp. 2, 28-32.
63. Crummell, Alexander, *Hope for Africa*, pp. 2-5, 114-117, 28-32, Crummell, *Africa and America*, pp. 418-22.
64. *Africa and America*, *Ibid.*, pp. 436-37, *Hope for Africa*, pp. 43-44.
65. Crummell, *Africa and America*, 1891, pp. 407-420, 436-67.
66. Sacar, Howard M., *Farewell Espana: The World of the Sephardim Remembered*, New York, Alfred A. Knopf, 1994, p. 72 et seq. Stanley Lane Poole, *The Moors in Spain*, London, 1886.
67. Crummell, Alexander, *Hope for Africa*, pp. 11, 15-16.
68. *Ibid.*, pp. 17-18.
69. *Ibid.*, pp. 17-18 et seq.. See also his *Africa and America*, pp. 418-422.
70. Halpern, Ben, *The Idea of the Jewish State*, pp. 212-20.
71. Crummell, *Africa and America*, pp. 421 & 429. The quotation is from the Book of Pslams.
72. Crummell, *Africa and America*, pp. 408-409.
73. *Ibid.*, p. 409.
74. Crummell, *Hope for Africa*, p. 17, note.
75. Crummell, Africa and America, pp. 418-19 quoting from *The Acts of the Apostles*, Ch. 26, v. 17.
76. Crummell, *Ibid.*, p. 421.
77. *Ibid.*, pp. 436-37.
78. Kubowitzki, A. Leon, *Unity in Dispersion: A History of the World Jewish Congress*, preface. For a variant on this thought Crummell had written: "Who shall these Saviours of our people be?" (a) Surely they will not come from afar. It is the rarest of things, that the men who raise and redeem

people are of foreign blood. The great regenerators of races and nations spring, generally, for their own ranks. (b) so must it be with us... The revival, the strength, the regeneration of a people, - of any people, must come from within; they cannot come from without. Our leaders must be men and women of their own Race, of our own blood! Quoted from "Tracts for the NEGRO Race No. 1, 1898" in *op. cit.* Oldfield (ed.), p. 218.

79. Crummell, *Africa and America*, pp. 409-10. Italics in original.
80. See Crummell, Alexander, " A Defence of the Negro Race in America from the Assaults on Charges of Rev. J. L. Tucker, D. D. of Jackson Mississippi" in J. R. Oldfield (ed.) *Civilization and Black Progress: Selected Writings of Alexander Crummell on the South*, Charlottesville and London, 1995, pp. 78-100. Also Crummell, Alexander, *The Negro Race is Not Under a Curse*, London, 1863.
81. Martin, Tony, "Garvey and Scattered African", in J. E. Harris (ed.), *Global Dimensions of the African Diaspora*, Washington, D.C., Howard University Press, 1982, pp. 243-49.
82. *Ibid.*, p. 243

EPILOGUE

The foundations of the modern African Diaspora or Dispersion were laid by the Trans-Atlantic slave trade and, to a limited extent, by the Trans-Indian Oceanic slave trade. But while the extent of the latter is still unascertained in any depth, apart from the assertions that it was not conceived on as large a scale as the Trans-Atlantic one, the fact remains that the African Diaspora did not originate with the Trans-Atlantic or Trans-Indian Ocean slave trade. There is evidence reaching back to antiquity of the presence of persons of African origin in various communities outside the African continent or of black communities outside Africa believed to have been African in origin. Herodotus, for instance, suggested that the Colchians around the Black Sea were a race of Egyptians.[1] Scholars debated whether the Dravidians of the Indian sub-continent were related to Africans.[2] Despite the uncertainties, we must not lose sight of the fact that Africans have experienced other periods of dispersion in ancient and medieval times, some forced and others voluntary, some on a gigantic scale and others more modest. The ancient Egyptian incursions into Asia Minor and the recurrent invasions of Egypt by outsiders have all contributed to the movement of Africans beyond the confines of their home continent. Some current studies have begun to reveal the movements of Africans out of their continent in ancient times. After the destruction of Carthage in 146 B.C., the Romans carried no less than 50,000 Carthaginians (Africans) into slavery; Roman recklessness also resulted in the destruction of wildlife and the impoverishment of the environment.[3] But the core period of the modern African diaspora, from the fifteenth through the nineteenth centuries (and its peculiar permutation in the twentieth) saw that systematic destruction of lives in a process of warfare aimed at capturing free human beings for their enslavement in the Americas. The numbers were in the millions, with many of them dying in the notorious "Middle Passage" and the survivors "beached" in the Americas, where they and their descendants survived to bear the burden of their degradation there.

However, since the early diaspora is still not well and systematically studied, the present study is confined to that modern dispersion which contributed to the growth of communities comprising descendants of Africa in the New World setting occasioned by the activities of Europeans and Euro-Americans between the fifteenth and the nineteenth centuries. There is justification for taking this period, so well-documented, to enable others to proceed with the task of observing even earlier periods of the African dispersion and helping to determine whether any real links existed between the ancient Egyptians or other Africans and the people of Olmec (Mexico) and others in South America, as well as relationships which may have existed between Africa and those known as the Dravidians in Asia and the Melanesians, Polynesians, and Indonesians in South East Asia. The latter groups are beyond the scope of this study, while works of some significance in this connection have begun to appear.[4]

It is necessary to stress that the history of the African people in the Americas since the sixteenth century has been one of tumult and upheaval. It is out of these upheavals and perceptions arising therefrom that programs were fashioned for coping with the weight of oppression, injury, and prejudice heaped upon these unfortunate people. It is out of these crises that leadership began to emerge.[5] A result of this development was the formulation of a variety of programs for either accommodating to the situation or transcending it. It was not unlike the Jewish experience in foreign lands during the exilic period which spanned two millennia, when opinion was divided between accommodation, assimilation, and the preservation of a separate identity. The Jewish hope was also sustained by the revival and preservation of cultural patterns, the most fundamental being that of the Judaic religion and the hope it promised for a national home. The revival of cultural patterns, saw the revival of the ancient Jewish language, Hebrew, and the evolution of a modern one, Yiddish. These revivals in themselves mirrored a consciousness of degradation and attempts to undermine the dominant culture.

In the case of Africans in the Americas, they had come from many societies and they spoke a variety of languages. It was in the diaspora, as Dr. DuBois informed us, that they began to think of

Africa "as one land[6] and one idea." The diaspora, therefore, forced them to a consciousness of Africa that they had not had prior to their enslavement from the parent continent. Thus, the diaspora became for them the melting pot and the place in which by an interchange of ideas they began to fuse various ideas into one composite mould to constitute the African diaspora consciousness. It was the basis of the forging of a Pan-African outlook among the few, in the first instance, and many more later on. But, as the Jews had learned in Europe and the Americas, the manipulative tactics of their enslavers, such as the technique of "divide and rule," sometimes kept them from forging solidarity. These divisive tactics pervaded their experiences from the days of enslavement until their emancipation and after. As with the Jews, these led to the emergence of many and divergent perspectives on issues consistent with status and class interests. But whatever the source, the divisive tendencies took their toll.

Moreover, the Africans in the dispersion came with their own peculiar, particular religious beliefs and languages, which, except in a few cases, were whipped out of them and were retained only in part under cover. In the nineteenth century, however, the African Diaspora experienced upheavals, change, and the rise of ideas similar to those of Zionism, notions of a "return" to the original homeland in Africa. It would, of course, be inappropriate to refer to them as "Zionist," since the Africans in the diaspora had conceived their emigrationist ideas and evolved the emigrationist ethos prior to the rise of "Zionism" in 1897 by Theodore Hertzl. But we must not belabor this point because, like the Zionism of the Jews, the roots of the emigrationist ethos of the Africans in the Americas are very difficult to determine. It might even be argued that from the beginning of their enslavement to Europe and the Americas, Africans who undid their chains or took advantage of the opportunity to throw themselves into the sea were expressing that "return" ethos. But through experience, the Africans from various communities had to redefine themselves in a manner distinct from the definitions imposed on the majority by their depressed status in society. But a time came when the majority of these Africans and African-descended people began to see themselves as members of a single, if despised people, bound by common descent and a common set of beliefs and rituals (whether original or synthetic) and a common history of collective oppression.

While the Jewish diaspora was accomplished partly by force and partly voluntarily, for the Africans the core period of their modern diaspora was forcibly imposed. While the first two displacements of the Jews (i.e., the Assyrian invasion and the Babylonian captivity) constitute what the Jews regard as exile, and the one following the destruction of the second Temple is seen as dispersion, both historic experiences together comprise the totality of the Jewish Diaspora.

The last of these periods would actually correspond to the more contemporary African dispersion, with its desire to seek better opportunities, whether driven by war, famine, or political retreat from an oppressive colonial power or oppressive African regime. But these emigrations fall outside the scope of the present work, for they belong to the twentieth century. These were dispersions forced on Africans by sheer necessity and these migrations have been for the sake of betterment, in search of employment, education, or just peace. But, as we have indicated earlier, the African Diaspora with which this study is concerned is the one that resembles that of the first two periods of the Jewish exile.

While the Jews saw their exile as resulting from Divine Will and his wrath for their transgressions, they also pinned their hopes on a restoration and return which would herald their redemption and the emergence of a national homeland. Thus, it is significant that Rabbi Abraham Ben Halpern, in one of his sermons published in the *Jewish Recorder* of August 1950, could say:

> Zionism too was to be motivated by moral, cultural and spiritual idealism of Judaism so the establishment of the Jewish homeland would reflect the hope and prayers of our people since the destruction of the Temple.[7]

Africans did not think in these terms until they came in contact-in the Americas—with the ideas contained in the Judaeo-Christian scriptures, when their prelates began to conceive of their own experiences in symbolic scriptural terms akin to those of the Jews, and began to apply this aspect of the Jewish promise to the African experience. Their perceptions of their own potential restoration were articulated by messengers ("missionaries") from the diaspora carrying the message of Christianity (which they equated with "civilization") back to their brethren in Africa. However misguided the missionaries' motives, they sincerely hoped this would herald the redemption of the African people. They also believed that it could not be achieved by any other means or agencies than by them, who had acquired the Christian faith as a result of their enslavement in a foreign land. It was in keeping with this sentiment that Fisk University, in its Catalog for 1876, indicated as one of its principal objectives under Religious Aims that:

> Its students being mainly descendants of the African race, its special efforts are directed toward that class in this land, and it hopes at no distant day to do something for Africa. At present, its main work must be done nearer home; but it is hoped and prayed by those who labor in the institution that its ultimate and best work will be that of redeeming Africa.[8]

Dispersion, exile, and return for the Jews had also implied eschatological considerations in terms of destiny and the re-establishment of a national home. This came to be the stock-in- trade of many fundamentalist religious prelates among the African-derived people in the United States, much more so than in the rest of the Americas. This was predominantly a North American perception, preoccupation, and phenomenon and, to a limited extent, in the British West Indies, where a leadership of prelates was prevalent from the late eighteenth century through the nineteenth century.

Edward Blyden, a nineteenth-century prelate and scholar of African descent, returned to Africa and became very prominent in West African affairs and became an inspiration to many West African nationalist leaders both in his own day and in the early twentieth century. In sentiments not dissimilar from those quoted above, with respect to the Jews, he had said:

> My heart is in Liberia, and longs for the welfare of Africa. An African nationality is the great desire of my soul. I believe nationality to be an ordinance of nature; and no people can rise to an influential position among the nations without the distinct and efficient nationality.... For myself and my children, I desire no wider field of labour, and no greater privilege than I enjoy in that country. And could my voice reach every descendant of Africa in America, I would say to him: "Come away from the land of caste and oppression, to freedom of our young Republic. Come help us build a nationality in Africa."[9]

Blyden had further insisted as follows: "We believe that the establishment of an African nationality in Africa is the great need of the African race; and the men who have gone or may hereafter go to assist in laying the foundations of empire... are the truest heroes of the race."[10] Blyden's protége, Casely-Hayford, was also to express his understanding of "providential design" in his approval of the Garvey Universal Negro Improvement Association and the "Black Star Line". He saw its organizers as descendants of Africa abroad, whose activities he approved of, hoping that in time their ships would come out to West Africa to engage in commerce. In his effusion he uttered sentiments consistent with providential design when he said, "God works in a mysterious way" and remembered them as "thousands of our people, right over in America, who were carried away from our country years and years back. We may not care to follow what they are doing, but sooner or later, we shall have to know."[11]

The leadership which continued to emerge in the diaspora in the Americas came, principally, from the United States. Time and space will not allow the discussion of the reasons behind the failure of leadership to emerge in the other theaters of slavery in the Americas. These will become apparent in later excursions into leadership in the twentieth century. But the leadership that continued to emerge in the United States was varied in kind, orientation, and methods. Initially, their objectives were the same—to secure freedom; and later, to achieve elevation and all the benefits of equality in the society. The latter proved more problematic and resulted in cleavages and some manifestations of the need to create an African nationality. The debates were intense, sometimes acrimonious, and some of those who despaired of ever realizing manhood left for other theaters such as Canada, Haiti, Mexico, and Africa but the majority remained in the United States, each of them bearing in their consciousness varying perceptions of Africa, some distancing themselves from the thought of being African, others recognizing their African origins. In time, however, the intellectual activities of a few were to beget that African consciousness in their organizations, which was later to bear fruit after World War II at the middle of the twentieth century. Emigration became a less dominant idea and the energies were concentrated on the internal situation within the United States for the enhancement of their status. But later leadership built its own struggles on the foundations laid by early leadership. In both periods the conceptualization of leadership as physical force, moral suasion, and activism could be discerned, but the later period saw a preponderance of the latter two types. The issues of equality continued to preoccupy them. In 1920, African-Americans reached the "Nadir" and their leaders were still concerned with their destiny and it was into this situation that the Afro-Caribbean leader from Jamaica, Marcus Mosiah Garvey, entered to advocate an African nationality and the unity of all the African descended peoples of the globe. That development belongs to the next phase in the evolution of leadership. That intrusion into the American mainland from the islands was neither the first nor was it to be the last in this protracted period of the evolution of leadership.

Some Considerations

If in the nineteenth century the West Indies was thinking in the religious terms of an "exodus" back to the parent continent of Africa, in the twentieth century, with the increasing global consciousness, West Indians were in the forefront in the ideology and organization of Pan-Africanism and their political and cultural ramifications. Among them were the pioneers, Henry Sylvester-Williams, first Secretary of the Pan-African Association formed in London in 1896. Two others who became driving forces in visualizing the African predicament were George Padmore, who himself wrote books about Pan-Africanism and colonial policies in Africa. Two of his most outstanding works were *How Britain Rules in Africa* and *Africa, Britain's Third Empire*. Many others appeared in pamphlet and journalistic venues. But his Pan-Africanism was the culminating point of his acceptance of Africa in an age when many Africans of the diaspora in the Americas were silent about Africa. He and C. L. R. James were instrumental, along with others both in America and Europe, in forming the Association for the Defense of Ethiopia after the brutal assault on that country by Facist Italy in 1936. But he also ended his career in Africa when Dr. Nkrumah invited him to become his adviser on African Affairs where he also headed the Bureau. Later, after his death, Nkrumah also brought another of his Pan-African stalwarts, James Nathaniel Griffiths (alias T. Ras Makonnen), originally from British Guiana (now Guyana), who headed the Africa Bureau until the army's overthrow of Nkrumah, when he was invited to Kenya by then president Jomo Kenyatta, where he ended his days. In the meantime, he had also written his book *Pan-Africanism from Within*. His attachment to Africa never waned and he continued even in his old age to advocate a Pan-African outlook and approach to problems of the continent and its link with the diaspora.

Then there were the labor unions from the Caribbean which were drawn into Pan-African activity in Manchester in 1945. But all of these belong to the later period. Nevertheless, the re-emergence of an African consciousness in the Caribbean as well as the U.S.A. in the post-World War II era helped the emergence of that consciousness in South American societies, with Brazil in the lead and to some extent Cubans at home and in the Diaspora in North America. That consciousness, though manifested in the arts in Haiti, has yet to express itself abroad in the North American and Canadian diasporas in such a manner as to find common ground for a diasporan perspective. But these communities are not living in isolation; ideas continue to permeate their consciousness and their communities. In fact, these communities in the Diaspora have manifested the desire for a Pan-African conference of the Diaspora and some initiatives have been taken and some gatherings assembled. But those events do not fall within the scope of this work. They belong to a later period in the evolution of leadership in the African Diaspora, which has the potential of bringing Africans from the parent continent and Africans throughout the "American" hemisphere to consider their destiny and devise solutions to their predicament.

NOTES

1. See Herodotus, *The History*, Bk. II, para 104 translated by Daniel Greene, p. 173.
2. William, Sue, Leo Hansberry *African History Notebook: Africa and Africas As Seen by Classical Writers*, (J.E. Harris ed.), Vol. 2, pp. 51-52; also W. E. B. DuBois, *The World of Africa*, pp. 176-77.
3. See Birley, Anthony, *Septimus Severus: The African Emperor*, London, Eyre and Spottiswoode, 1971, p. 215.
4. Sertima, Ivan Van, *The African Presence in America: They Came Before Columbus*, New York, Random House, 1976; Jairazbhoy, R. A., *Ancient Egyptians in Middle and South America*, London, 1981; Bradley, Michael, *Dawn Voyage: The Black African Discovery of America*, Toronto, Summerhill Press, Lt., 1987.
5. See Thompson, V. B., *The Making of the African Diaspora etc. op. cit.*, also by the same author: "Leadership in the Àfrican Diaspora in the Americas Prior to 1860", *Journal of Black Studies*, Vol. 24, No. 1 (Sept. 1993) pp. 42-76.
6. DuBois, W. E. B., *The World and Africa*, New York, International Publishers, 1965, p. 7, 1st edition, 1946.
7. Cf. *A Son of Faith From the Sermons of Abraham E. Halpern*, (ed. Bernard Paskas), Block Publishing Company, New York, 1963, p. 85.
8. *Fisk University, Catalogue for 1876*, p. 25.
9. Blyden, E. W., *Liberia's Offering*, New York, 1862, pp. v-vi.
10. *Ibid.*, p. 80 *et. seq.*
11. See Hayford, J. E. Casley, "Opening speech to the First Session of the National Congress of British West Africa," Accra, March 1920, in Sampson, Magnus, *West African Leadership*, Devon, 1949, pp. 65-5.

Select Bibliography

A. Primary Sources in Foreign Archives

PRO London. CO 14 and CO 806, esp. CO 14/59, CO 806/130
FO 2, esp. FO 2/28

B. Printed Primary Sources

Adams, Charles Francais. *Memoirs of John Quincy Adams.* Vol IV. Philadelphia: J. B. Lippincott & Co., 1874-1877.

The African Repository, several issues.

Annual Report of the American Colonization Society, 1817-

Aptheker, Herbert., (ed.) *'One Continued Cry': David Walker's Appeal to the Colored Citizens of The World (1829-1839) Its Setting and Its Meaning, Etc.* New York: Humanities Press, 1965.

Aptheker, Herbert. *A Documentary History of the Negro in the United States.* Vol. 1, New York: Citadel Press, 1968.

Basterd, Roy P., (ed.) *The Collected Works of Abraham Lincoln.* Vol. III. New Brunswick, NJ, 1953.

Bell, Howard., (ed.) *Minutes and Procedures of the National Negro Conventions 1830-1864.* New York: Arno Press and the *New York Times,* 1969.

Brotz, Howard. *Negro Social and Political Thought 1850-1920.* Representative Texts, New York and London: Basic Books, 1966.

Concise Dictionary of American Biography. ed. Joseph G. E. Hopkins. New York: Charles Scribner's Sons, 1964.

Crummell, Alexander. *Africa and America: Addresses and Discourses.* Springfield, MA: Willey and Co., 1891.

Douglass, Frederick. *Life and Times of Frederick Douglass.* ed. John Lobb, Christian Age Press, London, 1882; New York, 1881. Several New Editions.

Fitzpatrick, J. C. *The Writings of George Washington.* Washington D.C., 1931-1940, several volumes - Vol. 31.

Foner, Philip, S. *The Life and Writings of Frederick Douglass.* New York: International Publishers, 1950, 4 vols.

Foner, Philip, S., ed. with introduction. *The Teachings of Rev. George Washington Woodbey and His Disciple Rev. G. W. Slater, jr.* . Forward by Congressman Ronald V. DeGras, San Francisco, CA: Synthesis Publications, 1982.

Foner, Philip, S. *The Voice of Black America: Speeches by Negroes in the United States, 1797-1971.* New York: Simon & Schuster, 1972.

Jefferson, Thomas, *Notes on the State of Virginia in 1781, etc.* London: J. Sstockdale, 1787.

Kilson, Martin and A. C. Hill. *Apropos of Africa.* London: Frank Cass and Co., 1969.

Parish, William, ed. *The Life, Travels and Opinions of Benjamin Lundy with a sketch of Contempory Events, etc.* Philadelphia, PA, 1847. (Containing extracts from the Genisis of Universal Emancipation published in 1825, edited jointly by Garrison and Lundy).

The Public Statutes at Large of the United States of America. Vol. III. Boston, Little and J. Brown, 1846-1848

Sancho, Ignatius. *Letters of the Late Ignatius Sancho: An African* in two volumes to which were prefixed *Memoirs* of his life. London: J. Nichols, 1782.

Sancho, Ignatius. *Writings and Speeches.*

Singleton, G. A., ed. *The Life Experience and Gospel Labors of the Rt. Rev. Richard Allen to which is Annexed the Rise and Progress of The African Methodist Episcopal Church in the United States of America written by himself and published at his request.* n.d. New York,Nashville, Tennessee: Abingdon Press, reprint, 1960.

Still, William. *The Underground Railroad.* Philadelphia: Porter and Coates, 1872, 1879; New York: Arno Press: 1968.

Tragle, Henry Irving. *The Southampton Slave Revolt of 1831: a Compilation of Source Material.* Amherst: The University of Amherst, 1971.

Woodbey, Rev. George Washington. 'What to Do and How to Do It', *Waylands Monthly.* Published by Girard, Kansas: (J. A.

Wayland) No. 40, August 1903.

Woodson, Carter G. *The Mind of the Negro as Reflected in Letters Written during the Crisis 1800-1860.* Washington D.C.: The Association for the Study of Negro Life and History, 1926.

Woodson, Carter G. *Negro Orators and their Orations.* Washington D.C.: The Associated Publishers, 1925.

C. Secondary Sources

Adams, Russell L. *Great Negroes Past and Present.* Chicago: Afro-American Publishing Co., 1969.

Ahuma, Attoh (Rev. S. B. R. Solomon). *The Gold Coast Nation and National Consciousness.* Liverpool: D. Marples and Co., 1911.

Ahuma, Attoh. *Memoirs of West African Celebrities.* Liverpool: D. Marples and Co., 1905.

Ajayi, J. F. A. *Christian Missions in Nigeria, 1841-1891.* London: Longman, 1965, Evanston: Northwestern University Press.

Ajayi, J. F. A., and I. Espie, ed. *A Thousand Years of West Africa History.* Ibadan and Edinburgh: Ibadan University Press, 1965.

Aptheker, Herbert. *American Negro Slave Revolts.* 2nd printing. New York: Colombia University Press, 1944.

Aptheker, Herbert. "American Negro Slave Revolts." *Science and Society,* Summer, 1937.

Aptheker, Herbert. *Nat Turner's Slave Rebellion, together with the Full Text of the so-called 'Confessions' of Nat Turner made in Prison in 1831.* New York: Humanities Press, 1965.

Asiegbu, Johnson. *Slavery and the Politics of Liberation 1787- 1861.* London and Harlow: Longman, 1969.

Azikiwe, N. N. *Liberia in World Politics,* London, 1934.

Barber, J. Max. "The Niagara Movement." Voice of the Negro, II (1905) What's the Niagara Movement? (Pamphlet) Howard University Library, 1905.

Bastide, Roger. *African Religions of Brazil.* Baltimore and London: Johns Hopkins University Press, 1978.

Bell, Howard, ed. and intro. *Search for a Place, Black Separatism and Africa,1860:* M. R. Delany and Robert Campbell. Ann Arbor Paperbacks: The University of Michigan Press, 1971.

Bell, Howard. *The Early History of the Colored Convention Movement.* New York: Arno Press, 1969.

Birley, Anthony. *Septimus Severus: African Emperor.* London: Eyre and Spottiswoode, 1971.

Bennett, Harry J. Jr. *Bondsmen and Bishops: Slavery and Apprenticeship in the Codrington Plantation, 1710-1838.* Berkeley: University of California Press, 1958.

Blassingame, J. W. and Mary Berry. *Long Memory.* New York: Oxford University Press, 1982.

Blyden, E. W. *The Origins and Purpose of African Colonization Annual Discourse at the Sixty-sixth anniversary of the American Colonization Society, June 14, 1883.* Washington City, 1883.

Blyden, Edward Wilmot. *Christianity, Islam and the Negro Race.* Edinburgh: Edinburgh University Press, 1967.

Blyden, E. *Liberia's Offering.* New York: J. A. Gray, 1862.

Bontemps, Arna. *Any Place But Here.* New York: Hill and Wang, 1966.

Bontemps, Arna. *Black Thunder.* Boston: Beacon Press, 1968. earlier edition: The Macmillan Company, 1936, renewed 1963; new introduction 1992.

Bradford, Sarah. *Harriet: The Moses of her People.* New York: Corinth Books, reprint, 1961 and other issues.

Bradford, Sarah. *Scenes in the Life of Harriet Tubman.* New York: W. J. Moses-Printer, 1869.

Bradley, Michael. *Dawn Voyage: The Black African Discovery of America.* Toronto: Summerhill Press, 1987.

Brawley, Benjamin. *A Social History of the American Negro.* New York: MacMillan Co., 1921.

Brawley, Benjamin. *Early Negro American Writers.* Chapel Hill, North Carolina, 1934.

Brown, William Wells. *The Black Man: His Antecedents, His Genius and His Achievements.* London: T. Hamilton, 1863.

Buchner, J. H. *The Moravians in Jamaica: History of the Mission of the United Brethren's Church to the Negroes in the Island of Jamaica from the Year 1754-1854.* London: Longman and Co., 1854.

Buckmaster, Henrietta, *Let My People Go: The Story of the Underground railroad and the Growth of the Abolition Movement.* New York and London: Harper and Bros., 1941.

Buell, R. L. *The Native Problem in Africa.* New York: MacMillan Co., 1928, 2 vols.; Connecticut: Anchor Books, 1965.

Buell, R. L. *Liberia: A Century of Survival,* African Hand Books 7. Philadelphia: University of Pennsylvania Press, 1947.

Butcher, Margaret Just. *The Negro in American Culture,* (based on materials left by Alain Locke). A Mentor Book, New York, The New American Library, 1957.

Caldecott, Alfred. *The Church in the West Indies.* London, 1898.

Carroll, Charles. "The Negro as Beast" or "In the Image of God," St. Louis, MO., 1900.

Carwell, Hattie. *Blacks in Science.* Hicksville, NY: Exposition Press, 1977.

Casley-Hayford, J. E. *Ethiopia Unbound.* London: Cass, 1969.

Clarke, John Henrik, ed. *William Styron's Nat Turner: Ten Black Writers Respond.* Boston: Beacon Press, 1968.

Cohen, Israel I. *The Zionist movement.* New York, 1946.

Cohen, Chapman. *Christianity, Slavery and Labor.* London, 1931.

Cooke, J. E., ed. *The Early Anti-Slavery Movement and African Colonization.* Norman, Oklahoma, 1957.

Coupland, Reginald. *The British Anti-Slavery Movement.* 2nd edn. New York: Barnes and Noble, 1964.

Cromwell, J. W. *The Negro in American History.* Washington D.C.: The American Negro Academy, 1914.

Crummell, Alexander. *The Duty of a Rising Christian State* (Annual Oration). London: Wertheim and Mackintosh, 1856.

Crummell, Alexander. *The Negro Race Not Under a Curse.* New York and London, 1863.

Crummell, Alexander. *Hope for Africa.* London, 1853.

Cuffee, Paul (W. Alexander). *Memoirs of Captain Paul Cuffee: A Man of Color.* Liverpool: Liverpool Mercury, Egerton, Smith and Co., 1811.

Cuffee, Paul. *Memoirs of Captain Paul Cuffee with the Epistle of the Sierra Leone Society.* York, England: W. Alexander and Co., 1811. Paul Cuffee: *The Black Hero founded on Facts.* Edinburgh: William Oliphant and Co., 1872.

Cuguano, Ottobah (John Stewart). *Thoughts and Sentiments on the Evils of Slavery.* London: Dawsons, 1787.

Curry, Leonard P. *The Free Black in Urban America 1800-1850: The Shadow of the Dream.* Chicago: University of Chicago Press, 1981.

D'Auvergne, Edmund. *Human Livestock.* London, 1933.

Davidson, Basil. *Black Mother.* London: Victor Gollancz, 1961.

Davis, John P. *The American Negro Reference Book.* 2 vols. New Jersey: Prentice-Hall, 1966.

Delany, M. R. *Official Report of the Niger Valley Exploring Party,* No. 48. New York: Thomas Hamilton; London: Webb Millington and Co., 1861.

Dew, T. R. *The Pro-slavery Argument "Review of the Debate in the Virginia Legislature of 1831 and 1832".* Philadelphia: Lippincott, Grambo and Co., 1853.

Diggs, Irene. *Black Inventors.* Chicago: Third World Press, 1975.

Douglass, Frederick. *My Bondage and My Freedom.* New York: Miller, Orton

and Mulligan, 1855.
Douglass, Frederick. *The Narrative of the Life of Frederick Douglass: An American Slave.* New York, 1845, later eds. Penguin Books, 1982. 2nd edition.
Douglass, Frederick. *Oration Delivered in Corinthian Hall, Rochester, July 5, 1852.* Published by Request, Printed by Lee, Mann and Co., American Building, 1852.
Drake, St. Clair and Horace R. Cayton. *Black Metropolish: A Study of Negro Life in a Northern City.* 2 vols. New York and Evanston: Harper and Row, 1962.
Drake, St. Clair. *The Redemption of Africa and Black Religion.* Chicago: Third World Press, Atlanta: Institute of the Black World, 1970, 1st edition.
Draper, Theodore. *The Rediscovery of Black Nationalism.* New York: Viking Press, 1973.
Drewry, W. S. *The Southampton Insurrection.* Washington: Neale Company, 1900.
Drinkwater, John. *Abraham Lincoln.* London: Sidgwick and Jackson, 1918.
DuBois, W. E. B. *Black Folk Then and Now.* New York: Octagon Books, 1970.
DuBois, W. E. B. *Black Reconstruction: An Essay Toward aHistory of the Part Which Black Folk Played in the Attempt To Reconstruct Democracy in America 1860-1880.* New York: Harcourt, Brace and Co., 1935.
DuBois, W. E. B. *Dusk of Dawn.* New York: Harcourt, Brace & Co., 1935.
DuBois, W. E. B. *John Brown* (American Crisis Biographies, E. P. Oberholzer, ed.) Philadelphia, 1909.
DuBois, W. E. B. *The Amenia Conference: An Historical Negro Gathering at Troutbeck.* Leaflets No. 8, 1916, and 1925.
DuBois, W. E. B. *The Negro.* Home Universities Library, 1915.
DuBois, W. E. B. *Souls of Black Folk.* New York: Blue Heron, 1953. Several issues. First published in 1903.
DuBois, W. E. B. *The World and Africa.* New York: Viking Press, 1947. Several reissues.
Equiano, Olaudan (Gustavus Vassa). *The Interesting Narrative of the Life of Olaudan Equiano or Gustavus Vassa, The African.* 2nd edition. London, 1789. 2 vols.
Flemming, Walter. "Pap" Singleton, The Moses of the Colored Exodus,' *American Journal of Sociology,* Vol. 15, July 1909, pp. 61-82.
Franklin, J. H. and Meier August, eds. *Black Leaders of the Twentieth Century.* Urbana and Chicago: University of Illinois Press, 1982.
Franklin, J. H. *Reconstruction After the Civil War.* 1961, 8th imp. 1966. Chicago: University of Chicago Press, 1994 (2nd edition).
Franklin, J. H. *The Emancipation Proclamation.* Edinburgh: Edinburgh University Press, 1963.
Franklin, J. H. and Alfred Moss. *From Slavery to Freedom.* 7th ed. New York: McGraw Hill, 1994.
Frazier, E. F. *The Negro in the United States.* New York: MacMillan Co., 1949, 1957 revised.
Frazier, E. F. *The New Negro in the United States.* Revised edition 1961, first published in 1957.
Fredickson, George M. *The Black Image in the White Mind...* 1817-1914. Hanover, New Hampshire, 1987. New York: Harper and Row, 1971 (1st edition).
Freud, Sigmund. *Moses and Monotheism.* New York: A. A. Knopf, 1939.
Fryer, Peter. *Staying Power.* London: Pluto Press, 1984.

Fyfe, Christopher. *A History of the Sierra Leone*. London: Oxford University Press, 1962; reprint 1968.

Garrison, William Lloyd. *Thoughts on African Colonization, or an Impartial Exhibition of the Doctrine, Principles and Purposes of the American Colonization Society*. Boston: Garrison and Knapp, 1832.

George, Carol V. R. *Segregated Sabbaths.* New York: Oxford University Press, 1975.

Gilbert, Olive. *Narrative of Sojourner Truth: A Bondswoman of Olden time with a history of the Labors and Correspondence drawn from her book of life*. Michigan, 1878, reprinted London, 1968.

Goodwell, William. *The American Slave Code in Theory and Practice*. original edition: 1853; New York: Negro Universities Press, 1958.

Greene, David, tr. *Herodotus: The History.* Chicago and London: University of Chicago Press, 1987; also Penguin classics translated by Aubrey de Sélincourt, Revised with an Introduction by A. R. Burn, Penguin Books, 1972; also Harmondsworth, Middlesex; Baltimore: Penguin Books, 1972.

Haber, Louis. *Black Pioneers of Science and Invention.* New York: Harcourt Brace, 1970.

Halevi, Ilan. *A History of the Jews: Ancient and Modern*. London and New Jersey: Zed Books Ltd., 1987.

Halpern, Abraham E. *A Son of Faith: From the Sermon of A. T.* Halpern. New York: Block Publishing Company, 1963.

Halpern, Ben. *The Idea of the Jewish State,* Cambridge: Harvard University Press, 1961.

Harris, Sheldon H. *Paul Cuffee: Black America and The Africa Return.* New York, 1972.

Harris, J. E., ed. *Global Dimensions of the African Diaspora.* Washington, D.C.: Howard University Press, 1982.

Harris, J. E., *William Leo Hansberry African History Notebook: African and Africans As Seen By Classical Writers,* Howard University Press, Washington, DC, 1981, Vol. 2.

Hart, Ansell, Jr. *The Life of George William Gordon.* Kingston, Jamaica: Institute of Jamaica, 1972.

Hart, A. B., ed. *Slavery and Abolition, 1831-1841.* Vol. 16 of the American Nation Series. New York and London, 1906.

Hayden, Robert C. *Eight Black American Inventors.* Reading, Massachusetts: Addison-Wesley, Co., 1972.

Hayford, J. E. Casely. *Ethiopia UnBound.* London: G. M. Phillips, 1911; 2nd edition, Frank Cass, 1969.

Heartman, Charles F., ed. *Phyllis Wheatley: Poems and Lectures.* New York: C. F. Heastman, 1915.

Hebert, Hilary A. *The Abolition Crusade and Its Consequences,* etc. New York: C. Scribner's Sons, 1912.

Helg, Aline. *Our Rightful Share: The Afro-Cuban Struggle for Equality, 1886-1912.* Chapel Hill and London: University of North Carolina Press, 1995.

Hoare, Prince. *Memoirs of Granville Sharp, Esq.* London: Henry Colburn and Co., 1820.

Holt, Thomas C. *Black Over White: Negro Political Leadership in South Carolina During Reconstruction.* Urbana and Chicago: University of Chicago Press, 1979.

Hooker, H. R. *Henry Sylvester Williams: Imperial Pan-Africanist*. London, 1975.

Horton, G. M. *Hope for Liberty (Poems of George Moses Horton),* 1829; later reprinted as: *Poems of a Slave*. Raleigh, North Carolina: Gales and Sons, 1837.

Horton, George Moses. *Poems of a Slave*. Boston, Massachusetts: Isaac Knapp, 1837.

Hughes, Langston. *Famous American Negroes*. New York, 1954. 1st edition: Capetown: Weeden, 1944.

Jairazbhoy, R. A. *Ancient Egyptians in Middle and South America*. 1981. Old World Origins of American Civilization Vol. 3. Printed in England by Pika Print Ltd., Enfield, Middlesex Ru *Publication*

James, C. L. R. *Black Jacobins*. London: Wishart Brothers, 1938 and subsequent reissues.

Jay, W. *Inquiry into the Character of the American Colonization and American Anti-Slavery*. 6th edition. New York: R. G. Willams for the American Anti-Slavery Society, 1838.

Jay, William. *Miscellaneous Writings on Slavery*. Boston: John P. Jewett & Co.; Cleveland, Ohio: Jewett, Proctor, and Worthington; London: Sampson, Sampson Low and Co., 1853.

Jordan, A. Wilkerson. *The African Methodist Episcopal Church in Africa*. N. D., 1973.

July, Robert. *The Origin of Modern African Thought*. London: Faaber and Faber, 1968.

Kaplan, Sydney. *The Black Presence in the Era of the American Revolution, 1770-1800*. Greenwich, CT, New York: Graphic Society, 1973.

Karenga, Maulana. *Introduction to Black Studies*. Los Angeles: 1984, 3rd printing.

Katz, W. L., ed. *Five Slave Narratives*. New York: Arno Press, 1968.

King, K. J. *Pan-Africanism and Education*. Oxford: Clarendon Press, 1971.

Klein, Aaron E. *The Hidden Contributors: Black Scientists and Inventors in America*. New York: Doubleday and Co., 1971.

Klingberg F. J. ed. *Coderington Chronicle: An Experiment in Anglican Altruism on a Barbados Plantation 1710-1834*. Berkeley and Los Angeles: University of California Press, 1949.

Kubowitzki, A. Leon. *Unity in Dispersion: A History of the World Jewish Congress*. New York, 1948.

Lane, Lunsford. *Narrative of Lunsford Lane, Formerly of Raleigh \ North Carolina, Published by Himself*. Boston, Massachusetts: J. G. Torrey, 1842 and 1848.

Laotan, A. B. *The Torch Bearers or Brazilian Colony in Lagos*. Lagos, 1943.

Leon, Abram. *The Jewish Question: A Marxist Interpretation*. New York: Pathfinder Press Inc., 1970 2nd edition; 1st edition, 1965.

Lewis, David L. *When Harlem was in Vogue*. 1st editon, New York: Knopf: distributed by Random House, 1981.

Litwack, Leon and August Meier. *Black Leaders of the Nineteenth Century*. Blacks in the New World Series. Urbana and Chicago: University of Illinois Press, 1988.

Litwack, Leon. *North of Slavery; The Negro in the Free States, 1790-1860*. Chicago: University of Chicago Press, 1963.

Loggins, Vernon. *The Negro Author: His development in America to 1900*. New York: Colombia University Press, 1931. Reprint 1959, Washington and New

York, Kenwikat Press Inc. 1964.

Logan, Rayford W. *The Betrayal of the Negro.* New York: Collier Books, 1965.

Lundy, Benjamin. *Life, Travels and Opinions of Benjamin Lundy.* Philadelphia, 1847. 2nd edition, New York: Arno Press, 1969.

Lynch, Hollis R. *Black Spokesman.* London: Cass, 1971.

Mabee, Carleton and Susan. *Sojourner Truth, Slave, Prophet and Legend.* London and New York, New York University Press, 1993.

MacInnes, C. M. *England and Slavery.* Bristol: Arrowsmith, 1934.

Martin, Tony. *Race First.* Westport, Connecticut: Greenwood Press, 1976.

Martineau, Harriet. *Society in America.* New York and London: Sauders and Othley, 1837 4th edn., 2 vols.

Mason, Julian D., ed. *Poems of Phyllis Wheatley.* Chapel Hill: University of North Carolina Press, 1966.

Mathieson, W. L. *British Slave Emancipation 1838-1849.* London: Longman, Green and Co., 1932.

Mathieson, W. L. *Great Britain and the Slave Trade 1839-1865.* London: Longman, Green and Co., 1929.

Maury, Ann., ed. *Memoirs of a Huguenot Family.* New York, 1853. Putnam, 1907, 2nd edition.

McKay, Claude. *A Long Way From Home.* New York: Harcourt, Brace and World, 1970.

Meier, August. *Negro Thought in America 1880-1915.* Ann Arbor: The University of Michigan Press, 1963; New York: Basic Books, 1966.

Mellor, G. R. *British Imperial Trusteeship 1783-1850.* London: Faber and Faber, 1951.

Miller, Floyd Jr. *The Search for a Black Nationality: Black Emigration and Colonization 1787-1863.* Urbana, Illinois: University of Illinois Press, 1975.

Miller, Kelly. *Race Adjustment.* New York and Washington: The Neale Publishing Company, 1908.

Mittleholtzer, Edgar. *Kaywana Stock.* Corgi Books: London, 1976.

Mittleholtzer, Edgar. *Kaywana Heritage.* Corgi Books: London, 1976 earlier 1952.

Mittleholtzer, Edgar. *Children of Kaywana.* London: 1954. 1st edition New York: J. Day Co., 1952.

Morel, E. D. *The Black Man's Burden.* London and Manchester: The National Labor Press, 1919.

Nascimento, Abdias do. *Brazil: Mixture or Massacre.* Dover, Massachusetts: The Majority Press, 1979 and 1989.

The Negro Problem. New York: James Pott and Co., 1902.

Niagara Movement Declaration of Principles (pamphlet, 1905) Howard University Library.

Nye, R. B. and J. E. Morpurgo. *A History of the United States.* Penguin Books, 1955. 2 vols.

Oldfield, ed. *Civilization and Black Progress: Selected Writings of Alexander Crummell on the South.* Charlottesville and London, 1995.

Omer-Cooper, J. D., ed. *The Making of Modern Africa.* London and Harlow, Longman, 1968 2 vols.

Ovington, Mary White. *The Walls Came Tumbling Down.* New York, 1974. 2nd edition New York: Arno Press, 1969.

Paquette, Robert L. *Sugar is Made with Blood: The Conspiracy of La Escalera and the Conflict between Empires over Slavery in Cuba.* Middletown, Connecticut:

Wesleyan University Press, 1988.
Pauli, Hertha. *Her Name was Sojourner Truth.* New York, 1962, Camelot Printing, 1971.
Pike, James S. *The Prostrate State: South Carolina Under Negro Government.* 1874. 2nd edition New York: Loring and Mussey, 1935.
Poole, Stanley Lane. *The Moors in Spain.* London, 1886. Reprint Baltimore: Black Classic Press, 1990.
Porter, Arthur. *Creoledom: A Study of Development of Freetown Society*. London: Oxford University Press, 1963.
Purvis, Robert. *Appeal of Forty Thousand Citizens Threatened with Disfranchisement to the People of Pennsylvania.* (pamphlet), 1838.
Quarles, Benjamin. *Black Abolitionists.* New York; Oxford University Press, 1969.
Ranger, T. O. and I. Kimambo, eds. *Emerging Themes of African History.* Nairobi, Kenya: East Africa Publishing House, 1968.
Redding, Saunders J. *The Lonesome Road.* New York: Doubleday, 1958.
Redkey, Edwin. *Black Exodus*. New Haven: Yale University Press, 1969.
Riley, B. F. *The Life and Times of Booker T. Washington.* London and Edinburgh: Fleming H. Revell Coy, 1916.
Robert Vaux to Thomas Clarkson, Philadelphia, May 13, 1819, Moorland Spingarn Collections, Howard University.
Rout Leslie B. Jr. *The African Experience in Spanish America 1502-the present Day.* London, New York and Melbourne: Cambridge University Press, 1976.
Roux, Edward. *Time Longer Than Rope.* Madison, Wisconsin, 1972, 2nd edition, University of Wisconsin Press.
Rudwick, Elliot. *W. E. B. DuBois: Propagandist of The Negro-Protest*. New York: Athenum, 1972.
Sachar, Howard M. *Farewell Espana: The World of the Sephardim Remembered* New York: Alfred A. Knopf, 1994.
Sachar, Howard M. *A History of Israel from the Rise of Zionism to Our Time*. New York: Alfred A. Knopf, 1989.
Sachar, Howard M. *The Course of Modern Jewish History.* New York: A Delta Book, 1958 and 1977.
Sampson, Magnus. *West African Leadership.* Devon, 1949. London: F. Cass, 1969.
Sarduy, Pedro Perez and Jean Stubbs, ed. *Afro-Cuba: An Anthology of Cuban Writings on Race, Politics and Culture.* New York: Ocean Press, 1993.
Sertima, Ivan Van, ed. *The African Presence in Early America.* New Brunswick: U.S.A. Transaction Publishers, 1992.
Sertima, Ivan Van. *They Came Before Colombus.* New York: Random House, 1976 and subsequent reprints.
Shepperson, George and Thomas Price. *Independent African.* Edinburgh: Edinburgh University Press, 1958.
Schuler, Monica. "Alas Alas Kongo", Baltimore: Johns Hopkins University Press, 1979.
Simmons, Rev. William J. *Men of Mark, Eminent, Progressive and Rising.* New York, 1887. reprint 1968 Negro Universities Press.
Sibert, W. H. *The Underground Railroad.* New York, 1899.
Staudenraus, P. *The African Colonization Movement 1816-1865.* New York: Colombia University Press, 1961.
Swift, David. *Black Prophets of Justice: Activist Clergy Before the Civil War.* Baton

Rouge and London: Louisiana State University Press, 1989.

Tannenbaum, Frank. *Slave and Citizen: The Negro in the Americas.* New York: Alfred A. Knopf, 1947.

Tappan, Lewis. *Life of Arthur Tappan.* New York, Hurd and Houghton; Cambridge: Riverside Press, 1871.

Tate, Gayle T. "Prophesy and Transformation: The Contours of Lewis Woodsons Nationalism," *Journal of Black Studies,* Vol. 29, No. 2 (Nov. 1998) Sage Publications.

Thomas, Lamont D. and Paul Cuffee: *Black Entrepreneur and Pan-Africanism.* Urbana and Chicago, University of Illinois Press, 1988.

Thompson, V. B. *Africa and Unity: The Evolution of Pan- Africanism.* London: Longman, 1969, London and New York: Humanities Press, 1969 and subsequent reprints to 1984.

Thompson, V. B. *The Making of the African Diaspora in the Americas 1441-1900.* London and Harlow: Longman Group, 1987.

Thwaite, D. *The Seething African Pot.* London: Constable & Co., 1936.

Van Dusen, John G. "The Exodus of 1879," *Journal of Negro0 History,* Vol. 21, No. 2, (1936), pp. 111-129.

Wadstrom, C. B. *Essay on Colonization*. London, 1794.

Walters, Alexander. *My Life and Work, Fleming H.* London: Revel Coy, 1917.

Ward, Samuel Ringgold. *The Autobiography of a Fugitive Negro.* London: John Snow, 1855.

Washington, B. T. and W. E. B. DuBois. *The American Negro* (Southern States), London: T. Fisher Unwin, 1909.

Washington, Booker T. 'Industrialization for the Negro' in *The Negro Problem.* New York: James Pott and Co., 1903.

Wegelin, Oscar. *Jupiter Hammon: American Negro Poet; Selections from his Writings and a Bibliography,* Heartmen's Historical Set No. 13, New York: Charles Fred Heartman, 1915.

Weisbord, Robert G. *Ebony Kinship: Africa, Africans, and the African-Americans.* Westport, Connecticut: Greenwood Press, 1973.

Wesley, Charles H. *Richard Allen: Apostle of Freedom.* Washington D.C.: Associated Publishers, 1935 subsequent publications.

Wesley, Charles H. *Negro Labor in the United States 1850-1925.* New York: Vanguard Press, 1927.

West, Richard. *Back to Africa: A History of Sierra Leone and Liberia.* London: Jonathan Cape, 1970.

Wheatley, Phyllis. *Poems on Various Subjects, Religious and Moral.* London: A. Bell, 1773.

Williams, Eric E. *British Historians and the West Indies.* London: Andre Deutsch, 1966.

Williams, Eric E. *From Colombus to Castro.* New York, Vintage Books, 1970.

Williams, Eric E. *Capitalism and Slavery.* Chapel Hill: University of North Carolina Press, 1944, also subsequent reissues.

Williams, George Washington. *History of the Negro Race in America.* London, 1883, 2 vols. 1st edition, New York: G. P. Putnam's Sons, 1883.

Williams, Peter (Rev.). *A Discourse Delivered on the Death of Captain Paul Cuffee: A Man of Color.* New York, 1818.

Winterbottom, Thomas. *An Account of the Native Africans in the Neighborhood of Sierra Leone.* London, 1803, 2 vols. printed.

Woodson, C. G. *The Education of the Negro Prior to 1861.* New York and London: G. Putnam and Sons, 1915.

Woodson, C. G. *History of the Negro Church.* Wasington D.C.: Associated Publishers, 1921 and subsequent reprints.

Woodson, Carter G. *A Century of Negro Migration.* Washington D.C.: The Association for the Study of Negro Life and History, 1918.

Woodson, Carter G. *The Negro in Our History.* Washington D.C.: The Associated Publishers, several reprints.

Wyndham, H. A. *Problems of Imperial Trusteeship: The Atlantic and Slavery.* London: Oxford University Press, Humphrey Milford, 1935.

Wyndham, H. A. *The Atlantic and Emancipation.* London, New York, Toronto: O. U. P., 1937. Chapters 1 & 2 for humanitarian concept.

D. Articles consulted are not included here as reference has

been made to them in notes already.

E. Newspapers and Magazines

The African Repository

The American Colonization Society: Annual Report

The AME Christian Recorder

American Journal of Sociology

The Anti-Slavery Vanguard

Atlanta Independent

Boston Guardian

The Colored American Magazine

The Crisis

Frederick Douglas paper

The Horizon

Freedom's Journal

Indianapolis Freeman

Jamaica Journal

Journal of Black Studies

Journal of Negro History

Journal of Negro Education

The Liberator

The New York Age

Journal of American Sociology

Rights of All

Voice of Missions

Washington Bee

Washington Colored America

INDEX

Colonization, 9, 17-19, 35, 58, 67, 82, 90, 95-96, 100, 105-106, 113-150, 158-159, 203-204, 206-210, 212, 214-216, 219, 240, 254, 259-260

Cuba, 6, 10, 27, 37-39, 47-48, 99, 216, 249, 255

DATE DUE
MAY 01 2002
MAR 20 2002